college

Other titles in this series include:

college
A READER *for* WRITERS

Todd James Pierce
California Polytechnic State University

New York   Oxford
Oxford University Press

Oxford University Press is a department of the University of Oxford.
It furthers the University's objective of excellence in research,
scholarship, and education by publishing worldwide.

Oxford   New York
Auckland   Cape Town   Dar es Salaam   Hong Kong   Karachi
Kuala Lumpur   Madrid   Melbourne   Mexico City   Nairobi
New Delhi   Shanghai   Taipei   Toronto

With offices in
Argentina   Austria   Brazil   Chile   Czech Republic   France   Greece
Guatemala   Hungary   Italy   Japan   Poland   Portugal   Singapore
South Korea   Switzerland   Thailand   Turkey   Ukraine   Vietnam

For titles covered by Section 112 of the US Higher Education Opportunity Act,
please visit www.oup.com/us/he for the latest information about pricing and
alternate formats.

Published by Oxford University Press
198 Madison Avenue, New York, New York 10016
http://www.oup.com

Library of Congress Cataloging-in-Publication Data
Names: Pierce, Todd James, 1965- author.
Title: College : a reader for writers / Todd Pierce, California Polytechnic
   State University.
Description: New York : Oxford University Press, [2016]
Identifiers: LCCN 2015037602| ISBN 9780190279950 | ISBN 9780190279974
Subjects: LCSH: College readers. | English language--Rhetoric--Problems,
   exercises, etc. | Report writing--Problems, exercises, etc. |
   Readers--Education. | College students--Conduct of life.
Classification: LCC PE1417 .P473 2016 | DDC 808/.0427--dc23
LC record available at http://lccn.loc.gov/2015037602

Printing number: 9 8 7 6 5 4 3 2 1

Printed in the United States of America
on acid-free paper

brief table of contents

contents

"The University of Florida broadcasts and archives Dr. Rush's lectures less for the convenience of sleepy students like Mr. Patel than for a simple principle of economics: 1,500 undergraduates are enrolled and no lecture hall could possibly hold them."

"Skipping class undetected for a game of ultimate Frisbee might become a thing of the past as more universities adopt mandatory-attendance policies and acquire high-tech trackers that snitch when students skip."

"Though the technology is relatively new, preliminary studies at Harvard and Ohio State, among other institutions, suggest that engaging students in class through a device as familiar to them as a cellphone—there are even applications that convert iPads and BlackBerrys into class-ready clickers—increases their understanding of material that may otherwise be conveyed in traditional lectures."

"What's your major? It's the defining question for college students—and the cliché that's launched a thousand friendships and romances. It's also a question that has become harder for students to answer."

"Since last fall, when [Laura Gayle] uploaded her macroeconomics notes onto Flashnotes.com to pay for a birthday gift for her mother, Ms. Gayle has sold more than 500 copies of the study guides that she's put together for her courses, made over $3,285 and tapped into a growing, if controversial, online marketplace."

"Some courses we naturally loved because the subject just spoke to us and some because we were blessed with a fabulous professor who could make

"To me, as a college administrator, the underlying problem is that many big-sport schools fail to educate student-athletes on proper behavior, which leads to delinquency in the pros."

7   Campus Life   269

"Perhaps students are both more demanding and more fragile today. Perhaps colleges are more committed to their students. Perhaps [the increase in student services] is part of a trend that has turned college into a luxury-resort experience, a consumer-oriented product."

"Nationally, marijuana use among young adults has clearly been trending upward. The percentage of college students who reported smoking within the previous year plummeted from a high of 51 percent in 1981 to a low of 26.5 percent in 1991, and has been zigzagging back up, to some 36 percent in 2013."

"Internships have long been a part of the collegiate learning experience, but have never been more closely tied to permanent hiring than they are today."

"More than ever before, students will need to know how to think, evaluate, and explore, even as what they think about may change and expand. They will need the creativity and the courage to challenge traditional ways of doing and working, and forge new paths and solutions."

"Women's colleges across the country are reconsidering their admission policies to adapt to a changing world in which gender norms are being challenged and more transgender students are seeking to enroll."

"[L.L. Nunn's] idea was to form 'whole men'—and only men, it being Nunn's contention that a single-sex institution was the ideal way to achieve his goals—who would be as comfortable at a desk as in the field."

rhetorical contents

argument and persuasion

personal experience

cause and effect

comparison and contrast

description

article

advice

Students come to college for a variety of reasons. Some want to pursue academic or artistic subjects for personal fulfillment. Some see college as the fast track to a good job. Some feel family or peer pressure to get a degree. Regardless of their reasons, most first-year students find college to be a surprising and exciting experience, a community complete with its own methods, goals, values, and power centers, a place of personal and intellectual transformation. This textbook is an invitation for students to explore the system in which they are currently members, *college*, a system whose imprint they will likely carry for the rest of their lives.

Many college courses are forward-looking: communication classes help students gain confidence for speeches they will someday give; computer science classes help students master programming skills for jobs they will someday hold; studio art classes help students prepare for masterpieces they will someday create. Though a few articles in this reader look to the future, this book primarily asks students to examine the present: to become informed citizens of an individual college and knowledgeable observers of the college experience in general.

The readings in *College: A Reader for Writers* are designed to help students better understand their college experience and more deeply appreciate their time in school. The selections largely avoid the simplicity of "how to succeed" articles. Instead many selections wrestle with large subjects: William Deresiewicz, in "The Disadvantages of an Elite Education," explores how the socioeconomics of individual campus cultures prepare (or underprepare) students for specific social and workplace communities after graduation. Eric Hoover, in "The Comfortable Kid," examines the problems with viewing the student as a *marketplace consumer* of education. Caitlin Flanagan, in "The Dark Power of Fraternities," discusses how the Greek system has shifted the center point of the college experience away from academics and toward alcohol and party culture. And in "The Day the Purpose of College Changed," Dan Berrett investigates recent events that changed college from an experience in which students explored academic interests and developed a deep sense of intellectual curiosity to one in which students train for entry-level jobs.

At the end of each selection, the Analyze and Explore questions help classes to examine important issues, particularly as they relate to their own college. One sample question asks students to explore the difference between a liberal education, a technical education, and a moral education and how those definitions relate to their own college expectations. Another asks students what new subjects of cultural or professional importance, such as computer science or creative studies, should be included in the general education requirements at their school. Multiple questions ask students to explore the role they play in advancing their own education.

This book is divided into seven chapters, with each exploring one area of the college experience: from Admissions to Campus Life. The selections represent competing educational philosophies and opposing views on the social value of college. The selections include a variety of written forms: political arguments, personal reflections, nonfiction narratives, op-eds, and journalistic exposés. In this book students will find the voices of educational reformers, college presidents and professors, recent graduates, and one current college sophomore. Taken together these selections ask students to better understand the process of a college education as they pass through it and to take ownership of the journey that lies before them.

College: A Reader for Writers is part of a series of brief single-topic readers from Oxford University Press designed for today's college writing courses. Each reader in this series approaches a topic of contemporary conversation from multiple perspectives.

- **Timely**: Most selections were originally published in 2010 or later.
- **Global**: Sources and voices from around the world are included.
- **Diverse**: Selections come from a range of nontraditional and alternate print and online media, as well as representative mainstream sources.

- **Curated**: Every author of a volume in this series is a teacher-scholar whose experience in the writing classroom, as well as expertise in a volume's specific subject area, informs his or her choices of readings.

In addition to the rich array of perspectives on topical (even urgent) issues addressed in each reader, each volume features an abundance of different genres and styles—from the academic research to the pithy Twitter argument. Useful but nonintrusive pedagogy includes:

- **Chapter introductions** provide a brief overview of the chapter's theme and a sense of how the chapter's selections relate to both the overarching theme and each other.
- **"Analyze" and "Explore" questions** after each reading scaffold and support student reading for comprehension, as well as rhetorical considerations, providing prompts for reflection, classroom discussion, and writing assignments.
- **"Forging Connections" and "Looking Further"** prompts after each chapter encourage critical thinking by asking students to compare perspectives and strategies among readings both within the chapter and with readings in other chapters, suggesting writing assignments (many of which are multimodal) that encourage students to engage in larger conversations in the academy, the community, and the media.
- **An appendix on "Researching and Writing About College"** guides student inquiry and research in a digital environment. Co-authored by a research librarian and a writing program director, this appendix provides real-world, transferable strategies for locating, assessing, synthesizing, and citing sources in support of an argument.

about the author

Todd James Pierce is the author of many books of fiction and nonfiction, including *Newsworld* (University of Pittsburgh Press, 2006), *Three Years in Wonderland* (University of Mississippi Press, 2016), and winner of the Drue Heinz Literature Prize. He is the co-author of two other college textbooks, *Visual Storytelling* (Oxford University Press, 2016) and *Behind the Short Story: From First to Final Draft* (Pearson, 2007). He is a professor of English at Cal Poly University in San Luis Obispo, California, where he directs the creative writing program.

 college

Admissions

Few experiences are as transformational as college.
High school students prepare for college by taking AP courses, by striving for good grades, by studying for the SAT and ACT. Teenagers spend hours on university webpages exploring their options. Some even take trips to visit schools that interest them. The end result: high school students select a pool of colleges—or maybe even just one—to which they will send their transcripts, their test scores, maybe a writing sample and letters of recommendation. In doing so, they enter the admissions process.

The admissions process is far more complicated than it appears. Admissions departments solicit applications from targeted students—such as those with high SAT scores. Most admissions departments use a fairly complex set of criteria to determine who is admitted, who is waitlisted, who is denied. Some admissions officers look for personality or creativity in a writing sample; others seek candidates with deep but narrow interests; still others look for well-rounded individuals, students with civic, artistic, and academic aspirations.

In many ways the admissions process explains why you are where you are right now.

In this section Malcolm Gladwell explores the history of the admissions process, in particular the way admissions criteria have evolved in North America. Eric Hoover defends his position that schools are over-soliciting applications from students simply to form an impressive applicant pool. Robert J. Sternberg suggests that scores and GPA are poor tools to truly judge the merits of prospective students; instead, he proposes essays in which students write creatively. And Dalton Conley explores how social media have changed roommate selection for students at many schools, fondly recalling the days when roommates were randomly assigned by the student housing office.

In these selections, a bit of the mystery is pulled back from the admissions process, with an eye toward explaining how you've landed at the school where you currently study. These readings will not only allow you to reflect on your college journey, as it stands now, but also ask you to reimagine the admissions process for your school: what is your school doing well, and what might it do better?

Malcolm Gladwell
Getting In: The Social Logic of Ivy League Admissions

Malcolm Gladwell is a staff writer for *The New Yorker*, where he contributes articles on cultural trends and the ways social science research explains contemporary experience. He is the author of five books, all of which have become New York Times Bestsellers. In 2005, *Time Magazine* named him one of its 100 most influential people.

I applied to college one evening, after dinner, in the fall of my senior year in high school. College applicants in Ontario, in those days, were given a single sheet of paper which listed all the universities in the province. It was my job to rank them in order of preference. Then I had to mail the sheet of paper to a central college-admissions office. The whole process probably took ten minutes. My school sent in my grades separately. I vaguely remember filling out a supplementary two-page form listing my interests and activities. There were no S.A.T. scores to worry about, because in Canada we didn't have to take the S.A.T.s. I don't know whether anyone wrote me a recommendation. I certainly never asked anyone to. Why would I? It wasn't as if I were applying to a private club.

I put the University of Toronto first on my list, the University of Western Ontario second, and Queen's University third. I was working off a set of brochures that I'd sent away for. My parents' contribution consisted of my father's agreeing to drive me one afternoon to the University of Toronto campus, where we visited the residential college I was most interested in. I walked around. My father poked his head into the admissions office, chatted with the admissions director, and—I imagine—either said a few short words about the talents of his son or (knowing my father) remarked on the loveliness of the delphiniums in the college flower beds. Then we had ice cream. I got in.

Am I a better or more successful person for having been accepted at the University of Toronto, as opposed to my second or third choice? It strikes me as a curious question. In Ontario, there wasn't a strict hierarchy of colleges. There were several good ones and several better ones and a number of programs—like computer science at the University of Waterloo—that were world-class. But since all colleges were part of the same public system and tuition everywhere was the same (about a thousand dollars a year, in those days), and a B average in high school pretty much guaranteed you a spot in college, there wasn't a sense that anything great was at stake in the choice of which college we attended. The issue was *whether* we attended college, and—most important—how seriously we took the experience once we got there. I thought everyone felt this way. You can imagine my confusion, then, when I first met someone who had gone to Harvard.

There was, first of all, that strange initial reluctance to talk about the matter of college at all—a glance downward, a shuffling of the feet, a mumbled mention of Cambridge. "Did you go to Harvard?" I would ask. I had just moved to the United States. I didn't know the rules. An uncomfortable nod would follow. Don't define me by my school, they seemed to be saying, which implied that their school actually could define them. And, of course, it did. Wherever there was one Harvard graduate, another lurked not far behind, ready to swap tales of late nights at the Hasty Pudding, or recount the intricacies of the college-application essay, or wonder out loud about the whereabouts of Prince So-and-So, who lived down the hall and whose family had a place in the South of France that you would *not* believe. In the novels they were writing, the precocious and sensitive protagonist always went to Harvard; if he was troubled, he dropped out of Harvard; in the end, he returned to Harvard to complete his senior thesis. Once, I attended a wedding of a Harvard alum in his fifties, at which the best man spoke of his college days with the groom as if neither could have accomplished anything of greater importance in the intervening thirty years. By the end, I half expected him to take off his shirt and proudly display the large crimson "H" tattooed on his chest. What is this "Harvard" of which you Americans speak so reverently?

In 1905, Harvard College adopted the College Entrance Examination Board tests as the principal basis for admission, which meant that virtually any academically gifted high-school senior who could afford a private college had a straightforward shot at attending. By 1908, the freshman class was seven per cent Jewish, nine per cent Catholic, and forty-five per cent from public schools, an astonishing transformation for a school that historically had been the preserve of the New England boarding-school complex known in the admissions world as St. Grottlesex.

As the sociologist Jerome Karabel writes in "The Chosen" (Houghton Mifflin; $28), his remarkable history of the admissions process at Harvard, Yale, and Princeton, that meritocratic spirit soon led to a crisis. The enrollment of Jews began to rise dramatically. By 1922, they made up more than a fifth of Harvard's freshman class. The administration and alumni were up in arms. Jews were thought to be sickly and grasping, grade-grubbing and insular. They displaced the sons of wealthy Wasp alumni, which did not bode well for fund-raising. A. Lawrence Lowell, Harvard's president in the nineteen-twenties, stated flatly that too many Jews would destroy the school: "The summer hotel that is ruined by admitting Jews meets its fate . . . because they drive away the Gentiles, and then after the Gentiles have left, they leave also."

The difficult part, however, was coming up with a way of keeping Jews out, because as a group they were academically superior to everyone else. Lowell's first idea—a quota limiting Jews to fifteen per cent of the student body—was roundly criticized. Lowell tried restricting the number of scholarships given to Jewish students, and made an effort to bring in students from public schools in the West, where there were fewer Jews. Neither strategy worked. Finally, Lowell—and his counterparts at Yale and Princeton—realized that if a definition of merit based on academic prowess was leading to the wrong kind of student, the solution was to change the definition of merit. Karabel argues that it was at this moment that the history and nature of the Ivy League took a significant turn.

The admissions office at Harvard became much more interested in the details of an applicant's personal life. Lowell told his admissions officers to elicit information about the "character" of candidates from "persons who know the applicants well," and so the letter of reference became mandatory. Harvard started asking applicants to provide a photograph. Candidates had to write personal essays, demonstrating their aptitude for leadership, and list their extracurricular activities. "Starting in the fall of 1922," Karabel writes, "applicants were required to answer questions on 'Race and Color,' 'Religious Preference,' 'Maiden Name of Mother,' 'Birthplace of Father,' and 'What change, if any, has been made since birth in your own name or that of your father? (Explain fully).'"

At Princeton, emissaries were sent to the major boarding schools, with instructions to rate potential candidates on a scale of 1 to 4, where 1 was "very desirable and apparently exceptional material from every point of view" and 4 was "undesirable from the point of view of character, and, therefore, to be excluded no matter what the results of the entrance examinations might be." The personal interview became a key component of admissions in order, Karabel writes, "to ensure that 'undesirables' were identified and to assess important but subtle indicators of background and breeding such as speech, dress, deportment and physical appearance." By 1933, the end of Lowell's term, the percentage of Jews at Harvard was back down to fifteen per cent.

If this new admissions system seems familiar, that's because it is essentially the same system that the Ivy League uses to this day. According to Karabel, Harvard, Yale, and Princeton didn't abandon the elevation of character once the Jewish crisis passed. They institutionalized it.

Starting in 1953, Arthur Howe, Jr., spent a decade as the chair of admissions at Yale, and Karabel describes what happened under his guidance:

> The admissions committee viewed evidence of "manliness" with particular enthusiasm. One boy gained admission despite an academic prediction of 70 because "there was apparently something manly and distinctive about him that had won over both his alumni and staff interviewers." Another candidate, admitted despite his schoolwork being "mediocre in comparison with many others," was accepted over an applicant with a much better record and higher exam scores because, as Howe put it, "we just thought he was more of a guy." So preoccupied was Yale with the appearance of its students that the form used by alumni interviewers actually had a physical characteristics checklist through 1965. Each year, Yale carefully measured the height of entering freshmen, noting with pride the proportion of the class at six feet or more.

At Harvard, the key figure in that same period was Wilbur Bender, who, as the dean of admissions, had a preference for "the boy with some athletic interests and abilities, the boy with physical vigor and coordination and grace." Bender, Karabel tells us, believed that if Harvard continued to suffer on the football field it would contribute to the school's reputation as a place with "no college spirit, few good fellows, and no vigorous, healthy social life," not to mention a "surfeit of 'pansies,' 'decadent esthetes' and 'precious sophisticates.'" Bender concentrated on improving Harvard's techniques for evaluating "intangibles" and, in particular, its "ability to detect homosexual tendencies and serious psychiatric problems."

By the nineteen-sixties, Harvard's admissions system had evolved into a series of complex algorithms. The school began by lumping all applicants into one of twenty-two dockets, according to their geographical origin. (There was one docket for Exeter and Andover, another for the eight Rocky Mountain states.) Information from interviews, references, and student essays was then used to grade each applicant on a scale of 1 to 6, along four dimensions: personal, academic, extracurricular, and athletic. Competition, critically, was within each docket, not between dockets, so there was no way for, say, the graduates of Bronx Science and Stuyvesant to shut out the graduates of Andover and Exeter. More important, academic achievement was just one of four dimensions, further diluting the value of pure intellectual accomplishment. Athletic ability, rather than falling under "extracurriculars," got a category all to itself, which explains why, even now, recruited athletes have an acceptance rate to the Ivies at well over twice the rate of other students, despite S.A.T. scores that are on average more than a hundred points lower. And the most important category? That mysterious index of "personal" qualities. According to Harvard's own analysis, the personal rating was a better predictor of admission than the academic rating. Those with a rank of 4 or worse on the personal scale had, in the nineteen-sixties, a rejection rate of ninety-eight per cent. Those with a personal rating of 1 had a rejection rate of 2.5 per cent. When the Office of Civil Rights at the federal education department investigated Harvard in the nineteen-eighties, they found handwritten notes scribbled in the margins of various candidates' files. "This young woman could be one of the brightest applicants in the pool but there are several references to shyness," read one. Another comment reads, "Seems a tad frothy." One application— and at this point you can almost hear it going to the bottom of the pile— was notated, "Short with big ears."

Social scientists distinguish between what are known as treatment effects and selection effects. The Marine Corps, for instance, is largely a treatment-effect institution. It doesn't have an enormous admissions office grading applicants along four separate dimensions of toughness and intelligence. It's confident that the experience of undergoing Marine Corps basic training will turn you into a formidable soldier. A modelling agency, by contrast, is a selection-effect institution. You don't become beautiful by signing up with an agency. You get signed up by an agency because you're beautiful.

At the heart of the American obsession with the Ivy League is the belief that schools like Harvard provide the social and intellectual equivalent of Marine Corps basic training—that being taught by all those brilliant professors and meeting all those other motivated students and getting a degree with that powerful name on it will confer advantages that no local state university can provide. Fuelling the treatment-effect idea are studies showing that if you take two students with the same S.A.T. scores and grades, one of whom goes to a school like Harvard and one of whom goes to a less selective college, the Ivy Leaguer will make far more money ten or twenty years down the road.

The extraordinary emphasis the Ivy League places on admissions policies, though, makes it seem more like a modelling agency than like the

Marine Corps, and, sure enough, the studies based on those two apparently equivalent students turn out to be flawed. How do we know that two students who have the same S.A.T. scores and grades really are equivalent? It's quite possible that the student who goes to Harvard is more ambitious and energetic and personable than the student who wasn't let in, and that those same intangibles are what account for his better career success. To assess the effect of the Ivies, it makes more sense to compare the student who got into a top school with the student who got into that same school but chose to go to a less selective one. Three years ago, the economists Alan Krueger and Stacy Dale published just such a study. And they found that when you compare apples and apples the income bonus from selective schools disappears.

"As a hypothetical example, take the University of Pennsylvania and Penn State, which are two schools a lot of students choose between," Krueger said. "One is Ivy, one is a state school. Penn is much more highly selective. If you compare the students who go to those two schools, the ones who go to Penn have higher incomes. But let's look at those who got into both types of schools, some of whom chose Penn and some of whom chose Penn State. Within that set it doesn't seem to matter whether you go to the more selective school. Now, you would think that the more ambitious student is the one who would choose to go to Penn, and the ones choosing to go to Penn State might be a little less confident in their abilities or have a little lower family income, and both of those factors would point to people doing worse later on. But they don't."

Krueger says that there is one exception to this. Students from the very lowest economic strata do seem to benefit from going to an Ivy. For most students, though, the general rule seems to be that if you are a hardworking and intelligent person you'll end up doing well regardless of where you went to school. You'll make good contacts at Penn. But Penn State is big enough and diverse enough that you can make good contacts there, too. Having Penn on your résumé opens doors. But if you were good enough to get into Penn you're good enough that those doors will open for you anyway. "I can see why families are really concerned about this," Krueger went on. "The average graduate from a top school is making nearly a hundred and twenty thousand dollars a year, the average graduate from a moderately selective school is making ninety thousand dollars. That's an enormous difference, and I can see why parents would fight to get their kids into the better school. But I think they are just assigning to the school a lot of what the student is bringing with him to the school."

Bender was succeeded as the dean of admissions at Harvard by Fred Glimp, who, Karabel tells us, had a particular concern with academic underperformers. "Any class, no matter how able, will always have a bottom quarter," Glimp once wrote. "What are the effects of the psychology of feeling average, even in a very able group? Are there identifiable types with the psychological or what-not tolerance to be 'happy' or to make the most of education while in the bottom quarter?" Glimp thought it was critical that the students who populated the lower rungs of every Harvard class weren't so driven and ambitious that they would be disturbed by their status. "Thus the renowned (some would say notorious) Harvard admission practice known as the 'happy-bottom-quarter' policy was born," Karabel writes.

It's unclear whether or not Glimp found any students who fit that particular description. (He wondered, in a marvellously honest moment, whether the answer was "Harvard sons.") But Glimp had the realism of the modelling scout. Glimp believed implicitly what Krueger and Dale later confirmed: that the character and performance of an academic class is determined, to a significant extent, at the point of admission; that if you want to graduate winners you have to admit winners; that if you want the bottom quarter of your class to succeed you have to find people capable of succeeding in the bottom quarter. Karabel is quite right, then, to see the events of the nineteen-twenties as the defining moment of the modern Ivy League. You are whom you admit in the élite-education business, and when Harvard changed whom it admitted, it changed Harvard. Was that change for the better or for the worse?

In the wake of the Jewish crisis, Harvard, Yale, and Princeton chose to adopt what might be called the "best graduates" approach to admissions. France's École Normale Supérieure, Japan's University of Tokyo, and most of the world's other élite schools define their task as looking for the best students—that is, the applicants who will have the greatest academic success during their time in college. The Ivy League schools justified their emphasis on character and personality, however, by arguing that they were searching for the students who would have the greatest success *after* college. They were looking for leaders, and leadership, the officials of the Ivy League believed, was not a simple matter of academic brilliance. "Should our goal be to select a student body with the highest possible proportions of high-ranking students, or should it be to select, within a reasonably high range of academic ability, a student body with a certain variety of talents, qualities, attitudes, and backgrounds?" Wilbur Bender asked. To him, the answer was obvious. If you let in only the brilliant, then you produced bookworms and bench scientists: you ended up as socially irrelevant as the University of Chicago (an institution Harvard officials looked upon and shuddered). "Above a reasonably good level of mental ability, above that indicated by a 550-600 level of S.A.T. score," Bender went on, "the only thing that matters in terms of future impact on, or contribution to, society is the degree of personal inner force an individual has."

It's easy to find fault with the best-graduates approach. We tend to think that intellectual achievement is the fairest and highest standard of merit. The Ivy League process, quite apart from its dubious origins, seems subjective and opaque. Why should personality and athletic ability matter so much? The notion that "the ability to throw, kick, or hit a ball is a legitimate criterion in determining who should be admitted to our greatest research universities," Karabel writes, is "a proposition that would be considered laughable in most of the world's countries." At the same time that Harvard was constructing its byzantine admissions system, Hunter College Elementary School, in New York, required simply that applicants take an exam, and if they scored in the top fifty they got in. It's hard to imagine a more objective and transparent procedure.

But what did Hunter achieve with that best-students model? In the nineteen-eighties, a handful of educational researchers surveyed the students who attended the elementary school between 1948 and 1960. [The results were published in 1993 as "Genius Revisited: High IQ Children Grown Up," by Rena Subotnik, Lee Kassan, Ellen Summers, and Alan Wasser.] This was a group with an average I.Q. of 157—three and a half standard deviations above the mean—who had been given what, by any measure, was one of the finest classroom experiences in the world. As graduates, though, they weren't nearly as distinguished as they were expected to be. "Although most of our study participants are successful and fairly content with their lives and accomplishments," the authors conclude, "there are no superstars . . . and only one or two familiar names." The researchers spend a great deal of time trying to figure out why Hunter graduates are so disappointing, and end up sounding very much like Wilbur Bender. Being a smart child isn't a terribly good predictor of success in later life, they conclude. "Non-intellective" factors—like motivation and social skills—probably matter more. Perhaps, the study suggests, "after noting the sacrifices involved in trying for national or world-class leadership in a field, H.C.E.S. graduates decided that the intelligent thing to do was to choose relatively happy and successful lives." It is a wonderful thing, of course, for a school to turn out lots of relatively happy and successful graduates. But Harvard didn't want lots of relatively happy and successful graduates. It wanted superstars, and Bender and his colleagues recognized that if this is your goal a best-students model isn't enough.

Most élite law schools, to cite another example, follow a best-students model. That's why they rely so heavily on the L.S.A.T. Yet there's no reason to believe that a person's L.S.A.T. scores have much relation to how good a lawyer he will be. In a recent research project funded by the Law School Admission Council, the Berkeley researchers Sheldon Zedeck and Marjorie Shultz identified twenty-six "competencies" that they think effective lawyering demands—among them practical judgment, passion and engagement, legal-research skills, questioning and interviewing skills, negotiation skills, stress management, and so on—and the L.S.A.T. picks up only a handful of them. A law school that wants to select the best possible lawyers has to use a very different admissions process from a law school that wants to select the best possible law students. And wouldn't we prefer that at least some law schools try to select good lawyers instead of good law students?

This search for good lawyers, furthermore, is necessarily going to be subjective, because things like passion and engagement can't be measured as precisely as academic proficiency. Subjectivity in the admissions process is not just an occasion for discrimination; it is also, in better times, the only means available for giving us the social outcome we want. The first black captain of the Yale football team was a man named Levi Jackson, who graduated in 1950. Jackson was a hugely popular figure on campus. He went on to be a top executive at Ford, and is credited with persuading the company to hire thousands of African-Americans after the 1967 riots. When Jackson was tapped for the exclusive secret society Skull and Bones, he joked, "If my name had been reversed, I never would have made it." He had a point. The strategy of discretion that Yale had once used to exclude Jews was soon being used to include people like Levi Jackson.

In the 2001 book "The Game of Life," James L. Shulman and William Bowen (a former president of Princeton) conducted an enormous statistical analysis on an issue that has become one of the most contentious in admissions: the special preferences given to recruited athletes at selective universities. Athletes, Shulman and Bowen demonstrate, have a large and growing advantage in admission over everyone else. At the same time, they have markedly lower G.P.A.s and S.A.T. scores than their peers. Over the past twenty years, their class rankings have steadily dropped, and they tend to segregate themselves in an "athletic culture" different from the culture of the rest of the college. Shulman and Bowen think the preference given to athletes by the Ivy League is shameful.

Halfway through the book, however, Shulman and Bowen present what they call a "surprising" finding. Male athletes, despite their lower S.A.T. scores and grades, and despite the fact that many of them are members of minorities and come from lower socioeconomic backgrounds than other students, turn out to earn a lot more than their peers. Apparently, athletes are far more likely to go into the high-paying financial-services sector, where they succeed because of their personality and psychological makeup. In what can only be described as a textbook example of burying the lead, Bowen and Shulman write:

> One of these characteristics can be thought of as drive—a strong desire to succeed and unswerving determination to reach a goal, whether it be winning the next game or closing a sale. Similarly, athletes tend to be more energetic than the average person, which translates into an ability to work hard over long periods of time—to meet, for example, the workload demands placed on young people by an investment bank in the throes of analyzing a transaction. In addition, athletes are more likely than others to be highly competitive, gregarious and confident of their ability to work well in groups (on teams).

Shulman and Bowen would like to argue that the attitudes of selective colleges toward athletes are a perversion of the ideals of American élite education, but that's because they misrepresent the actual ideals of American élite education. The Ivy League is perfectly happy to accept, among others, the kind of student who makes a lot of money after graduation. As the old saying goes, the definition of a well-rounded Yale graduate is someone who can roll all the way from New Haven to Wall Street.

I once had a conversation with someone who worked for an advertising agency that represented one of the big luxury automobile brands. He said that he was worried that his client's new lower-priced line was being bought disproportionately by black women. He insisted that he did not mean this in a racist way. It was just a fact, he said. Black women would destroy the brand's cachet. It was his job to protect his client from the attentions of the socially undesirable.

This is, in no small part, what Ivy League admissions directors do. They are in the luxury-brand-management business, and "The Chosen," in the end, is a testament to just how well the brand managers in Cambridge, New Haven, and Princeton have done their job in the past seventy-five years. In the nineteen-twenties, when Harvard tried to figure out how many Jews they had on campus, the admissions office scoured student records and assigned each suspected Jew the designation j1 (for someone who was "conclusively Jewish"), j2 (where the "preponderance of evidence" pointed to Jewishness), or j3 (where Jewishness was a "possibility"). In the branding world, this is called customer segmentation. In the Second World War, as Yale faced plummeting enrollment and revenues, it continued to turn down qualified Jewish applicants. As Karabel writes, "In the language of sociology, Yale judged its symbolic capital to be even more precious than its economic capital." No good brand manager would sacrifice reputation for short-term gain. The admissions directors at Harvard have always, similarly, been diligent about rewarding the children of graduates, or, as they are quaintly called, "legacies." In the 1985–92 period, for instance, Harvard admitted children of alumni at a rate more than twice that of non-athlete, non-legacy applicants, despite the fact that, on virtually every one of the school's magical ratings scales, legacies significantly lagged behind their peers. Karabel calls the practice "unmeritocratic at best and profoundly corrupt at worst," but rewarding customer loyalty is what luxury brands do. Harvard wants good graduates, and part of their definition of a good graduate is someone who is a generous and loyal alumnus. And if you want generous and loyal alumni you have to reward them. Aren't the tremendous resources provided to Harvard by its alumni part of the reason so many people want to go to Harvard in the first place? The endless battle over admissions in the United States proceeds on the assumption that some great moral principle is at stake in the matter of whom schools like Harvard choose to let in—that those who are denied admission by the whims of the admissions office have somehow been harmed. If you are sick and a hospital shuts its doors to you, you are harmed. But a selective school is not a hospital, and those it turns away are not sick. Élite schools, like any luxury brand, are an aesthetic experience—an exquisitely constructed fantasy of what it means to belong to an élite—and they have always been mindful of what must be done to maintain that experience.

In the nineteen-eighties, when Harvard was accused of enforcing a secret quota on Asian admissions, its defense was that once you adjusted for the preferences given to the children of alumni and for the preferences given to athletes, Asians really weren't being discriminated against. But you could sense Harvard's exasperation that the issue was being raised at all. If Harvard had too many Asians, it wouldn't be Harvard, just as Harvard wouldn't be Harvard with too many Jews or pansies or parlor pinks or shy types or short people with big ears.

Analyze

1. In your opinion, what are the best markers in determining future success as a college student (grades, SAT/ACT, writing sample, extracurricular interests, focused expertise in sports or the arts, letters of reference, entrance interview, or some other factors)?
2. In a classroom discussion, explain ways that you prepared for college—such as taking AP courses, studying for the SAT, focusing on extracurricular activities, and so forth. In your opinion, which of these experiences helped you develop in meaningful ways as a person? Which did not?
3. Gladwell's essay explores ways in which Ivy League colleges have historically excluded or included certain student groups, allowing some campuses to foster a lack of diversity in its student population. In your opinion, to create well-rounded environments, which areas of diversity are *most* important for colleges to encourage through the admissions process: race, socioeconomics, religion, gender, sexual orientation, political orientation, geographic background (urban, suburban, or rural), or some other consideration?
4. Many colleges target students with unique abilities for admissions, often offering them incentives to attend with scholarships or non-need-based grants. In other words, the admissions process often lowers

the cost of college for students with certain abilities. These targeted abilities often include sports, music, high academic achievement, and the arts. But targeted abilities may include other areas, such as an entrepreneurial spirit, exceptional ability in writing, outstanding scores on a standardized test (e.g., the SAT), or a spirit of volunteerism. If you could target two student groups with unique abilities to receive scholarships or non-need-based grants, which two areas would you choose—and why?

Explore

1. Considering all of the things you have so far accomplished in life, what best prepared you for college?

2. Gladwell suggests that colleges are often known for key benefits. For example, Harvard is known for preparing individuals to work in high-paying business jobs, often in the financial sector. What is your college known for?

3. SHORT WRITING PROMPT: Most colleges "brand" themselves by cultivating a distinct image on their webpage. Spend some time on your college's webpage, with an eye toward exploring photos included on pages directed at perspective students. What experiences are valued in these photos? Are students studying? Are students participating in sports or the arts? Are students engaged in compelling social experiences? Are the students represented diverse in terms of gender and race? Do students appear to come from urban or rural environments? Is there a mix of economically comfortable and economically struggling students? Are students pictured in suits, lab coats, or other professional clothes in such a way as to suggest an emphasis on career training? How do these photos define your college's values for prospective students?

4. FULL WRITING PROMPT: Gladwell's essay explores connections between college and later happiness, future income, and career success. Spend some time talking with upper-class members (juniors and seniors) about the college experience that most mattered to them. In your opinion, how do you expect a college education to change your life? How do you expect it will change your personality or the way you think about yourself?

Eric Hoover
Application Inflation: When Is Enough Enough?

Eric Hoover is a senior writer for *The Chronicle of Higher Education*, where he has written about standardized testing, the process of college admissions, and social media and gender issues within universities.

Colleges and universities boast of their large applicant pools. The University of Chicago, long seen as a place for social misfits and scholarship, had lagged. The home of the "Uncommon App" now takes the Common Application, and is reframing its image. Result: a leap in students applying.

The numbers keep rising, the superlatives keep glowing. Each year, selective colleges promote their application totals, along with the virtues of their applicants.

For this fall's freshman class, the statistics reached remarkable levels. Stanford received a record 32,022 applications from students it called "simply amazing," and accepted 7 percent of them. Brown saw an unprecedented 30,135 applicants, who left the admissions staff "deeply impressed and at times awed." Nine percent were admitted.

The biggest boast came from the University of California, Los Angeles. In a news release, U.C.L.A. said its accepted students had "demonstrated excellence in all aspects of their lives." Citing its record 57,670 applications, the university proclaimed itself "the most popular campus in the nation."

Such announcements tell a story in which colleges get better—and students get more amazing—every year. In reality, the narrative is far more complex, and the implications far less sunny for students as well as colleges caught up in the cruel cycle of selectivity.

To some degree, the increases are inevitable: the college-bound population has grown, and so, too, has the number of applications students file, thanks in part to online technology. But wherever it is raining applications, colleges have helped seed the clouds—by recruiting widely and aggressively for ever more applicants.

Admissions officers are chasing not so much a more perfect student as a more perfect class. In a given year, this elusive ideal might require more violinists, goalies, aspiring engineers or students who can pay the full cost of attendance. Colleges everywhere want more minority students, more out-of-state students and more students from overseas. The pursuit reveals the duality of the modern college. It's a place that serves the public interest, and a business with a bottom line.

Although the tension between mission and marketing has long defined admissions, many believe the balance has tilted too far toward the latter. Many colleges have made applying as simple as updating a Facebook page. Some deans and guidance counselors complain that it's too easy. They question the ethics of intense recruitment by colleges that reject the overwhelming majority of applicants.

"It's like needing a new stereo and buying the whole Radio Shack," says Mark Speyer, director of college counseling at the Columbia Grammar and Preparatory School in New York. "With these bigger pools, colleges are getting a lot of students who have no chance."

Fred Hargadon, former dean of admissions at Princeton and Stanford, doubts that more and more applicants make for a stronger class. "I couldn't pick a better class out of 30,000 applicants than out of 15,000," he says. "I'd just end up rejecting multiples of the same kid."

The tide shows no signs of ebbing. This year, the University of Chicago, Duke and Tulane—the last juggling 43,816 submissions—surpassed their previous application records by double-digit percentages. Applications are, of course, a proxy for popularity and metric of merit. Such is the allure of exclusivity, and the appeal of simplicity. Measuring quality is difficult; measuring quantity is as easy as counting. The more apps a college receives, and rejects, the more impressive it seems.

Today's application inflation is a cause and symptom of the uncertainty in admissions. As application totals soar, colleges struggle to predict yield—the number of admitted students who actually attend—leading to longer wait lists and other competitive enrollment tactics. Students hedge against the plummeting admissions rates by flooding the system with even more applications.

Sarah Markhovsky sees the uncertainty in the students she counsels at Severn School, in Maryland. "They'll say, 'Oh, my gosh, I should apply to a million schools—if I shoot lots of arrows, maybe I'll hit something,'" she says. "This translates into hype that's not useful. It feels like the kids are commodities."

That's how Shaun Stewart felt when he started receiving brochures from colleges. "They want you so they can reject you," says Mr. Stewart, a senior in Burnsville, Minn., who has a 3.5 grade-point average and scored a 27 (out of 36) on the ACT. Those numbers are well below the freshman averages at some of the big-name colleges that sent him applications along with brochures.

"Colleges are there to educate you, but they make it all about who's the best college," he says. "They make it too stressful. Then we make it too stressful on ourselves." He is considering liberal arts colleges like Carleton and Gustavus Adolphus, which he says have shown a more personal touch.

The scale of rejection worries Karl M. Furstenberg, dean of admissions and financial aid at Dartmouth from 1992 to 2007. "When people keep hearing that they're not good enough, this has an undermining psychological effect," he says. Over the last 15 years, he says, growing applicant pools reflected an earnest push for greater diversity among the wealthiest institutions. Yet he believes many have reached a point of diminishing returns.

"It's a classic arms race—escalation for not a whole lot of gain," he says. "I don't think these larger applicant pools are materially improving the quality of their classes. Now what's driving it is the institutional self-interest factor, where bigger pools mean you're more popular, you're better."

Never has the University of Chicago been more popular. It received a record 19,347 applications for this fall—a 43 percent increase over last year—for a freshman class of about 1,400 students. Those numbers would have been noteworthy anywhere, but here they were startling. Chicago had been a holdout, attracting fewer applicants than other intellectual powerhouses. What changed—and why—reveals the dynamics of admissions in the 21st century.

The University of Chicago was founded in the South Side's Hyde Park neighborhood in 1890, but its Gothic buildings look centuries older. Its "Common Core" curriculum steeps undergraduates in the liberal arts. Many deep thinkers—Saul Bellow, Milton Friedman, Carl Sagan—have come here to ponder big questions. Even the wide-eyed gargoyles here seem struck by inspiration.

For years, Chicago's admissions office emphasized the university's distinctiveness: one offbeat mailing was a postcard ringed with a coffee stain. Its application has long included imaginative essay prompts, like "If you could balance on a tightrope, over what landscape would you walk? (No net)." This became known as the "Uncommon Application," in contrast to the Common Application, the standardized form that allows students to apply to any of hundreds of participating colleges.

That some students wouldn't like Chicago's quirky questions was the point. "If understood properly, no given college will appeal to everyone—that wouldn't be possible," says Theodore A. O'Neill, the university's dean of college admissions from 1989 to 2009. "It's important to signal something true and meaningful about yourself. The more signals, the more honest you're being, and doing that does limit the applications."

Mr. O'Neill was not opposed to attracting more applicants. Over time, the admissions staff had expanded outreach and increased diversity.

Yet some of Chicago's leaders concluded that the admissions office had trapped the university in a niche. It had long been dogged by a stereotype as a place for nerds and social misfits who shun sunlight and conversation. T-shirts created by students lovingly mock the university (the most famous is "Where Fun Comes to Die"). In recent years, the university has built new residential complexes, and expanded its study-abroad programs, career-counseling services and recreational offerings.

"It's not that we weren't getting students of quality that we wanted, because we were—they were terrific," says John W. Boyer, dean of the college since 1992. "But we still had the feeling that, as much progress as we were making, there were still a lot of people out there who had these older images of the place. We were not using our admissions office to the maximum degree to say what the college was to the American people."

Conventional wisdom holds that colleges seek more applicants to improve their rankings, but this is a narrow view of the issue. In fact, a college's admissions rate accounts for just 1.5 percent of its score in U.S. News & World Report's ratings. Still, rising selectivity can please alumni, aid fund-raising and help attract top professors.

Bond rating agencies also study application totals. Roger Goodman, vice president and senior credit officer at Moody's Investment Services, says applications are one measure of demand, an indicator of market position and financial health, which affect the cost of borrowing. "If an institution is not growing and improving selectivity, that would probably be more of a concern than it would have been a decade ago," Mr. Goodman says. "Even at a place that's highly selective, there can be very good reasons to expand its applicant base, as long it's coming from wanting to attract a diverse class."

In 2006, under a new president, Robert J. Zimmer, Chicago announced that it would join the Common Application, which many admissions deans say attracts more applicants, especially low-income and minority students.

Although the university vowed to retain its essays in a required supplement, the demise of the "Uncommon Application" sparked a student protest.

Mr. Zimmer, who attended Stuyvesant High School in Manhattan, told officials he wanted more applicants, especially top students from the New York area. The university commissioned market research to meet that goal.

Last year, Mr. O'Neill, one of the profession's most respected members, stepped down (he's now a lecturer at the university). In his place, Chicago hired James G. Nondorf as vice president and dean of college admissions and financial aid.

Colleagues describe Mr. Nondorf as a "super-marketer," a man who gets results. At Yale, he helped diversify the applicant pool and pioneered the university's use of a "likely letter," sent to top applicants before official acceptances. In three years as the top enrollment official at Rensselaer Polytechnic Institute, he oversaw a doubling of applications, which brought record numbers of women.

At Chicago, Mr. Nondorf's first priority was to create a recruitment booklet that contained many photographs of students engaged in group activities, including music, dance, tennis and football. Later, Chicago sent tailored letters to students who had expressed an interest in the arts or in medicine. Admissions officers talked up pre-professional opportunities and career preparation. Visiting families received special rates from the Hilton, where a letter from Mr. Nondorf and a pouch of chocolates awaited them. Over the last year, Chicago's admissions representatives visited about twice as many high schools as they had the previous year. Mr. Nondorf sent three to California instead of one, and for the first time, the university received more applications from the Golden State than from Illinois.

Chicago officials have cited many reasons for this year's application explosion, including the popularity of President Obama, who taught at the university. But some credit should go to Royall & Company, a direct-marketing firm hired last spring to help conduct an expansive recruitment campaign. This included a series of short e-mails sent in rapid succession; some students received nearly 20 in all. This year, Royall's clients averaged a 7 percent increase in applicants.

To each applicant, Chicago assigns a "fit" rating based on holistic measures—say, intellectual curiosity or evidence that a student applied a favorite subject to life. This year it admitted more top students with high ratings than in the past, according to Mr. Nondorf. "The number of applications reflects something, but they're not necessarily what we're after," he says. "Crafting a better educational experience through a better class is the goal."

Still, at an admissions conference in Rhode Island this May, Mr. Nondorf described the pressure on deans. "Don't kid yourselves, the presidents and trustees want you to have more applications," he said. "If you don't think that's the case, I don't know what schools you're working at, but it's true."

Mr. Boyer has compared Chicago's application total with that of Columbia University, which also has a strong liberal arts curriculum. "I believe we are a better university than they are, so I think we should have more applications than they do," he told the student newspaper last winter. The remark was a "friendly, competitive gesture," Mr. Boyer says today. "I don't think Chicago should stand behind New York on this one. We deserve the same number of applications, if not more."

Such talk worries Andre Phillips, who left Chicago last year after two decades as associate director of admissions. "By changing the admissions culture, Chicago has gone in for the quick fix," he says. "My concern is that the institution is marketing itself as something it isn't."

Colleges operate in a realm of perceptions influenced by numbers, yet admissions rates can be a statistical mirage.

As Caroline M. Hoxby noted in a 2009 paper published by the National Bureau of Economic Research, admissions rates fall even when students apply who don't have a shot. Moreover, while increasing selectivity suggests better students than in years past, in truth the most competitive applicants couldn't get more amazing if they levitated. The number of such all-stars isn't multiplying, either. Instead, they are jumping into more applicant pools, which Ms. Hoxby, a Stanford economist, describes as the nationwide "re-sorting" of students as more attend college far from home.

So it behooves colleges to cast wide nets. Most colleges start by buying the names of students whose standardized test scores and grade-point averages fall within a particular range. In the early 1990s, the College Board sold 35 million names a year; now it sells 80 million to about 1,200 colleges, at 32 cents a name. More colleges are buying names of sophomores to jump-start interest.

Over time, the nature of the application has changed. Dozens of colleges send "fast-track" applications, with some information already filled in—and no fee. Tulane mails its "V.I.P. Application" to 130,000 students annually. In an e-mail to the campus this year, its president, Scott S. Cowen, described Tulane's nearly 44,000 applications as "the largest of all private universities in the country."

Earl Retif, Tulane's vice president for enrollment management, credits aggressive recruitment and a new community-service emphasis for helping the university attract more applicants after Hurricane Katrina.

"We don't need 44,000 applications—it just means more people to choose from," Mr. Retif says. "Some people see it as a sign of our popularity. I keep saying it's a double-edged sword." For one, most of the winning applicants did not come. Only about 16 percent of the 10,000 students Tulane admitted ended up enrolling. And the volume of applications has taxed the admissions office, which processed a million pieces of paper this year. Counselors must review 1,200 to 1,500 applications per cycle, compared with 700 to 800 a few years ago.

And it's hard telling so many students no, Mr. Retif says. "Some people say, 'Hey, you invited me.'"

This year, Duke faced similar challenges, with more than 26,000 applications and an evaluation process meant to handle half that. Christoph Guttentag, dean of undergraduate admissions, says the deluge left his staff with too little time to trim its wait list of nearly 3,400 students, roughly twice the size of its freshman class.

Mr. Guttentag believes that application increases heighten anxiety for everyone involved, but he doesn't anticipate much change. "The pressure for more applications isn't offset by an equal pressure for less," he says, "and no college wants to consciously put itself in a weaker competitive position."

Some deans say they have all the applicants they need. Among them is Charles A. Deacon, dean of undergraduate admissions at Georgetown University, which reviewed 18,000 applications this year. Sitting behind a long wooden table, with admissions reports fanned out in front of him, Mr. Deacon explains why he refuses to adopt the Common Application. The ease of the form, he says, would bring Georgetown thousands more applicants. Yet he fears that adding the application would weaken Georgetown's admissions process, in which nearly all applicants are interviewed. "We believe this is a personal relationship between a student and a college," Mr. Deacon says. "With our own application, we know people are applying who want to apply."

Georgetown buys names of students with PSAT scores equivalent to 1270 on the SAT critical reading and math sections, and grade-point averages of A- or better. There are only so many students with these attributes to go around—about 44,000 a year, out of 1.5 million test takers. Georgetown lowers that threshold to search for another 5,000 or so under-represented minority students.

This year, Georgetown enrolled a record 142 black students, selected from a pool of 1,400. Mr. Deacon doubts he could have chosen a more accomplished group from a pool of 2,800. "The question is, what's a good enough class?" he says. "We're not going to say, 'Come one, come all' just to find that one gem of a student and devastate the dreams of all the rest."

William R. Fitzsimmons, Harvard's dean of admissions, describes his university's recruitment as "aggressive"—and crucial. "Nobody wants to go back to the bad old days, when getting into America's top colleges was like knowing a secret handshake," Mr. Fitzsimmons says. "If we started cutting back, applications would go down from the students who need real outreach."

Harvard enlists students to call and e-mail thousands of prospective minority applicants with high test scores. Lucerito Ortiz, who graduated last spring, grew up in Los Angeles, the daughter of two immigrants. Although she earned good grades in high school, she did not think about Harvard. "People like me didn't go to places like that," she recalls.

Her thinking changed when Harvard sent her a search letter. After enrolling at the university, Ms. Ortiz helped the admissions office contact students from backgrounds like hers. She says she always explained the long odds of getting in (Harvard's admissions rate was just under 7 percent this year). "In a way, it's sad, but I don't feel bad about it," says Ms. Ortiz, now an admissions officer at Harvard. "I don't feel guilty for giving students the chance to have their lives changed."

A Harvard representative contacted Sally Nuamah her junior year of high school in Chicago. Ms. Nuamah had good grades but an ACT score she describes as low. Her parents, who came from Ghana, had little money. As she welcomed the admissions rep into her living room one day, she was nervous. "I was like, 'Oh, goodness, I don't want to disappoint anyone,'" she says.

Ensuing conversations brought mixed emotions. "I felt that I was pushed and given motivation," she says, "but on the other hand, I wondered if what they were telling me was feasible." She knew her scores were below the average for Harvard students. Nonetheless, she applied. Months later, a rejection letter came.

Ms. Nuamah, now a senior at George Washington University, asserts that such outreach can help low-income students who lack confidence, but she sees a potential downside. "Many of those students are so conditioned to disappointment," she explains. "If colleges are targeting hundreds of students somewhere and not one is accepted, they may need to re-evaluate their efforts. Some people might say, 'Those colleges come here and do that to us, and nobody ever ends up going.'"

A half century ago, B. Alden Thresher wrote a prescient book called "College Admissions and the Public Interest." Thresher, a former director admissions at the Massachusetts Institute of Technology, described colleges' justifications for increasing selectivity as "rationalizations for a kind of insensate avarice: we want the best and only the best, we are never satisfied." But he saw something noble, too, in the relentless search: "It is also deeply connected with the highest virtues of academic man—the impulse toward perfection."

The quest for the perfect class involves irony: the push for more inclusiveness inevitably leads to more exclusivity. Andrew Delbanco, professor of humanities at Columbia and author of a forthcoming book about higher education, has pondered the meaning of declining admissions rates. He describes his students as smart, engaged and imaginative but not necessarily more than they were 10 years ago, when Columbia had far fewer applicants.

Ever-increasing selectivity, Mr. Delbanco says, has shaped the way some students think about education.

"If you succeed in getting into a selective college, it would take a pretty extraordinary person not to think you've already done something pretty terrific," he says. "One of the hazards of this arms race is that it can inculcate a feeling of self-satisfaction on the part of the student, as well as the institution."

William M. Shain, an educational consultant and former admissions dean at three private colleges, believes that bigger applicant pools can bring better students—up to a point. "You'll always get a class where things that can be measured, like testing, go up," he says. "But you won't necessarily get a class that thinks better or enhances the classroom."

Moreover, because so many seats go to "hooked" students, Mr. Shain questions the benefits of recruiting by colleges that accept fewer than 20 percent of applicants. Take Mr. Shain's alma mater, Princeton, whose freshman class this year is 37 percent minority students, 17 percent athletes, 13 percent legacies and 11 percent international students. "Among very, very good schools, a huge percentage of the class is not in play on academic grounds," he says. "How much can you improve the class when you're only working with half or less?"

Susan Tree, director of college counseling at the Westtown School, a college-prep academy in Pennsylvania, attends about 100 college presentations a year. She's often struck by the cookie-cutter nature of recruitment pitches. "It seems colleges have lost the sense of presenting places so that some kids are turned on and others are turned off," she says. She believes the University of Chicago had something that many colleges desired—an identity: "The risk they run is that they're joining the ranks of generic, highly selective colleges."

But selectivity speaks. Maya Lozinski, a freshman at Chicago, grew up in Menlo Park, Calif. She had never heard of the university until it sent her a postcard.

Ultimately, Chicago was her first choice. She says the university is becoming "normal," more career oriented. She liked the maroon scarf it sent her. She also liked its declining admissions rate. In 2004, Chicago accepted 40 percent of its applicants, compared with 18 percent this year. "I wouldn't have applied a few years ago—I would have felt overqualified," says Ms. Lozinski, who had an A average in high school and scored a 2370 (out of 2400) on the SAT. "A college's admissions rate says something about the quality of students who go there and the prestige of it."

Perhaps the University of Chicago will end up trading one kind of exclusivity for another. Marshall Knudson says that some students on the campus fret that the university will lose its niche as it attracts more applicants, while other students see the declining admissions rate as adding value to their degrees.

Mr. Knudson, who graduated from Chicago last spring, chose the university for its "feverish intellectual vapors." As a freshman, he protested the adoption of the Common Application, fearing it would diminish the culture of the university. Looking back, Mr. Knudson is skeptical of such "utopian visions." He doubts any university could deliver an experience that matches the story it tells the world beyond its gates. "People like to promote a vision of what makes them unique, but it's just wishful thinking," he says. "It was a great education. I'm glad I went there. But I don't think it ever lived up to its ideal."

"And maybe that's the value of an education," he says. "It helps you realize the limits of an ideal."

Analyze

1. Eric Hoover suggests that the appearance of selectivity and popularity drives some universities to expand their student applicant pool, even when they are aware many students in the pool will not meet admission standards. In your opinion, what other factors may spur colleges to over-fill their applicant pools?
2. In 2014, Harvard received 34,295 applications and accepted 2,048 students. In other words, it had a 1700% surplus of applications. In your opinion, how many additional applications should a college solicit beyond those it has the ability to accept?
3. Do you believe that colleges should be forbidden from accepting application packets—and application fees—from students whose GPA and SAT/ACT scores fall substantially below the general admission range for the college?
4. One student interviewed in the article, Maya Lozinski, speculates that the college admission pool has grown because the college experience currently is "more career oriented." If college didn't help determine your future employability, how would that have changed where you applied to college and what programs of study you considered?

Explore

1. In reviewing your own experience in applying for college, what one change would make the process easier or more meaningful for you?
2. At what age should kids start exploring their college possibilities? And why do students need this amount of time to consider their college options?
3. SHORT WRITING PROMPT: Visit your college admissions office and ask an admissions officer to explain the criteria that your school uses to review applications. Write up your notes into a one-page memo for the class.
4. FULL WRITING PROMPT: Using the form of a letter, write a two-page note to freshmen at your high school alma mater, explaining what you wish you had understood about the college application process and college itself at their age.

Thomas Frank
The Price of Admission

Thomas Frank is a historian and journalist whose work is focused on popular culture, American politics, and economic trends. He has been a columnist for *Harper's Magazine* and *The Wall Street Journal*. He is the author of nine books, including *What's the Matter with Kansas?*, which was adapted into a documentary film.

A vignette from the campaign trail, circa March 2012: The Republican front-runner was taking questions at a town-hall meeting in Mahoning Valley, Ohio. A high school senior rose to explain that he was on his way to college, but that he worried about the cost. Although the student didn't mention it—he scarcely needed to—tuition increases have been outpacing inflation for decades, and these days college graduates routinely begin their working lives deep in debt. What was Mitt Romney going to do about it?

In response, Romney gave one of his patented lessons in managerial smugness. The solution was to "recognize that college is expensive" but that competition "works." No "government money" would be forthcoming under a Romney regime, the candidate went on, to the kind of applause that these days seems to follow any public declaration of tightfisted self-righteousness. And so it was up to the student-consumer himself to "shop around," compare the goods offered up in the freewheeling marketplace of educational choice, and make the best decision he could.

Ordinarily, conservatives are willing to believe the absolute worst about the groves of academe. In their view, college is a gilded re-education camp, where innocent children of the entrepreneurial class are turned into brainwashed Maoist cadres, chanting slogans and grinding away the hours in a sexual frolic. The university's scholarly departments, they believe, are filled with political extremists; its graduates are snobs; its concern with diversity is a form of censorship; its scientists tell lies in order to further the "global warming" power grab or prepare the ground for more stem-cell monkey business.

Academia's pricing, however, is apparently A-OK. Nothing wrong here. Consumers shop around, they compare and contrast, and they get the best deal they can, reassured all the while by their awareness that competition works. Just don't come whining to the government for help.

But what if competition doesn't work? What if academia's pricing, which has hung student debt like a millstone around the neck of an entire generation, is completely out of whack?

This is not the first time such questions have been posed. Twenty years ago, under the presidency of George H. W. Bush, the Department of Justice charged the Ivy League universities and MIT with conspiring to restrict financial-aid awards, and thus to fix prices. Officers of the various Ivy League schools, it seems, were then in the habit of meeting several times a year to discuss tuition increases, faculty salaries, and financial-aid packages with their supposed competitors. It was classic price-fixing behavior— Attorney General Dick Thornburgh called the schools a "collegiate cartel"—and the antitrust violation seemed obvious on its face. The Ivies settled immediately after the suit was filed in 1991, signing a consent decree that forbade them to collude over tuition, salary, or financial-aid awards. (The decree expired in 2001.)[1]

To judge from newspaper reports, the Ivy League antitrust suit was to some degree a reaction against out-of-control tuition costs, of the sort that still rankle us today. The 1980s were, after all, the first great period of galloping tuition inflation. Parents of college students were understandably outraged as the total price of a year at, say, Princeton outpaced the cost of a new car and began to approach the annual income of the typical American. (When the Justice Department launched its antitrust investigation, annual tuitions at Ivy League schools were in the neighborhood of $16,000; today they are around $41,000, and once you factor in room and board, the tab is closer to $54,000.)

Looking back from twenty years on, it's clear that the antitrust suit did little to rein in tuition increases. Some believe it may have driven costs even higher. But the central facts are worth remembering: the most prestigious universities in America were acting like a cartel, consumers screamed in protest, and thanks to the quaint democratic dynamic that still sometimes prevailed in those days—even when Republicans were in power— government acted.

---

[1] MIT chose to fight on alone. The school was convicted of price fixing in U.S. District Court in 1992, but the following year, an appeals court sent the case back for review. Before the trial could begin again, MIT settled as well, working out a compromise with the Justice Department that was subsequently written into law.

Today, of course, we know better. The situation may be exponentially worse, and we may have a Democrat who burbles constantly from the presidential throne about the wonders of an educated public, but we have seen the light: we have learned about Markets. As Mitt Romney says, we know that competition exists, and that it will always guarantee us the best possible deal.

Oh, government can help in some regards. It can shovel out the student loans that subsidize the booming education industry. It can enforce tough bankruptcy standards, which make it virtually impossible for students to escape their indebtedness and thereby encourage private companies to write even more loans. And, of course, government can take the blame when the whole structure comes toppling down in a cascade of defaults, involving not only the loans themselves but also the asset-backed securities into which those loans have been so cunningly packaged. All we will need on that occasion is another Rick Santelli to rail against the liberal-arts deadbeats—those government-funded loafers responsible for ruining millions of hardworking derivatives investors.[2]

But do something to control costs? Draft a bailout plan for students in debt? Resolve to make state schools so cheap and so excellent that they drive down tuition everywhere? We might as well collectivize agriculture, or embark on a five-year plan for tractor production.

One of the arguments that the Ivy League brass made in their defense back in 1991 was that universities were not businesses but charitable institutions. This struck them as axiomatic, because of a very simple economic fact: tuition costs were high, but they could have been much, much higher.

After all, what universities were selling then, and what they are selling today, is an extremely valuable commodity: entry into what sociologists call the professional-managerial class. There's a reason that Lexus LX 570 that almost ran you down in the crosswalk the other day had a Harvard sticker neatly centered on its rear window. And it isn't because the driver believes we would all profit from immersing ourselves in theories of intersectionality, or because of a lifelong attachment to Crimson field hockey. That sticker is there because "Harvard" is a crucial part of who that SUV driver is. A college degree from a prestigious school is the credential that matters

---

[2] When that day comes, you can be pretty sure that tomorrow's Tea Partiers will also blame the usual scapegoats: college professors who teach inexcusably airy subjects like English and philology (but never the professors who teach marketing or civil procedure).

most in American life, and growing college-enrollment figures suggest that an increasing number of Americans have figured this out.

Why do they think this? Because just about everyone tells them that it is so. We live in a "knowledge economy," the consensus assures us, and awesome universities are both America's great competitive advantage over the rest of the world and every child's ticket to personal financial success.

In such a situation, the fact that the cost of attending an elite college has spiraled up like a runaway ICBM is utterly unsurprising, and it has little to do with the expenses involved in transferring wisdom from the professor's head into yours.[3] An annual pass to Disneyland would also cost $54,000 if society believed that what it took to make you eligible for success was a great many hours spent absorbing the subtle lessons of the Finding Nemo Submarine Voyage. And absent any flood of top-tier, quaintly antique universities into the marketplace, such costs will continue to increase until they hit the limit that people will pay for such a golden ticket. Ten years from now, in fact, college students may well look back with jealousy on their predecessors who got away with a mere hundred grand in debt.

Even in 1991, it had been a long time since anyone took seriously what the universities offered as their all-purpose defense: that everything they do is permissible because they are charitable institutions. Charitable institutions do not exploit the labor of their charges, nor do they relentlessly bid down their wages, as universities do with the grad students and new Ph.D.'s who take on much of the teaching nowadays. They don't run their endowments as you would a hedge fund (or, as is often the case, invest them directly in such concerns). They don't take kickbacks to steer kids into the toothy mouths of expensive private lenders. They don't sell their souls for seats on corporate boards or research grants from tobacco companies or a Division I title. They don't replace scholarly leaders with armies of professional managers who proceed to fiddle with the curriculum, funnel resources to business schools, and strive for supremacy as (in the winning words of one expert on the subject) "one among many industries that pursue intellectual properties." These are the deeds of profit-maximizing entities. The fact that universities don't have shareholders and don't pay exorbitant bonuses to top officers is merely a matter of organizational detail.

---

[3] The ascending cost of state universities is propelled by an obvious, additional cause: cutbacks in state funding.

Then again, given the valuable cultural real estate that universities control, one wonders why it took them so long to actualize their inner corporation. We are living in a golden age of price discovery, in which our masters have figured out that no one is going to stop them from charging as much as they want for necessities that ought to be or used to be considered public goods. Medicine, of course, is the classic example: how much can you get Americans to pay for the chemotherapy they need to stay alive? Electric power was also, briefly, an arena for this kind of behavior, back when Enron was selectively plunging millions of California households into darkness. And before long, our masters will no doubt have figured out ways to extend the logic to other necessities: food, highways, public safety, political representation, a prime poolside spot in the afterlife, all of them yielding whatever the traffic will bear.

It is easy to criticize the corporatization of education, since the examples are so plentiful and almost no one denies that it's taking place. But criticizing it is different from actually halting its progress—a political step we seem unable to take.

Indeed, the trends all point in the opposite direction. Until recently, the United Kingdom, which has long had one of the best higher-education systems in the world, capped university fees at the annual equivalent of $5,200. (Before 1998, tuition was free throughout the United Kingdom.) Now Britain is moving rapidly toward the American model, with its galaxy of private, for-profit institutions and its staggering price tags. It is doing so because British leaders, like their American brethren, have convinced themselves that what universities are really about is getting rich; that they exist to deliver the goods in the knowledge economy; and that in order to prepare students for wealth accumulation in a lean-and-mean knowledge-transmission sector, those students must be made to pay for what they receive. Without indebtedness to sharpen the point of the stick (and make the carrot seem that much juicier), students will just sit around in their quadrangles as they always have, wallowing in pointless disciplines and tossing Frisbees.

Massive indebtedness changes a person, maybe even more than a college education does, and it's reasonable to suspect that the politicos who have allowed the tuition disaster to take its course know this. To saddle young people with enormous, inescapable debt—total student debt is now more than one trillion dollars—is ultimately to transform them into profit-maximizing machines. I mean, working as a schoolteacher or an editorial assistant at a publishing house isn't going to help you chip away at that forty grand you owe. You can't get out of it by bankruptcy, either. And our political leaders, lost in a fantasy of punitive individualism, certainly won't propose the bailout measures they could take to rescue the young from the crushing burden.

What will happen to the young debtors instead is that they will become *Homo economicus*, whether or not they studied that noble creature. David Graeber, the anthropologist who wrote the soon-to-be-classic *Debt: The First 5,000 Years*, likens the process to a horror movie, in which the zombies or the vampires attack the humans as a kind of recruitment policy. "They turn you into one of them," as Graeber told me.

Actually, they do worse than that. Graeber relates the story of a woman he met who got a Ph.D. from Columbia University, but whose $80,000 debt load put an academic career off-limits, since adjuncts earn close to nothing. Instead, the woman wound up working as an escort for Wall Street types. "Here's someone who ought to be a professor," Graeber explains, "doing sexual services for the guys who lent her the money."

The story hit home for me, because I, too, wanted to be a professor once. I remember the waves of enlightenment that washed over me in my first few years in college, the ecstasy of finally beginning to understand what moved human affairs this way or that, the exciting sense of a generation arriving at a shared sensibility. Oh, I might have gone on doing that kind of work forever, whether or not it made me rich, if journalism had not intervened.

It's hard to find that kind of ecstasy among the current crop of college graduates. The sensibility shared by their generation seems to revolve around student debt, which has been clamped onto them like some sort of interest-bearing iron maiden. They've been screwed—that's what their moment of enlightenment has taught them.

As for my own cohort, or at least the members of it who struggled through and made it to one of the coveted positions in the knowledge factory, the new generational feeling seems to be one of disgust. Our enthusiasm for learning, which we trumpeted to the world, merely led the nation's children into debt bondage. Consider the remarks of Nicholas Mirzoeff, a professor of media at New York University, who sums up the diminishing returns of the profession on his blog: "I used to say that in academia one at least did very little harm. Now I feel like a pimp for loan sharks."

Analyze

1. Thomas Frank suggests that we live in a knowledge economy, where knowledge is essential to success. In your opinion, then, what obligation does a government have to ensure that students can afford a college education? Does the government have an obligation to ensure that all students can attend *private* colleges?
2. According to presidential candidate Mitt Romney, how is "competition" designed to lower the cost of college?
3. Should universities be arranged more as businesses or as charitable institutions? What are the differences between those two models? Which model offers a better experience for students?
4. In your opinion, should a college education be considered a public good (something available to all, generally useful to the society as a whole) or a private good (something available only to those who can afford it, primarily valuable to the person who receives it)?

Explore

1. College is expensive, but there are various ways to pay for it. In Norway students pay no tuition to receive a college education, but the country has a high total tax burden of roughly 45%—about twice the total tax rate of the United States. Would you be willing to pay higher taxes for life in exchange for a tuition-free college experience? What other models might exist for a society to pay for college?
2. Currently the average level of student debt in the United States for a student receiving a bachelor's degree is $30,000. Using the Internet, explore likely starting salaries for individuals within your major. For a moment consider college strictly in financial terms: Is a debt load of $30,000 a worthwhile financial investment in your future? What about a debt load of $50,000?
3. SHORT WRITING PROMPT: The actual cost for one full-time student to attend a California state university for one year is roughly $14,000—some of which is paid by the student, some of which is paid by the state, and some of which is paid by an endowment or other institutional resource. Develop a plan whereby society lowers the amount a student pays to attend college and provides the $14,000 through other means. How can a society shift money from other resources to universities? What must a society "give up" to better fund students?

4. FULL WRITING PROMPT: Interview someone at least thirty years
older than you—such as a grandparent—to learn how previous generations paid for college. How much did college cost back in the 1980s,
1970s, or earlier? What resources were available to students? How
much debt did the average student take on in those years?

Robert J. Sternberg
College Admissions, Beyond
the No. 2 Pencil

Robert J. Sternberg holds a PhD in Psychology from Stanford University.
He has worked as a professor at Yale and as a provost at Oklahoma State
University. At present he is Professor of Human Development at Cornell
University.

Wait list. That was the outcome of my application to Yale. It was
better than the outcome at Harvard, which was a rejection, and not
as good as the outcome at Princeton, which was an acceptance. I was eventually admitted to Yale, and I later had an opportunity that very few applicants ever have: I got to find out why I had been wait-listed.

My first job after college was in the Yale admissions office, and one day
(with the encouragement of some colleagues) I sneaked up into the attic
where old records were kept and read my interview report, which described
me as having a "flaky personality." I did not read the rest of my admissions
file—I felt too guilty—so I cannot say whether it was the interviewer's
assessment that consigned me to the wait list or whether I owe that honor
to some other perceived deficiency in my application. I do know that when
I finally got in, it was through the intervention of the admissions officer for
my area, who saw something special in me.

Most students, of course, don't benefit from this kind of intervention;
SAT scores and GPAs are much of what make or break a college application. And yet, over the course of my years in the Yale admissions office, I
found myself continually surprised by how many of the students we

accepted had sky-high SAT scores but seemed to lack basic practical and creative skills, whereas others with more modest scores were stunning successes at Yale, both academically and personally.

Great schools, as we know, don't always produce great people. But it's not just what happens after students arrive on campus that's the problem. By and large, our best schools don't always pick the best people in the first place. Many students who appear to have tremendous potential at age 17, based on their SAT scores and GPAs, don't look so wonderful 20 years later.

An executive at a major investment bank told me a while ago, looking back on his 25 years on Wall Street, that he had found that SAT scores predicted quite well who would be good analysts at his bank—that is, they predicted the technical skills needed to evaluate investments. What they did not signal, he said, is who would be able to take the next step, who would have the capacity to envision where various markets are going, to see larger trends and to make decisions that go beyond individual stock or bond picks.

We can do a much better job of college admissions if we start thinking about student abilities differently than we have for the past century. We should assess and value analytical, creative and practical skills and wisdom, not just the ability to memorize or do well on tests. And we should admit people on the basis of their potential for leadership and active citizenship—people who will make a positive, meaningful and enduring difference to the world.

Of course, many admissions offices try to do this already, through essays and the like, but their applications nonetheless remain anchored on test scores and grades. This is in part because scores and grades can be quantified and therefore get more weight than more abstract, seemingly "fluffy" qualities.

There is, however, a way to test these other important skills and thereby to pick more promising classes of future leaders.

And get this: the kids we select using this new method, which puts more emphasis on things other than GPAs? They'll have higher GPAs in college. I know, because this is what has happened at Tufts University.

"Use one of the following topics to create a short story: a. The Spam Filter, b. Seventeen Minutes..., c. Two by Two, d. Facebook, e. Now There's the Rub..., f. No Whip Half-Caf Latte, g. The Eleventh Commandment."

This was one of seven questions that appeared on the Tufts undergraduate application for the Class of 2013. How did it get there? The short answer is that it was crafted by a clever group of Tufts admissions officers, led by Dean of Admissions Lee Coffin.

The long answer goes back a few years. Inspired in part by my time in the admissions office, I went on to become a professor of psychology at Yale. In 1997, I proposed a theory of successful intelligence, based on the idea that people are meaningfully intelligent only to the extent that they can formulate and achieve their goals by synthesizing their creative, analytical and practical skills and their wisdom. People need creative skills to generate new ideas, analytical skills to determine if they are good ideas, practical skills to implement their ideas and wisdom to ensure that their ideas help achieve a common good. This theory, in turn, inspired me to design two projects to improve college admissions.

In the early 2000s, when I was still a Yale professor, I collaborated with teachers and researchers at two high schools and 13 colleges and universities of varying selectivity on a study we called the Rainbow Project. Our goal was to determine whether including a mix of creative, analytical and practical questions on a college admissions test might have positive effects on the admissions process. We found that it did: Incorporating the results of our tests made predictions of freshman grade-point average twice as accurate as those based on the SAT alone, and 50 percent better than those based on SATs and high school grades combined. We also found that differences between ethnic groups were substantially smaller on our questions than on the SAT.

In 2005, I became dean of arts and sciences at Tufts and helped start the Kaleidoscope Project, which added to the Tufts application optional questions designed to assess creative, analytical and practical skills and general wisdom. Above is one example of a "creative" question; others might ask students to draw something, such as a design for a new product; to post a video on YouTube; or to imagine an alternate history (what if the Nazis had won World War II?). An analytical question, meanwhile, might ask a student what his favorite book is and why. A practical question might ask a student how he convinced a friend of an idea. And a wisdom-oriented question might ask him how a high school passion might be turned toward the common good later in life.

This model provides a simple way of quantifying important qualities so they can become more central to the selection process. Some might wonder how we could evaluate answers to questions that seem so subjective. The answer is through well-developed scoring rubrics, backed up by a training program on how to use them. For example, one can score creative responses based on how original and compelling they are and how appropriately they accomplish the task at hand.

This system has been in place for five years, with about two-thirds of Tufts's roughly 15,500 annual applicants choosing to answer one of the optional questions. My collaborators and I have just published a study in the journal *College and University* looking at the results. Among our key findings: After controlling for high school grades and SATs, Tufts's new admissions questions, like those posed by the Rainbow Project before them, improved prediction of college grades. They also helped forecast which students would shine as active citizens and leaders on campus, and they virtually eliminated the admissions edge enjoyed by some ethnic groups.

The approach we tried at Tufts is one that any college can adopt by merely adding a few questions to its application. But some schools, in their rush to improve their U.S. News & World Report rankings, are moving in the opposite direction. They are stripping their applications to the bare bones, removing essays and other components that provide insight into a student's character and talents, so as to make their applications easier to fill out. They hope to thereby increase application numbers, and thus rejection rates and the appearance of "selectivity." But they should ask themselves how, exactly, this approach makes their schools any better.

It certainly doesn't make the world better. Many of the major messes confronting us today—in corporate boardrooms and on Wall Street, in politics and even in churches—have been created by people who tested very well and earned high grades at prestigious institutions. They are smart, but foolish. The world might improve if we deliberately and systematically selected students not only for their knowledge and analytical skills, but also for their creative and practical skills—and their wisdom.

Analyze

1. Robert Sternberg suggests that high school students highly focused on academics don't always succeed well in college or life in general. Do you agree with his assessment? How does one balance academics and other skills?

2. Sternberg suggests that students should memorize less and instead focus on "analytical, creative and practical skills and wisdom." At a

university, what classes or subject areas best encourage students to develop those skills?

3. Do you agree that the ability to write a short story might be a better criterion for college admissions than a high school GPA? What are the strengths and weaknesses of both means of evaluation?

4. Sternberg believes that the college admissions process should incorporate materials that examine applicants' "creative, analytical and practical skills and their wisdom." Aside from the examples in the essay, what are some ways that this can be accomplished in an application packet?

Explore

1. One of the areas that Sternberg is interested in is wisdom in high school students—even though wisdom is stereotypically imbued on the old. Outside of books and labs, how do students in high school acquire wisdom? Can you offer an example of a high school student you knew acting in a way that was noticeably wise?

2. Likewise, Sternberg is interested in locating high school students who will become "excellent citizens." In your opinion, what qualities in high school students are the best markers that they will later become "excellent citizens"?

3. SHORT WRITING PROMPT: Robert Sternberg suggests that a short story might be an excellent, though non-traditional, criterion for judging college admissions. In your opinion, what might also be another non-traditional criterion or skill for judging college admissions? The ability to memorize the names of thirty people at a party? The ability to express oneself with a drawing, painting, or other piece of visual art? An intimate entry from a personal diary? The ability to take an engine apart and put it back together again? What would this skill reveal about college applicants to admissions officers?

4. FULL WRITING PROMPT: After college Robert Sternberg was able to sneak "up into the attic where old records were kept" and learn why he wasn't initially accepted to Yale. The report said he had a "flaky personality." Write a narrative essay about a personal experience in which you applied to a program, such as a sports team, music camp, an art program, even college, only to have your application denied. Speculate on the reasons your application wasn't accepted. What did you learn from the experience? And how did this experience change you?

Dalton Conley
When Roommates Were Random

Dalton Conley is Professor of Sociology at New York University, where he studies racial and class inequalities and how health is related to socioeconomic positions. He holds two PhDs, one in Sociology from Columbia University and a second in Biology (Genomics) from New York University. He has received grants from the National Science Foundation and the Guggenheim Foundation.

Eager to throw off my nerdy past and reinvent myself at college, I wrote "party animal" on my roommate application form where it asked incoming freshmen whether they wanted to bunk with a smoker or a nonsmoker. When I told my mother about this later, she laughed and bought me a T-shirt that sported the image of Spuds MacKenzie, the 1980s Budweiser beer mascot, under the words "the original party animal."

I ended up with Tony from Sacramento, a very quiet, Republican son of a judge. (I suppose it's good policy to separate the party animals from those who request them.) I learned to appreciate his taste in music (U2 and The Smiths, as opposed to my predilection for reggae and jazz), and we agreed to disagree about politics during the reelection campaign of Alan Cranston, then one of the most liberal members of the United States Senate. I had never met anyone like Tony. And I'm pretty sure he hadn't come across many half-Jewish, Democratic children of New York artists. We learned to get along that first year at Berkeley, and every now and then even tried on each other's values and beliefs, just to see how they fit.

Today I am a college professor, and I am sad that most of my students will not experience what I did back when Mark Zuckerberg was in diapers. While the Internet has made it easy to reconnect with the lost Tonys of our lives, it has made it a lot more difficult to meet them in the first place, by taking a lot of randomness out of life. We tend to value order and control over randomness, but when we lose randomness, we also lose serendipity.

As soon as today's students receive their proverbial fat envelope from their top choice college, they are on Facebook meeting other potential freshmen. They are on sites like roomsurf.com and roomsync.com, scoping out prospective friends. By the time the roommate application forms arrive, many like-minded students with similar backgrounds have already connected and agreed to request one another.

It's just one of many ways in which digital technologies now spill over into non-screen-based aspects of social experience. I know certain people who can't bear to eat in a restaurant they haven't researched on Yelp. And Google now tailors searches to exactly what it thinks you want to find.

But this loss of randomness is particularly unfortunate for college-age students, who should be trying on new hats and getting exposed to new and different ideas. Which students end up bunking with whom may seem trivial at first glance. But research on the phenomenon of peer influence—and the influences of roommates in particular—has found that there are, in fact, long-lasting effects of whom you end up living with your first year.

David R. Harris, a sociologist at Cornell, studied roommates and found, in 2002, that white students who were assigned a roommate of a different race ended up more open-minded about race. In a 2000 study, the economist Bruce Sacerdote found that randomly assigned roommates at Dartmouth affected each other's G.P.A.'s.

(Of course, influences can sometimes be negative. Roommates can drive each other's grades up or down. In 2003, researchers at four colleges discovered that male students who reported binge drinking in high school drank much more throughout college if their first-year roommate also reported binge drinking in high school.)

These studies are important because we know that much education takes place not through the formal classroom curriculum but in the peer-to-peer learning that occurs in places like dorm rooms.

Other than prison and the military, there are not many other institutions outside the college dorm that shove two people into a 10-foot-by-10-foot space and expect them to get along for nine months. Can you think of any better training for marriage? In fact, in my research with Jennifer A. Heerwig, we have found that Vietnam-era military service actually lowers the risk of subsequent divorce. It's possible that the military teaches you how to subsume your individual desires for the good of the collective—in other words, how to get along well with others.

The drive to tame randomness into controllable order is a noble impulse, but letting a little serendipity flourish isn't such a bad thing. Nor is getting to know someone different from yourself. All colleges should follow the lead of Hamilton, where roommate choice is not allowed. And if you end up with the roommate from hell? You'll survive, and someday have great stories to tell your future spouse, with whom you'll probably get along better.

Analyze

1. Author Dalton Conley claims that he was "eager to throw off my nerdy past and reinvent myself at college." College, for many people, is an act of reinvention. How was your identity in high school different than the identity you now have at college?
2. College is also a period in which many students are confronted with individuals whose experience and worldviews are different from people found in their hometown or high school. In what ways have you been confronted with new experiences since arriving at college? How has this changed you?
3. Conley longs for the days in which chance defined dorm room pairings. In your opinion, what has been lost by allowing students to "choose" their roommates? What has been gained?
4. Conley suggests that the Internet has allowed freshmen to find living situations among "like-minded students," which limits the new experiences they will face in college. In your opinion, should a college force freshmen out of their comfort zones by engaging them with "non-like-minded students" or should a college allow students to take ownership of their own experience, even if that ownership limits the varieties of new experiences they will engage in on campus?

Explore

1. Spend some time walking through your dorm. Which room has the best roommate situation? What contributes to a successful roommate relationship?
2. Conley suggests that students, when left to their own impulses, will likely migrate to people who share some of their identity concerns, such as race. Test this theory. Scroll through your friends on Facebook. Identify those who share your race. Then identify those who share your religious outlook (Catholic, Jewish, Muslim, atheist, etc.). Lastly, identify those whose home economic lifestyle is similar to your own

(situated below the poverty line, working middle class, upper middle class, etc.). How deep are the similarities between you and your friends on Facebook?

3. SHORT WRITING PROMPT: Assuming that you are living in a dorm or other cooperative housing arrangement (such as a fraternity), list ten qualities helpful for students to develop to be a good roommate. In which of these areas do you excel? And in which do you fall short?

4. FULL WRITING PROMPT: Write a narrative essay in which you discuss the ways that you have changed since arriving at college. Which challenges have been most significant for you to overcome? Which areas of independence have most challenged you? Relate your experiences with concrete details and dialogue, as best you remember it.

Forging Connections

1. In general, Americans feel that childhood ends at a later age than it did in the 1950s. What would be the pros and cons of *all* students experiencing their first two years of college in their hometown, on their high school campus, while living with their parents, before applying to go elsewhere for a bachelor's degree?

2. For many high school students, the college admissions process is difficult and time consuming. For standardized tests, such as the SAT, students are asked to learn vocabulary, review principles of algebra, produce strong writing samples, and master the components of reasoning. For applications, students often create an admissions essay (or essays) when applying to top-tier private schools. Do you believe that high schools should offer an *extra* class for juniors that covers both the standardized test review and the application process? Assume the class would meet after school for one hour each day, much like extracurricular activities. In your opinion, what specifically should such a class offer to better prepare students for both the admissions process and for college itself?

Looking Further

1. In 2003, a group of psychologists presented an alternative to the SAT/ACT standardized tests to determine which students would best

succeed in college called the Rainbow Project test. These psychologists believed that the SAT/ACT primarily rewarded analytical and memory skills. "Creative and practical skills can be more useful in real-world settings," one of the test's developers noted. "For example, the Rainbow Project test includes multiple-choice items in which students must ascertain the meaning of a word from context—tapping analytical skills . . . To measure creative skills, the exam asks students to complete more imaginative tasks, such as solving math problems using novel operations, thinking up cartoon captions, writing a short story based on a given title and dictating a short story based on a picture collage." The test seeks to measure aptitude, not practiced skills or memorized facts; therefore, studying for the test would have minimal impact on an individual's score. Data suggest that the test is a slightly better predictor of college success than the SAT. What would be the pros and cons of using the Rainbow Project test in place of the SAT/ACT? Consider the difference between aptitude and practiced skills; consider the connection between studying and score on the SAT/ACT; consider how using an aptitude test as the basis for college admission might change the core educational elements of many high school classes.

2. The American admissions system is run, in ways, as a popularity contest, with colleges vying for the most application packets. In your opinion, should admission to public colleges be taken over by the state? For example, California has 23 public universities in the CSU system and another 10 in the UC system. Instead of applying to individual colleges, a prospective student could simply apply to a central state office. The state, then, could review each application packet and, based on the applicant's interests, GPA, test scores, and so forth, offer the student a place in up to three different universities. This system would substantially minimize cost (both for the student and the universities) but limit student choice and university control of an incoming class. Is this a better system than the one currently in place? If you do not like this proposal, can you think of a more cost-effective way to manage admissions to public institutions?

What Is College?

So what exactly is college?

This question goes back centuries—arguments over the pursuit of knowledge, the exploration of the arts, and skills that translate easily into successful employment. Thomas Jefferson argued that college should be focused on a liberal education, such as the arts and sciences, so college graduates might become informed citizens and defenders of liberty. Benjamin Franklin, on the other hand, believed that a liberal education was mostly suitable for the wealthy and that most students needed a practical education that would better help them earn a living. Still other early Americans argued that college should provide a moral education, focusing neither on academic pursuits or practical training, but on experiences and discussions that would develop principles and a strong sense of character.

These early ideas, in part, explain the enormous variety of college experiences available to students today. Students on a polytechnic campus will likely focus much of their studies on engineering, architecture, or agriculture. Students at a liberal arts college will find their coursework directed largely at the arts and sciences, with many courses focused on literature, history, and philosophy. Students at religious colleges may take many courses in religion, morals, and ethics, perhaps even enough to earn a minor in religious studies.

The debate as to what experiences a college should provide is an old one. Yet in recent years, this debate has absorbed a new element: not only do educators disagree on what should make up a college education, they now argue over how it should be delivered: in face-to-face classroom experiences, by computer, by video, by a system of self-learning?

Graeme Wood, in his article "The Future of College?," explores an online format in which students work with a professor only through a video interface. This futuristic college has no traditional classrooms, no gym, no student center; it has only the most basic dormitory, and all of its small-group classes are taught online. In "The Day the Purpose of College Changed," Dan Barrett explores how American colleges shifted from the goals of a liberal education to those of career training over the past four decades. William Deresiewicz considers the way in which Ivy League schools prepare their students to have targeted social and career goals, while under-preparing them for some of life's essential experiences. Vauhini Vara wonders if college is now the new minimum level of education we expect most individuals to have in Western countries. And Derek Newton investigates whether college classes—and even majors—should be unbundled from their universities, allowing students to select those courses and professors they most want to take, even if they aren't offered at their home institution.

As colleges evolve toward the future, educators are exploring what it means to have a college education in the twenty-first century and how this educational experience might be best delivered to students.

Graeme Wood
The Future of College?

Graeme Wood is a contributing editor to *The Atlantic* and *The New Republic*, where he's written on America's involvement in the Middle East, the culture of U.S. prisons, and higher education. At Yale University, he is a lecturer in political science.

On a Friday morning in April, I strapped on a headset, leaned into a microphone, and experienced what had been described to me as a type of time travel to the future of higher education. I was on the ninth floor of a building in downtown San Francisco, in a neighborhood whose streets are heavily populated with winos and vagrants, and whose buildings host hip new businesses, many of them tech start-ups. In a small room, I was flanked by a publicist and a tech manager from an educational venture called the Minerva Project, whose founder and CEO, the 39-year-old entrepreneur Ben Nelson, aims to replace (or, when he is feeling less aggressive, "reform") the modern liberal-arts college.

Minerva is an accredited university with administrative offices and a dorm in San Francisco, and it plans to open locations in at least six other major world cities. But the key to Minerva, what sets it apart most jarringly from traditional universities, is a proprietary online platform developed to apply pedagogical practices that have been studied and vetted by one of the world's foremost psychologists, a former Harvard dean named Stephen M. Kosslyn, who joined Minerva in 2012.

Nelson and Kosslyn had invited me to sit in on a test run of the platform, and at first it reminded me of the opening credits of *The Brady Bunch*: a grid of images of the professor and eight "students" (the others were all Minerva employees) appeared on the screen before me, and we introduced ourselves. For a college seminar, it felt impersonal, and though we were all sitting on the same floor of Minerva's offices, my fellow students seemed oddly distant, as if piped in from the International Space Station. I half expected a packet of astronaut ice cream to float by someone's face.

Within a few minutes, though, the experience got more intense. The subject of the class—one in a series during which the instructor, a French physicist named Eric Bonabeau, was trying out his course material—was inductive reasoning. Bonabeau began by polling us on our understanding of the reading, a *Nature* article about the sudden depletion of North Atlantic cod in the early 1990s. He asked us which of four possible interpretations of the article was the most accurate. In an ordinary undergraduate seminar, this might have been an occasion for timid silence, until the class's biggest loudmouth or most caffeinated student ventured a guess. But the Minerva class extended no refuge for the timid, nor privilege for the garrulous. Within seconds, every student had to provide an answer, and Bonabeau displayed our choices so that we could be called upon to defend them.

Bonabeau led the class like a benevolent dictator, subjecting us to pop quizzes, cold calls, and pedagogical tactics that during an in-the-flesh seminar would have taken precious minutes of class time to arrange. He split us into groups to defend opposite propositions—that the cod had disappeared because of overfishing, or that other factors were to blame. No one needed to shuffle seats; Bonabeau just pushed a button, and the students in the other group vanished from my screen, leaving my three fellow debaters and me to plan, using a shared bulletin board on which we could record our ideas. Bonabeau bounced between the two groups to offer advice as we worked. After a representative from each group gave a brief presentation, Bonabeau ended by showing a short video about the evils of overfishing. ("Propaganda," he snorted, adding that we'd talk about logical fallacies in the next session.) The computer screen blinked off after 45 minutes of class.

The system had bugs—it crashed once, and some of the video lagged—but overall it worked well, and felt decidedly unlike a normal classroom. For one thing, it was exhausting: a continuous period of forced engagement, with no relief in the form of time when my attention could flag or I could doodle in a notebook undetected. Instead, my focus was directed relentlessly by the platform, and because it looked like my professor and fellow edu-nauts were staring at me, I was reluctant to ever let my gaze stray from the screen. Even in moments when I wanted to think about aspects of the material that weren't currently under discussion—to me these seemed like moments of creative space, but perhaps they were just daydreams—I felt my attention snapped back to the narrow issue at hand, because I had to answer a quiz question or articulate a position. I was forced, in effect, to learn. If this was the education of the future, it seemed vaguely fascistic. Good, but fascistic.

Minerva, which operates for profit, started teaching its inaugural class of 33 students this month. To seed this first class with talent, Minerva gave every admitted student a full-tuition scholarship of $10,000 a year for four years, plus free housing in San Francisco for the first year. Next year's class is expected to have 200 to 300 students, and Minerva hopes future classes will double in size roughly every year for a few years after that.

Those future students will pay about $28,000 a year, including room and board, a $30,000 savings over the sticker price of many of the schools—the Ivies, plus other hyperselective colleges like Pomona and Williams—with which Minerva hopes to compete. (Most American students at these colleges do not pay full price, of course; Minerva will offer financial aid and target middle-class students whose bills at the other schools would still be tens of thousands of dollars more per year.) If Minerva grows to 2,500 students a class, that would mean an annual revenue of up to $280 million. A partnership with the Keck Graduate Institute in Claremont, California, allowed Minerva to fast-track its accreditation, and its advisory board has included Larry Summers, the former U.S. Treasury secretary and Harvard president, and Bob Kerrey, the former Democratic senator from Nebraska, who also served as the president of the New School, in New York City.

Nelson's long-term goal for Minerva is to radically remake one of the most sclerotic sectors of the U.S. economy, one so shielded from the need for improvement that its biggest innovation in the past 30 years has been to double its costs and hire more administrators at higher salaries.

The paradox of undergraduate education in the United States is that it is the envy of the world, but also tremendously beleaguered. In that way it resembles the U.S. health-care sector. Both carry price tags that shock the conscience of citizens of other developed countries. They're both tied up inextricably with government, through student loans and federal research funding or through Medicare. But if you can afford the Mayo Clinic, the United States is the best place in the world to get sick. And if you get a scholarship to Stanford, you should take it, and turn down offers from even the best universities in Europe, Australia, or Japan. (Most likely, though, you won't get that scholarship. The average U.S. college graduate in 2014 carried $33,000 of debt.)

Financial dysfunction is only the most obvious way in which higher education is troubled. In the past half millennium, the technology of learning has hardly budged. The easiest way to picture what a university looked like 500 years ago is to go to any large university today, walk into a lecture hall, and imagine the professor speaking Latin and wearing a monk's cowl. The most common class format is still a professor standing in front of a group of students and talking. And even though we've subjected students to lectures for hundreds of years, we have no evidence that they are a good way to teach. (One educational psychologist, Ludy Benjamin, likens lectures to Velveeta cheese—something lots of people consume but no one considers either delicious or nourishing.)

In recent years, other innovations in higher education have preceded Minerva, most famously massive open online courses, known by the unfortunate acronym MOOCs. Among the most prominent MOOC purveyors are Khan Academy, the brainchild of the entrepreneur Salman Khan, and

Coursera, headed by the Stanford computer scientists Andrew Ng and Daphne Koller. Khan Academy began as a way to tutor children in math, but it has grown to include a dazzling array of tutorials, some very effective, many on technical subjects. Coursera offers college-level classes for free (you can pay for premium services, like actual college credit). There can be hundreds of thousands of students in a single course, and millions are enrolled altogether. At their most basic, these courses consist of standard university lectures, caught on video.

But Minerva is not a MOOC provider. Its courses are not massive (they're capped at 19 students), open (Minerva is overtly elitist and selective), or online, at least not in the same way Coursera's are. Lectures are banned. All Minerva classes take the form of seminars conducted on the platform I tested. The first students will by now have moved into Minerva's dorm on the fifth floor of a building in San Francisco's Nob Hill neighborhood and begun attending class on Apple laptops they were required to supply themselves.

Each year, according to Minerva's plan, they'll attend university in a different place, so that after four years they'll have the kind of international experience that other universities advertise but can rarely deliver. By 2016, Berlin and Buenos Aires campuses will have opened. Likely future cities include Mumbai, Hong Kong, New York, and London. Students will live in dorms with two-person rooms and a communal kitchen. They'll also take part in field trips organized by Minerva, such as a tour of Alcatraz with a prison psychologist. Minerva will maintain almost no facilities other than the dorm itself—no library, no dining hall, no gym—and students will use city parks and recreation centers, as well as other local cultural resources, for their extracurricular activities.

The professors can live anywhere, as long as they have an Internet connection. Given that many academics are coastal-elite types who refuse to live in places like Evansville, Indiana, geographic freedom is a vital part of Minerva's faculty recruitment.

The student body could become truly global, in part because Minerva's policy is to admit students without regard to national origin, thus catering to the unmet demand of, say, prosperous Chinese and Indians and Brazilians for American-style liberal-arts education.

The Minerva boast is that it will strip the university experience down to the aspects that are shown to contribute directly to student learning. Lectures, gone. Tenure, gone. Gothic architecture, football, ivy crawling up the walls—gone, gone, gone. What's left will be leaner and cheaper. (Minerva has already attracted $25 million in capital from investors who think it can undercut the incumbents.) And Minerva officials claim that their methods will be tested against scientifically determined best practices, unlike the methods used at other universities and assumed to be sound just because the schools themselves are old and expensive. Yet because classes have only just begun, we have little clue as to whether the process of stripping down the university removes something essential to what has made America's best colleges the greatest in the world.

Minerva will, after all, look very little like a university—and not merely because it won't be accessorized in useless and expensive ways. The teaching methods may well be optimized, but universities, as currently constituted, are only partly about classroom time. Can a school that has no faculty offices, research labs, community spaces for students, or professors paid to do scholarly work still be called a university?

If Minerva fails, it will lay off its staff and sell its office furniture and never be heard from again. If it succeeds, it could inspire a legion of entrepreneurs, and a whole category of legacy institutions might have to liquidate. One imagines tumbleweeds rolling through abandoned quads and wrecking balls smashing through the windows of classrooms left empty by students who have plugged into new online platforms.

The decor in the lobby of the Minerva office building nods to the classical roots of education: enormous Roman statues dominate. (Minerva is the Roman goddess of wisdom.) But where Minerva's employees work, on the ninth floor, the atmosphere is pure business, in a California-casual sort of way. Everyone, including the top officers of the university, works at open-plan stations. I associate scholars' offices with chalk dust, strewn papers, and books stacked haphazardly in contravention of fire codes. But here, I found tidiness.

One of the Minerva employees least scholarly in demeanor is its founder, chief executive, and principal evangelist. Ben Nelson attended the University of Pennsylvania's Wharton School as an undergraduate in the late 1990s and then had no further contact with academia before he began incubating Minerva, in 2010. His résumé's main entry is his 10-year stint as an executive at Snapfish, an online photo service that allows users to print pictures on postcards and in books.

Nelson is curly-haired and bespectacled, and when I met him he wore a casual button-down shirt with no tie or jacket. His ambition to reform academia was born of his own undergraduate experience. At Wharton, he was dissatisfied with what he perceived as a random barrage of business instruction, with no coordination to ensure that he learned bedrock skills like critical thinking. "My entire critique of higher education started with curricular reform at Penn," he says. "General education is nonexistent. It's effectively a buffet, and when you have a noncurated academic experience, you effectively don't get educated. You get a random collection of information. Liberal-arts education is about developing the intellectual capacity of the individual, and learning to be a productive member of society. And you cannot do that without a curriculum."

Students begin their Minerva education by taking the same four "Cornerstone Courses," which introduce core concepts and ways of thinking that cut across the sciences and humanities. These are not 101 classes, meant to impart freshman-level knowledge of subjects. ("The freshman year [as taught at traditional schools] should not exist," Nelson says, suggesting that MOOCs can teach the basics. "Do your freshman year at home.") Instead, Minerva's first-year classes are designed to inculcate what Nelson calls "habits of mind" and "foundational concepts," which are the basis for all sound systematic thought. In a science class, for example, students should develop a deep understanding of the need for controlled experiments. In a humanities class, they need to learn the classical techniques of rhetoric and develop basic persuasive skills. The curriculum then builds from that foundation.

Nelson compares this level of direction favorably with what he found at Penn (curricular disorder), and with what one finds at Brown (very few requirements) or Columbia (a "great books" core curriculum). As Minerva students advance, they choose one of five majors: arts and humanities, social sciences, computational sciences, natural sciences, or business.

Snapfish sold for $300 million to Hewlett-Packard in 2005, and Nelson made enough to fund two years of planning for his dream project. He is prone to bombastic pronouncements about Minerva, making broad claims about the state of higher education that are at times insightful and at times speculative at best. He speaks at many conferences, unsettling academic administrators less radical than he is by blithely dismissing long-standing practices. "Your cash cow is the lecture, and the lecture is over," he told a gathering of deans. "The lecture model . . . will be obliterated."

In academic circles, where overt competition between institutions is a serious breach of etiquette, Nelson is a bracing presence. (Imagine the president of Columbia telling the assembled presidents of other Ivy League schools, as Nelson sometimes tells his competitors, "Our goal is not to put you out of business; it is to lead you. It is to show you that there is a better way to do what you are doing, and for you to follow us.")

The other taboo Nelson ignores is acknowledgment of profit motive. "*For-profit* in higher education equates to evil," Nelson told me, noting that most for-profit colleges are indeed the sort of disreputable degree mills that wallpaper the Web with banner ads. "As if nonprofits aren't money-driven!" he howled. "They're just corporations that dodge their taxes."

Minerva is built to make money, but Nelson insists that its motives will align with student interests. As evidence, Nelson points to the fact that the school will eschew all federal funding, to which he attributes much of the runaway cost of universities. The compliance cost of taking federal financial aid is about $1,000 per student—a tenth of Minerva's tuition—and the aid wouldn't be of any use to the majority of Minerva's students, who will likely come from overseas.

Subsidies, Nelson says, encourage universities to enroll even students who aren't likely to thrive, and to raise tuition, since federal money is pegged to costs. These effects pervade higher education, he says, but they have nothing to do with teaching students. He believes Minerva would end up hungering after federal money, too, if it ever allowed itself to be tempted. Instead, like Ulysses, it will tie itself to the mast and work with private-sector funding only. "If you put a drug"—federal funds—"into a system, the system changes itself to fit the drug. If [Minerva] took money from the government, in 20 years we'd be majority American, with substantially higher tuition. And as much as you try to create barriers, if you don't structure it to be mission-oriented, that's the way it will evolve."

When talking about Minerva's future, Nelson says he thinks in terms of the life spans of universities—hundreds of years as opposed to the decades of typical corporate time horizons. Minerva's very founding is a rare event. "We are now building an institution that has not been attempted in over 100 years, since the founding of Rice"—the last four-year liberal-arts-based research institution founded in this country. It opened in 1912 and now charges $53,966 a year.

So far, Minerva has hired its deans, who will teach all the courses for this inaugural class. It will hire rank-and-file faculty later in the year. One of Minerva's main strategies is to lure a few prominent scholars from existing institutions. Other "new" universities, especially fantastically wealthy ones like King Abdullah University of Science and Technology, in Saudi Arabia, have attempted a similar strategy—at times with an almost cargo-cult-like confidence that filling their labs and offices with big-shot professors will turn the institutions themselves into important players.

Among the bigger shots hired by Minerva is Eric Bonabeau, the dean of computational sciences, who taught the seminar I participated in. Bonabeau, a physicist who has worked in academia and in business, studies the mathematics of swarming behavior (of bees, fish, robots), and his research helped inspire Michael Crichton's terrible thriller *Prey*. Diane Halpern, a prominent psychologist, signed on this year as the dean of social sciences.

Minerva's first major hire, Stephen M. Kosslyn, is a man I met in the fall of 1999, when I went to have my head examined. Kosslyn taught cognitive psychology and neuroscience for 32 years at Harvard, and during my undergraduate years I visited his lab and earned a few dollars here and there as one of his guinea pigs. The studies usually involved sticking my head in an fMRI machine so he and his researchers could record activity in my brain and observe which parts fired when.

Around that time, Kosslyn's lab made news because it began to show how "mental imagery"—the experience of seeing things in your mind's eye—really works. (One study involved putting volunteers into fMRI machines and asking them to hold an image of a cat in their head for as long as possible. You can try this exercise now. If you're especially good at concentrating, the cat might vanish in a matter of a few seconds, as soon as your brain—distractible as a puppy—comes up with another object of attention.) Kosslyn served as Harvard's dean of social sciences from 2008 to 2010, then spent two years at Stanford as the director of its Center for Advanced Study in the Behavioral Sciences. In 2013, after a few months of contract work for Minerva, he resigned from Stanford and joined Minerva as its founding dean.

Kosslyn speaks softly and slowly, with little emotional affect. Bald and bearded, he has an owlish stare, and at times during my recent conversations with him, he seemed to be scanning my brain with his eyes. For purposes of illustration (and perhaps also amusement), he will ask you to perform some cognitive task, then wait patiently while you do it—explain a concept, say, or come up with an argument—before telling you matter-of-factly what your mind just did. When talking with him, you often feel as though your brain is a machine, and his job is to know how it works better than it knows itself.

He spent much of his first year at Minerva surveying the literature on education and the psychology of learning. "We have numerous sound, reproducible experiments that tell us how people learn, and what teachers can do to improve learning." Some of the studies are ancient, by the standards of scientific research—and yet their lessons are almost wholly ignored.

For example, he points to a 1972 study by Fergus I. M. Craik and Robert S. Lockhart in *The Journal of Verbal Learning and Verbal Behavior*, which shows that memory of material is enhanced by "deep" cognitive tasks. In an educational context, such tasks would include working with material, applying it, arguing about it (rote memorization is insufficient). The finding is hardly revolutionary, but applying it systematically in the classroom is. Similarly, research shows that having a pop quiz at the beginning of a class and (if the students are warned in advance) another one at a random moment later in the class greatly increases the durability of what is learned. Likewise, if you ask a student to explain a concept she has been studying, the very act of articulating it seems to lodge it in her memory. Forcing students to guess the answer to a problem, and to discuss their answers in small groups, seems to make them understand the problem better—even if they guess wrong.

Kosslyn has begun publishing his research on the science of learning. His most recent co-authored article, in *Psychological Science in the Public Interest*, argues (against conventional wisdom) that the traditional concept of "cognitive styles"—visual versus aural learners, those who learn by doing versus those who learn by studying—is muddled and wrong.

The pedagogical best practices Kosslyn has identified have been programmed into the Minerva platform so that they are easy for professors to apply. They are not only easy, in fact, but also compulsory, and professors will be trained intensively in how to use the platform.

This approach does have its efficiencies. In a normal class, a pop quiz might involve taking out paper and pencils, not to mention eye-rolls from students. On the Minerva platform, quizzes—often a single multiple-choice question—are over and done in a matter of seconds, with students' answers immediately logged and analyzed. Professors are able to sort students instantly, and by many metrics, for small-group work—perhaps pairing poets with business majors, to expose students who are weak in a particular class to the thought processes of their stronger peers. Some claim that education is an art and a science. Nelson has disputed this: "It's a science and a science."

Nelson likes to compare this approach to traditional seminars. He says he spoke to a prominent university president—he wouldn't say which one—early in the planning of Minerva, and he found the man's view of education, in a word, faith-based. "He said the reason elite university education was so great was because you take an expert in the subject, plus a bunch of smart kids, you put them in a room and apply pressure—and *magic* happens," Nelson told me, leaning portentously on that word. "That was his analysis. They're trying to sell magic! Something that happens by accident! It sure didn't happen when I was an undergrad."

To Kosslyn, building effective teaching techniques directly into the platform gives Minerva a huge advantage. "Typically, the way a professor learns to teach is completely haphazard," he says. "One day the person is a graduate student, and the next day, a professor standing up giving a lecture, with almost no training." Lectures, Kosslyn says, are pedagogically unsound, although for universities looking to trim budgets they are at least cost-effective, with one employee for dozens or hundreds of tuition-paying students. "A great way to teach," Kosslyn says drily, "but a terrible way to learn."

I asked him whether, at Harvard and Stanford, he attempted to apply any of the lessons of psychology in the classroom. He told me he could have alerted colleagues to best practices, but they most likely would have ignored them. "The classroom time is theirs, and it is sacrosanct," he says. The very thought that he might be able to impose his own order on it was laughable. Professors, especially tenured ones at places like Harvard, answer to nobody.

It occurred to me that Kosslyn was living the dream of every university administrator who has watched professors mulishly defy even the most reasonable directives. Kosslyn had powers literally no one at Harvard—even the president—had. He could tell people what to do, and they had to do it.

There were moments, during my various conversations with Kosslyn and Nelson, when I found I couldn't wait for Minerva's wrecking ball to demolish the ivory tower. The American college system is a frustrating thing—and I say this as someone who was a satisfied customer of two undergraduate institutions, Deep Springs College (an obscure but selective college in the high desert of California) and Harvard. At Deep Springs, my classes rarely exceeded five students. At Harvard, I went to many excellent lectures and took only one class with fewer than 10 students. I didn't sleepwalk or drink my way through either school, and the education I received was well worth the $16,000 a year my parents paid, after scholarships.

But the Minerva seminar did bring back memories of many a pointless, formless discussion or lecture, and it began to seem obvious that if Harvard had approached teaching with a little more care, it could have improved the seminars and replaced the worst lectures with something else.

When Eric Bonabeau assigned the reading for his class on induction, he barely bothered to tell us what induction was, or how it related to North Atlantic cod. When I asked him afterward about his decision not to spend a session introducing the concept, he said the Web had plenty of tutorials about induction, and any Minerva student ought to be able to learn the basics on her own time, in her own way. Seminars are for advanced discussion. And, of course, he was right.

Minerva's model, Nelson says, will flourish in part because it will exploit free online content, rather than trying to compete with it, as traditional universities do. A student who wants an introductory economics course can turn to Coursera or Khan Academy. "We are a university, and a MOOC is a version of publishing," Nelson explains. "The reason we can get away with the pedagogical model we have is because MOOCs exist. The MOOCs will eventually make lectures obsolete."

Indeed, the more I looked into Minerva and its operations, the more I started to think that certain functions of universities have simply become less relevant as information has become more ubiquitous. Just as learning to read in Latin was essential before books became widely available in other languages, gathering students in places where they could attend lectures in person was once a necessary part of higher education. But by now books are abundant, and so are serviceable online lectures by knowledgeable experts.

On the other hand, no one yet knows whether reducing a university to a smooth-running pedagogical machine will continue to allow scholarship to thrive—or whether it will simply put universities out of business, replace scholar-teachers with just teachers, and retard a whole generation of research. At any great university, there are faculty who are terrible at teaching but whose work drives their field forward with greater momentum than the research of their classroom-competent colleagues. Will there be a place for such people at Minerva—or anywhere, if Minerva succeeds?

Last spring, when universities began mailing out acceptance letters and parents all over the country shuddered as the reality of tuition bills became more concrete, Minerva sent 69 offers. Thirty-three students decided to enroll, a typical percentage for a liberal-arts school. Nelson told me Minerva would admit students without regard for diversity or balance of gender.

Applicants to Minerva take a battery of online quizzes, including spatial-reasoning tests of the sort one might find on an IQ test. SATs are not considered, because affluent students can boost their scores by hiring tutors. ("They're a good way of determining how rich a student is," Nelson says.) If students perform well enough, Minerva interviews them over Skype and makes them write a short essay during the interview, to ensure that they aren't paying a ghost writer. "The top 30 applicants get in," he told me back in February, slicing his hand through the air to mark the cutoff point. For more than three years, he had been proselytizing worldwide, speaking to high-school students in California and Qatar and Brazil. In May, he and the Minerva deans made the final chop.

Of the students who enrolled, slightly less than 20 percent are American—a percentage much higher than anticipated. (Nelson ultimately expects as many as 90 percent of the students to come from overseas.) Perhaps not surprisingly, the students come disproportionately from unconventional backgrounds—nearly one-tenth are from United World Colleges, the chain of cosmopolitan hippie high schools that brings together students from around the globe in places like Wales, Singapore, and New Mexico.

In an oddly controlling move for a university, Minerva asked admitted students to run requests for media interviews by its public-relations department. But the university gave me the names of three students willing to speak.

When I got through to Ian Van Buskirk of Marietta, Georgia, he was eager to tell me about a dugout canoe that he had recently carved out of a two-ton oak log, using only an ax, an adze, and a chisel, and that he planned to take on a maiden voyage in the hour after our conversation. He told me he would have attended Duke University if Minerva hadn't come calling, but he said it wasn't a particularly difficult decision, even though Minerva lacks the prestige and 176-year history of Duke. "There's no reputation out there," he told me. "But that means we get to make the reputation ourselves. I'm creating it now, while I'm talking to you."

Minerva had let him try out the same online platform I did, and Van Buskirk singled out the "level of interaction and intensity" as a reason for attending. "It took deep concentration," he said. "It's not some lecture class where you can just click 'record' on your tape." He said the focus required was similar to the mind-set he'd needed when he made his first hacks into his oak log, which could have cracked, rendering it useless.

Another student, Shane Dabor, of the small city of Brantford, Ontario, had planned to attend Canada's University of Waterloo or the University of Toronto. But his experiences with online learning and a series of internships had led him to conclude that traditional universities were not for him. "I already had lots of friends at university who weren't learning anything," he says. "Both options seemed like a wager, and I chose this one."

A young Palestinian woman, Rana Abu Diab, of Silwan, in East Jerusalem, described how she had learned English through movies and books (a translation of the Norwegian philosophical novel *Sophie's World* was a particular favorite). "If I had relied on my school, I would not be able to have a two-minute conversation," she told me in fluent English. During a year studying media at Birzeit University, in Ramallah, she heard about Minerva and decided to scrap her other academic plans and focus on applying there. For her, the ability to study overseas on multiple continents, and get an American-style liberal-arts education in the process, was irresistible. "I want to explore everything and learn everything," she says. "And that's what Minerva is offering: an experience that lets you live multiple lives and learn not just your concentration but how to think." Minerva admitted her, and, like a third of her classmates in the founding class, she received a supplemental scholarship, which she could use to pay for her computer and health insurance.

Two students told me that they had felt a little trepidation, and a need to convince themselves or their parents that Minerva wasn't just a moneymaking scheme. Minerva had an open house weekend for admitted students, and (perhaps ironically) the in-person interactions with Minerva faculty and staff helped assure them that the university was legit. The students all now say they're confident in Minerva—although of course they can leave whenever they like, with little lost but time.

Some people consider universities sacred places, and they might even see professors' freedom to be the fallible sovereigns of their own classrooms as a necessary part of what makes a university special. To these romantics, universities are havens from a world dominated by orthodoxy, money, and quotidian concerns. Professors get to think independently, and students come away molded by the total experience—classes, social life, extracurriculars—that the university provides. We spend the rest of our lives chasing mates, money, and jobs, but at university we enjoy the liberty to indulge aimless curiosity in subjects we know nothing about, for purposes unrelated to efficiency or practicality.

Minerva is too young to have attracted zealous naysayers, but it's safe to assume that the people with this disposition toward the university experience are least likely to be enthusiastic about Minerva and other attempts to revolutionize education through technical innovation. MOOCs are beloved by those too poor for a traditional university, as well as those who like to dabble, and those who like to learn in their pajamas. And MOOCs are not to be knocked: for a precocious Malawian peasant girl who learns math through free lessons from Khan Academy, the new Web resources can change her life. But the dropout rate for online classes is about 95 percent, and they skew strongly toward quantitative disciplines, particularly computer science, and toward privileged male students. As Nelson is fond of pointing out, however, MOOCs will continue to get better, until eventually no one will pay Duke or Johns Hopkins for the possibility of a good lecture, when Coursera offers a reliably great one, with hundreds of thousands of five-star ratings, for free.

The question remains as to whether Minerva can provide what traditional universities offer now. Kosslyn's project of efficiently cramming learning into students' brains is preferable to failing to cram in anything at all. And it is designed to convey not just information, as most MOOCs seem to, but whole mental tool kits that help students become more-thoughtful citizens. But defenders of the traditional university see efficiency as a false idol.

"Like other things that are going on now in higher ed, Minerva brings us back to first principles," says Harry R. Lewis, a computer-science professor who was the dean of Harvard's undergraduate college from 1995 to 2003. What, he asks, does it mean to be educated? Perhaps the process of education is a profound one, involving all sorts of leaps in maturity that do not show up on a Kosslyn-style test of pedagogical efficiency. "I'm sure there's a market for people who want to be more efficiently educated," Lewis says. "But how do you improve the efficiency of growing up?"

He warns that online-education innovations tend to be oversold. "They seem to want to re-create the School of Athens in every little hamlet on the prairie—and maybe they'll do that," he told me. "But part of the process of education happens not just through good pedagogy but by having students in places where they see the scholars working and plying their trades."

He calls the "hydraulic metaphor" of education—the idea that the main task of education is to increase the flow of knowledge into the student—an "old fallacy." As Lewis explains, "Plutarch said the mind is not a vessel to be filled but a fire to be lit. Part of my worry about these Internet start-ups is that it's not clear they'll be any good at the fire-lighting part."

In February, at a university-administrator conference at a Hyatt in downtown San Francisco, Ben Nelson spoke to a plenary session of business-school deans from around the world. Daphne Koller of Coursera sat opposite him onstage, and they calmly but assuredly described what sounded to me like the destruction of the very schools where their audience members worked. Nelson wore a bored smirk while an introductory video played, advertising the next year's version of the same conference. To a pair of educational entrepreneurs boasting the low price of their new projects, the slickly produced video must have looked like just another expensive barnacle on the hull of higher education.

"Content is about to become free and ubiquitous," Koller said, an especially worrying comment for deans who still thought the job of their universities was to teach "content." The institutions "that are going to survive are the ones that reimagine themselves in this new world."

Nelson ticked off the advantages he had over legacy institutions: the spryness of a well-funded start-up, a student body from all over the world, and deals for faculty (they get to keep their own intellectual property, rather than having to hand over lucrative patents to, say, Stanford) that are likely to make Minerva attractive.

Yet in some ways, the worst possible outcome would be for U.S. higher education to accept Minerva as its model and dismantle the old universities before anyone can really be sure that it offers a satisfactory replacement. During my conversations with the three Minerva students, I wanted to ask whether they were confident Minerva would give them all the wonderful intangibles and productive diversions that Harry Lewis found so important. But then I remembered what I was like as a teenager headed off to college, so ignorant of what college was and what it could be, and so reliant on the college itself to provide what I'd need in order to get a good education. These three young students were more resourceful than I was, and probably more deliberate in their choice of college. But they were newcomers to higher education, and asking them whether their fledgling alma mater could provide these things seemed akin to asking the passengers on the *Mayflower* how they liked America as soon as their feet touched Plymouth Rock.

Lewis is certainly right when he says that Minerva challenges the field to return to first principles. But of course the conclusions one reaches might not be flattering to traditional colleges. One possibility is that Minerva will fail because a college degree, for all the high-minded talk of liberal education— of lighting fires and raising thoughtful citizens—is really just a credential, or an entry point to an old-boys network that gets you your first job and your first lunch with the machers at your alumni club. Minerva has no alumni club, and if it fails for this reason, it will look naive and idealistic, a bet on the inherent value of education in a world where cynicism gets better odds.

In another sense, it's difficult to imagine Minerva failing altogether: it will offer something that resembles a liberal education to large segments of the Earth's population who currently have to choose between the long-shot possibility of getting into a traditional U.S. school, and the more narrowly career-oriented education available in their home country. That population might give Minerva a steady flow of tuition-paying warm bodies even if U.S. higher education ignores it completely. It could plausibly become the Amherst of the world beyond the borders of the United States.

These are not, however, the terms by which Ben Nelson defines success. To him, the brass ring is for Minerva to force itself on the consciousness of the Yales and Swarthmores and "lead" American universities into a new era. More modestly, we can expect Minerva to force some universities to justify what previously could be waved off with mentions of "magic" and a puff of smoke. Its seminar platform will challenge professors to stop thinking they're using technology just because they lecture with PowerPoint.

It seems only remotely possible that in 20 years Minerva could have more students enrolled than Ohio State will. But it is almost a certainty that the classrooms of elite universities will in that time have come to look more and more like Minerva classrooms, with professors and students increasingly separated geographically, mediated through technology that alters the nature of the student–teacher relationship. Even if Minerva turns out not to be the venture that upends American higher education, other innovators will crop up in its wake to address the exact weaknesses Nelson now attacks. The idea that college will in two decades look exactly as it does today increasingly sounds like the forlorn, fingers-crossed hope of a higher-education dinosaur that retirement comes before extinction.

At the university-administrator conference where Nelson spoke in February, I sat at a table with an affable bunch of deans from Australia and the United States. They listened attentively, first with interest and then with growing alarm. Toward the end of the conversation, the sponsoring organization's president asked the panelists what they expected to be said at a similar event in 2017, on the same topic of innovative online education.

("Assuming we're still in business," a dean near me whispered to no one in particular.)

Daphne Koller said she expected Coursera to have grown in offerings into a university the size of a large state school—after having started from scratch in 2012. Even before Nelson gave his answer, I noticed some audience members uncomfortably shifting their weight. The stench of fear made him bold.

"I predict that in three years, four or five or seven or eight of you will be onstage here, presenting your preliminary findings of your first year of a radical new conception of your undergraduate [or] graduate program . . . And the rest of you will look at two or three of those versions and say, 'Uh-oh.' " This was meant as a joke, but hardly anyone laughed.

Analyze

1. What advantages do you see for students in the Minerva system? What disadvantages?

2. Minerva is a for-profit college, developed with private money. In your opinion, how does the nature of a university change when it shifts from delivering a public good and being partially funded with tax dollars (such as a state university) to a for-profit college whose final goal is to make money by delivering education as a private or luxury good?

3. The social environment at Minerva will be exclusively students, with no face-to-face contact with professors. What will be lost—or perhaps gained—in a college environment in which students are geographically removed from professors?

4. One of the central questions in the essay is: "Can a school that has no faculty offices, research labs, community spaces for students, or professors paid to do scholarly work still be called a university?" In your opinion, how important is it for a university both to introduce students to knowledge (teaching) and to be a production center of new knowledge (research)?

Explore

1. Have you ever learned a skill or been introduced to a subject through online lectures or tutorials? If so, how is the online learning experience different from classroom-based experiences?

2. Consider your own personal and social development since starting college. How would those areas of your development be different in a Minerva-like setting?

3. SHORT WRITING PROMPT: The Minerva experiment asks observers to consider: what is a college? Make a list of twenty items that you feel are essential to a complete college experience. Consider areas such as a wide variety of classes, training in traditional academic subjects, dorm life, living apart from parents, participation in research, a well-developed library, exposure to individuals whose background is significantly different from your own, learning to express yourself with accuracy and authority, the mixing of poets and business majors, and so forth.

4. FULL WRITING PROMPT: Ben Nelson started Minerva in part as a response to his own frustrating experience at the University of Pennsylvania's Wharton School. After exploring your university, identify one area that you believe you could improve. It could be part of the freshman experience, a required sequence of classes, the level of student–faculty contact, a social or entertainment program, and so forth. What would you improve? How would it add to the cost of attending your college? Lastly, what would be the educational or social benefits to students?

Dan Berrett
The Day the Purpose of College Changed

Dan Berrett is a senior reporter for *The Chronicle of Higher Education*, where he covers issues pertaining to teaching and curriculum.

The governor had bad news: The state budget was in crisis, and everyone needed to tighten their belts. High taxes threatened "economic ruin," said the newly elected Ronald Reagan. Welfare stood to be curbed, the highway patrol had fat to trim. Everything would be pared down; he'd start with his own office.

California still boasted a system of public higher education that was the envy of the world. And on February 28, 1967, a month into his term, the Republican governor assured people that he wouldn't do anything to harm it. "But," he added, "we do believe that there are certain intellectual luxuries that perhaps we could do without," for a little while at least.

"Governor," a reporter asked, "what is an intellectual luxury?"

Reagan described a four-credit course at the University of California at Davis on organizing demonstrations. "I figure that carrying a picket sign is sort of like, oh, a lot of things you pick up naturally," he said, "like learning how to swim by falling off the end of a dock."

Whole academic programs in California and across the country he found similarly suspect. Taxpayers, he said, shouldn't be "subsidizing intellectual curiosity."

That phrase quickly brought Reagan scorn. The following week the *Los Angeles Times* editorial page warned that his budget cuts and "tampering" with higher education threatened to create second-rate institutions.

"If a university is not a place where intellectual curiosity is to be encouraged, and subsidized," the editors wrote, "then it is nothing."

The *Times* was giving voice to the ideal of liberal education, in which college is a vehicle for intellectual development, for cultivating a flexible mind, and, no matter the focus of study, for fostering a broad set of knowledge and skills whose value is not always immediately apparent.

Reagan was staking out a competing vision. Learning for learning's sake might be nice, but the rest of us shouldn't have to pay for it. A higher education should prepare students for jobs.

Those two theories had long existed in uneasy equilibrium. On that day in 1967, the balance started to tip toward utility in ways not even Reagan may have anticipated.

Sometimes, sea changes in attitude start small, gradually establishing assumptions until no one remembers thinking differently. This is how that happened to liberal education. It's a story of events on campus and beyond: the oil embargo, the canon wars, federal fiscal policies, the fall of the Soviet Union. On that day in 1967, Reagan crystalized what has since become conventional wisdom about college. In the early 1970s, nearly three-quarters of freshmen said it was essential to them to develop a meaningful philosophy of life. About a third felt the same about being very well off financially. Now those fractions have flipped.

The notion that a liberal education is of dubious value has become entrenched in the popular imagination, even as its defenders argue the opposite. The Association of American Colleges and Universities, liberal education's chief advocate, celebrates its 100th anniversary this month. Its choices have shaped the story of liberal education, too. The group appears to be in fine shape, with a $10-million budget, more than 1,300 member colleges, and high-profile projects on educational quality, funded by the Bill & Melinda Gates Foundation, and civic learning, commissioned by the U.S. Department of Education. But such projects and respect on many campuses haven't stopped the public from largely dismissing the idea of liberal education.

College is defined so narrowly and instrumentally now, AAC&U's president, Carol Geary Schneider, has said, that it's "ultimately dangerous both to democracy and to economic creativity."

Once prized as a worthy pursuit for all, liberal education that day in 1967 became pointless, an indulgence, a joke.

It wasn't always a punchline. Thomas Jefferson argued for increased access to liberal education—among white males. A broadly educated populace, he said, would strengthen democracy. People "with genius and virtue should be rendered by liberal education worthy to receive and able to guard the sacred deposit of the rights and liberties of their fellow citizens," he wrote in 1779. Such men wouldn't be easily swayed by tyrants.

Still, there were dissenters, Michael S. Roth notes in *Beyond the University: Why Liberal Education Matters*. Benjamin Franklin mocked liberal education for focusing on the frivolous accouterments of privilege. Harvard College's students "learn little more than how to carry themselves handsomely and enter a room genteely," Franklin wrote. When they graduated, they remained "great blockheads as ever, only more proud and self-conceited."

A century later, prominent thinkers were still striking a balance. Booker T. Washington believed "knowledge must be harnessed to the things of real life" so that newly emancipated black Americans could determine their own economic fates. W.E.B. Du Bois sought to broaden what counted as real life, so that "the pursuit of happiness wouldn't be reduced to the pursuit of dollars," Mr. Roth writes.

Du Bois lent grandeur to that vision in *The Souls of Black Folk*: "The final product of our training must be neither a psychologist nor a brickmason, but a man."

Tensions between the two visions lingered into the 20th century. In 1942, a consultant to what was then the Association of American Colleges worried that institutions had "lost sight of the value of a liberal education" and that their curricula had "deteriorated into a hodge-podge of training in technical skills."

Still, the prevailing consensus endorsed liberal education. A presidential commission chartered by Harry S. Truman recommended in 1947 that colleges strive to more fully realize democracy "in every phase of living," promote international understanding, and deploy creative intelligence to solve social problems. College wasn't a way to get a job or make a buck.

For a long time, the pushback to that philosophy was productive. It forced higher education to be dynamic, to respond to conditions beyond campus, says Mr. Roth, who is president of Wesleyan University and sits on the AAC&U board. People understood that liberal learning served individuals, regardless of their jobs, as well as society at large. That's no longer true, he says.

A farmer reading the classics or an industrial worker quoting Shakespeare was at one time an honorable character. Today's news stories lament bartenders with chemistry degrees. "Where once these 'incongruities' might have been hailed as signs of a healthy republic," Mr. Roth writes, "today they are more likely to be cited as examples of a 'wasted'—nonmonetized—education."

Reagan rose to power by highlighting how colleges had veered dangerously away from mainstream values. He seized on campus unrest at Berkeley to connect with voters who hadn't gone to college but wanted their kids to. But the buildings their tax dollars paid for were burning.

The new governor didn't spend time talking about the tension between Jefferson's and Franklin's visions. There was little political payoff in nuance. Reagan, one of his campaign aides told *The New York Times* in 1970, doesn't operate in shades of gray: "He lays it out there."

As his second term and the 1970s began, demographics, economic uncertainty, and world events reinforced Reagan's ideology. Two philosophical shifts, toward social egalitarianism and free-market orthodoxy, took hold.

Higher education felt those shifts. Professorial authority diminished. The unraveling consensus on the curriculum accelerated. Colleges increasingly viewed students as customers. Economic inequality and insecurity rose, as did the wage premium of a college degree. And that became one of higher education's main selling points.

The long postwar boom, for both the economy and for higher education, was ending, and the oil embargo, in 1973, further strained the economy. Enrollment data showed students fleeing from the liberal arts, disciplines commonly associated with a liberal education, and flocking to professional and pre-professional programs.

Higher education became more of a buyer's market. Overall enrollments dropped. As that trend continued, colleges sought out new customers, especially adults and first-generation students, many of whom wanted their investments to pay off in jobs.

Liberal education felt the squeeze. The Association of American Colleges went into the red as several cash-strapped colleges withdrew their membership. With money tight, all of higher education looked for help from Washington. "Although it may indeed be contrary to academic tradition, as it is distasteful to many of us personally, the hour is overdue for us all to become more involved politically," Frederic W. Ness wrote as the group's president in 1973.

Many of the sector's chief associations had long refrained from lobbying because they found it "vulgar," according to the higher-education scholar Harland G. Bloland. College leaders, he said, advocated not self-interest, but the dispassionate pursuit of knowledge. They spoke the language of liberal education.

But after some cajoling from lawmakers, most of the higher-education associations shifted tactics. The lone holdout was the AAC.

By 1976, it faced a crossroads. Five years earlier, it had set up a subsidiary group to represent independent colleges. But trying to be two things at once—a lobbyist for a particular type of institution and an advocate for liberal education in general—became untenable. So it spun off the National Association of Independent Colleges and Universities, a lobbying group for private institutions. Left behind was an AAC that would look after the curriculum and liberal education.

On one hand, that gave it freedom and broad appeal. Schools of business and engineering joined the fold. And not lobbying on behalf of liberal education meant not inviting the federal government into curricular matters. "We've been able to be more forthright and direct about needed change in higher education," says Ms. Schneider, the group's president, "because we never have to worry about what the House of Representatives has to say about our recommendations." Still, AAC&U has worked closely with several states' higher-education departments.

But not pressing for federal legislation has its minuses, says John R. Thelin, a professor of the history of higher education and public policy at the University of Kentucky. AAC&U, like most of the big higher-education associations, is in Washington, where political power determines winners and losers. "AAC&U doesn't see itself as a lobbying group," he says. "They see it as a more subtle game."

But being too subtle risks leaving you on the sidelines.

By the time Reagan won the presidency, in 1980, practical degrees had become the safe and popular choice.

That year students were most likely to major in business. The discipline's rise seemed inexorable. In the 1930s, around the time Reagan went to college, about 8 percent of students studied in "business and commerce." When he was elected governor, that share was 12 percent. By the time he moved into the White House, more students majored in business than anything else. It's held that top spot ever since. In the early 80s, most freshmen said they'd chosen their college because they thought it would help them get a better job. The previous top reason? Learning more about things that interested them.

It was a rational response to changing federal policy. Under the Reagan administration, the maximum Pell Grant decreased by about a quarter. Student loans became a more common way to pay for college, even as the president made their interest payments ineligible for tax deductions. As student debt rose, so did the urgency of earning a living after graduation.

Free-market ideas permeated higher education. "The curriculum has given way to a marketplace philosophy," wrote the authors of "Integrity in the College Curriculum: A Report to the Academic Community," commissioned by the AAC in 1985. "It is a supermarket where students are shoppers and professors are merchants of learning."

Meanwhile, liberal learning floated from its traditional moorings. After the associations' split, the concept no longer resided so clearly with liberal-arts colleges, and the next logical home, academic departments in the arts and sciences, didn't offer refuge for long. The fierce canon wars of the 1980s revealed little consensus on what belonged in the curriculum. How could anybody defend a liberal education when no one could agree on what it was?

The battles were especially passionate in the humanities, reflecting anxieties about demographic change in the country and on campuses, says Andrew Hartman, an associate professor of history at Illinois State University. Reagan showed little interest in the canon wars, but he is often associated with a strain of thought that grew out of the 1960s and gained strength when he was president. It saw professors as idle elites antagonistic toward the values of the white working class, says Mr. Hartman, author of the forthcoming *A War for the Soul of America*. "Liberal education," he says, "gets wrapped up in that."

While the ideal of liberal education faded during that period, it survived. The Sputnik crisis had justified a huge investment in education that lifted all boats, says Catherine Liu, a professor of film and media studies at the University of California at Irvine. Responding to the Soviet threat opened opportunities for generations of middle-class Americans, argues Ms. Liu, author of *The American Idyll: Academic Antielitism as Cultural Critique*. "Liberal education was the great dream of the postwar era," she says.

But the conclusion of the Cold War ended that dream, she says, and a more instrumentalist view of college has become a point of bipartisan agreement. President Obama, she says, "sees education as a redistributive process" in which "community and state colleges will teach vocational skills so people can get jobs."

Education once sought to develop people's potential, says Ms. Liu. Now it's all about training. "Training," she says, "is what you get through mindless repetition."

Liberal learning is now a luxury good, she says. "It's become the education of the 1 percent."

If the definition and value of liberal education are in doubt, so is the question of whom it's for.

Even Jefferson and Du Bois thought such a privilege should be limited—to those "endowed with genius and virtue" or belonging to the "talented tenth," respectively. The AAC&U pushes a more expansive vision: that a liberal education is for everyone who seeks to make meaning in their lives and to participate in democracy.

"The purpose is broad knowledge that enables you to navigate the world you inherit, to develop powers of the mind to make reasoned judgments and cultivate a sense of ethical responsibility, and to connect those goals to the world," says Ms. Schneider, the group's president.

Those objectives should not be restricted, she says, to liberal-arts majors. They are useful for teachers and technicians. "We argued in 1915 and we're arguing today that we need good citizens," she says. "A welder is a citizen, too."

That message appears to get some traction, at least on campus. Some deans of colleges in practical fields tout their liberal-education approach. They want engineers who can build a bridge and think about its effects on the environment and surrounding community. Nurses should know how to draw blood and consider the cultural influences that might keep patients from taking their medication.

And for students in traditional academic disciplines, liberal learning can't be purely theoretical. The AAC&U started the campaign Liberal Education and America's Promise a decade ago to encourage students to learn by tackling society's "big questions." More than 450 campuses have signed on, and this month the association said it would expand the campaign, pushing for every student to complete a project involving field research, an internship, a practicum, or community service.

Such projects, the AAC&U argues, draw on the vital skills of critical thinking, writing, quantitative reasoning, and teamwork that liberal education cultivates. That's what employers have consistently told the group they're looking for in new hires, Ms. Schneider says. "They just didn't use the words 'liberal education.'"

Those words are often confused or conflated with "liberal arts," not necessarily a positive association. The word "liberal," the association acknowledges, has become a term of opprobrium. Recent research in economics found that top students from low-income backgrounds reacted to the term "liberal arts" with comments like "I am not liberal" and "I don't like learning useless things."

When politicians mock particular disciplines, it doesn't exactly bolster popular opinion of liberal education. "If you want to take gender studies, that's fine, go to a private school," Pat McCrory, the Republican governor of North Carolina, said on a radio show a couple of years ago. "I don't want to subsidize that if that's not going to get someone a job." In other words, it's an intellectual luxury.

To people like Mr. McCrory, such luxuries are exclusively private goods. That said, plenty of governors through the years have understood that a liberal education also has a public benefit.

One governor, dedicating a library at small Eureka College in 1967, made the case.

Standing in front of the new building, the speaker invoked the accumulated wisdom behind him. "The truth is," he said, "the answers to all the problems of mankind, every one of them, even the most modern and the most complex, can be found in this building."

He grounded his remarks in sociological theory and sprinkled in references to Aristotle, Plato, Socrates, and Maimonides, counseling students to read them critically. Past democracies had become mobs when they didn't adequately protect minorities. Even the greats made mistakes.

"One of mankind's problems," the speaker said, "is we keep committing the same errors."

His name was Ronald Reagan.

Analyze

1. Ronald Reagan believed that taxpayers shouldn't be "subsidizing intellectual curiosity." What courses at a university might be defined as "intellectual curiosities"? Do you agree that state universities—that is, universities that are partially funded with state tax dollars—shouldn't teach these subjects? Relatedly, do you believe that intellectual curiosities should be reserved for those who can afford them?

2. Berrett's article introduces an interesting question: What topics, if any, when approached with college-level rigor might be considered outside the domain of a university education? Animation? Reality TV shows? Comic books? Video games? Rap music? Celebrity lifestyles?

3. Since the age of Reagan, most colleges have shifted from an environment of "intellectual curiosity" to an environment of utility and career training. In your opinion, is this a positive or negative change?

4. What classes, in your opinion, are most likely to develop flexible minds? And what classes develop career readiness? How much overlap do you see between the two groups? If you could select only one path—flexible mind or career readiness—which would you choose? What would be the long-term costs and benefits of your choice?

Explore

1. When you applied to college, did you spend more time considering how college would change you as a person or how college would prepare you for a career?

2. What percentage of a college classroom experience, in your opinion, should be directed at career preparation and what percentage should be directed at intellectual and artistic development?

3. SHORT WRITING PROMPT: Make an appointment with an advisor for a major that interests you to discuss how courses in that major relate to both intellectual development and career training. How does this major prepare you for a career? How do classes in this major path allow you to change jobs entirely (i.e., transferable skills) after college? How does this major allow students to find personal fulfillment outside of a career?

William Deresiewicz
The Disadvantages of an Elite Education

William Deresiewicz taught at Yale University for ten years, an experience that contributed to his best-selling book *Excellent Sheep: The Miseducation of the American Elite and the Way to a Meaningful Life.* His work regularly appears in *The Nation, The American Scholar, Harper's,* and *The Atlantic.*

It didn't dawn on me that there might be a few holes in my education until I was about 35. I'd just bought a house, the pipes needed fixing, and the plumber was standing in my kitchen. There he was, a short, beefy guy with a goatee and a Red Sox cap and a thick Boston accent, and I suddenly learned that I didn't have the slightest idea what to say to someone like him. So alien was his experience to me, so unguessable his values, so mysterious his very language, that I couldn't succeed in engaging him in a few minutes of small talk before he got down to work. Fourteen years of higher education and a handful of Ivy League degrees, and there I was, stiff and stupid, struck dumb by my own dumbness. "Ivy retardation," a friend of mine calls this. I could carry on conversations with people from other countries, in other languages, but I couldn't talk to the man who was standing in my own house.

It's not surprising that it took me so long to discover the extent of my miseducation, because the last thing an elite education will teach you is its own inadequacy. As two dozen years at Yale and Columbia have shown me, elite colleges relentlessly encourage their students to flatter themselves for being there, and for what being there can do for them. The advantages of an elite education are indeed undeniable. You learn to think, at least in certain ways, and you make the contacts needed to launch yourself into a life rich in all of society's most cherished rewards. To consider that while some opportunities are being created, others are being cancelled and that while some abilities are being developed, others are being crippled is, within this context, not only outrageous, but inconceivable.

I'm not talking about curricula or the culture wars, the closing or opening of the American mind, political correctness, canon formation, or what have you. I'm talking about the whole system in which these skirmishes play out. Not just the Ivy League and its peer institutions, but also the mechanisms that get you there in the first place: the private and affluent public "feeder" schools, the ever-growing parastructure of tutors and test-prep courses and enrichment programs, the whole admissions frenzy and everything that leads up to and away from it. The message, as always, is the medium. Before, after, and around the elite college classroom, a constellation of values is ceaselessly inculcated. As globalization sharpens economic insecurity, we are increasingly committing ourselves—as students, as parents, as a society—to a vast apparatus of educational advantage. With so many resources devoted to the business of elite academics and so many people scrambling for the limited space at the top of the ladder, it is worth asking what exactly it is you get in the end—what it is we all get, because the elite students of today, as their institutions never tire of reminding them, are the leaders of tomorrow.

The first disadvantage of an elite education, as I learned in my kitchen that day, is that it makes you incapable of talking to people who aren't like you. Elite schools pride themselves on their diversity, but that diversity is almost entirely a matter of ethnicity and race. With respect to class, these schools are largely—indeed increasingly—homogeneous. Visit any elite campus in our great nation and you can thrill to the heartwarming spectacle of the children of white businesspeople and professionals studying and playing alongside the children of black, Asian, and Latino businesspeople and professionals. At the same time, because these schools tend to cultivate liberal attitudes, they leave their students in the paradoxical position of wanting to advocate on behalf of the working class while being unable to hold a simple conversation with anyone in it. Witness the last two Democratic presidential nominees, Al Gore and John Kerry: one each from

Harvard and Yale, both earnest, decent, intelligent men, both utterly incapable of communicating with the larger electorate.

But it isn't just a matter of class. My education taught me to believe that people who didn't go to an Ivy League or equivalent school weren't worth talking to, regardless of their class. I was given the unmistakable message that such people were beneath me. We were "the best and the brightest," as these places love to say, and everyone else was, well, something else: less good, less bright. I learned to give that little nod of understanding, that slightly sympathetic "Oh," when people told me they went to a less prestigious college. (If I'd gone to Harvard, I would have learned to say "in Boston" when I was asked where I went to school—the Cambridge version of noblesse oblige.) I never learned that there are smart people who don't go to elite colleges, often precisely for reasons of class. I never learned that there are smart people who don't go to college at all.

I also never learned that there are smart people who aren't "smart." The existence of multiple forms of intelligence has become a commonplace, but however much elite universities like to sprinkle their incoming classes with a few actors or violinists, they select for and develop one form of intelligence: the analytic. While this is broadly true of all universities, elite schools, precisely because their students (and faculty, and administrators) possess this one form of intelligence to such a high degree, are more apt to ignore the value of others. One naturally prizes what one most possesses and what most makes for one's advantages. But social intelligence and emotional intelligence and creative ability, to name just three other forms, are not distributed preferentially among the educational elite. The "best" are the brightest only in one narrow sense. One needs to wander away from the educational elite to begin to discover this.

What about people who aren't bright in any sense? I have a friend who went to an Ivy League college after graduating from a typically mediocre public high school. One of the values of going to such a school, she once said, is that it teaches you to relate to stupid people. Some people are smart in the elite-college way, some are smart in other ways, and some aren't smart at all. It should be embarrassing not to know how to talk to any of them, if only because talking to people is the only real way of knowing them. Elite institutions are supposed to provide a humanistic education, but the first principle of humanism is Terence's: "nothing human is alien to me." The first disadvantage of an elite education is how very much of the human it alienates you from.

The second disadvantage, implicit in what I've been saying, is that an elite education inculcates a false sense of self-worth. Getting to an elite college, being at an elite college, and going on from an elite college—all involve numerical rankings: SAT, GPA, GRE. You learn to think of yourself in terms of those numbers. They come to signify not only your fate, but your identity; not only your identity, but your value. It's been said that what those tests really measure is your ability to take tests, but even if they measure something real, it is only a small slice of the real. The problem begins when students are encouraged to forget this truth, when academic excellence becomes excellence in some absolute sense, when "better at X" becomes simply "better."

There is nothing wrong with taking pride in one's intellect or knowledge. There is something wrong with the smugness and self-congratulation that elite schools connive at from the moment the fat envelopes come in the mail. From orientation to graduation, the message is implicit in every tone of voice and tilt of the head, every old-school tradition, every article in the student paper, every speech from the dean. The message is: You have arrived. Welcome to the club. And the corollary is equally clear: You deserve everything your presence here is going to enable you to get. When people say that students at elite schools have a strong sense of entitlement, they mean that those students think they deserve more than other people because their SAT scores are higher.

At Yale, and no doubt at other places, the message is reinforced in embarrassingly literal terms. The physical form of the university—its quads and residential colleges, with their Gothic stone façades and wrought-iron portals—is constituted by the locked gate set into the encircling wall. Everyone carries around an ID card that determines which gates they can enter. The gate, in other words, is a kind of governing metaphor—because the social form of the university, as is true of every elite school, is constituted the same way. Elite colleges are walled domains guarded by locked gates, with admission granted only to the elect. The aptitude with which students absorb this lesson is demonstrated by the avidity with which they erect still more gates within those gates, special realms of ever-greater exclusivity—at Yale, the famous secret societies, or as they should probably be called, the open-secret societies, since true secrecy would defeat their purpose. There's no point in excluding people unless they know they've been excluded.

One of the great errors of an elite education, then, is that it teaches you to think that measures of intelligence and academic achievement are measures of value in some moral or metaphysical sense. But they're not. Graduates of elite schools are not more valuable than stupid people, or talentless people, or even lazy people. Their pain does not hurt more. Their souls do not weigh more. If I were religious, I would say, God does not love them more. The political implications should be clear. As John Ruskin told an older elite, grabbing what you can get isn't any less wicked when you grab it with the power of your brains than with the power of your fists. "Work must always be," Ruskin says, "and captains of work must always be . . . [But] there is a wide difference between being captains . . . of work, and taking the profits of it."

The political implications don't stop there. An elite education not only ushers you into the upper classes; it trains you for the life you will lead once you get there. I didn't understand this until I began comparing my experience, and even more, my students' experience, with the experience of a friend of mine who went to Cleveland State. There are due dates and attendance requirements at places like Yale, but no one takes them very seriously. Extensions are available for the asking; threats to deduct credit for missed classes are rarely, if ever, carried out. In other words, students at places like Yale get an endless string of second chances. Not so at places like Cleveland State. My friend once got a D in a class in which she'd been running an A because she was coming off a waitressing shift and had to hand in her term paper an hour late.

That may be an extreme example, but it is unthinkable at an elite school. Just as unthinkably, she had no one to appeal to. Students at places like Cleveland State, unlike those at places like Yale, don't have a platoon of advisers and tutors and deans to write out excuses for late work, give them extra help when they need it, pick them up when they fall down. They get their education wholesale, from an indifferent bureaucracy; it's not handed to them in individually wrapped packages by smiling clerks. There are few, if any, opportunities for the kind of contacts I saw my students get routinely—classes with visiting power brokers, dinners with foreign dignitaries. There are also few, if any, of the kind of special funds that, at places like Yale, are available in profusion: travel stipends, research fellowships, performance grants. Each year, my department at Yale awards dozens of cash prizes for everything from freshman essays to senior projects. This year, those awards came to more than $90,000—in just one department.

Students at places like Cleveland State also don't get A-'s just for doing the work. There's been a lot of handwringing lately over grade inflation, and it is a scandal, but the most scandalous thing about it is how uneven it's been. Forty years ago, the average GPA at both public and private universities was about 2.6, still close to the traditional B-/C+ curve. Since then, it's gone up everywhere, but not by anything like the same amount. The average GPA at public universities is now about 3.0, a B; at private universities it's about 3.3, just short of a B+. And at most Ivy League schools, it's closer to 3.4. But there are always students who don't do the work, or who are taking a class far outside their field (for fun or to fulfill a requirement), or who aren't up to standard to begin with (athletes, legacies). At a school like Yale, students who come to class and work hard expect nothing less than an A-. And most of the time, they get it.

In short, the way students are treated in college trains them for the social position they will occupy once they get out. At schools like Cleveland State, they're being trained for positions somewhere in the middle of the class system, in the depths of one bureaucracy or another. They're being conditioned for lives with few second chances, no extensions, little support, narrow opportunity—lives of subordination, supervision, and control, lives of deadlines, not guidelines. At places like Yale, of course, it's the reverse. The elite like to think of themselves as belonging to a meritocracy, but that's true only up to a point. Getting through the gate is very difficult, but once you're in, there's almost nothing you can do to get kicked out. Not the most abject academic failure, not the most heinous act of plagiarism, not even threatening a fellow student with bodily harm—I've heard of all three—will get you expelled. The feeling is that, by gosh, it just wouldn't be fair—in other words, the self-protectiveness of the old-boy network, even if it now includes girls. Elite schools nurture excellence, but they also nurture what a former Yale graduate student I know calls "entitled mediocrity." A is the mark of excellence; A- is the mark of entitled mediocrity. It's another one of those metaphors, not so much a grade as a promise. It means, don't worry, we'll take care of you. You may not be all that good, but you're good enough.

Here, too, college reflects the way things work in the adult world (unless it's the other way around). For the elite, there's always another extension—a bailout, a pardon, a stint in rehab—always plenty of contacts and special stipends—the country club, the conference, the year-end bonus, the dividend. If Al Gore and John Kerry represent one of the characteristic products of an elite education, George W. Bush represents another. It's no coincidence that our current president, the apotheosis of entitled mediocrity, went to Yale. Entitled mediocrity is indeed the operating principle of his administration, but as Enron and WorldCom and the other scandals of the dot-com meltdown demonstrated, it's also the operating principle of corporate America. The fat salaries paid to underperforming CEOs are an adult version of the A-. Anyone who remembers the injured sanctimony with which Kenneth Lay greeted the notion that he should be held accountable for his actions will understand the mentality in question—the belief that once you're in the club, you've got a God-given right to stay in the club. But you don't need to remember Ken Lay, because the whole dynamic played out again last year in the case of Scooter Libby, another Yale man.

If one of the disadvantages of an elite education is the temptation it offers to mediocrity, another is the temptation it offers to security. When parents explain why they work so hard to give their children the best possible education, they invariably say it is because of the opportunities it opens up. But what of the opportunities it shuts down? An elite education gives you the chance to be rich—which is, after all, what we're talking about—but it takes away the chance not to be. Yet the opportunity not to be rich is one of the greatest opportunities with which young Americans have been blessed. We live in a society that is itself so wealthy that it can afford to provide a decent living to whole classes of people who in other countries exist (or in earlier times existed) on the brink of poverty or, at least, of indignity. You can live comfortably in the United States as a schoolteacher, or a community organizer, or a civil rights lawyer, or an artist—that is, by any reasonable definition of comfort. You have to live in an ordinary house instead of an apartment in Manhattan or a mansion in L.A.; you have to drive a Honda instead of a BMW or a Hummer; you have to vacation in Florida instead of Barbados or Paris, but what are such losses when set against the opportunity to do work you believe in, work you're suited for, work you love, every day of your life?

Yet it is precisely that opportunity that an elite education takes away. How can I be a schoolteacher—wouldn't that be a waste of my expensive education? Wouldn't I be squandering the opportunities my parents worked so hard to provide? What will my friends think? How will I face my classmates at our 20th reunion, when they're all rich lawyers or important people in New York? And the question that lies behind all these: Isn't it beneath me? So a whole universe of possibility closes, and you miss your true calling.

This is not to say that students from elite colleges never pursue a riskier or less lucrative course after graduation, but even when they do, they tend to give up more quickly than others. (Let's not even talk about the possibility of kids from privileged backgrounds not going to college at all, or delaying matriculation for several years, because however appropriate such choices might sometimes be, our rigid educational mentality places them outside the universe of possibility—the reason so many kids go sleepwalking off to college with no idea what they're doing there.) This doesn't seem to make sense, especially since students from elite schools tend to graduate with less debt and are more likely to be able to float by on family money for a while. I wasn't aware of the phenomenon myself until I heard about it from a couple of graduate students in my department, one from Yale, one from Harvard. They were talking about trying to write poetry, how friends of theirs from college called it quits within a year or two while people they know from less prestigious schools are still at it. Why should this be? Because students from elite schools expect success, and expect it now. They have, by definition, never experienced anything else, and their sense of self has been built around their ability to succeed. The idea of not being successful terrifies them, disorients them, defeats them. They've been driven their whole lives by a fear of failure—often, in the first instance, by their parents' fear of failure. The first time I blew a test, I walked out of the room feeling like I no longer knew who I was. The second time, it was easier; I had started to learn that failure isn't the end of the world.

But if you're afraid to fail, you're afraid to take risks, which begins to explain the final and most damning disadvantage of an elite education: that it is profoundly anti-intellectual. This will seem counterintuitive. Aren't kids at elite schools the smartest ones around, at least in the narrow academic sense? Don't they work harder than anyone else—indeed, harder than any previous generation? They are. They do. But being an intellectual is not the same as being smart. Being an intellectual means more than doing your homework.

If so few kids come to college understanding this, it is no wonder. They are products of a system that rarely asked them to think about something bigger than the next assignment. The system forgot to teach them, along the way to the prestige admissions and the lucrative jobs, that the most important achievements can't be measured by a letter or a number or a name. It forgot that the true purpose of education is to make minds, not careers.

Being an intellectual means, first of all, being passionate about ideas—and not just for the duration of a semester, for the sake of pleasing the teacher, or for getting a good grade. A friend who teaches at the University of Connecticut once complained to me that his students don't think for themselves. Well, I said, Yale students think for themselves, but only because they know we want them to. I've had many wonderful students at Yale and Columbia, bright, thoughtful, creative kids whom it's been a pleasure to talk with and learn from. But most of them have seemed content to color within the lines that their education had marked out for them. Only a small minority have seen their education as part of a larger intellectual journey, have approached the work of the mind with a pilgrim soul. These few have tended to feel like freaks, not least because they get so little support from the university itself. Places like Yale, as one of them put it to me, are not conducive to searchers.

Places like Yale are simply not set up to help students ask the big questions. I don't think there ever was a golden age of intellectualism in the American university, but in the 19th century students might at least have had a chance to hear such questions raised in chapel or in the literary societies and debating clubs that flourished on campus. Throughout much of the 20th century, with the growth of the humanistic ideal in American colleges, students might have encountered the big questions in the classrooms of professors possessed of a strong sense of pedagogic mission. Teachers like that still exist in this country, but the increasingly dire exigencies of academic professionalization have made them all but extinct at elite universities. Professors at top research institutions are valued exclusively for the quality of their scholarly work; time spent on teaching is time lost. If students want a conversion experience, they're better off at a liberal arts college.

When elite universities boast that they teach their students how to think, they mean that they teach them the analytic and rhetorical skills necessary for success in law or medicine or science or business. But a humanistic education is supposed to mean something more than that, as universities still dimly feel. So when students get to college, they hear a couple of speeches telling them to ask the big questions, and when they graduate, they hear a couple more speeches telling them to ask the big questions. And in between, they spend four years taking courses that train them to ask the little questions—specialized courses, taught by specialized professors, aimed at specialized students. Although the notion of breadth is implicit in the very idea of a liberal arts education, the admissions process increasingly selects for kids who have already begun to think of themselves in specialized terms—the junior journalist, the budding astronomer, the language prodigy. We are slouching, even at elite schools, toward a glorified form of vocational training.

Indeed, that seems to be exactly what those schools want. There's a reason elite schools speak of training leaders, not thinkers—holders of power, not its critics. An independent mind is independent of all allegiances, and elite schools, which get a large percentage of their budget from alumni giving, are strongly invested in fostering institutional loyalty. As another friend, a third-generation Yalie, says, the purpose of Yale College is to manufacture Yale alumni. Of course, for the system to work, those alumni need money. At Yale, the long-term drift of students away from majors in the humanities and basic sciences toward more practical ones like computer science and economics has been abetted by administrative indifference. The college career office has little to say to students not interested in law, medicine, or business, and elite universities are not going to do anything to discourage the large percentage of their graduates who take their degrees to Wall Street. In fact, they're showing them the way. The liberal arts university is becoming the corporate university, its center of gravity shifting to technical fields where scholarly expertise can be parlayed into lucrative business opportunities.

It's no wonder that the few students who are passionate about ideas find themselves feeling isolated and confused. I was talking with one of them last year about his interest in the German Romantic idea of *bildung,* the upbuilding of the soul. But, he said—he was a senior at the time—it's hard to build your soul when everyone around you is trying to sell theirs.

Yet there is a dimension of the intellectual life that lies above the passion for ideas, though so thoroughly has our culture been sanitized of it that it is hardly surprising if it was beyond the reach of even my most alert students. Since the idea of the intellectual emerged in the 18th century, it has had, at its core, a commitment to social transformation. Being an intellectual means thinking your way toward a vision of the good society and then trying to realize that vision by speaking truth to power. It means going into spiritual exile. It means forswearing your allegiance, in lonely freedom, to God, to country, and to Yale. It takes more than just intellect; it takes imagination and courage. "I am not afraid to make a mistake," Stephen Dedalus says, "even a great mistake, a lifelong mistake, and perhaps as long as eternity, too."

Being an intellectual begins with thinking your way outside of your assumptions and the system that enforces them. But students who get into elite schools are precisely the ones who have best learned to work within the system, so it's almost impossible for them to see outside it, to see that it's even there. Long before they got to college, they turned themselves into world-class hoop-jumpers and teacher-pleasers, getting A's in every class no matter how boring they found the teacher or how pointless the subject, racking up eight or 10 extracurricular activities no matter what else they wanted to do with their time. Paradoxically, the situation may be better at second-tier schools and, in particular, again, at liberal arts colleges than at the most prestigious universities. Some students end up at second-tier schools because they're exactly like students at Harvard or Yale, only less gifted or driven. But others end up there because they have a more independent spirit. They didn't get straight A's because they couldn't be bothered to give everything in every class. They concentrated on the ones that meant the most to them or on a single strong extracurricular passion or on projects that had nothing to do with school or even with looking good on a college application. Maybe they just sat in their room, reading a lot and writing in their journal. These are the kinds of kids who are likely, once they get to college, to be more interested in the human spirit than in school spirit, and to think about leaving college bearing questions, not résumés.

I've been struck, during my time at Yale, by how similar everyone looks. You hardly see any hippies or punks or art-school types, and at a college that was known in the '80s as the Gay Ivy, few out lesbians and no gender queers. The geeks don't look all that geeky; the fashionable kids go in for understated elegance. Thirty-two flavors, all of them vanilla. The most elite schools have become places of a narrow and suffocating normalcy. Everyone feels pressure to maintain the kind of appearance—and affect—that go with achievement. (Dress for success, medicate for success.) I know from long experience as an adviser that not every Yale student is appropriate and well-adjusted, which is exactly why it worries me that so many of them act that way. The tyranny of the normal must be very heavy in their lives. One consequence is that those who can't get with the program (and they tend to be students from poorer backgrounds) often polarize in the opposite direction, flying off into extremes of disaffection and self-destruction. But another consequence has to do with the large majority who can get with the program.

I taught a class several years ago on the literature of friendship. One day we were discussing Virginia Woolf's novel *The Waves,* which follows a group of friends from childhood to middle age. In high school, one of them falls in love with another boy. He thinks, "To whom can I expose the urgency of my own passion? . . . There is nobody—here among these grey arches, and moaning pigeons, and cheerful games and tradition and emulation, all so skilfully organised to prevent feeling alone." A pretty good description of an elite college campus, including the part about never being allowed to feel alone. What did my students think of this, I wanted to know? What does it mean to go to school at a place where you're never alone? Well, one of them said, I do feel uncomfortable sitting in my room by myself. Even when I have to write a paper, I do it at a friend's. That same day, as it happened, another student gave a presentation on Emerson's essay on friendship. Emerson says, he reported, that one of the purposes of friendship is to equip you for solitude. As I was asking my students what they thought that meant, one of them interrupted to say, wait a second, why do you need solitude in the first place? What can you do by yourself that you can't do with a friend?

So there they were: one young person who had lost the capacity for solitude and another who couldn't see the point of it. There's been much talk of late about the loss of privacy, but equally calamitous is its corollary, the loss of solitude. It used to be that you couldn't always get together with your friends even when you wanted to. Now that students are in constant electronic contact, they never have trouble finding each other. But it's not as if their compulsive sociability is enabling them to develop deep friendships. "To whom can I expose the urgency of my own passion?": my student was in her friend's room writing a paper, not having a heart-to-heart. She probably didn't have the time; indeed, other students told me they found their peers too busy for intimacy.

What happens when busyness and sociability leave no room for solitude? The ability to engage in introspection, I put it to my students that day, is the essential precondition for living an intellectual life, and the essential precondition for introspection is solitude. They took this in for a second, and then one of them said, with a dawning sense of self-awareness, "So are you saying that we're all just, like, really excellent sheep?" Well, I don't know. But I do know that the life of the mind is lived one mind at a time: one solitary, skeptical, resistant mind at a time. The best place to cultivate it is not within an educational system whose real purpose is to reproduce the class system.

The world that produced John Kerry and George Bush is indeed giving us our next generation of leaders. The kid who's loading up on AP courses junior year or editing three campus publications while double-majoring, the kid whom everyone wants at their college or law school but no one wants in their classroom, the kid who doesn't have a minute to breathe, let alone think, will soon be running a corporation or an institution or a government. She will have many achievements but little experience, great success but no vision. The disadvantage of an elite education is that it's given us the elite we have, and the elite we're going to have.

Analyze

1. The essay suggests that college experience helps define a person's later social life. What types of people will your university likely teach you to socialize with after graduation? Plumbers? Politicians? High school teachers? Investment bankers? Artists? The working poor? The upper one-percent of wealth holders? People whose worldviews are different than those with whom you grew up?

2. The essay suggests that SAT and ACT scores may not reflect all types of intelligence. What types of intelligence might not be best represented by a high standardized test score?

3. The essay says: "The opportunity not to be rich is one of the greatest opportunities with which young Americans have been blessed." How can this be considered a personal "blessing"?

4. The author suggests that "the loss of solitude" has diminished the emotional and expressive lives of students. How is solitude connected to important intellectual and emotional experiences? What barriers exist at your college for students who want to engage in meaningful solitude?

Explore

1. In your college experience, what classes have asked you to consider big questions? What big questions were explored?

2. SHORT WRITING PROMPT: The essay suggests that college trains individuals for the social life they will lead after college. Make a list of ten professional groups around whom, after graduation, you will feel comfortable in social situations. Make a second list of ten professional groups around whom, after graduation, you will not feel comfortable.

Professional groups would include bank tellers, plumbers, senators, stockbrokers, lawyers, elementary school teachers, small business owners, CEOs, and so forth.

3. FULL WRITING PROMPT: Agree or disagree: Your college has done a good job so far in helping you "build your soul." If you agree, offer personal examples of how your college has accomplished this. If you disagree, offer suggestions on how your college could be more effective in this pursuit.

Vauhini Vara
Is College the New High School?

Vauhini Vara is a former reporter for *The Wall Street Journal* and a former business editor for NewYorker.com. Currently she lives in San Francisco and writes about business and technology.

On Friday, President Obama travelled to Tennessee to outline a plan to provide free community college for all. Mere hours had passed since the federal government's announcement of the latest employment figures, which were encouraging. In December, the unemployment rate stood at 5.6 per cent, the lowest rate since the end of the recession. Beneath those promising numbers, though, clear gaps were evident. For high-school graduates without an advanced degree, the unemployment rate was 5.3 per cent, but for those with a bachelor's degree, the rate was more than two percentage points lower—2.9 per cent. At Pellissippi State Community College, in Knoxville, Obama told the students in his audience:

> You came to college to learn about the world and to engage with new ideas and to discover the things you're passionate about—and maybe have a little fun. And to expand your horizons. That's terrific—that's a huge part of what college has to offer. But you're also here, now more than ever, because a college degree is the surest ticket to the middle class. It is the key to getting a good job that pays

a good income—and to provide you the security where even if you don't have the same job for thirty years, you're so adaptable and you have a skill set and the capacity to learn new skills, it ensures you're always employable. And that is the key not just for individual Americans, that's the key for this whole country's ability to compete in the global economy. In the new economy, jobs and businesses will go wherever the most skilled, best-educated workforce resides. Because businesses are mobile now. Technology means they can locate anywhere. And where they have the most educated, most adaptable, most nimble workforce, that's where they're going to locate. And I want them to look no further than the United States of America.

Obama's comments reflected a significant shift in what college means to American society and the U.S. economy. For centuries, it functioned as a social rite of passage for people from a certain background—a place where young, well-to-do men learned about the world, discovered their passions, and had a little fun. It was only in the second half of the twentieth century, especially after blue-collar jobs became harder to find because of outsourcing and automation, that a bachelor's degree became something more pragmatic—a prerequisite to earning a good, middle-class living. In 1940, five per cent of people in the U.S. over the age of twenty-five had finished at least four years of college. By 2013, that figure had risen to thirty-two per cent. At this point, it's well understood that there exists a persistent gap in employment rates and wages between those with bachelor's degrees and those without. On average, those who graduate from four-year colleges are not only employed at higher rates but also earn over fifty per cent more than those with only a high-school degree.

Obama's response to this problem has been to make college a more practical choice for more people, and to that end he has recently undertaken a number of initiatives, including expanding Pell grants and capping student-loan payments at ten per cent of borrowers' income. But the community-college proposal is especially notable. It would cover the cost of two years of community college for any student who maintains a grade-point average of 2.5 (about a C+), or higher. The federal government would cover three-fourths of the student's expenses, at an estimated cost of sixty billion dollars over ten years, and states would be responsible for the rest.

This represents a huge investment, for one thing, but it also represents a shift in how the government—or one influential branch of it, at least—views higher education. The Obama Administration has framed its community-college proposal as the obvious next phase of an expansion that has taken place over the past several decades in the number of years of schooling seen as required for a young person to be educated and which, therefore, ought to be subsidized by the government. In other words, in the Obama Administration's view, college has become the new high school. The Obama argument in favor of supporting this transformation is, by and large, an economic one rather than a cultural one: people who are college-educated have better employment prospects, and a nation with more employable people is more competitive.

For now, Obama's proposal remains a proposal. Unlike some of the policy measures he has taken through executive actions, this one would require support from a Republican-led Congress, which isn't at all guaranteed. G.O.P. leaders have so far been circumspect, and Cory Fritz, a spokesman for the Republican Speaker of the House, John Boehner, has said, "With no details or information on the cost, this seems more like a talking point than a plan." Some of the proposal's most vocal critics, perhaps surprisingly, have been those who want to make higher education more affordable but are concerned that such a move would provide free community college to students regardless of their financial situations. An eighteen-year-old with affluent parents would be able to attend for free, just like someone less well off, which seems, to them, like a poor use of resources. In fact, Pell grants already cover the cost of community college for most low-income students, so more-affluent students could receive the greatest net benefit from the plan.

There's another issue, though, that has received less attention. What about the assumption underlying the proposal, that a college education makes a person more employable? In a blog post accompanying Obama's announcement, Betsey Stevenson, a member of the Council of Economic Advisers, included a chart showing that college graduates earn more than those who have only finished high school. That chart, however, compares the wages of high-school graduates with those of people who finished four years of college—not people who hold the associate's degrees conferred by community colleges, which Obama's plan would facilitate.

In fact, research suggests that people with associate's degrees don't hold jobs, or earn more money, at a substantially higher rate than high-school graduates. In December, for example, the unemployment rate of 5.3 per cent for high-school graduates wasn't much higher than the 4.9 per cent rate for people with associate's degrees or some other amount of college less than a bachelor's degree. Statistics about wages are harder to come by, but they generally suggest that people with associate's degrees tend to earn around ten per cent more than high-school graduates—a welcome income bump, for sure, but not a particularly large one.

Obama hopes, in part, that by making community college more affordable—and therefore encouraging more students to attend—he will make it likelier that they will move on to a four-year college and complete a bachelor's degree after earning an associate's degree. He told his audience in Tennessee about Caitlin McLawhorn, a graduate of Pellissippi State who is a beneficiary of a state program that is similar to what Obama hopes to offer. "She was raised by a single mom," he said. "She helped make ends meet, getting her first job almost the minute she could, two days after her sixteenth birthday. When it came time for college, the money wasn't there. But Caitlin lives in Tennessee, so she knew she had a great, free option. She completed two years at this institution. Now she's a senior at Maryville College. She's working full-time, just like she has since her first day of college."

In fact, situations like McLawhorn's are exceedingly rare. The National Student Clearinghouse Research Center found that, among students who started at two-year colleges, only about ten per cent had completed a degree at a four-year institution within six years; another thirty per cent had earned an associate's degree, while about sixty per cent had dropped out or were still enrolled. Let's assume that McLawhorn earns a bachelor's degree sometime in the next couple of years. For every McLawhorn, there will be nine students who don't make it that far.

Despite raising McLawhorn as an example, Obama seems to be aware of this shortcoming. Some aspects of his plan, which have been less discussed than the promise of free tuition, are meant both to improve graduation rates and to encourage community colleges to run programs that better prepare students for the workforce. According to a fact sheet released by the White House, colleges will be expected to "adopt promising and evidence-based institutional reforms to improve student outcomes"—for instance, offering academic advising and scheduling that better fits students' needs. Obama also wants to help fund community-college programs with "strong employer partnerships" and "work-based learning opportunities" that are meant to help workers get jobs in fast-growing fields such as energy, technology, and advanced manufacturing. The details of these aspects of Obama's plan have yet to be spelled out, but as Congress considers Obama's proposal and puts forth ideas of its own, they will be worth some attention. If Obama and

Congress can make higher education more accessible, that would be impressive. But making it more effective would be even more so.

Analyze

1. Do you believe that the United States should offer free two-year community college programs for all?
2. In the article, President Obama says that college is designed to give students "capacity to learn new skills"—that is, college is designed to teach students how to learn. What does he mean by this? How does college deliver the capacity to learn?
3. According to Obama, is college more of a private good (beneficial primarily for the student) or a public good (beneficial primarily for society at large)?
4. The Obama administration argues that the level of mandatory minimum education for Americans has shifted from a high school education to a community college education. What has caused this shift?

Explore

1. The article suggests that, with additional education, the age of maturity might also be now higher than 18. At what age do you believe most people are now full, self-supporting adults?
2. This article focuses on the connection between a college education and salary. As a class, create a list of reasons why students attend college in addition to future employability and future salary potential.
3. FULL WRITING PROMPT: The article claims that this proposal will cost $60 billion. Using the Internet, identify a few other programs that the government could fund with $60 billion. For example, $60 billion would triple the annual budget of the National Institutes of Health, allowing them more robust means to investigate possible treatments or even cures for cancer, mental illness, and heart disease. Sixty billion dollars would pay for universal preschool for all Americans. Sixty billion dollars would also give every household in America a $500 tax cut. In an argumentative essay, answer the following question: Do you believe that the U.S. government should spend $60 billion to provide free community college for all students?

Derek Newton
Higher Education Is Not a Mixtape

Derek Newton, a reporter based in New York, writes for *The Atlantic*.

Will higher education go the way of music albums and cable TV? Is it inevitable that the Internet will break apart degrees and colleges? Some entrepreneurs think so. Fortunately, they are wrong.

It's true that both cable TV and record albums have been "unbundled." By providing smaller units (individual songs and shows) on the Internet, they've offered customers lower prices, more content, and more options. With those examples as their guide, some entrepreneurs see higher education going the same way—being unbundled on the Internet—producing more choice and lower costs.

One of these entrepreneurs is Martin Smith, who wrote an essay last July for *Quartz* titled "What universities have in common with record labels." In the essay he made the case for a future in which education institutions separate their classroom-level courses from their related degrees the way individual songs have been broken away from albums. That could mean, for example, that someone could take an accounting course from a Columbia University professor and a marketing course offered at the University of Florida and build his or her own business degree, one class at a time, from the best professors.

Quoting Smith:

> The unbundling of albums in favor of individual songs was one of the biggest causes of the music industry's decline. It cannibalized the revenue of record labels as 99-cent songs gained popularity over $20 albums. It also changed the way music labels had to operate in order to maintain profitability.

This last decade of the music industry presages the coming decade of education. Choice is expanding at every level, from pre-K to graduate school. The individual course, rather than the degree, is becoming the unit of content. And universities, the record labels of education, are facing increased pressure to unbundle their services.

At first, it may appear that Smith has a point. Higher education is dominated by institutions that have not kept up with technology. And like cable TV and record companies, higher-education bundlers (colleges and universities) don't produce the content they sell—they package it for sale and provide support services such as marketing and quality control.

There are also unprecedented reform pressures circling higher education, which means that technology has made education content more efficient to deliver at the exact moment when traditional delivery methods are becoming more and more expensive. From the outside, this looks like a perfect reform storm.

Other pundits have joined Smith in his comparisons and predictions. Michael Staton, for example, wrote a 2012 draft paper for The American Enterprise Institute that includes:

> The Internet has challenged business models that serve bundled services by offering unbundled alternatives. Offering direct access to targeted services tends to disintermediate (the process of cutting out middlemen between producers and consumers) institutions whose value proposition relies on placing a premium on the aggregation of services and resources. We have seen these forces disrupt the music and journalism industries, and similar forces are beginning to affect the education sector.

It's worth noting that Smith, Staton, and many others who foresee this shift are all literally invested in the outcome they predict. They work for, run, or bankroll companies that sell the very platforms and services colleges would need to buy in order to deliver classroom content online.

That aside, it's a fantasy that higher education is careening toward an unbundled future of consumer choice, lower prices, and efficiency. Those making such predictions are peddling flawed analogies, while the technology they rely on is flawed. They just don't understand the economics of higher education.

Higher-education consumers—students and parents—behave exactly the opposite: They shop for schools, not for professors. The consumer choice is for the bundler—the brand, the label, university—and not the individual course content. Consumers buy Stanford or Princeton in a way no one ever bought EMI or Universal. College data underlines this reality. For example, the 2012 UCLA annual survey of incoming college freshmen found that nearly two-thirds said "a very good academic reputation" was "very important" in their decision on which college to attend.

Accepting the premise that professors and researchers are the content creators of higher education—analogous to the artists in the music industry—universities don't function as record labels do simply because they both bundle content. In music, the label is irrelevant. Consumers are buying the music and artist, not the companies behind them. No one ever waited in line for the newest song from Sony records. Television has a similar dynamic.

Moreover, the difference between a $0.99 downloaded song—or even a traditionally packaged $20 CD—and a $120,000 out-of-state, private college education is so vast it's insulting. A music purchase is an entertainment indulgence with minimal investment and limited risk of bad decision making. Choosing the right college, on the other hand, often involves years of research and planning.

Moreover, the rates of students who fail to either learn from or complete online college courses are exceedingly high. In 2011, Columbia University's Teachers College concluded a five-year study of online courses at community colleges in Washington and found that students in online courses were more likely to fail those courses and drop out of school than those in traditional, face-to-face courses. Another study, this one in 2013 by researchers at the University of Pennsylvania, found that only about half of students enrolled in massive open online courses, or MOOCs, view even a single online lecture and that the average completion rate is just 4 percent.

But the most spectacular failure of moving college classes online was in 2013, when San Jose State University launched a pilot program in partnership with Udacity, a for-profit online education company. The program offered online classes in a small number of subjects such as algebra and statistics. Fewer than one in four online students who enrolled in algebra courses passed their classes, for example, while just 12 percent of all newly enrolled college students made it through theirs. The results were so bad, the program was essentially scrapped after one year.

Moreover, the last 150 years are littered with examples of massive, technology-driven reforms that promised to expand learning and reduce costs of higher education but did neither. A 2013 report on a separate Columbia University study framed virtual college courses as simply the next iteration of distance education—the latest, unrevolutionary chapter in a history that includes millions of Americans in correspondence courses, the radio classrooms of the 1920s and 1930s, and TV lectures, which have been common since the 1960s.

Other unbundling proponents, like the New America Foundation's Kevin Carey, an education-policy researcher and writer who has a book due out in March, argue that the digitalization of learning will open up access to college. For its part, Carey's book, *The End of College: Creating the Future of Learning and the University of Everywhere*, contends that the "revolution" in technology and "the skyrocketing cost of college . . . are converging in ways that will radically alter the college experience, upend the traditional meritocracy, and emancipate hundreds of millions of people around the world."

But arguments for unbundling that are based on skyrocketing costs ignore that, in higher education, the traditional rules of cost and demand are inverted. The most expensive products are the most in demand. The top 25 universities in the country, according to the U.S. News and World Report's annual ranking for the 2013–14 school year, include some the best-known higher education brands—institutions such as Harvard, Stanford, MIT, and Johns Hopkins. These schools are some of the most expensive (average annual tuition of $46,600) and the most in demand in the country, with an average of 36,500 annual applicants each. Colleges in the next cohort of 25 on the U.S. News list, by contrast, are easier to purchase (40 percent average admission rate versus 11 percent) and less expensive. But they are far less in-demand, with an average annual applicant pool of just 16,000.

There are two other important factors that insulate colleges and universities from the type of cost-reform pressure that could alter other markets: government support and loans. It almost doesn't matter where someone goes to college; it's heavily subsidized by the government in one way or another. According to an analysis last year for *The Atlantic*, in 2012 the federal government allocated nearly $177 billion in financial-aid money, including loans, toward public higher-education institutions. Those same public schools collected just $62.6 billion total from undergraduate students in tuition. And that spending excludes private institutions. One report found that Northeastern University, a private university in Boston, received $90 million in public funding in 2011 alone in the form of tax subsidies and student-aid payments. And other research shows that Princeton is banking $54,000 per student per year in tax subsidies and other public support—not counting direct student aid and government loans.

With government chipping in more than three dollars for every dollar a student pays in tuition at public schools, and underwriting private ones as well, the real consumers of higher education aren't students at all. The real consumers are Congress and state legislatures—and so far they have exerted little cost pressure on higher-education institutions.

Further confusing the education cost-and-demand market is the fact that most students don't actually pay their college costs at the time of purchase. According to the Project on Student Debt, more than seven in 10 U.S. college students take loans to pay for college. If purchase-price considerations significantly affected higher-education consumption, at least some intuitions would be lowering costs to attract students. Instead, costs continue to escalate and the most expensive schools have the most buyers.

And even if unbundling were on the higher-education horizon, it would more likely be a problem rather than a solution. If colleges move in the direction of hiring and rewarding professors who gather large online audiences, like record labels signed rock stars, the line between professor and performer would blur. Rewarding performance would inevitably undercut substance, and unbundled colleges would then, ironically, be far more like record labels than they are now—finding, promoting, and selling edu-tainers.

Moreover, a build-it-yourself online degree program may, one day, offer great content to consumers—but little else. Less-popular and less-profitable academic fields could wither. In the current system, it may not be efficient to maintain fine-arts programs, but most people think it's important to have them. It has long been part of colleges' mission to expose students to new ideas and disciplines. On campus, even business students, for example, are typically required to study literature and other topics in the humanities. Some may call that inefficient; others call it essential.

Analyze

1. What might be the problems and benefits with allowing students to select classes from individual colleges or different departments to make up their own degree program?

2. Individual college classes often have limited goals. For example, a class in argumentative writing is likely designed to teach students the skills necessary to create strong essay-length arguments. Majors, however, bundle classes together into a well-considered educational path in which classes work in concert to produce sophisticated goals. What

some goals for college majors that can't be completed within individual classes?

3. Recently some colleges stopped taking AP credit; others limited transfer credit. Both groups argued that a college experience was best completed at one college, under one major and one set of general education requirements. What would be the benefits and costs of insisting that students complete a college degree primarily (or even exclusively) at one college?

4. If college were "unbundled," allowing students to sample classes from many different sources, how else would the college experience change for the average student? Consider social, athletic, residential, artistic, and cultural aspects of this problem.

Explore

1. MOOCs (massive open online courses), with lectures delivered by video, have proven to be largely unsuccessful at delivering a meaningful education to college students. A study at San Jose State University showed that very few of its students were able to pass a class when content was delivered in a MOOC environment. With this in mind, what successful roles do you see for Internet technology in the delivery of classroom content in the future?

2. This article suggests that education shouldn't draw too deeply on the attention-grabbing strategies of entertainment to engage a class: it uses the pejorative term "edu-tainer" to describe an instructor who uses entertainment or an entertaining style to capture students' attention, possibly undercutting substance to gain an audience. In your opinion, what role, if any, should entertainment or a pervasively entertaining style play in a college classroom? If the entertainment is primarily in the classroom to capture student interest, is this a type of pandering that devalues education? Or do you see some value in connecting entertainment and education? If so, what?

3. SHORT WRITING PROMPT: The required classes in a major are often designed to, collectively, deliver significant experiences and help students to develop complex skills. Visit an advisor or professor in a major that interests you to explore this question. What experiences or skills are the major classes designed to provide? How do the classes

work together to produce significant outcomes? How important is it that students take the classes in order, without skipping prerequisites? And why?

Forging Connections

1. Many articles in this chapter offer ideas—albeit conflicting ones—as to what college should offer students. These ideas range from technical training to a liberal arts education, from career readiness to moral exploration. A college's mission statement is a summary of its primary objectives, often focused on educational, social, and technical goals. In one page or less, write a mission statement for your ideal college: identify those goals central to the college experience of your dreams.

2. In "The Day the Purpose of College Changed," the author explains how, in 1967, Ronald Reagan began a process that would shift the emphasis of college from individual academic pursuits to job preparedness. In effect, through Reagan, colleges increased the number of classes focused on career training and decreased the number of classes focused on intellectual or artistic exploration. In your opinion, was this academic shift from "thinking" to "working" beneficial or detrimental to the country?

Looking Ahead

1. In her article "Is College the New High School?" Vauhini Vara suggests that young adults today, more so than in previous generations, need a college education to find career and personal success. Assuming this is true, how has our culture changed so as to require an additional two or four years of education? How have jobs and civic and personal obligations changed in the past fifty years to place a greater reliance on systems of higher education to prepare people for adult responsibilities?

2. In 1944, American philosopher and educational reformer John Dewey said, "If we teach today's students as we taught yesterday's, we rob them of tomorrow." In other words, he felt that the methods of education needed to change with the times to best prepare students

for the future. Relying on your own experience in college so far, what would you change about the methods of education to better prepare students for the future? Lecture hall classes? Scantrons? Classes that require memorization? Textbooks as a focal point of learning? Replacing consumer-driven classes with more challenging material? Moving from a teacher-based system to a one-on-one mentor-based system? Customizable majors? A decreased focus on career training? An emphasis on lab-based learning as opposed to lecture-based learning? Integration of video or visual projects to complement written assignments? A greater focus on collaboration and student learning groups?

3 Academic Life

Twenty years ago, professors took attendance by calling roll from the front of the class and recording those present in a grade book. Today professors can take roll with clickers and iPhone apps. Students sign in to an online page or complete a quiz—that doubles for attendance—on their laptops. In some cases, students don't even share physical space with the professor but log in remotely on a computer. They are present because the educational software logs their username as "active."

But attendance is only one way that academic life is changing to meet the desires and expectations of current students.

In this section, Eric Hoover explores the concept of "trigger warnings" on class syllabi, those brief descriptions some professors employ to prepare students for potentially distressing content; he also explores how trigger warnings have changed students' expectations for the college experience in general. Jacques Steinberg discusses electronic devices that professors are using to engage students raised on iPhones and handheld video games. Trip Gabriel visits a college that streams live lecture video to the dorm room, even though the lecture is occurring on the other side of the campus. And Douglas Belkin examines ways that geofencing and movement tracking technology might improve graduation rates at many colleges.

But this chapter doesn't simply explore new cultural and technological challenges shaping academic life; it also explores traditional problems faced by many students. Cecilia Capuzzi Simon examines how to pick a major. The problem of note taking—or rather of note taking as a small business—is analyzed by Laura Pappano. And Marcia Y. Cantarella offers advice on perhaps the oldest of all college problems: how to engage a course when the subject doesn't engage you.

The readings in this section, together, explore a variety of college experiences, placing traditional challenges shoulder to shoulder with ones that have emerged in the past decade. Together, these experiences define contemporary academic life.

Eric Hoover
The Comfortable Kid

Eric Hoover is a senior writer for *The Chronicle of Higher Education*, where he has written about standardized testing, the process of college admissions, and social media and gender issues within universities.

Go ahead, laugh at them. Call them thin-skinned, lily-livered, self-righteous. They always find a way to take offense. That's just how—as you've surely heard—today's college students roll.

Consider the evidence. Recently students have expressed many concerns that their elders describe as hypersensitivity gone haywire. In March, *The*

New York Times reported on campus discussions of "microaggressions," subtle slights of one's race, ethnicity, gender, or sexual orientation. This spring, commencement speakers at several prominent institutions withdrew amid students' opposition to their views or affiliations. By then the nation had heard all about "trigger warnings": Students on various campuses have called for alerts about assigned texts (yes, old sport, even *The Great Gatsby*) that might upset or traumatize them.

So when something awful happened this past May, perhaps nobody should've been surprised by how a student newspaper at the University of California at Santa Barbara reacted. After the fatal shootings of six students near the campus, *The Bottom Line*'s editors opted against immediately publishing an article, to protect student journalists from "emotional harm."

These developments raise a question. Are the future caretakers of civilization made of marshmallows?

Yes, say the pundits. Lately commentators have ridiculed students for an array of sins ("overreaching sensitivity," "longing for an 'offenseless' society"). The Daily Beast's jab at undergraduates ("The Oh-So-Fragile Class of 2014 Needs to STFU and Listen to Some New Ideas") bore this blunt conclusion: "Young people are the worst."

But the kids-these-days diss simplifies the complexity of 21st-century students. They are a diverse bunch with varying needs and wants, some more serious than others. They carry immense expectations through higher education's gates, and in the name of compassion and competition, colleges strive to serve. If students are soft, campuses help make them so.

"What happens on college campuses has as much to do with the institution and the adults within it as anything that the students bring," says Richard Arum, a professor of sociology and education at New York University. "There's a dynamic in place where colleges are catering to them as consumers and clients. They are increasingly making decisions to keep students happy."

That means trade-offs. The rise of the consumer ethos has sapped colleges' commitment to learning, argue Mr. Arum and Josipa Roksa, an associate professor of sociology at the University of Virginia, in *Academically Adrift: Limited Learning on College Campuses*. Yet the "delivery of elaborate and ever-expanding services," the authors concede, might also have positive consequences. Generally colleges have become more responsive to students, which hardly spells doom.

Just how responsive an institution should be, however, is debatable. The line between care and coddling can be blurry. Critiques of the college experience often mention the physical comforts that students now enjoy. The high-rise dorm. The fancy gym. The cafeteria featuring omelets with your choice of 17 locally sourced ingredients.

Those amenities are tangible expressions of a broader goal. Colleges continue to grapple with many dimensions of comfort—intellectual, cultural, social—and how much of it to provide. The challenge, some administrators and professors say, is making students uncomfortable in some ways but comfortable in others. Challenge their ideas and assumptions here, support their identities and interests there.

On an increasingly diverse campus, striking that balance is difficult. Some students stroll in, convinced that they own the place; others slink along, lugging problems and doubts. So, go ahead, laugh at college students. But maybe, just maybe, not all of them deserve it.

When colleges first entered the business of tending to students' personal needs, the streets were full of Model Ts. During the 1920s, the problems that students experienced as they adjusted to campus life became a widespread concern. Then, as now, those problems included frustration with large, impersonal classes, and depression.

Previously, college leaders had assumed that participation in extracurricular activities worked against students' academic performance. That notion faded as more and more research suggested a connection between personality development and achievement. Gradually a host of academic, social, and psychological programs grew. In 1924 the American College Personnel Association was founded to lead the burgeoning student-affairs profession.

Its purpose? To reduce the "psychic dislocation of college" by giving students more individualized attention, says Christopher P. Loss, an associate professor of public policy and higher education at Vanderbilt University, who describes the rise of student services in *Between Citizens and the State: The Politics of American Higher Education in the 20th Century*. Eventually educators were focused on the "whole student."

At least half of all students who enrolled in college in the 1920s left without earning a degree, typically in their first year. Although attrition then had many causes, Mr. Loss has found, colleges embraced extracurricular programs as the primary solution to the dropout problem (then known as "student mortality"). So began freshman week, orientation classes, clubs, honors programs, social events—myriad ways to make students feel at home.

"There's been an ongoing tension between being efficient and effective in handling this massive student body on the one hand," Mr. Loss says, "and providing personalized instruction and care on the other."

The influx of veterans on the original GI Bill cemented student services as a primary function of colleges. And long after the erosion of *in loco parentis* as the basis for discipline and social control, Mr. Loss writes in a forthcoming essay, the doctrine continued to compel colleges "to care for and nurture their students in order to help them steer clear of the innumerable academic and emotional challenges of going to school."

In the 1960s and 1970s, as institutions enrolled more and more black students, "diversity" was the key word in student affairs. Later, cultural programs and support services designed for students of various racial and ethnic backgrounds became the norm. Conceptions of diversity today go well beyond demographics. Many colleges now try to accommodate the broad spectrum of a student's identity: sexual orientation, religious beliefs, and political views, for instance, or hardships faced as a combat soldier or a victim of sexual assault.

"There's an almost infinite array of personal experiences, traumas, and tragedies that can shape or condition your capacities to be a member of a college community," says Mr. Loss. "What role does the college have to play in order to ensure that all students are treated fairly?"

An increasingly large one. Generally, educators believe they have a moral responsibility to develop students beyond the classroom. Those who are happy and "engaged" are more likely to succeed and graduate, which is also good for the bottom line. So colleges are canvassing students and alumni to gauge their satisfaction.

To that end, Augustana College, in Illinois, is trying to determine whether it inadvertently "privileges" extroverted students, making it easier for them to find a niche. In surveys of freshmen, the college includes a three-item scale, "Comfort With Social Interaction," which asks how they feel about meeting new people and interacting in unfamiliar settings. Researchers use the scores, along with responses to other questions, to determine how personality might affect students' sense of belonging on the campus. "We're asking, have we created this environment where we suck the oxygen out of the introverts in the room?" says Mark Salisbury, assistant dean and director of institutional research and assessment.

Such sophisticated inquiry suggests a level of concern that once would have seemed outlandish. In the age of Starbucks, where each cup bears a name, students—and the parents they call and text daily—expect a lot more than they used to. "It's part of the movement for individualization," says Jean Twenge, a professor of psychology at San Diego State University and author of *Generation Me: Why Today's Young Americans Are More Confident, Assertive, Entitled—and More Miserable Than Ever Before.* "On many campuses, there's this idea, 'I paid my money, thus I want this customized experience.'"

Customization means more options. But how many aspects of college should be optional?

Philip Wythe, a junior at Rutgers University, has thought carefully about that. In February, Mr. Wythe wrote a column for the New Brunswick campus newspaper in which he described trigger warnings on syllabi as "psychological protection for those who need it." Such warnings originated in feminist forums online, where they flag content that victims of sexual abuse might find distressing. Recently students on several campuses—Rutgers, UC-Santa Barbara, the University of Michigan—have called for their use in academic courses. A panel of students and faculty members at Oberlin College is weighing the issue.

Importing trigger warnings to the classroom, Mr. Wythe argues, would help students prepare themselves for emotionally hazardous material and avoid it if necessary. A trigger warning for *The Great Gatsby,* he suggests, might include the words "suicide" and "domestic abuse."

Mr. Wythe recounts in an email the experience of a close friend, a young woman at Rutgers, who suffered a panic attack in class. While watching a film in which the protagonist describes being sexually abused, Mr. Wythe writes, his friend started shaking and crying. Eventually she ran out of the room.

By his description, the woman had been "triggered," or reminded of a past trauma. Colleges have an obligation, he says, to try to prevent that, by warning students about material that deals with violence and sexual assault. "Trigger warnings aren't for able-minded students who are prone to sensitivity," he writes. "It's about individuals with disabilities, such as PTSD or severe anxiety disorder, which can disrupt daily life." More such students are going to college than ever before.

Mr. Wythe's views are informed by his experience in a high-school health class. During discussions of sensitive topics like depression and suicide, he explained in a recent interview on Huff Post Live, students were assured that if they felt uneasy at any point, they could approach the teacher and request "an alternate plan."

So Mr. Wythe has come to see the issue as a matter of transparency. "These are students trying to change the course of their own education, as in saying what they would like in the classroom, what they're comfortable with in the classroom," he said in the interview. In other words, they're consumers, making buying decisions. A trigger warning, he says, can help a student decide whether to skip a class on a given day—or whether to take that course in the first place.

That idea frustrates many professors who see an overstated problem. It's not as if students are always blindsided, as if instructors never preview assignments or contextualize them. One psychology professor who plans to assign a book about sexual abuse this fall says he will first discuss why reading it might be difficult. "Is that a trigger warning?" he asks. "Partly, it's being a good teacher."

The notion that a book, like a pack of cigarettes, needs a warning label strikes many professors as preposterous. Where to draw the line? Instructors aren't counselors, nor could they begin to anticipate all of the things that might traumatize someone.

Orange juice, for instance, triggers Mariah Woelfel, a student at DePaul University. She associates it with visiting her brother in the hospital after a car accident left him severely disabled. She opposes trigger warnings, however, because, as she wrote in *The DePaulia,* they go against "the main purpose of higher-level learning: to explore diversity in ideas, and challenge the ones that you already hold."

Trigger warnings are evidence that political correctness has given way to something broader, says Karen Swallow Prior, an English professor at Liberty University. "Now, instead of challenging the status quo by demanding texts that question the comfort of the Western canon," she wrote in *The Atlantic* this spring, "students are demanding the status quo by refusing to read texts that challenge their own personal comfort." She calls this "empathetic correctness."

Empathy is tricky. Where it exists, students may feel secure, and understanding might flow. But it's hard to cultivate.

Still, colleges should try, says Charles W. Green, a psychology professor at Hope College. Fifteen years ago, Mr. Green, who studies race and racism, helped start a residential academic program, or learning community, for freshmen interested in racial and cultural issues. The goal: to promote inclusion as the predominantly white campus diversified (today 15 percent of its students are nonwhite, up from 4 percent about a decade ago).

"If you're in the majority and it's all working for you, it's hard to see that other people might not be having this lovely time," he says. "Some people don't realize how common it is for students to have experiences that leave them feeling as if they are unwelcome on their own campus."

Mr. Green recalls a black student who was carrying a pizza back to the campus one evening when a group of teenagers surrounded her. When she refused to hand over her dinner, they called her the N-word. The next day, the young woman and several other black students came to his office. They were shaken.

Most incidents he hears about are more subtle. A white student tells a black student not to "play the race card" during a class discussion. A black woman reports that when professors ask students to discuss a topic in pairs, the white classmates to her left and right always turn away from her.

Whether a particular insult is also a microaggression—a subtle conveyance of bias or stereotype—is subjective ("No, where are you *really* from?" or "I have trouble telling Asians apart"). Some students say hurtful things because they're bigoted jerks; others, naïve or socially clumsy, don't mean to offend. The term "microaggression," like "trigger warning," comes from the realm of social justice, which increasingly informs discussions of diversity on campuses.

This is especially true at Emory University, where freshmen now discuss microaggressions during orientation. Throughout the year, students in the Issues Troupe write and perform skits to increase awareness of racial stereotypes and cultural differences.

Ajay Nair, senior vice president and dean of campus life at Emory, believes that the modern campus must move beyond traditional multicultural programs. "With multiculturalism, the destination is tolerance, not understanding," he says. "Our students are pushing back and saying, 'This doesn't work; tolerance doesn't lead to understanding.' Multiculturalism focuses on celebration instead of social justice and activism."

Mr. Nair envisions a "polycultural" model that acknowledges multiple identities. A student might be gay and Hispanic, or Asian-American and Christian. The dean has begun restructuring his entire division to reflect that model (think more collaboration, less compartmentalization). The shift serves another goal as well: persuading all students that they have a stake in diversity.

"A straight, white male student has a lot to offer, a particular way of understanding the world," says Mr. Nair. "As we think about a deeper understanding of diversity, the dialogue can't just be with certain parts of the community that have been marginalized."

Talking about microaggressions is a helpful way to frame that dialogue, Mr. Nair believes (as an Indian-American, he recalls being told that his English was "so good," even though he was born and raised in Philadelphia). Whether such discussions promote understanding, however, is complicated.

Jovonna Jones, a senior at Emory, says the term "microaggression" can help minority students describe their feelings to others. "There are many things my peers have experienced, but we didn't have a name for it before," says Ms. Jones, who is black. "It's another way of trying to explain how racism works to people who still don't want to hear it exists."

Sometimes, for instance, her peers call her "sassy," which she hears as a code word for the stereotype that black women have an attitude. Now and then, students ask to touch her hair; some have just gone ahead without asking. Framing her objections in terms of microaggressions, she says, can be empowering and productive.

But it's not always easy. When she hears someone say, "Oh, that's ghetto," she says, she has to decide whether to explain why that might offend not just her, but many black students. "It can become a very toxic position to be put in," she says. "What happened to it just mattering that you hurt someone's feelings?"

Some white students, meanwhile, have complained that diversity discussions shovel guilt down their throats. "Check your privilege," some are told, meaning that they should acknowledge their advantages in life, and maybe think twice about the views they're sharing. In April, Tal Fortgang, a white student at Princeton University, wrote a column describing the phrase as a rebuke that "threatens to strike down opinions without regard for their merits, but rather solely on the basis of the person that voiced them."

Exposing students to unfamiliar ideas has long been a core purpose of higher education. From temporary discomfort comes an essential struggle, writes Tricia A. Seifert, an assistant professor at the Ontario Institute for Studies in Education, at the University of Toronto. "Disequilibrium, cognitive dissonance, challenge—these are the building blocks of learning."

But is that still in vogue? A national survey of freshmen conducted annually by the Higher Education Research Institute at the University of California at Los Angeles suggests that many students wrestle with the concept. Generally, freshmen say they work well with others and tolerate those with different beliefs. Yet they rate themselves low on their "openness to having their own views challenged."

These days Netflix recommends a film based on those you like. Spotify suggests a band based on your listening habits. And curated news feeds deliver the political opinions you choose.

"As we have a greater expectation of physical comfort, of an ability to choose what media we want to see, what sources we want to read, it does cultivate, almost inevitably, seeking intellectual comfort," says Greg Lukianoff, president of the Foundation for Individual Rights in Education. "You want people to agree with you. It's part of human nature."

There's one problem, though. "It's just not intellectually healthy," he says.

Kathleen McCartney also thinks "ideological echo chambers" have diminished the appetite for true dialogue on campuses. She is president of Smith College, where some students and faculty members objected to the selection of Christine Lagarde, managing director of the International Monetary Fund, as this spring's commencement speaker, which they saw as an implicit endorsement. An online petition urging Smith to reconsider the invitation said the IMF had helped strengthen "imperialist and patriarchal systems that oppress and abuse women worldwide." A few students wrote to Ms. Lagarde, asking her not to come. A week before graduation, she withdrew.

Ms. McCartney insists that she wouldn't have minded if students had protested during the speech. "That's fair game," she says. What troubled her was the impulse to prevent anyone at Smith from hearing Ms. Lagarde. "They had many options between acquiescing and urging her to stay away," the president says.

Since the episode, Ms. McCartney has heard from members of the Class of 1964, recalling their objections to that year's commencement speaker, Dean Rusk, then the U.S. secretary of state, who supported the American role in the Vietnam War. Although many students wore black armbands in protest, they sat and listened to his speech.

What might explain why two generations responded so differently? Ms. McCartney cites social media, for one. "Before, you had to walk a petition around campus. Now you can put it online in a millisecond," immediately attracting like-minded classmates and a broader audience. But there's something deeper, too. "Maybe in 1964, students felt like the power to say 'don't come' wasn't there," she says. "Students are empowered today, and that's mostly good."

Mostly. Discussions of microaggressions and trigger warnings often flow from some wish, however vague, to make the world kinder, to make life easier for one's neighbor. And the pushback against commencement speakers challenges the notion that today's students are politically apathetic.

But there's a troubling side to those trends, all of which boil down to scrutiny of words—which words students should say, read, hear. "All these things," Ms. McCartney says, "can threaten free speech."

The attention to finely tuned sensitivities, the relentless delivery of more options, more alternatives can also convince students that the world stops for them. The comfortable kid can get far too comfortable.

Recently, Ms. McCartney heard a radio report about how younger students perceive criticism as especially harsh when their teachers grade assignments in red pen. Just for a moment, she imagined Smith students demanding that professors use only black or blue ink. "I hope," she says, "we don't have a red-pen movement."

Indeed, a national campaign about the harm caused by ink colors would be absurd. Life, we know, marks us up in whatever colors it wants. With wisdom drawn from our many years of experience, we tend to laugh at the kids, scoff at their ideas. But we should at least consider the possibility that old people are the worst.

Analyze

1. Do trigger warnings for college material protect students from potentially harmful experiences? Or do they harmfully shield students from the realities of the world around them?

2. How might a marketplace consumerism ethos at college—the desire to keep students happy—ultimately prevent them from receiving the best education possible? How might this same ethos play out in terms of course subjects, grades, and even graduation requirements?

3. Would you rather attend (a) a college with a modern, high-rise dorm, an elaborate gym, and a cafeteria that features "omelets with your choice of 17 locally sourced ingredients," but offers only mediocre courses that are not too difficult to pass or (b) a college with old-style,

cinderblock dorms, no fancy gym, and a cafeteria with food options no better than at an average food court, but with excellent courses that are challenging to pass?

4. Would you be willing to give up some comforts at college if it (a) reduced your tuition bill, (b) lowered your college debt, (c) allowed you better college resources for job placement, (d) allowed you more plentiful and varied class offerings, or (e) allowed you to take more small seminar-style courses instead of large hall lectures?

Explore

1. If you could pick only one area of comfort to receive at college, which would you pick: social (i.e., activities to foster friendships), educational (i.e., courses that support your individual learning needs), physical (i.e., comfortable beds), culinary (i.e., excellent food), recreational (i.e., modern gym), or entertainment (i.e., speakers and musicians performing on campus)? Why?

2. SHORT WRITING PROMPT: Write an opinion paper in which you argue for or against the use of syllabus-oriented trigger warnings on your campus. If you believe trigger warnings should be implemented at your college, what subject material should be covered under them?

3. FULL WRITING PROMPT: Write an essay about an experience—in class, on a sports team, in music or art, or while pursuing a hobby—that might have made you a better person if only the requirements were more stringent and difficult to achieve.

Trip Gabriel
Learning in Dorm, Because Class Is on the Web

Trip Gabriel, a journalist for the *New York Times*, primarily covers American politics, style, and higher education, including articles on college lifestyles and academic dishonesty.

Like most other undergraduates, Anish Patel likes to sleep in. Even though his Principles of Microeconomics class at 9:35 a.m. is just a five-minute stroll from his dorm, he would rather flip open his laptop in his room to watch the lecture, streamed live over the campus network.

On a recent morning, as Mr. Patel's two roommates slept with covers pulled tightly over their heads, he sat at his desk taking notes on Prof. Mark Rush's explanation of the term "perfect competition." A camera zoomed in for a close-up of the blackboard, where Dr. Rush scribbled in chalk, "lots of firms and lots of buyers." The curtains were drawn in the dorm room. The floor was awash in the flotsam of three freshmen—clothes, backpacks, homework, packages of Chips Ahoy and Cap'n Crunch's Crunch Berries.

The University of Florida broadcasts and archives Dr. Rush's lectures less for the convenience of sleepy students like Mr. Patel than for a simple principle of economics: 1,500 undergraduates are enrolled and no lecture hall could possibly hold them.

Dozens of popular courses in psychology, statistics, biology and other fields are also offered primarily online. Students on this scenic campus of stately oaks rarely meet classmates in these courses.

Online education is best known for serving older, nontraditional students who cannot travel to colleges because of jobs and family. But the same technologies of "distance learning" are now finding their way onto brick-and-mortar campuses, especially public institutions hit hard by declining state funds. At the University of Florida, for example, resident students are earning 12 percent of their credit hours online this semester, a figure expected to grow to 25 percent in five years.

This may delight undergraduates who do not have to change out of pajamas to "attend" class. But it also raises questions that go to the core of a college's mission: Is it possible to learn as much when your professor is a mass of pixels whom you never meet? How much of a student's education and growth—academic and personal—depends on face-to-face contact with instructors and fellow students?

"When I look back, I think it took away from my freshman year," said Kaitlyn Hartsock, a senior psychology major at Florida who was assigned to two online classes during her first semester in Gainesville. "My mom was really upset about it. She felt like she's paying for me to go to college and not sit at home and watch through a computer."

Across the country, online education is exploding: 4.6 million students took a college-level online course during fall 2008, up 17 percent from a year earlier, according to the Sloan Survey of Online Learning. A large majority—about three million—were simultaneously enrolled in face-to-face courses, belying the popular notion that most online students live far from campuses, said Jeff Seaman, co-director of the survey. Many are in community colleges, he said. Very few attend private colleges; families paying $53,000 a year demand low student–faculty ratios.

Colleges and universities that have plunged into the online field, mostly public, cite their dual missions to serve as many students as possible while remaining affordable, as well as a desire to exploit the latest technologies.

At the University of Iowa, as many as 10 percent of 14,000 liberal arts undergraduates take an online course each semester, including Classical Mythology and Introduction to American Politics.

At the University of North Carolina at Chapel Hill, first-year Spanish students are no longer offered a face-to-face class; the university moved all instruction online, despite internal research showing that online students do slightly less well in grammar and speaking.

"You have X amount of money, what are you going to do with it?" said Larry King, chairman of the Romance languages department, where budget cuts have forced difficult choices. "You can't be all things to all people."

The University of Florida has faced sweeping budget cuts from the State Legislature totaling 25 percent over three years. That is a main reason the university is moving aggressively to offer more online instruction. "We see this as the future of higher education," said Joe Glover, the university provost.

"Quite honestly, the higher education industry in the United States has not been tremendously effective in the face-to-face mode if you look at national graduation rates," he added. "At the very least we should be experimenting with other modes of delivery of education."

A sampling of Florida professors teaching online found both enthusiasm and doubts. "I would prefer to teach classes of 50 and know every student's name, but that's not where we are financially and space-wise," said Megan Mocko, who teaches statistics to 1,650 students. She said an advantage of the Internet is that students can stop the lecture and rewind when they do not understand something.

Ilan Shrira, who teaches developmental psychology to 300, said that he chose his field because of the passion of a professor who taught him as an undergraduate. But he thought it unlikely that anyone could be so inspired by an online course.

Kristin Joos built interactivity into her Principles of Sociology course to keep students engaged. There are small-group online discussions, and students join a virtual classroom once a week using a conferencing software called WiZiQ.

"Hi, everyone, welcome to Week 9. Hello!" Dr. Joos said in a peppy voice recently to about 60 students who had logged on. She sat at a desk in her home office; a live video feed she switched on at one point showed her in black librarian's glasses and a tank top.

Ms. Hartsock, the senior psychology major, followed the class from her own off-campus home, her laptop open on the dining room table. As Dr. Joos lectured, a chat box scrolled with students' comments and questions.

The topic was sexual identity, which Dr. Joos defined as "a determination made through the application of socially agreed-upon biological criteria for classifying persons as females and males."

She asked students for their own definitions. One, bringing an online-chat sensibility to an academic discussion, typed: "If someone looks like a chick and wants to be called a chick even though they're not, now they can be one."

Ms. Hartsock, 23, diligently typed notes. A hard-working student who maintains an A average, she was frustrated by the online format. Other members of her discussion group were not pulling their weight, she said. The one test so far, online, required answering five questions in 10 minutes—a lightning round meant to prevent cheating by Googling answers.

In a conventional class, "I'm someone who sits toward the front and shares my thoughts with the teacher," she said. In the 10 or so online courses she has taken in her four years, "it's all the same," she said. "No comments. No feedback. And the grades are always late."

As her attention wandered, she got up to microwave some leftover rice.

Analyze

1. If you had a choice between attending a lecture in person or watching it in your dorm, which would you choose? And why?
2. The essay asks readers to consider the connection between personal contact and learning. How much better do you learn material in an environment with "face-to-face contact with instructors and fellow students" than in a virtual environment of streaming video and pixels?
3. What is lost when learning shifts from classrooms and lecture halls to online environments? And what is gained?

Explore

1. One concern about online lecture classes is that they limit student involvement and discussion. In one model of education the professor is the expert who delivers information to an audience. In another model the professor is a facilitator who offers information in an attempt to create meaningful discussion between students. What are the pros and cons of each model?

2. Public universities often explain their interest in online education as an attempt to both (a) keep tuition costs low and (b) deliver classes to as many students as possible. Both of these goals are partially accomplished by limiting the face-to-face in-class time that students share with professors. In your opinion, for public universities, is this a good trade?

3. SHORT WRITING PROMPT: The article explains that some colleges ballooned lecture courses out to 1,500 students as a cost-savings measure, most likely designed to keep other classes small. To save money at your college, assuming its budget was cut, where would you reduce or change funding? Lower funding to health or fitness centers? Increase small discussion classes by five seats each? Increase lecture hall classes by offering video-streaming options? Reduce the quality of food on campus? Cut landscaping budgets? Cut student activities budgets? Cut funding to sports programs? After you have made your decisions, consider one more thing: what would be the social, educational, or institutional costs of these cuts?

Douglas Belkin
Cracking Down on Skipping Class: High-Tech Trackers Aim to Boost Attendance, as Colleges Seek Higher Graduation Rates

Douglas Belkin, a resident of Chicago, is a reporter who writes about higher education for *The Wall Street Journal*.

Skipping class undetected for a game of ultimate Frisbee might become a thing of the past as more universities adopt mandatory-attendance policies and acquire high-tech trackers that snitch when students skip.

At Villanova University, student ID cards track attendance at some lectures. Administrators at University of Arkansas last semester began electronically monitoring the class attendance of 750 freshmen as part of a pilot program they might extend to all underclassman. And at Harvard, researchers secretly filmed classrooms to learn how many students were skipping lectures.

The moves reflect the rising financial consequence of skipping too many classes and, consequently, dropping out. More than four in 10 full-time college students fail to graduate in six years. Many are stuck with crippling student debt and no credentials to help them pay it back. Graduation rates also figure into closely watched school rankings.

In response, schools are under pressure from taxpayers and parents to increase retention and graduation rates, said Mike Reilly, executive director of the American Association of Collegiate Registrars and Admissions Officers. Schoolwide policies on attendance are fairly rare but growing, Mr. Reilly said.

Many colleges are using "retention alert systems" that monitor behaviors that can lead to dropping out—including playing hooky. "There's just so much more at stake now than there was 20 years ago and parents want to protect their investment; they want to make sure their kids are in class," said Rosalind Alderman, who leads the retention effort at St. Mary's University in San Antonio. If professors report a student is skipping class at St. Mary's the student's "risk level" elevates from green to yellow to red in the school's monitoring system.

The latest entrant into the market of tracking student's whereabouts: Class120, a $199-a-year notification service that tracks a student through the GPS in their smartphone and alerts their parents (or another third party) in real time if their child isn't within a geofence mapped around the classroom where they are scheduled to be.

"For most students, if they miss too many classes, there is no safety net," said Jeff Whorley, whose company, Core Principle, has mapped about 2,000 college campuses to create the system. "Just three days of missed classes can completely unravel a semester."

The app's reminder was jarring for Caleb Hiltunen, a sophomore at Columbia College in Chicago who was a beta tester for Class120. One morning last semester he was sick in bed when the app pinged to alert him he missed class—a notification that would go to a student's parents once the app is live.

"I think it's good stuff," Mr. Hiltunen said. "I had a roommate freshman year kicked out of college for not attending enough classes. This kid was smart but he was lazy and had no motivation. I think something like this could have helped him."

Attendance is the best known predictor of college grades, even more so than scores on standardized admissions tests, said Marcus Crede, a professor of psychology at Iowa State University who studies the subject. The correlation is particularly high in science, engineering and math. And grades, in turn, seem linked to graduation rates, he said.

Mandatory attendance has long been a staple in high schools. At community colleges, such as Stark State in Ohio, financial aid is tied to attendance, a policy that dates back decades. At some Christian schools, such as Abilene Christian University in Texas, chapel attendance has been tracked with assigned seats since the 1980s.

At most four-year colleges, attendance policy has been left to the professors' discretion. Until recently, taking roll was especially tough in large lecture halls. But new technologies using chips in student IDs and interactive software that allows students to engage with professors through their laptops make the job easier.

At Villanova, student monitoring of some form has been in place in some form since 2007.

As online interactions have grown, schools have realized they have a trove of new data to look at, such as how much a student is accessing the syllabus, taking part in online discussions with classmates and reading assigned material. Such technology "shows faculty exactly where students are interacting outside as well inside the classroom," said Stephen Fugale, Villanova's chief information officer.

Not all such technology is foolproof. Dartmouth College accused 64 students of cheating in a sports-ethics class last semester when students used a clicker—individually linked to each student—for classmates who were absent.

At Harvard, Vice Provost Peter Bol said the lecture halls were filmed without student consent to gauge attendance without skewing the results by making students aware they were being measured. Many on campus were angered when the results were made public in November, but the test provided some insight into class attendance.

Among 10 lectures monitored, attendance averaged 60%, declining from 79% as the semester began to 43% as it ended. Attendance also fell more than 10 percentage points over an average week. Courses that incorporated attendance into the final grade averaged 87%, compared with 49% for those that didn't.

University of Arkansas began experimenting with mandatory attendance as a way to boost its 62% six-year graduation rate, said Provost Sharon Gaber. "We talk about helicopter parents," she said. "Well, some of these kids haven't learned how to get out of bed on their own yet."

Analyze

1. What would be gained and what would be lost if your college implemented an electronic attendance system by using ID cards or some other means?
2. College has traditionally been considered a place where teenagers have the freedoms and responsibilities of legal adults. A high-tech tracking system would suggest that college students today are less responsible than those of previous generations. Do you believe that college students today need more supervision to successfully manage college?
3. Previous generations have considered college an experience where students investigate ideas that matter, find themselves, prepare for life as adults, and explore cultural and scientific interests from a variety of academic disciplines. In this article, college is viewed primarily as an "investment," a training program designed to elevate students' earnings potential. Do you feel this is the best way to view the college experience?
4. Would you be more or less likely to attend a college with a "geofence" grid mapped over its campus? Why?

Explore

1. What would best motivate you to attend all class sessions—a system that rewards you with additional financial aid, a system that rewards you with a higher course grade, a system that threatens you with notifying your parents, or some other system?
2. In general, do you feel that poor class attendance is more closely tied to situation-specific problems (work schedules, poor sleep habits, late-night

studying) or to the overall general motivation of a student? That is, for most students, does a situation need to be changed or does the responsibility level of the student need to be improved?

3. FULL WRITING PROMPT: In an essay, propose an attendance policy and tracking system that would improve freshman attendance at your college. Your policy should tie good attendance to some benefit or punishment for students. Your policy should also take into account what you feel is a reasonable level of freedom and responsibility for college freshmen, most of whom are eighteen years old. The tracking system itself—such as roll call, ID cards, smartphone apps, and so forth—must be reasonable to implement and not place an unusual cost burden on the school or students. Most of all, it must be structured in a way to encourage students to better engage college learning.

Jacques Steinberg
More Professors Give Out Hand-Held Devices to Monitor Students and Engage Them

Jacques Steinberg spent 25 years as a reporter at the *New York Times* reporting on education. He is the author of *The Gatekeepers: Inside the Admissions Process of a Premier College* and now works with Say Yes to Education, a nonprofit that seeks to improve educational opportunities for children in the inner city.

If any of the 70 undergraduates in Prof. Bill White's "Organizational Behavior" course here at Northwestern University are late for class, or not paying attention, he will know without having to scan the lecture hall.

Their "clickers" will tell him.

Every student in Mr. White's class has been assigned a palm-size, wireless device that looks like a TV remote but has a far less entertaining purpose. With their clickers in hand, the students in Mr. White's class automatically clock in as "present" as they walk into class.

They then use the numbered buttons on the devices to answer multiple-choice quizzes that count for nearly 20 percent of their grade, and that always begin precisely one minute into class. Later, with a click, they can signal to their teacher without raising a hand that they are confused by the day's lesson.

But the greatest impact of such devices—which more than a half-million students are using this fall on several thousand college campuses—may be cultural: they have altered, perhaps irrevocably, the nap schedules of anyone who might have hoped to catch a few winks in the back row, and made it harder for them to respond to text messages, e-mail and other distractions.

In Professor White's 90-minute class, as in similar classes at Harvard, the University of Arizona and Vanderbilt, barely 15 minutes pass without his asking students to "grab your clickers" to provide feedback

Though some Northwestern students say they resent the potential Big Brother aspect of all this, Jasmine Morris, a senior majoring in industrial engineering, is not one of them.

"I actually kind of like it," Ms. Morris said after a class last week. "It does make you read. It makes you pay attention. It reinforces what you're supposed to be doing as a student."

Inevitably, some students have been tempted to see clickers as "cat and mouse" game pieces. Noshir Contractor, who teaches a class on social networking to Northwestern undergraduates, said he began using clickers in spring 2008—and, not long after, watched a student array perhaps five of the devices in front of him.

The owners had skipped class, but their clickers had made it.

Professor Contractor said he tipped his cap to the students' creativity—this was, after all, a class on social networking—but then reminded them that there "are other ways to count attendance," and that, by the way, they were all signatories to the school's honor principle. The practice stopped, he said.

Though the technology is relatively new, preliminary studies at Harvard and Ohio State, among other institutions, suggest that engaging students in class through a device as familiar to them as a cellphone—there are even applications that convert iPads and BlackBerrys into class-ready clickers—increases their understanding of material that may otherwise be conveyed in traditional lectures.

The clickers are also gaining wide use in middle and high schools, as well as at corporate gatherings. Whatever the setting, audience responses are received on a computer at the front of the room and instantly translated into colorful bar graphs displayed on a giant monitor.

The remotes used at Northwestern were made by Turning Technologies, a company in Youngstown, Ohio, and are compatible with PowerPoint. Depending on the model, the hand-helds can sell for $30 to $70 each. Some colleges require students to buy them; others lend them to students.

Tina Rooks, the chief instructional officer for Turning Technologies, said the company expected to ship over one million clickers this year, with roughly half destined for about 2,500 university campuses, including community colleges and for-profit institutions. The company said its higher-education sales had grown 60 percent since 2008, and 95 percent since 2006.

At Northwestern, more than three dozen professors now use clickers in their classrooms. Professor White, who teaches industrial engineering, was among the first here to adopt them about six years ago.

He smiled knowingly when asked about some students' professed dislike of the clickers.

"They should walk in with them in their hands, on time, ready to go," he said.

Professor White acknowledged, though, that the clickers were hardly a silver bullet for engaging students, and that they were just one of many tools he employed, including video clips, guest speakers and calling on individual students to share their thoughts.

"Everyone learns differently," he said. "Some learn watching stuff. Some learn by listening. Some learn by reading. I try to mix it all into every class."

Many of Professor White's students said the highlight of his class was often the display of results of a survey-via-clicker, when they could see whether their classmates shared their opinions. They also said that they appreciated the anonymity, and that while the professor might know how they responded, their peers would not.

Last week, for example, he flashed a photo of the university president, Morton Schapiro, onto the screen, along with a question, "Source of power?" followed by these possible answers:

"1. Coercive power" (sometimes punitive).
"2. Reward power."
"3. Legitimate power" (typically by virtue of one's office).

"4. Expert power" (more typically applied to someone like an electrician or a mechanic).

"5. Referent power" (usually tied to how the leader is viewed personally).

To Professor White's seeming relief, a clear majority, 71 percent, chose No. 3, a sign that they considered his ultimate boss to be "legitimate."

And then, to his delight, the students emerged from their electronic veils to register their opinions the old-fashioned way.

"They can be very reluctant to speak when they think they're in the minority," he said. "Once they see they're not the only ones, they speak up more."

Analyze

1. Do you believe an electronic method of tracking attendance would improve the level of education students receive at your college?

2. Are clickers or other monitoring devices an invasion of students' privacy—or an affront to their perceived levels of responsibility?

3. Are electronic tracking systems more likely to turn students into responsible adults or turn them into individuals who have difficulty managing their schedule without supervision?

Explore

1. The article suggests that electronic clickers—or similar iPhone or iPad apps—may help engender discussion in some lecture hall classes. Do you believe that electronic clickers or apps would better engage students at your college?

2. Clickers are used, primarily, to increase interest in lecture classes. What other methods might professors use to deepen student interest in a lecture hall environment without using hand-held electronics?

3. SHORT WRITING PROMPT: Clickers, in effect, crowd source opinions from a lecture hall class. Propose a plan, either with or without electronics, that would increase participation by *individual* students, with *individual* opinions, in a large lecture hall environment. In what situations might electronic opinion polls be valuable, and in what situations might individual discussion be valuable to a student's development?

Cecilia Capuzzi Simon
Major Decisions

Cecilia Capuzzi Simon is a regular contributor to *The New York Times,* where her articles often focus on education, psychology, and media. At present she teaches writing at American University's School of Communication.

What's your major? It's the defining question for college students—and the cliché that's launched a thousand friendships and romances. It's also a question that has become harder for students to answer.

Blame it on the growing number of possibilities. Colleges and universities reported nearly 1,500 academic programs to the Department of Education in 2010; 355 were added to the list over the previous 10 years as colleges, to stay competitive and current, adopted new disciplines like homeland security and global studies, cyberforensics and agroecology.

At the University of Michigan and Arizona State University, students choose from a dizzying 251 and 250 majors, respectively. DePaul University in Chicago offers 24 more majors than it did in 2002, for a total of 98.

And graduating with a double (or triple) major, minor or concentration as a way to hedge bets in an uncertain job market has become increasingly popular; the number of bachelor's degrees awarded with double majors rose 70 percent between 2001 and 2011, according to the Education Department.

Some students go to college knowing exactly what they want to do. But most don't. At Penn State, 80 percent of freshmen—even those who have declared a major—say they are uncertain about their major, and half will change their minds after they declare, sometimes more than once. How to decide?

The New Explorer

Colleges and universities have vested interests in students declaring early. Retention rates for declared students are better, and they are more likely to graduate in four years. But college officials also recognize that deciding on a major can be overwhelming, especially when coupled with the fear that a wrong choice will result in added semesters and tuition.

"Students no longer have the luxury of stumbling into a major or making mistakes," says Neeta P. Fogg, a research professor at Drexel University's Center for Labor Markets and Policy, and a co-author of "College Majors Handbook With Real Career Paths and Payoffs."

"Exploratory" is the new undeclared. Colleges have moved away from the negative-sounding "undecided" label to encourage students to experiment with unfamiliar disciplines and, perhaps, discover a passion and career path. "We want to remind them that they have an active role" in their academic choices, says Mary Beth Collier, the dean of academic advising at the State University of New York at New Paltz. At SUNY, exploratory students are urged to try new subjects using general education electives.

Ms. Collier tells students: "You've taken the same six subjects since kindergarten. If you don't know your major, don't come here and take the same subjects expecting to figure it out." That can mean fulfilling a U.S. studies requirement with a political science or black studies course instead of a rehash of U.S. history that you should have learned in high school.

Some schools have made exploration official. At the University of Florida, where 61 percent of students change their majors by the end of their second year, there are three exploratory tracks—engineering and science, humanities and letters, and social and behavioral—that students can declare for three semesters before choosing a specialized major. At the University of Cincinnati, undecided students can enroll in an exploratory studies program.

When in Doubt, Take It

Advisers caution: Don't abandon subjects that you may need later. Students often don't realize that many popular majors—psychology, social sciences, business—have math and science requirements. You might have to forgo majoring in economics, for example, if come junior year you have to make up courses in calculus and statistics.

This requires thinking ahead, says Fritz Grupe, the creator of MyMajors. com and an emeritus professor of computer science at the University of Nevada. You may not know what to do with the rest of your life at age 18, but you can cover your bases with prudent planning. Some majors have a curriculum that follows a tight sequence of courses. It's easier to switch out of engineering than it is to take it up (if that's possible at all) later in your college career.

The "biggest mistake" students make, Dr. Grupe adds, is failing to research what's required of the major, and the profession. Nursing may sound attractive because "you like to help people," he says, but nursing students take the same demanding math and science curriculum as pre-med students, and the work is often technical and not for every kindhearted soul.

The Bottom Line

Colleges "do not make decisions in a vacuum," Dr. Fogg says. They are constantly tweaking their offerings. The Department of Education's list shows clusters of new programs in established fields of study that mirror scientific, cultural and societal developments. Some are cross-disciplinary or specializations, like biosystems engineering, clinical nurse leadership, computational biology and international policy analysis.

Quirkier additions to the list obviously reflect marketplace trends and student demand, like culinary science/culinology, digital arts, casino management and sports communication. At Montclair State University in New Jersey, which offers 300 majors, minors and concentrations, a new fashion studies major has been hugely popular, thanks to the university's proximity to Manhattan; with Madison Square Garden and Giants Stadium in sight, it also saw opportunity in a sports industry and event-planning major within its business school.

Still, it's difficult to predict the employment market, says Michele Campagna, the executive director of the Center for Advising and Student Transitions at Montclair State. Many students choose majors they think will lead to jobs, but "four years from now," she says, "freshmen will be applying for jobs that don't even exist today."

Most employers are looking for transferable skills—the ability to problem solve, work in teams, write and communicate, and think critically, says Ms. Collier of SUNY New Paltz. These can be developed in any liberal arts discipline. It makes no sense, she says, to "suffer through a major" because you think it will lead to employment. "We tell students, 'Find a major that makes you intellectually engaged, that expands your brain and deepens your understanding of the world.'"

At the same time, cautions Dr. Fogg, the stakes for college students today couldn't be higher: 41 percent of graduates are employed in jobs that don't require a college degree. Many employers today lack the resources and patience for on-the-job training, she says, and are looking for college graduates who are "shelf-ready employees." So pick up professional direction, job-related skills and work experience, she says, and of course follow your heart.

Analyze

1. What was—or *is*—the most difficult aspect in deciding on your major?
2. "What's your major?" is often the first question that two students ask each other. What would be a different question that would reveal more meaningful information about students you meet at college? In your opinion, why are American students so focused on "majors" when they meet new people?
3. In your opinion, which would serve students better in the long run: a traditional major, such as history or math, or a newly developed, highly specialized major, such as international policy analysis? Why?
4. If you were to exclude career considerations from selecting a major— that is, if you were to study only a major that interested you in terms of your own curiosity and personal development—what would you study? And why? Would it be different than your current major or majors you are actively considering?

Explore

1. At most high schools, students do not have a major or even a declared major area of study. Discuss the pros and cons of colleges offering this model to *some* students: a four-year general education focused on transferable skills, such as writing, critical thinking, and creative problem solving. Assume students would obtain breadth in their education, taking multiple courses in math, science, social science, literature, arts, writing, humanities, business, and so forth, rather than an education focused primarily in one discipline.
2. SHORT WRITING PROMPT: With the help of the web, a career counselor, a school adviser, and/or a research librarian, answer the following questions: What are the long-term social and workplace benefits to majoring in engineering, English, and biology? Which of these majors, for you, would yield the highest personal satisfaction? Which

would give you broad skills to change careers as you move through life? Which would offer the highest potential salary for new graduates? Which would offer the highest potential salary for graduates twenty years after graduation? With which major do students express the highest degree of satisfaction?

3. FULL WRITING PROMPT: In the article: Dr. Grupe advises that "the 'biggest mistake' [students make when picking a major] . . . is failing to research what's required of the major, and the profession." In a full essay, chart your future path through a major on your campus. You choose the major. Identify the classes that will be most difficult for you to complete, and identify resources on campus (the math lab, peer tutoring, etc.) that will help you succeed. Use the web to explore possible entry-level jobs for new graduates in this major. Look at job ads to see if certain minors, certificate programs, or internships will be helpful in obtaining a job. Note starting salaries. Ask seniors or recent graduates how difficult jobs are to obtain in this field. Your final paper should be a road map through one major, noting projected difficulties and their solutions, leading to one or two possible entry-level jobs after college.

Laura Pappano
Take Notes from the Pros

Laura Pappano is the author of *Inside School Turnarounds* and *The Connection Gap*, as well as the co-author of *Playing with Boys*. Her articles on education regularly appear in *The New York Times*, *The Harvard Education Letter*, and *The Boston Globe*.

When it comes to taking lecture notes, Laura Gayle, a sophomore at Florida State University, has her methods. A smiley face connotes an important person. If the professor says, "Make sure you know this," she uses an asterisk. A triangular button signals a video clip played in class. Later, she will organize the notes, write a video summary and check uncertainties against the textbook or with the professor. For "Introduction to Classical Mythology," she'll even alphabetize a list of Greek gods and goddesses.

Then, a few days before the exam, she puts it all up for sale.

Since last fall, when she uploaded her macroeconomics notes onto Flash-notes.com to pay for a birthday gift for her mother, Ms. Gayle has sold more than 500 copies of the study guides that she's put together for her courses, made over $3,285 and tapped into a growing, if controversial, online marketplace.

In describing her approach, Ms. Gayle, a human resources major with a 3.8 grade-point average, sounds aggressive in the best way. "I sit in the front row center for every single class, whether I am selling notes or not," she says. "For me it is a matter of paying attention, being detail-oriented and," if something is unclear, "taking the initiative to go out and find the answer." Her study guides are rated five stars by users.

While borrowing, bartering and selling class notes is nothing new, the online market is just getting organized. Amazon-like sites matching note sellers and buyers have come and gone in recent years as students who started them graduate. NerdyNotes at Stony Brook University is surviving the graduation of a founder, but bigger players are arriving.

Flashnotes started up last fall on five campuses—Kent State, Ohio State, Florida State, Rutgers and University of Maryland—with 30,000 registered users. There are now about 100,000 at 100 campuses, and the company just bought Moola-guides, a Florida State start-up. The sites let student sellers set prices for notes (average is $9) but take a cut. Flashnotes gets 30 percent; NerdyNotes takes 50.

The marketplace has annoyed some professors, who bar their students from buying or selling notes. In 2010, California State University banned students on its 23 campuses from using NoteUtopia.com (since bought by Flashnotes), citing a little-known state education code prohibiting the selling of class notes for commercial purposes. Some argue that lectures are professors' intellectual property, including notes recording their ideas; others warn that notes are a student's interpretation of a class. Some say that selling them promotes laziness by enticing students to skip lectures.

Still others encourage it. "I want them to use any resource they can to do well on my tests," says Lora Holcombe, an economics professor at Florida

State. "It's not like with the notes you sleep on them and they'll go into your head. You have to do some heavy studying."

Michael Matousek, who graduated from Kent State in 2010, dreamed up Flashnotes during a statistics class in his senior year. He had switched majors twice so was taking a required class that covered topics he had previously studied. Students found the professor confusing, but Mr. Matousek "knew *how* they were confused."

After classmates repeatedly sought his help, he compiled and sold his notes to a friend. Soon others wanted copies, so Mr. Matousek collected $10 for each emailed copy, netting more than $1,000 for the semester. The experience showed him the power of peer education—and not necessarily led by brainiacs. "The 4.0 kids, they can't explain," he says. "The 3.5, the 3.6 kids understand what it takes to learn something." Mr. Matousek graduated with a 3.67 G.P.A. and now heads a staff of 22 at Flashnotes headquarters in Faneuil Hall in Boston.

The demand is not surprising. "Students are notoriously poor note-takers," says Kenneth Kiewra, professor of educational psychology at the University of Nebraska, Lincoln. They tend to record only a third of the important lecture points.

What makes notes great? "Completeness," Dr. Kiewra says.

Research shows that having detailed, comprehensive notes raises test performance. In his oft-cited 1985 study, published in *Human Learning*, Dr. Kiewra randomly assigned 100 students to one of seven groups. Forty-eight hours after a lecture, the groups had 25 minutes to review before a test. Each group was assigned a learning method: *Take your own notes and review* (1) your notes, (2) your notes as well as instructor notes, (3) without any notes. *Don't take notes but review* (1) instructor notes, (2) without any notes. *Skip the lecture but review* (1) instructor notes, (2) without any notes.

Groups that reviewed instructor notes performed best. "It didn't matter so much what you did during the lecture," Dr. Kiewra explains. "It mattered what notes you had." Even those who didn't attend the lecture but reviewed instructor notes did better than those who attended and "reviewed their own crummy notes."

He concludes: "The real value of note-taking is not so much in the taking as in the having."

Getting down details along with main points is easier said than done. Average lecture speed is 100 to 125 words a minute, but college students listening to a lecture write 22 words a minute by hand; they type just 33 words a minute. In his latest research Dr. Kiewra has found that when the professor pauses three times to let students catch up and fill in missing information, they have more "original, additional and total notes" than those who waited to revise immediately after a lecture. If a student fails to note a particular point, Dr. Kiewra says, there is only a 5 percent chance of recalling it later.

Videotaped lectures help. When students viewed a video twice, they recorded 53 percent of the details, up from 38 percent, Dr. Kiewra says. Watching three times raised it to 60 percent.

Memory is a weak tool, but thinking about the information—paraphrasing rather than writing everything verbatim—improves retention, according to a series of studies at Princeton, published last April in *Psychological Science*. Students who took notes by hand rather than laptop wrote less but performed better. Laptop users tended to merely transcribe a lecture "rather than processing and reframing it in their own words"; they scored strikingly lower on conceptual tests.

Alexandra E. Hadley, a Boston College junior who has posted 29 different offerings on Flashnotes in the last year, uses paper for small discussion classes and a laptop for lectures. An English and communications major, she says she thinks hard about points the professor stresses. "I try to be very present in all of my classes," she says. "That is key—focusing on what I am doing." That means considering points as you take notes and connecting new ideas with information from earlier lectures. "I was taking notes in my research methods class and we were talking about pop culture," she says. "We touched on two theories, but it reminded me of another one, so I threw that in my notes."

Umar Zaidi, a Stony Brook senior from Queens double-majoring in political science and sociology, prefers to grab a seat near a power outlet and tap away. "When you are typing you can look at your professor," he says. He reads over the syllabus before class, "so when the professor mentions something that rings a bell, I type it up." While typing he organizes material into sections with main ideas, bullet points and asterisks.

Mr. Zaidi uploaded a semester's worth of lecture notes for "Urban Politics," an upper-level course, when NerdyNotes started up last spring. Sales, at $10 a packet, were slow at first. (Biology notes are the most in demand on campus.) Classmates didn't take notes, he says, because they thought political science was a breeze—until the midterm. After, he netted $150. "If they're too lazy to make notes," he says, "then I'll make notes and take advantage."

But Mr. Zaidi won't sell the study guides he makes for himself. One doesn't want to make it too easy for classmates. Indeed, some campuses are not good note-selling territory because students don't want to help competitors. In other words, at Flashnotes, Mr. Matousek says, "we're not putting a huge emphasis on Harvard."

Analyze

1. Do online class note sources do more to help students or harm students? Consider those who use the notes, those who make and receive payment for the notes, and the ways that the class environment is changed by having a note option available.
2. Do professional notes, with complete lecture outlines, help students to learn more efficiently or undercut a student's education?
3. In your opinion, who owns the content of a lecture class: the college, the professor, the students, or some combination of all three?

Explore

1. Is it a better learning experience to write down exactly what a professor says in your class notes? Or is it better to rephrase the professor's ideas into your own language? That is, do you learn better through the language of an expert or by digesting information and assimilating it into your own vocabulary? What are the pros and cons of each approach?
2. In terms of using notes to engage difficult material, when is your optimal time to review notes: before each class, at the end of each week, or in the days leading up to a test? How does your mind best absorb new concepts in a way that you understand them with depth and familiarity?
3. SHORT WRITING PROMPT: Identify a class subject where professional notes might deepen your understanding of the course material. How would professional notes accomplish this? Likewise, identify a class subject where professional notes might lessen your own engagement with the course material.

Marcia Y. Cantarella
Just Not Feeling It—Or When You Don't Love a Subject You Have to Take

---

Marcia Y. Cantarella is the president of Cantarella Consulting, where she explores issues of college access, diversity, and student success. She has worked at Hunter College, Princeton University, New York University, and Metropolitan College of New York, where she has served as a dean and a vice president of student affairs.

I had a great email when I got back to a work focus after the holidays. The topic was what to do when you are just not loving the subject you have to take. It was from a student I had met when I did a workshop this past summer for students heading off to college for the first time. I usually give out cards and tell students that the winners will reach out to me. And generally a few do. And Timothy did. And he wanted "to ask you for your opinion on the best way to consistently absorb information that you have no interest in or that doesn't challenge you much. What did you/do you do when you need to memorize/learn things that don't interest you much?" A really great question.

We have all been there—the A+ students and those of us who struggled more. Some courses we naturally loved because the subject just spoke to us and some because we were blessed with a fabulous professor who could make reading the phone book fascinating. But there was always the one (or more) course that was meeting a requirement and just did not work for us. Today students are focused on the relationship of what they study to the jobs they see themselves having. So everything is also seen through the lens of relevance. Given that perspective a course won't be interesting if it does not relate to the perceived future career goal. There is the reality too that every professor does not teach like a rock star. I had one in graduate school who would literally doze off reading his yellowing notes and on a hot summer evening that meant most of the class wanted to doze off too.

But there are ways to approach this problem of not loving a subject. And it is a problem because lack of interest leads to less focus and attention to the class and maybe then to a lower grade. Readings do not get read. Dozing or texting in class happens. Hands do not go up when questions are asked. GPAs can be damaged. Think of 25 percent of your grade for class participation being shot because of boredom.

So here is what I told Timothy. First unpack the course. What are the skills you are going to get from it? Does it push you to read, research, write, collaborate with others, and solve problems? Which of these skills are you likely to need in the workplace where you see yourself? Your motivation can be to really perfect those skills because they will be useful to you for achieving your dreams.

Second, what might you learn about the world that could be good to know? Does it help to know something about how the body fights disease when you have a sick grandmother? Does it help to know something about the political process when the outcome of an election can change your quality of life? How does this subject relate to your life?

Does it help to know enough of literature or the arts that you don't feel like a dummy when your work colleagues are talking about books or a joke has a reference to Shakespeare and you don't get it? Or you are the idiot who does not know who Paul McCartney is when collaborating with Kanye and gets laughed at all over the internet. Some of what you learn just helps you be part of the conversation but those who are part of the conversation get ahead. Again it is tied to your dreams of success. You are keeping your eyes on the prize.

A magic way to become engaged and, maybe the most important, is to ask your professor what drew them to the subject in the first place. They have spent their lives deeply immersed in a field. They do it for the love of the subject. I know from my own experience that I had to love my field (American Studies focused on Business) in order to spend the 6+ years it took to earn my doctorate and then to teach it for several years after. They want you to love it too. They can get excited talking about it. Getting to know your professors is always a smart strategy. And so getting them going on what they love will endear you and also maybe turn on the light bulb for you. Both outcomes are good for your grades. And a strong GPA is good for your goals.

Similarly talk to upperclassmen who are doing this as a major. I remember assembling a panel of students of different majors to share with underclassmen what they liked about their chosen fields. And each was wildly enthusiastic about their own major. So use the experience of those who are immersed in the subject but closer to your own goals and life experience to see what they see through their eyes. How do they study? What professors do they love? What questions excite them?

Finally maybe you are not studying effectively. The struggle to get a subject can also be because you are not approaching the study effectively. Study groups can energize a subject because you have several minds and skill sets being brought to bear. Figure out how you learn best—if you are a visual learner then charts and pictures may help, for example. Learning social sciences is not the same as studying poetry or the memorization Bio requires. Use your school's tutoring centers to learn how to best approach each subject so you have a better chance of getting it.

One thing you may not realize is that you need to learn how to read for college. Yes, you might make it to college, but that does not mean you know how to read. With a heavy reading load—more than in high school—you learn that different kinds of reading work for different classes. Some academic disciplines require close reading, some require memorizing key concepts, and still others involve a process of skimming and comprehending. Some sciences, like biology, may require a lot of memorization, but you also have to understand what you are memorizing. So reading with access to a glossary or dictionary is wise. It is easy to be "bored" when the issue is really not understanding.

If reading in the humanities (history, philosophy, art) or social sciences (psychology, sociology, economics), look for themes or key concepts and evidence to support them. Once you know what you're looking for, it is easy to skim or read faster. A key skill in learning is to argue with evidence, so note where you disagree with the author's premises and why. Having that kind of debate can also get your interest up in a subject.

Sometimes it helps get interested if you have to explain material to those who are not familiar with it as a way of testing your own understanding. Students who tutor younger kids find it helps them too.

And finally do what Timothy did. Ask someone for help! So smart! Love may follow and bring success with it.

Analyze

1. The central question for this article is a good one for new college students: "What did you/do you do when you need to memorize/learn things that don't interest you much?" What advice can you contribute beyond those answers offered in the essay?

2. Many experts believe that college should serve a larger purpose than simple career training. How can students move beyond a career-readiness understanding of college—"study to the jobs they see themselves having"—to one that speaks to a model in which college helps students improve in many areas of life?

3. The article suggests that this is a good way to better engage the fullness of the college experience: "Getting to know your professors is always a smart strategy." Can you think of other strategies that would likely help students get more out of the college classroom experience in general?

Explore

1. Some employers see college as a process in which students learn to pursue long-term goals with focus and passion, while struggling through difficult classes or classes that merely meet "a requirement." This skill—sometimes called grit or drive—shows that a student has developed perseverance, which is a marker of future career success. Aside from technical and academic abilities, what other life skills, such as perseverance, do students often develop while completing a college degree?

2. Most colleges have multiple committees and substantial oversight when developing both general education and major requirements. Review the list of classes for your major—or a major that interests you—to identify a class for which you don't immediately understand its value. Either through email or in a brief meeting, ask an advisor how this class will help you develop as a student. Many students find that understanding the rationale for requiring a class—or how a class fits into a larger educational program—helps them to better engage the material.

3. SHORT WRITING PROMPT: Develop a complete list of tutoring centers and study-skills programs offered on your campus. Most colleges have a writing center and a math lab. Many offer occasional (and often free) short classes in speed-reading, note taking, test taking, and essay research. Lasting only a single evening or two, these classes are usually not offered for college credit but informally, as a means to help students succeed in college. To develop this list, review your college's website, ask juniors and seniors, and visit the writing center and various student support areas at your school.

Paul Fain
Competent at What?

Paul Fain, a journalist, writes for *Inside Higher Ed*. His work has also appeared in *The New York Times*, *Washington City Paper*, and *Mother Jones*.

Competency-based education appears to be higher education's "next big thing." Yet many academics aren't sure what it is. And that goes double for lawmakers and journalists.

A new group is stepping in to try to clear up some of the confusion. The nascent Competency-Based Education Network (C-BEN) will include up to 20 institutions that offer competency-based degrees or are well on their way to creating them.

The Lumina Foundation is funding the three-year effort. Public Agenda, a nonprofit research organization, is coordinating the work.

The group's overarching goals are to share intelligence and discuss "best practices" on competency-based education, while also influencing the national conversation, according to the invitation for applications, which are due at the end of next month.

"This national network will consist of representatives from colleges and universities willing to commit time and effort to solving common challenges around developing quality competency-based models capable of scaling or spreading to affordably serve more students," the invitation document said.

The reason for the project's creation, said several officials who are working on it, is a growing need for shared guiding principles. Interest in online education is high, and many college leaders want competency-based education to avoid the hype, misconceptions and resulting backlash massive open online courses have received.

"There's really a danger of people just repackaging what they're doing and calling it competency-based education because it's the buzzword du jour," said Amy Laitinen, a former Education Department and White House official who is deputy director of the New America Foundation's higher education program.

Network and Incubator

Laitinen is a consultant for the project. Joining her is Mike Offerman, an expert on competency-based education, and Sally Johnstone, vice president for academic advancement at Western Governors University.

The group will focus on the nitty-gritty details of building a new program, including how to design sound assessments, comply with financial aid policies and make tweaks to business processes and information technology systems.

Participants will also discuss how to talk about and market their new degrees. Everything will be on the table, said several officials, even the term "competency."

A separate Lumina grant will help pay for a website that will make public much of the network's work and research. Southern New Hampshire University is responsible for creating the website.

"We're going to share as much of that as possible," said Paul LeBlanc, the university's president.

Southern New Hampshire, which has moved aggressively into competency-based education, will also host quarterly meetings at its campus for the group's members.

The network will be limited to colleges that are at least close to creating competency-based degrees. However, a separate, somewhat similar new effort is aimed at institutions that are interested in getting into the space.

That project is an "incubator" that the Bill and Melinda Gates Foundation is funding through its Next Generation Learning Challenges grant, which is managed by Educause. To participate, colleges will need to submit a plan to begin creating a competency-based program by January 2015, according to a draft document about the grant.

"C-BEN and the incubator share the goals of developing and advancing competency-based business models capable of scaling and serving many more students from all backgrounds," the document said. "Both will offer exposure to subject matter experts and will encourage the development and testing of relevant tools for institutions."

Carol Geary Schneider, president of the Association of American Colleges and Universities, welcomed the deepening conversation over competency-based education. She said she hopes the network can provide some clarity on the emerging delivery model, which the association has viewed warily.

The competency-based movement does have promise, she said. Ideally, Schneider said, competency-based programs share goals with the Degree Qualifications Profile (DQP), a Lumina-funded effort that attempts to define what degree holders should know and be able to do. Schneider helped author the profile.

However, Schneider said competency-based education could also lead to degrees that are based on a haphazard grouping of one-off competencies rather than a holistic curriculum. And she said competency is "now being used to define so many experiments."

Defining Competency

Competency-based education's defining feature, experts said, is that it places a priority on the assessment of defined learning outcomes, regardless of where the learning occurs. That typically means breaking credit requirements into discrete "competencies" that indicate a student has mastered concepts.

The idea is hardly new. Decades ago pioneering institutions like Alverno College, Excelsior College, Thomas Edison State College and others with a focus on adult students began assessing competencies and issuing college credit for experiential learning. As with Advanced Placement tests, students could pass assessments and earn credit for knowledge and skills they gained outside the traditional classroom.

Western Governors offers a twist on this model. Created in 1997, the online university added the element of self-paced instruction. Students at Western Governors can work through automated, asynchronous online course material at their own speed. And the university's instructors act more like tutors than professors in a lecture hall.

A third style first hit the scene this year. This approach, which is called "direct assessment," drops the credit-hour standard and completely severs the link between competencies and the amount of time students spend mastering them.

Earlier this year the federal government and regional accreditors gave a green light to new direct assessment offerings from College for America, a subsidiary of Southern New Hampshire, and Capella University.

Northern Arizona University has also pursued a direct-assessment program. So has the University of Wisconsin System, with its growing

"Flexible Option." More are on the way, including one from Brandman University. The Western Association of Schools and Colleges (WASC), a regional accreditor, this week approved Brandman's new, competency-based, bachelor degree in business administration.

Even advocates for competency-based education say it raises plenty of questions.

For example, Laitinen, who is a prominent critic of the credit hour, has begun publicly worrying about moving too fast on competency-based education. She said lawmakers in particular might be overeager to help spur the creation of new programs by making changes to legislation before academics even know what changes might help.

The work around competency-based education "needs to be done responsibly and thoughtfully, and with the right motivation" said Laitinen, adding that "the right motivation is outcomes."

Schneider agreed. "We're in a long-term change from a higher education system organized around credit hours" to one based on "demonstrated achievements of capabilities."

That's a difficult undertaking, she said. "We're trying to invent something new."

The Lumina-funded group's creators want its members to help lead conversations around those big-ticket questions.

A steering committee composed of representatives from 10 or so colleges with experience on competency-based education will help set the network's agenda, said several officials who are involved in the effort.

The committee's first co-chairs are Laurie Dodge, vice chancellor of institutional assessment and planning and vice provost at Brandman University, and David Schejbal, dean of continuing education, outreach and e-learning at University of Wisconsin-Extension.

Dodge said the project will seek to create a set of shared guiding principles. "The big thing is quality and rigor," she said.

One key to the work being helpful, said Schneider, is whether colleges share meaningful details about their assessments. Competency-based education relies heavily on assessments, so it's important to know what they measure.

"Ultimately we're going to need to reach some ground rules," Schneider said.

The invitation for applications said institutions must commit to sharing information about assessments, such as details about testing principles and how to formulate good assessments. They will not, however, be required to share "trade secrets." Western Governors, for example, has taken some heat for allegedly not being open about its competencies and assessments.

Johnstone recently responded to that criticism by saying "there are few people that ask" about course-level competencies.

LeBlanc said he was confident that participants would get specific about the creation of quality assessment tools. "We have to have transparency."

In the meantime, LeBlanc has been busy discussing competency-based education with accreditors. In a recent span of five days he spoke at three meetings held by regional accrediting agencies.

No "Single Model"

Colleges will be asked to do a substantial amount of work to participate in the group. And just sending their president to quarterly meetings won't cut it.

To apply, institutions must identify a team of up to seven employees, including faculty members, academic leaders, business and financial aid officers, information technology leaders, institutional researchers and marketing officials.

Several of the project's leaders said they want a broad range of competency-based programs to be represented.

"It is not our intention to push for a single model or approach," said Alison Kadlec, a senior vice president at Public Agenda, who will help lead the project.

Schejbal said the group hopes to come up with some sort of "standard, working definition" for competency-based education. But that doesn't mean they will be prescriptive.

"We don't have any intention of being exclusionary or telling people how to do it," he said.

The effort grew out of an April meeting Lumina held with representatives of approximately 25 institutions that were working on competency-based degrees. During the planning of that meeting and other, related discussions there was controversy over whether or not to include for-profit institutions.

Some advocates of competency-based education worry that for-profits might create lower-quality programs that could hurt the movement.

However, it appears the group will be open to participation by at least some for-profits. Capella, for example, which is widely viewed as a leader on competency-based education, is planning to contribute, said officials from the university.

No group is ever big enough for everyone, however. And some college leaders have grumbled about Lumina's outsized role in organizing conversations about competency-based education. But the network's leaders said few colleges actually have competency-based programs up and running.

"A lot of the right players are around the table," said Deb Bushway, Capella's chief academic officer.

Analyze

1. One advocate of competency-based education sees college primarily as a set of knowledge and skills that graduates "should know and be able to do." What important aspects of your experience would not fit into this description of a college education? And which would?
2. Assuming you are enrolled in a traditional college, what would be lost or gained if you transferred to a "competency-based" program?
3. In competency-based education, students can "earn credit for knowledge and skills they gained outside the traditional classroom." What college-level skills have you learned outside the classroom? And how did you learn them?
4. This model of competency-based education acknowledges that some college subjects take more than a single term to master, others take less, yet all are fixed into semester-length (or quarter-length) courses. In your opinion, which subjects need more time to master and which less?

Explore

1. Competency-based education would reduce the time a student spends in college. It may lower the overall cost of tuition, and it would limit the time a student was removed from the workforce. Both of these outcomes have potential advantages. But what experiences or skill development would be lost if the overall college experience were shortened by a year or two?
2. SHORT WRITING PROMPT: Make two lists. On the first list, identify a set of college subjects with which you might engage well,

without a class, as a self-directed learner. On the second, list a set of college subjects with which you would likely not engage well, without a class, as a self-directed learner.

3. FULL WRITING PROMPT: In an essay, relate an experience in which you taught (or tried to teach) yourself a complex skill or engage in a difficult subject. How well were you able to accomplish this? What were the strengths of self-guided learning? And the shortcomings?

Forging Connections

1. In "The Comfortable Kid," the author suggests that trigger warnings infantilize college students—that is, trigger warnings deny college students the opportunity to gain maturity through challenging situations. In your experience at college so far, can you identify other areas where classes protect students from challenging or disturbing information? Is this protection helpful to students or does it delay their entry into the adult world?

2. Multiple articles in this chapter describe colleges acting with a "consumer ethos"—that is, colleges want to make the student (i.e., the consumer) happy, perhaps with slightly higher-than-average grades, professors who aren't too strict, and classes that aren't too challenging. This consumer ethos is reinforced with websites like Rate My Professors, which places a premium on easygoing instructors and interesting classes that don't require heavy workloads. As you consider your campus, where do you see evidence of this "consumer ethos"? In your opinion, is a consumer ethos a beneficial or detrimental force on a college campus?

Looking Further

1. Multiple articles in this chapter discuss ways that technology can be integrated into the college experience, such as with clickers or attendance devices. Technology, no doubt, will continue to be an important element at college. Which technology-related experiences in the classroom have helped you learn a subject with depth and complexity? And which technology-related experiences have placed more emphasis on the technology than on learning? How can colleges better focus on meaningful technology-related experiences?

2. A few articles in this chapter offer practical advice for students—on choosing a major, for example, and how to pass a class you don't love. As you look ahead into your career as a college student, what is the one area of concern for which you would most like useful advice, an area not covered in this book and also not yet covered in your class?

The Ever-Changing Curriculum

If you had attended the University of Pennsylvania in the mid-1800s, your class list would likely have included courses in classical literature and classical languages (such as Latin and ancient Greek), religious studies, and various math subjects (such as geometry and calculus). Classes recently added to the curriculum included offerings in mechanics, constitutional law, electricity, and magnetism. But over time curriculums change. Most students today are not required to take courses in Latin or religion. If students explore magnetism, they likely explore it as part of a physics sequence.

The needs of students—and the expectations for higher education—change over time. In today's college, students are more likely to take Spanish or Chinese than they are ancient Greek, as skills of international business have a higher perceived value than skills relating to antiquity. In ways, it might be ideal if college lasted five or six years, allowing students to pursue both Spanish and ancient Greek. But for most programs, a college education is capped at four years of study, 120 semester hours, or 180 quarter hours. The curriculum debate always focuses on this: to best serve contemporary students, what subjects should be included in those four years, and to make room for new requirements, what old classes should fall away?

In the past decade or so, colleges have explored many new requirements: many of these classes carry official college credit, though some are noncredit requirements to cover social concerns. Laura Pappano explores the possibility of requiring a course in creativity or creative thinking, while Rajat Bhageria suggests that, in an age of iPhones and tablet computers, all students should take at least one course in programming code. Scott Carlson investigates what is lost when colleges remove physical education courses to make way for new requirements. Rich Barlow, Diana Divecha, and Robin Stern explore two new social courses, one on alcohol abuse, the other on emotional health. These articles discuss the ways in which the college experience is changing, removing some traditions to make way for new ones. Together, these authors point to what a college curriculum might look like in the near future and the way new classes help students adapt to our ever-changing world.

Laura Pappano
Learning to Think Outside the Box: Creativity Becomes an Academic Discipline

Laura Pappano is the author of *Inside School Turnarounds* and *The Connection Gap*, as well as the co-author of *Playing with Boys*. Her articles on education regularly appear in *The New York Times*, *The Harvard Education Letter*, and *The Boston Globe*.

It bothers Matthew Lahue and it surely bothers you: enter a public restroom and the stall lock is broken. Fortunately, Mr. Lahue has a solution. It's called the Bathroom Bodyguard. Standing before his Buffalo State College classmates and professor, Cyndi Burnett, Mr. Lahue displayed a device he concocted from a large washer, metal ring, wall hook, rubber bands and Lincoln Log. Slide the ring in the crack and twist. The door stays shut. Plus, the device fits in a jacket pocket.

The world may be full of problems, but students presenting projects for Introduction to Creative Studies have uncovered a bunch you probably haven't thought of. Elie Fortune, a freshman, revealed his Sneaks 'n Geeks app to identify the brand of killer sneakers you spot on the street. Jason Cathcart, a senior, sported a bulky martial arts uniform with sparring pads he had sewn in. No more forgetting them at home.

"I don't expect them to be the next Steve Jobs or invent the flying car," Dr. Burnett says. "But I do want them to be more effective and resourceful problem solvers." Her hope, she says, is that her course has made them more creative.

Once considered the product of genius or divine inspiration, creativity—the ability to spot problems and devise smart solutions—is being recast as a prized and teachable skill. Pin it on pushback against standardized tests and standardized thinking, or on the need for ingenuity in a fluid landscape.

"The reality is that to survive in a fast-changing world you need to be creative," says Gerard J. Puccio, chairman of the International Center for Studies in Creativity at Buffalo State College, which has the nation's oldest creative studies program, having offered courses in it since 1967.

"That is why you are seeing more attention to creativity at universities," he says. "The marketplace is demanding it."

Critical thinking has long been regarded as *the* essential skill for success, but it's not enough, says Dr. Puccio. Creativity moves beyond mere synthesis and evaluation and is, he says, "the higher order skill." This has not been a sudden development. Nearly 20 years ago "creating" replaced "evaluation" at the top of Bloom's Taxonomy of learning objectives. In 2010 "creativity" was the factor most crucial for success found in an I.B.M. survey of 1,500 chief executives in 33 industries. These days "creative" is the most used buzzword in LinkedIn profiles two years running.

Traditional academic disciplines still matter, but as content knowledge evolves at lightning speed, educators are talking more and more about "process skills," strategies to reframe challenges and extrapolate and transform information, and to accept and deal with ambiguity.

Creative studies is popping up on course lists and as a credential. Buffalo State, part of the State University of New York, plans a Ph.D. and already offers a master's degree and undergraduate minor. Saybrook University in San Francisco has a master's and certificate, and added a specialization to its psychology Ph.D. in 2011. Drexel University in Philadelphia has a three-year-old online master's. St. Andrews University in Laurinburg, N.C., has added a minor. And creative studies offerings, sometimes with a transdisciplinary bent, are new options in business, education, digital media, humanities, arts, science and engineering programs across the country.

Suddenly, says Russell G. Carpenter, program coordinator for a new minor in applied creative thinking at Eastern Kentucky University, "there is a larger conversation happening on campus: 'Where does creativity fit into the E.K.U. student experience?' " Dr. Carpenter says 40 students from a broad array of fields, including nursing and justice and safety, have enrolled in the minor—a number he expects to double as more sections are added to introductory classes. Justice and safety? Students want tools to help them solve public safety problems and deal with community issues, Dr. Carpenter explains, and a credential to take to market.

The credential's worth is apparent to Mr. Lahue, a communication major who believes that a minor in the field carries a message. "It says: 'This person is not a drone. They can use this skill set and apply themselves in other parts of the job.' "

On-demand inventiveness is not as outrageous as it sounds. Sure, some people are naturally more imaginative than others. What's igniting campuses, though, is the conviction that everyone is creative, and can learn to be more so.

Just about every pedagogical toolbox taps similar strategies, employing divergent thinking (generating multiple ideas) and convergent thinking (finding what works). The real genius, of course, is in the *how*.

Dr. Puccio developed an approach that he and partners market as Four-Sight and sell to schools, businesses and individuals. The method, which is used in Buffalo State classrooms, has four steps: clarifying, ideating, developing and implementing. People tend to gravitate to particular steps, suggesting their primary thinking style. Clarifying—asking the right question—is critical because people often misstate or misperceive a problem. "If you don't have the right frame for the situation, it's difficult to come up with a breakthrough," Dr. Puccio says. Ideating is brainstorming and calls for getting rid of your inner naysayer to let your imagination fly. Developing is building out a solution, and maybe finding that it doesn't work and having to start over. Implementing calls for convincing others that your idea has value.

Jack V. Matson, an environmental engineer and a lead instructor of "Creativity, Innovation and Change," a MOOC that drew 120,000 in September, teaches a freshman seminar course at Penn State that he calls "Failure 101." That's because, he says, "the frequency and intensity of failures is an implicit principle of the course. Getting into a creative mind-set involves a lot of trial and error."

His favorite assignments? Construct a résumé based on things that didn't work out and find the meaning and influence these have had on your choices. Or build the tallest structure you can with 20 Popsicle sticks. The secret to the assignment is to destroy the sticks and reimagine their use. "As soon as someone in the class starts breaking the sticks," he says, "it changes everything."

Dr. Matson also asks students to "find some cultural norms to break," like doing cartwheels while entering the library. The point: "Examine what in the culture is preventing you from creating something new or different. And what is it like to look like a fool because a lot of things won't work out and you will look foolish? So how do you handle that?"

It's a lesson that has been basic to the ventures of Brad Keywell, a Groupon founder and a student of Dr. Matson's at the University of Michigan. "I am an absolute evangelist about the value of failure as part of creativity," says Mr. Keywell, noting that Groupon took off after the failure of ThePoint. com, where people were to organize for collective action but instead organized discount group purchases. Dr. Matson taught him not just to be willing to fail but that failure is a critical avenue to a successful end. Because academics run from failure, Mr. Keywell says, universities are "way too often shapers of formulaic minds," and encourage students to repeat and internalize fail-safe ideas.

Bonnie Cramond, director of the Torrance Center for Creativity and Talent Development at the University of Georgia, is another believer in taking bold risks, which she calls a competitive necessity. Her center added an interdisciplinary graduate certificate in creativity and innovation this year. "The new people who will be creative will sit at the juxtaposition of two or more fields," she says. When ideas from different fields collide, Dr. Cramond says, fresh ones are generated. She cites an undergraduate class that teams engineering and art students to, say, reimagine the use of public spaces. Basic creativity tools used at the Torrance Center include thinking by analogy, looking for and making patterns, playing, literally, to encourage ideas, and learning to abstract problems to their essence.

In Dr. Burnett's Introduction to Creative Studies survey course, students explore definitions of creativity, characteristics of creative people and strategies to enhance their own creativity. These include rephrasing problems as questions, learning not to instinctively shoot down a new idea (first find three positives), and categorizing problems as needing a solution that requires either action, planning or invention. A key objective is to get students to look around with fresh eyes and be curious. The inventive process, she says, starts with "How might you . . ."

Dr. Burnett is an energetic instructor with a sense of humor—she tested Mr. Cathcart's martial arts padding with kung fu whacks. Near the end of last semester, she dumped Post-it pads (the department uses 400 a semester) onto a classroom desk with instructions: On pale yellow ones, jot down what you learned; on rainbow colored pads, share how you will use this learning. She then sent students off in groups with orders that were a litany of brainstorming basics: "Defer judgment! Strive for quantity! Wild and unusual! Build on others' ideas!"

As students scribbled and stuck, the takeaways were more than academic. "I will be optimistic," read one. "I will look at tasks differently," said another. And, "I can generate more ideas."

Asked to elaborate, students talked about confidence and adaptability. "A lot of people can't deal with things they don't know and they panic. I can deal with that more now," said Rony Parmar, a computer information systems major with Dr. Dre's Beats headphones circling his neck.

Mr. Cathcart added that, given tasks, "you think of other ways of solving the problem." For example, he streamlined the check-in and reshelving of DVDs at the library branch where he works.

The view of creativity as a practical skill that can be learned and applied in daily life is a 180-degree flip from the thinking that it requires a little magic: Throw yourself into a challenge, step back—pause—wait for brilliance to spout.

The point of creative studies, says Roger L. Firestien, a Buffalo State professor and author of several books on creativity, is to learn techniques "to make creativity happen instead of waiting for it to bubble up. A muse doesn't have to hit you."

Analyze

1. The article claims that though creativity was once considered part of an ethereal process called inspiration, "ability to spot problems and devise smart solutions—is being recast as a prized and teachable skill." In your opinion, how is "creativity" a teachable skill?
2. How is "creative thinking" different from "critical thinking"?
3. How is "creative thinking" different from "being imaginative"?
4. What is a "process skill"? How is the acquisition of a process skill different from the acquisition of a body of knowledge?

Explore

1. The article claims that universities encourage students to develop skills for which they already have an aptitude: university classes are "way too often shapers of formulaic minds," rewarding students with high grades for taking familiar subjects and punishing them with low grades for taking subjects in which they don't have much previous experience. If all college classes were ungraded—with students receiving full credit for a good faith effort on each assignment— what new or additional classes might you take that you would otherwise avoid?
2. The article suggests that creativity skills are particularly important at the intersection between two seemingly unrelated areas of study, such as engineering and visual arts. Why is creativity important in intersecting disciplines? The article also suggests that in the near future, many jobs will develop in interdisciplinary intersections. Do you agree?
3. SHORT WRITING PROMPT: Jack V. Matson, an environmental engineer at Penn State, suggests that there is value in failure. Relate a story in which you failed—and explore what you learned from the experience.
4. FULL WRITING PROMPT: Agree or disagree: your college should *require* all students to take one course in creative studies. This will add one course to your school's general education requirements and remove one course from free electives. What benefits do you believe students would receive from a course in creative studies? Is this benefit large enough to mandate that students take such a course as a general education requirement?

Rajat Bhageria
Should We Require Computer Science Classes?

Rajat Bhageria is an eighteen-year-old entrepreneur and engineer who is the author of *What High School Didn't Teach Me: A Recent Graduate's Perspective on How High School Is Killing Creativity*. He is also the inventor of ThirdEye, a Google Glass app that assists the sight impaired.

Computer science: most of us don't even know what it is. It may seem distant and even a bit threatening. What does it mean? How is it used? Indeed, most students—and even more adults—don't know anything about computer science. There are so many misconceptions that too many people are afraid to even *try* it.

Moreover, since computer science is a relatively recent field—at least compared to chemistry, English or history—administrators high in the schooling hierarchy are not willing to substitute it for a subject that has existed for some time and *works*. But it is precisely because we live in this modern world that this recent subject is so incredibly important; most everything around us was in some sense affected by code, and yet most of us cannot even write a simple program that calculates how much gas we use in a year.

Now, there is no doubt that some colleges do require all students to take one CS class. The problem: not enough do. This scenario is especially nonsensical considering that CS teaches problem solving like no other—even theoretical math and physics courses. Why? Computer science is all about finding the easiest way to do something—the method that is most efficient and requires the least lines of code.

So, let's say I want to create a program for my theoretical t-shirt business that tracks profits. It seems pretty easy, right? Find revenue and then subtract costs. But something you may not have realized is how many unique routes a programmer may take to create a program that accomplishes this task. Unlike a paper-and-pencil logbook, programs are dynamic since there are always many different ways of accomplishing the same thing.

Nevertheless, some methods are more practical than others. This is the programmer's job. He or she must identify the "easiest" method to implement a particular assignment. And thus, programming is "difficult," mainly because it requires a programmer to think deeply about how to do a particular task, locating the most efficient and economical approach. Once the programmer has this "algorithm"—just a fancy term for a series of instructions the computer follows, kind of like a recipe—most of the hard work is done. Actually typing the code into the computer is a fairly simple task.

Unlike many of those math and physics courses, computer science is an extremely versatile tool. Indeed, you can use programming to enhance your lifestyle for almost any situation. Want to create a business? You'll need a website. Want to do college research? Many labs around the world use MATLAB to assist in creating accurate data-tables and graphs. Want to create video games like *Halo, Call of Duty* or *Mario Brothers*? Programming is a must.

Furthermore, in terms of numbers, CS pays off; computer science majors make on average $60,000 right out of college. That's second only to engineering (and even that by only $3,000) and is significantly higher than business (at $54,000), math and sciences (at $42,000), and humanities & social sciences (at $37,000).

But not enough students even know what computer science is because their schools don't teach it to everyone. And thus, schools are discarding tremendous opportunities for their students. So what's the solution? The basic response after weighing the enormous number of positives over the small number of negatives of CS is to give the green light: go ahead add more CS classes; require some CS for everyone. But here's the problem: finding enough qualified instructors willing to teach can be a challenge.

Still, there is a simple solution to this problem—a way to help a few instructors teach CS to large numbers of students. Indeed, precisely because of computer science and the Internet revolution, there is a plethora of online resources focused on computer programming—many of which are free. These websites (e.g., CodeAcademy.com, Code.org, and Treehouse) cover basic concepts, offer tests, and help students apply the concepts to practical projects.

These classes are revolutionary as they help students to learn outside a traditional classroom. In fact, an instructor is only necessary to ensure that students are *doing* the work; the website takes care of the rest. Once the students start working, the addictive nature of programming usually entices them to more deeply explore the topic. Indeed, there is almost no reason *not* to teach students how to program with so little negatives to bear.

Even a study hall supervisor with a minimal background in CS can easily convert a study hall into an Intro to Computer Programming through these programming websites.

More and more, the ability to independently run a business (a club, an organization, a non-profit, or a team) is significantly more important than having a formal education in terms of earning and then succeeding in a job. And in any of these cases, having a programming background—especially in creating websites—is almost imperative in today's fast-changing business culture.

Analyze

1. What level, if any, of computer programing should all students with a college education possess?
2. What core skills in a CS course—apart from understanding and writing code—might translate well to other disciplines? That is, how might the intellectual skills acquired in a CS course, such as problem solving and critical thinking, help students in other majors, even if those students won't write code for a living?
3. The author believes that colleges might employ study hall monitors to supervise students in a self-directed CS course, with much of the class content provided by free online tutorials. Do you believe that this would be an effective or meaningful method of college study?

Explore

1. The author feels that computer programing, a relatively recent field of study at most colleges, is essential for all college graduates. Are there other relatively new fields of study that, in your opinion, should be arranged as introductory courses required for all students?
2. The author is a college student himself, who is interested in improving education. In your opinion, what role should students play in shaping educational experiences—especially considering that professors are usually considered experts within their disciplines? Is student input likely to make a class easier or more challenging; more or less career-focused; more lecture-oriented or discussion-centered? What opportunities exist at your college for students to shape its educational environment?

3. FULL WRITING PROMPT: Agree or disagree: your college should *require* all students to take one course in computer science, with an emphasis on programming. This will add one course to your school's general education requirements and remove one course from free electives. What benefits do you believe students would receive from a course in computer science? Is this benefit large enough to mandate that students take such a course as a general education requirement?

Diana Divecha and Robin Stern
Why College Freshmen Need to Take Emotions 101

Diana Divecha is a developmental psychologist and research affiliate of the Yale Center for Emotional Intelligence. **Robin Stern** is a psychoanalyst and associate director of the Yale Center for Emotional Intelligence.

You've dropped your kid off at college. You may feel sad and nostalgic in spite of newfound freedom, or even that parenting as you know it is behind you. Your child, at the same time, has a new roommate—or two or three—has started classes, and has received grades on her first set of assignments. You exhale, believing that she's well on her way.

But mid-autumn, when students get their first real feedback on their academic performance, is when college counselors see the first big spike in anxiety. And in general, anxiety on college campuses is on the rise. Why? There's a lot more going on for students than buying books, writing papers, playing sports, and pledging fraternities and sororities.

In fact, many college students are struggling, even suffering.

College life for most freshmen is emotionally challenging. The security and comfort of old relationships are interrupted, bringing feelings of grief, or loss, or of being at sea—in spite of being surrounded by hundreds (often thousands) of new peers. In the context of those ruptures, the desire to connect can lead kids to make unsatisfying or poor choices, perhaps even socializing with people they don't really like. Some freshmen bring with them unresolved interpersonal difficulties from high school or family life, which complicates their adjustment.

On a deeper level, at college there are new and often unexpected challenges to their identity and sense of efficacy: Perhaps the freshman was a high performer with career plans in high school and is shocked by the lower grades in college; or maybe it is her first time out of her community and she can't find people like herself. Many students have financial pressures, leading them to take too many classes at once, or to take on an extra job, or even to skimp on meal plans, leaving them hungry. Rising inequality in an increasingly competitive economy has raised all the stakes.

A 2013 survey of 380 college counseling departments across the country shows that anxiety is the most common presenting problem in their offices, followed by depression and relationship problems. A quarter of students seen in counselors' offices are on psychotropic medications, and though American students are famously medicated more than students from other countries, it still signals a problem for individuals. And many counselors privately say that their students are surprisingly lonely. Karen Gee, a health educator at UC Berkeley said that on a single day, she saw six students who were painfully, tearfully lonely. "Many have suffered in silence due to the stigma of loneliness," she said.

A 2013 survey of over 123,000 students across 153 campuses confirmed that over half of students feel overwhelming anxiety, and about a third experience intense depression, sometime during the year. Almost a third report that their stress has been high enough at some point to interfere with their academics—lowering their grades on exams or courses or projects—and 44% say that academic or career issues have been traumatic or difficult to handle. The majority of college students don't get enough sleep, and half say that they've felt overwhelmed and exhausted, lonely or sad sometime during the year. Colleges often blame parents, but the problem is likely more systemic: American children rank 26th out of 29 developed countries on overall measures of well-being.

Colleges are trying to meet students' emotional needs, but efforts and resources vary. Many universities report upping their budgets, adding staff, increasing their outreach to students, and/or experimenting with innovative programs. This fall, Gee started a "friendliness" campaign at UC Berkeley to help students connect in healthy ways—and when one lonely freshman posted that he wanted to make friends, he received 180 "likes" and ten offers to "hang out." For those that do take advantage of counseling, the majority say it helps with academic difficulties. But data show that the reach is constrained: Counseling centers serve only about 10 percent of students on campus, and there is an inverse relationship between the size of the college and the ratio of mental health workers to students (in other words, larger campuses have proportionally fewer resources available). According to students, it's not unusual to experience long wait times (even two to three months) and inconsistent, insufficient meetings.

We can do better.

Students need real emotional skills. There is a large and growing body of research that suggests that the skills of emotional intelligence—the ability to reason with and about emotions to achieve goals—are correlated with positive outcomes across the entire age spectrum, from preschool through adulthood. Emotions affect learning, decision-making, creativity, relationships, and health, and people with more developed emotion skills do better. Among college students, skills of emotional intelligence are linked to engaging in fewer risky behaviors whereas self-esteem is not.

And, our research at the Yale Center for Emotional Intelligence with children in classrooms shows us that these abilities can be taught. In classrooms where children learn to recognize, understand, label, express, and regulate their emotions, they are rated as having a greater range of skills: they have better relationships and social skills and are more connected to each other and their teachers; they are better at managing conflict; they are more autonomous and show more leadership skills; and they perform better in academic subjects (it's easier to concentrate when they feel better).

Colleges would do well to go beyond the therapeutic model and integrate positive emotional skill-building into their orientations, their freshman seminars, and their dormitory lives. Pace University and McCaulay Honors College in New York City are already experimenting with this: Pace is incorporating a short course in emotion skills into their freshman seminar, and McCaulay purchased a mobile app for all of their freshmen to help them recognize their feelings, make decisions about how to regulate them, and track them over time. Many graduate schools are beginning to recognize that emotion skills are necessary to their students' future success. Our neighbor, the Yale School of Management, has incorporated into their program a standardized test of emotional intelligence and a mobile app that teaches emotional skills. Several medical schools have approached us for advice on how to incorporate emotional intelligence into their training of doctors.

When college students are aware of what they're feeling, they can make conscious decisions about how to manage those emotions, rather than escalate, act out, or medicate. When they identify emotional patterns and clearly see preceding triggers, they can reflect on how and with whom they spend that time and employ strategies to manage the things that "set them off." When students are anxious and pressured, they can use strategies to calm themselves and proceed on tasks with lowered anxiety. When they inevitably discover new aspects of themselves in college, e.g., sexual or religious or political orientations, they can share these discoveries with trusted family or friends so they don't feel alone in their journey. When they are more masterful at reading others' cues, they'll be better able to resolve interpersonal conflicts. They might not be able to solve the problem, but they can have empathy for the other person, de-escalate, and take care of themselves.

And what about parents?

Parenting is an ongoing renegotiation of the balance between expectations and supports, and parents can recognize that college kids need them in different ways from before. College personnel say that kids' confidence is undermined when parents intervene on their behalf. Instead, when a campus issue arises, it is better to be a coach from the sidelines and encourage kids to "work the system," seek out resources, and advocate for themselves. At the same time, kids need to draw on their attachments to parents—and research shows that in families where parents offer it, kids do better in the long run.

Of course, it can take real emotional skills to figure out how to best support a student who is growing and changing away from home. Parents can listen carefully for cues that a student may be struggling. Then parents can set the stage for a successful conversation by "putting on their own oxygen mask first"—that is, pausing, checking in with themselves, and regulating their own—possibly intense—emotions. Without that personal "check-in," strong feelings of parental anxiety, disappointment, or anger will likely interfere with clear thinking and the outcome of helping the student.

It's easy to think that once kids go off to college, they are fully-launched and independent adults who no longer need our help. But the needle on adulthood has inched up the age range since medieval times, when children were considered adults as soon as they could dress, feed and toilet themselves. These days, based on brain, psychological, and social development, the field of developmental science considers adulthood to begin at around age 25-30.

Of course parents already invest a lot in their children's education. But investing in their emotional lives by teaching real skills is an important foundation to their success and can yield great returns. While it certainly won't solve all of our kids' problems, we can certainly keep an intentional focus on teaching them skills that they will need to successfully negotiate their freshman experience . . . and every year of their lives.

Imagine trying to solve complex mathematical problems without the tools of algebra or calculus. Emotions are constantly at play—you're probably having some right now—but every day we ask our children, ourselves, and each other to solve complex emotional problems with few real tools. An ongoing education in emotions from preschool through college, based on the emerging field of emotion science, will go a long way toward equipping our youth for adulthood—and easing the journey along the way.

Analyze

1. How is the emotional experience of college different than that of high school?

2. Aside from grades, in your experience, what factors contribute to a heightened sense of anxiety for most students at your college?

3. Many students experience tremendous personal change during the first term of college—so much so that many first-year students see their "college identity" as distinct from their "high school identity." What elements of the college experience most strongly contribute to this change in identity?

4. Describe one activity or new service that your college could provide that would make students feel more connected to each other on your campus.

Explore

1. The article claims "the needle on adulthood has inched up the age range since medieval times." With this in mind, when do you believe

that college students are emotionally independent (though perhaps not financially independent) from their parents?

2. For whom is the college journey more difficult—assuming it's a journey *away* from home—students or their parents?

3. SHORT WRITING PROMPT: In an annotated list, name the top seven sources of anxiety for freshman/sophomore students at your college as you understand them.

4. FULL WRITING PROMPT: Agree or disagree: your college's orientation program should require a one-day seminar on emotional skills for all new students, even if this adds one day to the orientation program.

Rich Barlow
BU Mandates Online Alcohol Course for First-Year Students

Rich Barlow, a graduate of Dartmouth College and a former reporter for *The Boston Globe*, is a staff writer for *BU Today*.

More than a third (35 percent) of first-year BU students don't drink alcohol. But many students may not know that, misled by urban myth about universal, *Animal House* imbibing on college campuses.

This year, the University is requiring first-year students to take an online alcohol course to separate truthful wheat from mythic chaff, starting before they even arrive on campus.

Those students will receive log-in instructions midsummer for AlcoholEdu for College. The course includes two parts: the first, featuring educational material and surveys before and after the material is studied, takes between one and a half and two and a half hours to complete. (It needn't all be done in one sitting.) Part 2 is a third, 15-minute survey.

In recent years, the University has offered students another online survey, iHealth, to dispel misconceptions, but has not required it. The hope is that through the mandatory course, students will be more responsible about alcohol use.

"It is used by most of our peer institutions as a prevention-level intervention for first-year college students" to curb dangerous drinking, says Elizabeth Douglas, manager of wellness and prevention services at Student Health Services. "We are using AlcoholEdu because it has the capacity to track student completion, in addition to having evidence of its being an effective intervention."

That evidence comes from a three-year, 30-campus study that found reduced frequency of drinking, including binge drinking, and related problems among students who participated in AlcoholEdu, as compared with students who did not.

Part 1 must be completed before students arrive on campus for the academic year. They will be required to finish Part 2 sometime in October; the University will send them a reminder email. AlcoholEdu is designed to be taken by both drinkers and nondrinking students. The surveys and intersecting information touch on such topics as how many drinks are in a bottle of wine or beer, factors influencing whether people drink, exaggerated notions of heavy drinking on campuses, alcohol's effects on the body and mind, and tactics students can use to protect themselves and friends from harm in a variety of drinking situations.

The course also provides information for parents about discussions they should have with their children: about alcohol, about its possible effects on schoolwork, and about drinking laws. It asks their views on college alcohol policies, issues they deem important to discuss with their kids, and demographic information about their families.

The new program follows a drop in alcohol-related violations and hospital runs on campus last year, which officials attribute to their recent alcohol enforcement program, entering its third academic year this fall. That program features increased police patrols of known party neighborhoods, dispersing parties, issuing citations, and publishing fall's enforcement statistics on *BU Today*.

Meanwhile, a city ordinance allows Boston police to arrest landlords and tenants in so-called problem properties—rentals with four documented complaints of loud parties or alcohol violations.

Douglas says the University likely will use AlcoholEdu in coming years, since BU chooses responsible drinking programs "based on research and evidence of effectiveness."

Analyze

1. The article suggests that *Animal House*–style parties are a "myth" at many universities—that is, disorderly, drunken house parties are events that new students often associate with the college experience but rarely happen in real life. In your opinion, why are images of drunken house parties so closely associated with college life? Consider how movies, TV shows, books, and magazines might contribute to this myth.

2. Why do you think that Boston University (BU) requires students to complete part of the alcohol education program *before* arriving at college?

3. The AlcoholEdu program, according to the article, helps educate students on alcohol consumption (such as how many servings are in a bottle of wine) and the effects of alcohol use (such as the effects of alcohol on the body). How successful do you believe an online program would be on your campus in reducing problem drinking among students?

Explore

1. AlcoholEdu is an online program. On your campus, do you believe an online program (one that allows students to participate anonymously, without peer engagement) would be more or less effective than a face-to-face program (a student discussion group led by a counseling professional)? In what type of environment, private or semi-public, would students on your campus be more likely to participate honestly?

2. The BU program strongly advises parents to initiate discussions about alcohol use with their college-age children, even though these "children" are legal adults. In your opinion, what is the best role parents can play in their children's life when it comes to issues of drinking, sexual experimentation, and financial responsibility?

3. FULL WRITING PROMPT: Agree or disagree: your college should require a non-credit online alcohol education program for all incoming students.

Scott Carlson
When Colleges Abandon Phys Ed, What Else Is Lost?

Scott Carlson is a senior writer for *The Chronicle of Higher Education*, where he writes on college management, the cost of higher education, and sustainability.

It's warm-up time at 7:45 a.m., with sunlight just starting to stream into a mat room in the kinesiology building at Los Angeles City College. A dozen students—most of them Latinas, all dressed in thick, white judo uniforms—stand at one end of the room, breathing hard, their hands over their heads or resting heavily on their hips. It's too early to be up, their faces say, and way too early to bear crawl, somersault, or drag yourself across the room using only your arms.

"Ready," comes a new command, "let's shrimp!" It's like a sit-up, combined with scooting butt-first along the mat. One young woman curses under her breath, while the rest bend to the floor in resignation. This is only the beginning: Later this morning, they will repeatedly toss one another to the ground, wrestle a partner into submission, or escape from a heavy pin.

Hayward Nishioka stands quietly on one side of the room, looking for signs of a transformation he has seen in scores of judo students at LACC. Most had almost no physical education leading up to college, he says, speculating that if they had known what his judo course entailed, they would have quit. Now, midway through the semester, he sees grit.

"By the time they get out of here, they'll be different people," says Mr. Nishioka, a professor emeritus of physical education at LACC. "Just this type of movement says to them: 'I can move, I can roll. I can also go against somebody. These people are trying really hard to try to beat me up, but I am able to survive this.'"

Decades ago, Mr. Nishioka used judo in his own bid to survive. It was an escape route from a rough East LA neighborhood, to travel the world as an international judo champion. After his competitive career was over, he spent 40 years here at LACC—eight years as chair of the physical-education department—helping students with backgrounds much like his own discover the vitality of their bodies, the connection of that body to the mind, and the new confidence, character, and life lessons that might come from a little soreness and sweat.

"We are physical creatures, first and foremost," he says. "Everything we do in education is about improving the brain. But how do we improve the brain? Through our physical acts. Our physical senses are our antennae."

Mr. Nishioka's focus on the body runs counter to prevailing trends, from kindergarten through college, where recess and physical education have been given up in favor of more sit-down classroom time. Although colleges have built lots of swanky recreation centers in recent years, studies indicate that college physical-education requirements are at an all-time low. Meanwhile, researchers have seen alarming trends among the college-aged population: significant rates of obesity, hypertension, depression, anxiety.

Paradoxically, colleges are cutting back on physical education just as a growing body of research indicates that regular physical activity is key to cognitive development and helps people focus, process information faster, and remember things more easily. John J. Ratey, an associate clinical professor of psychiatry at Harvard Medical School, has called exercise "Miracle-Gro for the brain."

Bradley J. Cardinal, a professor of public health and human sciences at Oregon State University, has researched the decline of physical education at colleges. "There is definitely a point of irony with schools saying we want to focus on academics, so we are going to cut back on physical activity or physical education," he says. "We do research showing the benefits of physical activity, and the federal government funds this stuff, and we don't use it."

Moreover, Mr. Nishioka, reaching back to the idealistic founders of judo, says physical educators are losing the opportunity to teach life lessons that go beyond fitness and health. The field or the judo mat, for example, can be a place to learn about loyalty, resolve, or courage in the face of sure defeat—a lesson rarely conveyed so effectively in a classroom. "Physical education should be more about teaching values, morals, losing with honor, friendship," he says. "Even physical educators these days don't think about these things."

Mr. Nishioka made his fame through combat on the judo mat, and he seems to have spent his whole life fighting. He was born in 1942 to a single mother and never knew his father, whom he suspects was a criminal. He spent the first few years of his life in a Japanese internment camp before returning to East LA, where he was always in one scrap or another. Kids would hunt him down after school and call him a "Jap."

"That was a war cry," he says. They'd gang up on him. But the young Nishioka adhered to a Japanese principle of *kataki-uchi,* or blood revenge. He would follow kids home from school or go looking for them at their houses, when they'd be alone, and he'd give a licking right back.

When he was about 12, Dan Oka, the man who would become Mr. Nishioka's stepfather, took the boy to watch a judo contest. "I was taken by their throws and flying through the air," he says. "When we got back to the house, I said, 'What's that like? I want to try that.'" Mr. Oka put an old army jacket on the boy, grabbed him by the collar, and tossed him onto the wood floor several times. Despite the bumps and bruises, Mr. Nishioka was hooked.

Judo is a Japanese form of wrestling. Two fighters try to hurl each other to the mat. A perfect throw, landing a player flat on his back, will end the match. An imperfect throw might bring the fight to the ground, where the fighters try to pin their opponents or make them submit using stranglehold or potentially bone-breaking armlocks.

Compared with street fighting, Mr. Nishioka says, judo seemed easy. It had rules—and beauty in turning an opponent's force into a sailing throw. But Mr. Nishioka went out on the mat with the same primal instinct for survival he'd carried to the streets. From 1965 to 1970, he won three national championships and a gold medal in the Pan-American Games. Judo took him around the world—on a goodwill tour of Europe with teammates like Ben Nighthorse Campbell, who would later become a U.S. senator, and to Japan, where he studied with Shigeru Egami, a legendary karate instructor.

As his competitive career waned in the 1970s, he began teaching judo at Los Angeles City College. It was a transition that put Mr. Nishioka more firmly on a path set by judo's founder, Jigoro Kano.

Kano, who studied philosophy and economics under Western professors, was a director in Japan's Ministry of Education and is now considered the country's "father of physical education." Trained in samurai jiujitsu from his teenage years in the 1870s to early adulthood, Kano was strongly influenced by the philosopher Herbert Spencer, who described the ideal education as one that blends mind, morals, and body. In 1908,

Kano's judo, a recreational form of jiujitsu, became a requirement in Japanese schools.

John Stevens, a former professor of Buddhist studies at Tohoku Fukushi University who wrote a biography of Kano, says the ideal person of the samurai era—which lasted into Kano's childhood—was a physical force on the battlefield as well as an accomplished statesman, poet, or philosopher. After the Meiji Restoration, "scholarly people became kind of wimpy," Mr. Stevens says. "When Kano was teaching high school, he was appalled at how weak the students were—a lot of them had servants that would carry their books to class." When Kano visited the legislature, he would stop officials and tell them they looked ill and should exercise more.

"You cannot be a well-rounded person if you don't know your body, or be confident, or be aware of your surroundings—all of those things you get from judo training." Mr. Stevens says. "Ideally, that's what he wanted."

At the grade-school level in the United States, parents and teachers have lamented how schools have shortened recess and gym classes to make room for written exercises and testing. After-school entertainment, meanwhile, has become more sedentary: gaming, surfing the Internet, texting friends. That has led to what some physical educators call a "pipeline problem" for college PE programs.

"A lot of these students were not physically active as kids," says Jared A. Russell, an associate professor of kinesiology at Auburn University. "We have students coming to campus who have never swung a tennis racket or a baseball bat, or who can't swim at all."

The trend among grade-school physical-education programs has been seen in college programs, too. Mr. Cardinal, of Oregon State, was a co-author of a 2012 study showing that among 354 institutions, fewer than 40 percent had maintained any physical-education requirement, down from 67 percent in 1993 and 87 percent in 1968. Public institutions were more likely than private ones to have dropped the requirement.

Mr. Cardinal points to several possible explanations. For one, physical-education departments might be politically weaker than other departments on campus, and lose ground as administrators shift more resources and emphasis to science, math, and other academic subjects. PE programs are also professionalizing—as they rebrand under the more scientifically oriented "kinesiology," the departments focus more on sending students into health fields like physical therapy or nutrition, and less on "service" courses like swimming or basketball.

The departments' facilities have also, to some extent on campuses across the country, been replaced by opulent recreation centers. Administrators look at those rec centers and wonder why they need to spend money on physical-education departments.

Some of those factors seem to have gone into a decision earlier this year at the University of Notre Dame to eliminate the physical-education department and requirements to take two PE courses and pass a swimming test. Next year the requirements will be replaced by two courses that spend more time on university orientation, community standards, strategies for academic success, and spiritual life, as well as helping students set goals for physical activity.

Hugh R. Page Jr., dean of the First Year of Studies program, says the new courses are "placing a greater degree of the onus for wellness on the shoulders of individual students" by encouraging them to take "ownership of their physical well-being." Notre Dame, he says, is not diminishing its emphasis on physical activity. He points out that three-quarters of the students played on varsity teams in high school and will play some intramural, club, or intercollegiate sport during their time at the university. "You don't necessarily have to require students to take a volleyball course or a tennis course to generate their involvement" in physical activity, he says.

It's a different story at Los Angeles City College. As chair of the PE department, Mr. Nishioka spent the past several years fighting for more prominence for physical education, only to see administrators cut the square footage of a new kinesiology building by half. When Mr. Nishioka started at LACC, in the 1970s, students were required to take one PE class every semester; today they're required to take only one during their time at the college.

And over the years, the "pipeline problem" in Los Angeles has become just as challenging as in any other city. In 2013, student advocates sued 37 California school districts for not providing the physical-education hours mandated by state law. Some critics have highlighted the condition of PE at the Los Angeles Unified School District as particularly egregious. Studies found that 25 to 40 percent of students from the district were obese, and 75 percent failed state fitness standards.

Under pressure to jam more math, reading, social studies, and science into each semester with fewer resources, schools and colleges have found room by cutting back on exercise time. "All of my research flies in the face of that, and that is actually contrary and counterproductive to normal growth and development," says Darla M. Castelli, an associate professor of physical-education pedagogy at the University of Texas at Austin, who studies the connection between exercise and brain health.

Her studies and others show that regular exercise allows people to process information more accurately, allocate more working memory to a given task, and improve attention span—even among people in their cognitive peak years, from age 21 to 27.

There are several competing theories to explain those effects: Aerobic activity might help oxygenate the brain through increased blood flow, stimulating the growth of new brain cells or helping to maintain neuroplasticity, or the connection of synapses. Physical activity might also activate the production of "brain-derived neurotropic factor," or BDNF, a protein that stimulates the growth of the hippocampal region, which is responsible for memory.

Ms. Castelli says one study suggests that people get cognitive benefits from coordinated movements—as in, say, dance, where a person has to work off of and respond to a partner. And there are new theories that active people can build up a cognitive "reserve" that will stave off decline as they head into their 30s and beyond.

Unfortunately, her studies of people in the peak college years show nearly 50 percent with signs of cardiometabolic risk factors, like high glucose or high blood-lipid levels. "They're at risk and they don't even know it, and they're largely inactive," she says. Most believe that they are getting all the exercise they need by walking to class.

There is an ancient ideal that goes beyond brain or bodily health: The classroom instructs in one way, but the field, judo mat, and dance floor hold other invaluable lessons, especially as educators emphasize the importance of collaboration. Mr. Cardinal often discusses the topic with his wife, who teaches dance at Western Oregon University: Dance harnesses creativity in the moment, working in space and time to challenge an individual in a whole new way—to say nothing of the courage it takes to cut loose in front of an audience.

Or he mentions times when he has seen groups of colleagues take on a ropes course: There, the person who is a leader in the office or classroom often becomes a follower. "And someone who is not typically the leader now has to be in the leadership position," he says, "and people see him in a new light."

That is what Kano intended when he created judo, more than 100 years ago. Old samurai fighting techniques, through a marriage of mind and body, would teach principles that people could use everywhere. "Judo began with the study of martial arts, and then it gradually became clear that it could be applied to physical education, intellectual training, moral education, social interaction, management, and people's everyday lives," Kano wrote. "It is wrong to assume that judo ends in the dojo."

At judo practice in Los Angeles, as tangled bodies roll on the ground, it's clear that the close contact, aggression, pain—and, occasionally, the unexpectedly graceful throws—push some students to discover things about themselves. For Marilyn Hernandez, who is studying biochemistry, the class was her first experience with a contact sport. "I really fell in love with it," she says. Every tussle on the mat gave her lessons in improvisation and determination, and she lost 30 pounds to boot. "You have to say, I can do this. You are the person who is going to win. It's mental." She dreams of transferring to San Jose State University, which has a top-ranked judo team.

Sintia Diaz, who is studying early-childhood education, has decided that she wants to become a professional fighter, and she was thrilled to land in a class led by a martial-arts luminary. She's tiny, about five feet tall and slight. Yet she's a pit bull—walking up to men a foot taller than her and challenging them to fight. She says she once lacked self-esteem, in part because of her size. "Judo gave me a totally different perspective about myself," she says. Now if she makes a mistake or fails at something, she shrugs it off. "It's about how did I grow, or what did I learn? It's crazy to take a class for a few months and feel totally empowered. I had never felt that before."

Mr. Nishioka observes all of this from the sidelines or while walking through the grappling bodies, stopping now and then to adjust a pin or a cranking arm. At the end of the class, he tells the students to encircle the mat, and he reminds them why they are here. "What is judo about? Is it just technique?" he prods. No. "Small judo" is just the throws and pins and how they work.

"But 'large judo' is taking the techniques and concepts and applying them to your everyday lives," he says. To meet a challenge, to do the impossible, to have courage. "This is one of the few activities at City College that will teach you about bravery," he says, gesturing to the mat, "because you have to be brave to get out here."

Analyze

1. What role, if any, should your college play in combating obesity and promoting physical well-being in its students?

2. The article suggests that physical education classes might offer students a unique learning experience (promoting values, morals, honor, and friendship) that are more difficult to acquire in traditional "sit-down" classes. Aside from activity skills (such as how to throw a football or how to swim freestyle), what lessons, in your opinion, might be best learned in a physical education class?

3. The article claims that at many colleges the responsibility of physical education has shifted from the school (through required PE classes) to the individual (through voluntary participation at a student gym or activity center). In your opinion, are the majority of college students mature enough to take full responsibility for their physical well-being by the age of 18?

Explore

1. The article takes the position that colleges should participate in a student's moral education—an education that exceeds academic exploration, technical training, and career preparation. In your opinion, what is a college's obligation to help develop a student's sense of morals and values?

2. Most colleges cap programs of study at 120 semester credit hours or 180 quarter credit hours for a bachelor's degree—or half of that for an associate's degree. Adding one required class often means removing a different requirement—or reducing free electives. Most colleges revise their general education requirements every few years. Assuming you wish to add three or four units of physical activity to the general education requirements of your college, what three- or four-unit current requirement (or free electives) would you remove?

3. FULL WRITING PROMPT: Agree or disagree: your college should increase the number of required physical education classes, a decision that will lower the number of free electives available to students.

Forging Connections

1. Writers in this section take note of ways that college can change to serve both professional goals and personal development. Laura Pappano and Rajat Bhageria, respectively, recommend courses in creativity and coding (professional skills), while Scott Carlson advocates for physical education (personal development). Beyond those courses discussed in this chapter, name one class not currently required at your college that you believe all students should take for career readiness in the twenty-first century. Also identify one course, not currently required, that all students should take for personal development. Be prepared to discuss your rationale.

2. With required courses on emotional health and drinking, some colleges are taking on a parental role, particularly with freshmen and sophomores. Explore your campus to find examples of paternalism in how the college relates to younger students—that is, how it guides students toward responsible, respectful, and moral behavior, a duty that was once centered inside the family. Do you believe that paternalism within a college setting is helpful or detrimental to students?

Looking Further

1. The author of "When Colleges Abandon Phys Ed, What Else Is Lost?" suggests that American colleges have relinquished physical activities "in favor of more sit-down classroom time." That is, colleges place a premium on sedentary activities, such as reading, writing, and studying. Through this, colleges increase the value of the mind and decrease the value of the body. Do you believe that this is a positive trend, to so heavily privilege mental development for four years? Has college, with its emphasis on learning as opposed to doing, changed how we think about the human experience in general, to place a higher premium on mental activity than physical activity?

2. The article "Learning to Think Outside the Box" suggests that creativity—once thought to be the domain of genius and inspiration—can to some extent be a teachable process skill. What other areas, once thought to be the domain of genius and inspiration, might someday be offered as a class?

5 The Greek System

Perhaps the oldest Greek-letter organization in the United States was Phi Beta Kappa, founded in 1776, a few months after America declared its independence from England. Though there were earlier social clubs at American universities, Phi Beta Kappa was likely the first Greek organization. Its goals, like those of later fraternities and sororities, were centered on friendships, charitable pursuits, and a desire to expand from its founding university (the College of William and Mary) to other institutions, such as Yale and Harvard. Unlike contemporary fraternities and sororities, Phi Beta Kappa saw itself as a political and literary organization, with gatherings held to discuss American principles of self-rule, taxation, and national autonomy.

Fraternities and sororities today are largely social and residential organizations for college students. Fraternities and sororities offer students a sense of belonging, often centered around a chapter house where many members live. They may engage in philanthropic or civic events, such as raising money for a local charity; they may establish GPA minimums to ensure its members graduate on time; they may offer classes in safe alcohol practices, but they are still largely known for their party culture, an image established by the movie *Animal House*. In recent years fraternities in particular have fallen under public scrutiny for fostering a culture of sexism, racism, binge drinking, and hazing, which occasionally leads to a student death.

In this chapter, you'll explore the pros and cons of fraternity and sorority life. Caitlin Flanagan offers a deeply researched exposé on the culture of fraternities—a culture so troubling that the editors of Bloomberg News called for an outright ban of the Greek organizations. Peter Jacobs, a recent graduate, explains the positive values he sees in fraternity culture, claiming that "joining a fraternity was one of the best decisions" he has made as an adult. Lastly, Risa C. Doherty explores the actual cost—both in terms of money and time—of joining a sorority.

Though most college administrations have a love/hate relationship with Greek houses—they love how Greek alums tend to support their college after graduating, yet they hate the problems caused by party culture—many students see the Greek experience as central to their college years. In these articles, you'll confront both the advantages and troubles for those who pledge themselves to a fraternity or sorority.

Caitlin Flanagan
The Dark Power of Fraternities

Caitlin Flanagan is a regular contributor to *The Atlantic* and a former staff writer for *The New Yorker*. She holds an MA in art history from the University of Virginia and is the author of the book *To Hell with All That: Loving and Loathing Our Inner Housewife*.

One warm spring night in 2011, a young man named Travis Hughes stood on the back deck of the Alpha Tau Omega fraternity house at Marshall University, in West Virginia, and was struck by what seemed to him—under the influence of powerful inebriants, not least among them the clear ether of youth itself—to be an excellent idea: he would shove a bottle rocket up his ass and blast it into the sweet night air. And perhaps it *was* an excellent idea. What was not an excellent idea, however, was to misjudge the relative tightness of a 20-year-old sphincter and the propulsive reliability of a 20-cent bottle rocket. What followed ignition was not the bright report of a successful blastoff, but the muffled thud of fire in the hole.

Also on the deck, and also in the thrall of the night's pleasures, was one Louis Helmburg III, an education major and ace benchwarmer for the Thundering Herd baseball team. His response to the proposed launch was the obvious one: he reportedly whipped out his cellphone to record it on video, which would turn out to be yet another of the night's seemingly excellent but ultimately misguided ideas. When the bottle rocket exploded in Hughes's rectum, Helmburg was seized by the kind of battlefield panic that has claimed brave men from outfits far more illustrious than even the Thundering Herd. Terrified, he staggered away from the human bomb and fell off the deck.

Fortunately for him, and adding to the Chaplinesque aspect of the night's miseries, the deck was no more than four feet off the ground, but such was the urgency of his escape that he managed to get himself wedged between the structure and an air-conditioning unit, sustaining injuries that would require medical attention, cut short his baseball season, and—in the fullness of time—pit him against the mighty forces of the Alpha Tau Omega national organization, which had been waiting for him.

It takes a certain kind of personal-injury lawyer to look at the facts of this glittering night and wrest from them a plausible plaintiff and defendant, unless it were possible for Travis Hughes to be sued by his own anus. But the fraternity lawsuit is a lucrative mini-segment of the personal-injury business, and if ever there was a deck that ought to have had a railing, it was the one that served as a nighttime think tank and party-idea testing ground for the brain trust of the Theta Omicron Chapter of Alpha Tau Omega and its honored guests—including these two knuckleheads, who didn't even belong to the fraternity. Moreover, the building codes of Huntington, West Virginia, are unambiguous on the necessity of railings on elevated decks.

Whether Helmburg stumbled in reaction to an exploding party guest or to the Second Coming of Jesus Christ is immaterial; there should have been a railing to catch him.

And so it was that Louis Helmburg III joined forces with Timothy P. Rosinsky, Esq., a slip-and-fall lawyer from Huntington who had experience also with dog-bite, DUI, car-repossession, and drug cases. The events of that night, laid out in Helmburg's complaint, suggested a relatively straight-forward lawsuit. But the suit would turn out to have its own repeated fail-ures to launch and unintended collateral damage, and it would include an ever-widening and desperate search for potential defendants willing to foot the modest bill for Helmburg's documented injuries. Sending a lawyer without special expertise in wrangling with fraternities to sue one of them is like sending a Boy Scout to sort out the unpleasantness in Afghanistan. Who knows? The kid could get lucky. But it never hurts—preparedness and all that—to send him off with a body bag.

College fraternities—by which term of art I refer to the formerly all-white, now nominally integrated men's "general" or "social" fraternities, and not the several other types of fraternities on American campuses (reli-gious, ethnic, academic)—are as old, almost, as the republic. In a sense, they are older: they emanated in part from the Freemasons, of which George Washington himself was a member. When arguments are made in their favor, they are arguments in defense of a foundational experience for mil-lions of American young men, and of a system that helped build American higher education as we know it. Fraternities also provide their members with matchless leadership training. While the system has produced its share of poets, aesthetes, and Henry James scholars, it is far more famous for its success in the powerhouse fraternity fields of business, law, and politics. An astonishing number of CEOs of *Fortune* 500 companies, congressmen and male senators, and American presidents have belonged to fraternities. Many more thousands of American men count their fraternal experience—and the friendships made within it—as among the most valuable in their lives. The organizations raise millions of dollars for worthy causes, contribute millions of hours in community service, and seek to steer young men toward lives of service and honorable action. They also have a long, dark history of violence against their own members and visitors to their houses, which makes them in many respects at odds with the core mission of college itself.

Lawsuits against fraternities are becoming a growing matter of public interest, in part because they record such lurid events, some of them ludicrous, many more of them horrendous. For every butt bomb, there's a complaint of manslaughter, rape, sexual torture, psychological trauma. A recent series of articles on fraternities by Bloomberg News's David Glovin and John Hechinger notes that since 2005, more than 60 people—the majority of them students—have died in incidents linked to fraternities, a sobering number in itself, but one that is dwarfed by the numbers of serious injuries, assaults, and sexual crimes that regularly take place in these houses. Many people believe that violent hazing is the most dangerous event associated with fraternity life, but hazing causes a relatively small percentage of these injuries. Because of a variety of forces, all this harm—and the behaviors that lead to it—has lately been moving out of the shadows of private disciplinary hearings and silent suffering, and into the bright light of civil lawsuits, giving us a clear picture of some of the more forbidding truths about fraternity life. While many of these suits never make it to trial, disappearing into confidential settlements (as did that of Louis Helmburg III, nearly two years after he filed his lawsuit) or melting away once plaintiffs recognize the powerful and monolithic forces they are up against, the narratives they leave behind in their complaints—all of them matters of public record—comprise a rich and potent testimony to the kinds of experiences regularly taking place on college campuses. Tellingly, the material facts of these complaints are rarely in dispute; what is contested, most often, is only liability.

I have spent most of the past year looking deeply into the questions posed by these lawsuits, and more generally into the particular nature of fraternity life on the modern American campus. Much of what I found challenged my beliefs about the system, assumptions that I came to see as grossly outdated, not because the nature of fraternity life has changed so much, but rather because life at the contemporary university has gone through such a profound transformation in the past quarter century. I found that the ways in which the system exerts its power—and maintains its longevity—in the face of the many potentially antagonistic priorities in contemporary higher education commanded my grudging respect. Fraternity tradition at its most essential is rooted in a set of old, deeply American, morally unassailable convictions, some of which—such as a young man's right to the freedom of association—emanate from the Constitution itself. In contrast, much of the policy governing college campuses today is rooted in the loose soil of a set of political and social fashions that change with the season, and that tend not to hold up to any kind of penetrating challenge.

And this is why—to answer the vexing question "why don't colleges just get rid of their bad fraternities?"—the system, and its individual frats, have only grown in power and influence. Indeed, in many substantive ways, fraternities are now mightier than the colleges and universities that host them.

The entire multibillion-dollar, 2,000-campus American college system—with its armies of salaried professors, administrators, librarians, bursars, secretaries, admissions officers, alumni liaisons, development-office workers, coaches, groundskeepers, janitors, maintenance workers, psychologists, nurses, trainers, technology-support staffers, residence-life personnel, cafeteria workers, diversity-compliance officers, the whole shebang—depends overwhelmingly for its very existence on one resource: an ever-renewing supply of fee-paying undergraduates. It could never attract hundreds of thousands of them each year—many of them woefully unprepared for the experience, a staggering number (some 40 percent) destined never to get a degree, more than 60 percent of them saddled with student loans that they very well may carry with them to their deathbeds—if the experience were not accurately marketed as a blast. They show up on campus lugging enormous Bed Bath & Beyond bags crammed with "essentials," and with new laptop computers, on which they will surf Facebook and Tumblr while some coot down at the lectern bangs on about Maslow's hierarchy and tries to make his PowerPoint slides appear right side up. Many of these consumer goods have been purchased with money from the very student loans that will haunt them for so long, but no matter: it's college; any cost can be justified. The kids arrive eager to hurl themselves upon the pasta bars and the climbing walls, to splash into the 12-person Jacuzzis and lounge around the outdoor fire pits, all of which have been constructed in a blatant effort to woo them away from competitors. They swipe prepaid cards in dormitory vending machines to acquire whatever tanning wipes or ear-buds or condoms or lube or energy drinks the occasion seems to require. And every moment of the experience is sweetened by the general understanding that with each kegger and rager, each lazy afternoon spent snoozing on the quad (a forgotten highlighter slowly drying out on the open pages of *Introduction to Economics*, a Coke Zero sweating beside it), they are actively engaged in the most significant act of self-improvement available to an American young person: college!

That all of this fun is somehow as essential as the education itself—is somehow part of a benevolent and ultimately edifying process of "growing up"—is one of the main reasons so many parents who are themselves in rocky financial shape will make economically ruinous decisions to support a four-year-residential-college experience for their children. There are many thousands of American undergraduates whose economic futures (and those of their parents) would be far brighter if they knocked off some of their general-education requirements online, or at the local community college—for pennies on the dollar—before entering the Weimar Republic of traditional-college pricing. But college education, like weddings and funerals, tends to prompt irrational financial decision making, and so here we are. Add another pesto flavor to the pasta bar, Dean Roland! We just lost another kid to online ed!

That pursuing a bachelor's degree might be something other than a deeply ascetic and generally miserable experience was once a preposterous idea. American colleges came into being with the express purpose of training young men for the ministry, a preparation that was marked by a chilly round of early risings, Greek and Latin recitations, religious study, and strict discipline meted out by a dour faculty—along with expectations of both temperance and chastity. Hardly conditions that would augur the current trillion-dollar student-loan balloon that hovers over us like a pre-ignition *Hindenburg*. But sexual frustration and homiletics would not last forever as the hallmarks of American college life.

In 1825, at Union College, in upstate New York (hardly a garden of earthly delights in the best of circumstances, but surely a gulag experience for those stuck at Union; imagine studying Thessalonians in the ass-cracking cold of a Schenectady February), a small group of young men came up with a creative act of rebellion against the fun-busters who had them down: the formation of a secret club, which they grandly named the Kappa Alpha Society. Word of the group spread, and a new kind of college institution was founded, and with it a brand-new notion: that going to college could include some pleasure. It was the American age of societies, and this new type fit right in. As Nicholas Syrett observes in his excellent history of white men's college fraternities, *The Company He Keeps*, these early fraternities were in every way a measure of their time. They combined the secret handshakes and passwords of small boys' clubs; the symbols and rituals of Freemasonry; the new national interest in Greek, as opposed to Roman, culture as a model for an emerging citizenry; and the popularity of literary societies, elements of which—oratory, recitation, and the presentation of essays—the early fraternities included. Fraternities also gave young college men a way of behaving and of thinking about themselves that quickly took on surprisingly modern dimensions. An 1857 letter that a Sigma Phi member named Jenkins Holland sent to one of his fraternity brothers suggests the new system was already hitting full stride: "I did get one of the nicest pieces of ass some day or two ago."

From the very beginning, fraternities were loathed by the grown-ups running colleges, who tried to banish them. But independence from overbearing faculties—existing on a plane beyond the reach of discipline—was, in large measure, the point of fraternity membership; far from fearing the opprobrium of their knock-kneed overlords, the young men relished and even courted it. When colleges tried to shut them down, fraternities asserted that any threat to men's membership in the clubs constituted an infringement of their right to freedom of association. It was, at best, a legally delicate argument, but it was a symbolically potent one, and it has withstood through the years. The powerful and well-funded political-action committee that represents fraternities in Washington has fought successfully to ensure that freedom-of-association language is included in all higher-education reauthorization legislation, thus "disallowing public Universities the ability to ban fraternities."

Perhaps the best testament to the deep power of fraternities is how quickly and widely they spread. Soon after Gold Rush money began flowing into the newly established state of California—giving rise to the improbable idea of building a great American university on the shores of the Pacific Ocean—fraternity men staked their own claim: a campus in Berkeley had existed barely a year before the brothers of Phi Delta Theta arrived to initiate new members. The thing to remember about fraternities is that when Kappa Alpha was founded at Union, in all of the United States there were only 4,600 college students; fraternities exist as deeply in the groundwater of American higher education as religious study—and have retained a far greater presence in the lives of modern students.

In fairly short order, a paradox began to emerge, one that exists to this day. While the fraternities continued to exert their independence from the colleges with which they were affiliated, these same colleges started to develop an increasingly bedeviling kind of interdependence with the accursed societies. To begin with, the fraternities involved themselves very deeply in the business of student housing, which provided tremendous financial savings to their host institutions, and allowed them to expand the number of students they could admit. Today, one in eight American students at four-year colleges lives in a Greek house, and a conservative estimate of the collective value of these houses across the country is $3 billion. Greek housing constitutes a troubling fact for college administrators (the majority of fraternity-related deaths occur in and around fraternity houses, over which the schools have limited and widely varying levels of operational oversight) and also a great boon to them (saving them untold millions of dollars in the construction and maintenance of campus-owned and -controlled dormitories).

Moreover, fraternities tie alumni to their colleges in a powerful and lucrative way. At least one study has affirmed what had long been assumed: that fraternity men tend to be generous to their alma maters. Furthermore, fraternities provide colleges with unlimited social programming of a kind that is highly attractive to legions of potential students, most of whom are not applying to ivy-covered rejection factories, but rather to vast public institutions and obscure private colleges that are desperate for students. When Mom is trying—against all better judgment—to persuade lackluster Joe Jr. to go to college, she gets a huge assist when she drives him over to State and he gets an eyeful of frat row. Joe Jr. may be slow to grasp even the most elemental concepts of math and English (his first two years of expensive college study will largely be spent in remediation of the subjects he should have learned, for free, in high school), but one look at the Fiji house and he gets the message: kids are getting laid here; kids are having fun. Maybe he ought to snuff out the joint and take a second look at that application Mom keeps pushing across the kitchen table.

Will he be in increased physical jeopardy if he joins one of these clubs? The fraternity industry says no. When confronted with evidence of student injury and death in their houses, fraternities claim they are no worse than any other campus group; that they have become "target defendants," prey to the avarice of tort lawyers excited by their many assets and extensive liability coverage. It is true that fraternity lawsuits tend to involve at least one, and often more, of the four horsemen of the student-life apocalypse, a set of factors that exist far beyond frat row and that are currently bringing college presidents to their knees. First and foremost of these is the binge-drinking epidemic, which anyone outside the problem has a hard time grasping as serious (everyone drinks in college!) and which anyone with knowledge of the current situation understands as a lurid and complicated disaster. The second is the issue of sexual assault of female undergraduates by their male peers, a subject of urgent importance but one that remains stubbornly difficult even to quantify, let alone rectify, although it absorbs huge amounts of student interest, outrage, institutional funding, and—increasingly—federal attention. The third is the growing pervasiveness of violent hazing on campus, an art form that reaches its apogee at fraternities, but that has lately spread to all sorts of student groups. And the fourth is the fact that Boomers, who in their own days destroyed the doctrine of *in loco parentis* so that they could party in blissful, unsupervised freedom, have grown up into the helicopter parents of today, holding fiercely to a pair of mutually exclusive desires: on the one hand that their kids get to experience the same unfettered personal freedoms of college that they remember so fondly, and on the other that the colleges work hard to protect the physical and emotional well-being of their precious children.

But it's impossible to examine particular types of campus calamity and not find that a large number of them cluster at fraternity houses. Surely they have cornered the market in injuries to the buttocks. The number of lawsuits that involve paddling gone wrong, or branding that necessitated skin grafts, or a particular variety of sexual torture reserved for hazing and best not described in the gentle pages of this magazine, is astounding. To say nothing of the University of Tennessee frat boy who got dropped off, insensate, at the university hospital's emergency room and was originally assumed to be the victim of a sexual assault, and only later turned out to have damaged his rectum by allegedly pumping wine into it through an enema hose, as had his pals.

Or, to turn away from the buttocks, as surely a good number of fraternity men would be well advised to do, consider another type of fraternity injury: the tendency of brothers and their guests to get liquored up and fall off—or out of—the damn houses is a story in itself.

The campuses of Washington State University and the University of Idaho are located some eight miles apart in the vast agricultural region of the Northwest known as the Palouse. It was at the latter institution that the 19-year-old sophomore and newly minted Delta Delta Delta pledge Amanda Andaverde arrived in August of 2009, although she had scarcely moved into the Tri Delta house and registered for classes before she was at the center of events that would leave her with brain damage and cast her as the plaintiff in a major lawsuit filed on her behalf by her devastated parents.

It would have been an unremarkable Wednesday evening—focused on the kind of partying and hooking up that are frequent pleasures of modern sorority women—save for its hideous end. Andaverde and her sorority sisters began the night at Sigma Chi, where the "sorority ladies" drank alcohol and spent the evening with "dates" they had been assigned during a party game. (The language of Andaverde's legal complaint often seems couched in a combination of '50s lingo and polite euphemism, intended perhaps to preclude a conservative Idaho jury from making moralistic judgments about the plaintiff's behavior.) The charms of Andaverde's assigned date ran thin, apparently, because close to midnight, she left him and made her way over to the Sigma Alpha Epsilon house, where she quickly ended up on the third-floor sleeping porch.

Many fraternity houses, especially older ones, have sleeping porches—sometimes called "cold airs" or "rack rooms"—typically located on the top floor of the buildings' gable ends. They are large rooms filled with bunks, some of which are stacked in triple tiers, and their large windows are often left open, even in the coldest months. Many fraternity members have exceedingly fond memories of their time on the porches, which they view—like so many fraternity traditions—as a simultaneously vexing and bonding experience. Although these group sleeping arrangements were once considered an impediment to a young man's sex life, the hookup culture, in which privacy is no longer a requirement of sexual activity, has changed that, and the sleeping-porch experience is once again coming into favor. For a variety of reasons, sleeping porches feature in a number of lawsuits, pointing to an astonishing fact: despite fraternity houses' position as de facto residence halls for so many American college students, safety features are decidedly spotty; about half of them don't even have fire sprinklers.

According to the complaint, shortly after arriving at SAE, Andaverde ran into a friend of hers, and he took her up to the sleeping porch, where he introduced her to a pal of his named Joseph Cody Cook. Andaverde and Cook talked, then climbed into Cook's bunk, where the two began kissing. It is at this point that the language of the suit finally frees itself of euphemism and reveals the fearsome power of the unambiguous, declarative sentence: "Amanda rolled onto her shoulder toward the exterior wall, and suddenly, quickly, and unexpectedly dropped off Cook's mattress into the open exterior window, falling from the third-floor 'sleeping porch' to the cement approximately 25 feet below."

The injuries were devastating and included permanent brain injury. Andaverde was airlifted to a trauma center in Seattle, where she remained for many weeks; in the early days of her care, it seemed she might not survive.

Eventually, however, she improved enough to leave the hospital and was transferred to a series of rehabilitation centers, where she spent many months learning to regain basic functions. Police, interviewed about the case, defended themselves the way police departments in college towns all over the country reasonably defend themselves when accused of not preventing a fraternity-house disaster: "We just can't send undercover people into private houses or private parties," said David Duke, the Moscow, Idaho, assistant chief of police.

Local news outlets covered Andaverde's plight widely and sympathetically, although the optimism with which her "miraculous" recovery was celebrated was perhaps exaggerated. A television news report dedicated to that miracle revealed a young woman who, while she had escaped death, had clearly been grievously injured. As the reporter interviewed her mother, Andaverde sat in a wheelchair. When her hands were not propped on a black lap tray latched to the chair, she struggled to grasp a crayon and run it across the pages of a children's coloring book, or to place the six large pieces of a simple puzzle—square, triangle, circle—into their spaces. She eventually improved from this desperate state—learning to walk and dress herself—but she was a far cry from the student of veterinary medicine she had once been.

The local inclinations to see a badly injured college student as a figure deserving of community support, and to view even a limited recovery as evidence of the goodness of God, are not unaligned with regional preferences for self-reliance and for taking responsibility for one's own actions, however dire the consequences. The inevitable court case—in which the Andaverde family named not only SAE and Tri Delta as defendants, but also the University of Idaho and the Idaho State Board of Education—was dismissed on summary judgment because there was no dispute that Andaverde fell out of an open window, and because there was no evidence of an inherently dangerous condition in the house: that the window was open was obvious to anyone who walked into the room. The court determined that no other person or institution had a duty to protect Amanda from the actions and decisions—the decision to drink alcohol, as a minor; the decision to climb into a bunk bed; the impulse to roll over—that led to her accident.

Andaverde's case seemed to me to be an isolated tragedy, until I sent away to the Latah County courthouse for a copy of the complaint and discovered within it this sentence: "Amanda's fall was the second fall of a student from an upper-story fraternity house window at the University of Idaho within approximately a two-week period." This struck me as an astonishing coincidence. I looked into the matter and found that, indeed, a 20-year-old man named Shane Meyer had fallen from the third-floor window of the Delta Tau Delta house just 12 days before Andaverde's fall from SAE; not surprisingly, the police reported that "alcohol may have been a factor." He, too, had been airlifted to Seattle, and incredibly, the two fought for their lives in the same critical-care unit at Harborview Medical Center. I became intrigued by this kind of injury and began to do some more checking into the subject. I discovered that two months *after* Andaverde's fall, a 20-year-old student at Washington State—"quite intoxicated," in the laconic assessment of a local cop—pitched forward and fell from a third-floor window of Alpha Kappa Lambda, escaping serious injury when his fall was broken by an SUV parked below. That these three events were not greeted on either campus by any kind of clamoring sense of urgency—that they were, rather, met with a resigned sort of "here we go again" attitude by campus administrators and with what appeared to be the pro forma appointment of an investigative task force—sparked my interest, and so it was that I entered the bizarre world of falls from fraternity houses, which, far from being freakish and unpredictable events, are in fact fairly regular occurrences across the country.

During the 2012–13 school year on the Palouse—where students from the two campuses often share apartments and attend parties at each other's schools—the falls continued. In September, a student suffered serious injuries after falling off the roof of the Alpha Tau Omega house at the University of Idaho, and two days later a Washington State student fell three stories from a window at Phi Kappa Tau. In November, a 19-year-old suffered critical head injuries when he fell backwards off a second-floor balcony at the Washington State Lambda Chi Alpha house, necessitating the surgical removal of part of his skull. In April, a University of Idaho student named Krysta Huft filed a suit against the Delta Chi fraternity, seeking damages for a broken pelvis resulting from a 2011 fall, which she claims was from the house's third-story sleeping porch onto a basketball court beneath it.

I decided to widen my search, and quickly discovered that this is not a phenomenon particular to the Northwest. Across the country, kids fall—disastrously—from the upper heights of fraternity houses with some regularity. They tumble from the open windows they are trying to urinate out of, slip off roofs, lose their grasp on drainpipes, misjudge the width of fire-escape landings. On February 25, 2012, a student at the University of California at Berkeley attempted to climb down the drainpipe of the Phi Gamma Delta house, fell, and suffered devastating injuries; on April 14 of the same year, a 21-year-old student at Gannon University, in Pennsylvania, died after a fall from the second-floor balcony of the Alpha Phi Delta house the night before; on May 13, a Cornell student was airlifted to a trauma center after falling from the fire escape at Delta Chi; on October 13, a student at James Madison University fell from the roof of the three-story Delta Chi house and was airlifted to the University of Virginia hospital; on December 1, a 19-year-old woman fell eight feet from the Sigma Alpha Mu house at Penn State.

This summer brought little relief. On July 13, a man fell more than 30 feet from a third-story window at the Theta Delta Chi house at the University of Washington and was transported to Harborview Medical Center (which must by now be developing a subspecialty in such injuries); that same day, a Dartmouth College employee, apparently having consumed LSD and marijuana, fell out of a second-story window of the Sigma Nu house and was seriously injured. On August 13, a student at the University of Oklahoma fell face-first off a balcony of the SAE house; the next day, a woman fell from a second-story fire escape at Phi Kappa Tau at Washington State University.

The current school year began, and still the falls continued. In September, a student at Washington State fell down a flight of stairs in the Delta Chi house and was rendered unconscious; a University of Minnesota student was hospitalized after falling off a second-floor balcony of the Phi Kappa Psi house; a Northwestern student was listed in critical condition after falling out of a third-floor window of the Phi Gamma Delta house; and an MIT student injured his head and genitals after falling through a skylight at the Phi Sigma Kappa house and landing some 40 feet below.

These falls, of course, are in addition to the many other kinds of havoc and tragedy associated with fraternities. On the Palouse, such incidents include the January 2013 death of 18-year-old Joseph Wiederrick, a University of Idaho freshman who had made the dean's list his first semester, and who had plans to become an architect. He had attended a party at SAE (of which he was not a member) and then wandered, apparently drunk and lost, for five miles before freezing to death under a bridge. They also include the March 2013 conviction of Jesse M. Vierstra, who, while visiting Sigma Chi over the University of Idaho's homecoming weekend, raped an

18-year-old freshman in the bushes outside the house. (He is appealing the decision.)

The notion that fraternities are target defendants did not hold true in my investigation. College students can (and do) fall out of just about any kind of residence, of course. But during the period of time under consideration, serious falls from fraternity houses on the two Palouse campuses far outnumbered those from other types of student residences, including privately owned apartments occupied by students. I began to view Amanda Andaverde's situation in a new light. Why are so many colleges allowing students to live and party in such unsafe locations? And why do the lawsuits against fraternities for this kind of serious injury and death—so predictable and so preventable—have such a hard time getting traction? The answers lie in the recent history of fraternities and the colleges and universities that host them.

What all of these lawsuits ultimately concern is a crucially important question in higher education, one that legal scholars have been grappling with for the past half century. This question is perhaps most elegantly expressed in the subtitle of Robert D. Bickel and Peter F. Lake's authoritative 1999 book on the subject, *The Rights and Responsibilities of the Modern University: Who Assumes the Risks of College Life?*

The answer to this question has been steadily evolving ever since the 1960s, when dramatic changes took place on American campuses, changes that affected both a university's ability to control student behavior and the status of fraternities in the undergraduate firmament. During this period of student unrest, the fraternities—long the unquestioned leaders in the area of sabotaging or ignoring the patriarchal control of school administrators—became the exact opposite: representatives of the very status quo the new activists sought to overthrow. Suddenly their beer bashes and sorority mixers, their panty raids and obsession with the big game, seemed impossibly reactionary when compared with the mind-altering drugs being sampled in off-campus apartments where sexual liberation was being born and the Little Red Book proved, if nothing else, a fantastic coaster for a leaky bong.

American students sought to wrest themselves entirely from the disciplinary control of their colleges and universities, institutions that had historically operated *in loco parentis*, carefully monitoring the private behavior of undergraduates. The students of the new era wanted nothing to do with that infantilizing way of existence, and fought to rid themselves of the

various curfews, dorm mothers, demerit systems, and other modes of institutional oppression. If they were old enough to die in Vietnam, powerful
enough to overthrow a president, groovy enough to expand their minds
with LSD and free love, then they certainly didn't need their own colleges—
the very places where they were forming their radical, nation-changing
ideas—to treat them like teenyboppers in need of a sock hop and a chaper-
one. It was a turning point: American colleges began to regard their students not as dependents whose private lives they must shape and monitor,
but as adult consumers whose contract was solely for an education, not an
upbringing. The doctrine of *in loco parentis* was abolished at school after
school. Through it all, fraternities—for so long the repositories of the most
outrageous behavior—moldered, all but forgotten. Membership fell
sharply, fraternity houses slid into increasing states of disrepair, and hundreds of chapters closed.

Animal House, released in 1978, at once predicted and to no small extent
occasioned the roaring return of fraternity life that began in the early '80s
and that gave birth to today's vital Greek scene. The casting of John Belushi
was essential to the movie's influence: no one had greater credibility in the
post-'60s youth culture. If something as fundamentally reactionary as
fraternity membership was going to replace something as fundamentally
radical as student unrest, it would need to align itself with someone whose
bona fides among young, white, middle-class males were unassailable. In this
newly forming culture, the drugs and personal liberation of the '60s would
be paired with the self-serving materialism of the '80s, all of which made
partying for its own sake—and not as a philosophical adjunct to solving
some complicated problem in Southeast Asia—a righteous activity for the
pampered young collegian. Fraternity life was reborn with a vengeance.

It was an entirely new kind of student who arrived at the doors of those
great and crumbling mansions: at once deeply attracted to the ceremony
and formality of fraternity life and yet utterly transformed by the social
revolutions of the past decades. These new members and their countless
guests brought with them hard drugs, new and ever-developing sexual attitudes, and a stunningly high tolerance for squalor (never had middle- and
upper-middle-class American young people lived in such filth as did '60s
and '70s college kids who were intent on rejecting their parents' bourgeois
ways). Furthermore, in 1984 Congress passed the National Minimum
Drinking Age Act, with the ultimate result of raising the legal drinking age
to 21 in all 50 states. This change moved college partying away from bars

and college-sponsored events and toward private houses—an ideal situation for fraternities. When these advances were combined with the evergreen fraternity traditions of violent hazing and brawling among rival frats, the scene quickly became wildly dangerous.

Adult supervision was nowhere to be found. Colleges had little authority to intervene in what took place in the personal lives of its students visiting private property. Fraternities, eager to provide their members with the independence that is at the heart of the system—and responsive to members' wish for the same level of freedom that non-Greek students enjoyed—had largely gotten rid of the live-in resident advisers who had once provided some sort of check on the brothers. With these conditions in place, lawsuits began to pour in.

The mid-1980s were a treacherous time to be the defendant in a tort lawsuit. Personal-injury cases had undergone a long shift to the plaintiff's advantage; the theory of comparative negligence—by which an individual can acknowledge his or her own partial responsibility for an injury yet still recover damages from a defendant—had become the standard; the era of huge jury verdicts was at hand. Americans in vast numbers—motivated perhaps in part by the possibility of financial recompense, and in part by a new national impetus to move personal suffering from the sphere of private sorrow to that of public confession and complaint—began to sue those who had damaged them. Many fraternity lawsuits listed the relevant college or university among the defendants, a practice still common among less experienced plaintiff's attorneys. These institutions possess deep reservoirs of liability coverage, but students rarely recover significant funds from their schools. As Amanda Andaverde's attorneys discovered the hard way, a great deal of time and money can be spent seeking damages from institutions of higher learning, which can be protected by everything from sovereign immunity and damage caps (in the case of public universities), to their limited ability to monitor the private behavior of their students. But for the fraternities themselves, it was a far different story.

So recently and robustly brought back to life, the fraternities now faced the most serious threat to their existence they had ever experienced. A single lawsuit had the potential to devastate a fraternity. In 1985, a young man grievously injured in a Kappa Alpha–related accident reached a settlement with the fraternity that, over the course of his lifetime, could amount to some $21 million—a sum that caught the attention of everyone in the Greek world. Liability insurance became both ruinously expensive and increasingly difficult to obtain. The insurance industry ranked American fraternities as the sixth-worst insurance risk in the country—just ahead of toxic-waste-removal companies. "You guys are nuts," an insurance representative told a fraternity CEO in 1989, just before canceling the organization's coverage; "you can't operate like this much longer."

For fraternities to survive, they needed to do four separate but related things: take the task of acquiring insurance out of the hands of the local chapters and place it in the hands of the vast national organizations; develop procedures and policies that would transfer as much of their liability as possible to outside parties; find new and creative means of protecting their massive assets from juries; and—perhaps most important of all—find a way of indemnifying the national and local organizations from the dangerous and illegal behavior of some of their undergraduate members. The way fraternities accomplished all of this is the underlying story in the lawsuits they face, and it is something that few members—and, I would wager, even fewer parents of members—grasp completely, comprising a set of realities you should absolutely understand in detail if your son ever decides to join a fraternity.

Self-insurance was an obvious means for combating prohibitive insurance pricing and the widening reluctance to insure fraternities. In 1992, four fraternities created what was first called the Fraternity Risk Management Trust, a vast sum of money used for reinsurance. Today, 32 fraternities belong to this trust. In 2006, a group of seven other fraternities bought their own insurance broker, James R. Favor, which now insures many others. More important than self-insurance, however, was the development of a risk-management policy that would become—across these huge national outfits and their hundreds of individual chapters—the industry standard. This was accomplished by the creation of something called the Fraternal Information and Programming Group (FIPG), which in the mid-1980s developed a comprehensive risk-management policy for fraternities that is regularly updated. Currently 32 fraternities are members of the FIPG and adhere to this policy, or to their own even more rigorous versions. One fraternity expert told me that even non-FIPG frats have similar policies, many based in large measure on FIPG's, which is seen as something of a blueprint. In a certain sense, you may *think* you belong to Tau Kappa Epsilon or Sigma Nu or Delta Tau Delta—but if you find yourself a part of life-changing litigation involving one of those outfits, what you really belong to is FIPG, because its risk-management policy (and your adherence to or violation of it) will determine your fate far more than the vows you made during your initiation ritual—vows composed by long-dead men who had never even heard of the concept of fraternity insurance.

FIPG regularly produces a risk-management manual—the current version is 50 pages—that lays out a wide range of (optional) best practices. If the manual were *Anna Karenina*, alcohol policy would be its farming reform: the buzz-killing subplot that quickly reveals itself to be an authorial obsession. For good reason: the majority of all fraternity insurance claims involve booze—I have read hundreds of fraternity incident reports, not one of which describes an event where massive amounts of alcohol weren't part of the problem—and the need to manage or transfer risk presented by alcohol is perhaps the most important factor in protecting the system's longevity. Any plaintiff's attorney worth his salt knows how to use relevant social-host and dramshop laws against a fraternity; to avoid this kind of liability, the fraternity needs to establish that the young men being charged were not acting within the scope of their status as fraternity members. Once they violated their frat's alcohol policy, they parted company with the frat. It's a neat piece of logic: the very fact that a young man finds himself in need of insurance coverage is often grounds for denying it to him.

So: alcohol and the fraternity man. Despite everything you may think you know about life on frat row, there are actually only two FIPG-approved means of serving drinks at a frat party. The first is to hire a third-party vendor who will sell drinks and to whom some liability—most significant, that of checking whether drinkers are of legal age—will be transferred. The second and far more common is to have a BYO event, in which the liability for each bottle of alcohol resides solely in the person who brought it. If you think this is in any way a casual system, then you have never read either the FIPG risk-management manual or its sister publication, an essay written in the surrealist vein titled "Making Bring Your Own Beverage Events Happen."

The official BYO system is like something dreamed up by a committee of Soviet bureaucrats and Irish nuns. It begins with the composition—no fewer than 24 hours before the party—of a comprehensive guest list. This guest list does not serve the happy function of ensuring a perfect mix of types and temperaments at the festivity; rather, it limits attendance—and ensures that the frat is in possession of "a witness list in the event something does occur which may end up in court two or more years later." Provided a fraternity member—let's call him Larry—is older than 21 (which the great majority of members, like the great majority of all college students, are not), he is allowed to bring six (and no more) beers *or* four (and no more) wine coolers to the party. (FIPG's admiration for the wine-cooler four-pack suggests that at least some aspects of the foundational document—including its recommendation for throwing a *M*A*S*H*-themed party as recently as 2007—have not received much of an overhaul since its first edition, published in the mid-'80s.) Okay, so Larry brings a six-pack. The first stop, depending on which fraternity he belongs to: a "sober check point," at which he is subjected to an examination. Does he appear to have already consumed any alcohol? Is he in any way "known" to have done so? If he passes, he hands over his ID for inspection. Next he must do business with a "sober monitor." This person relieves him of the six-pack, hands him a ticket indicating the precise type of beer he brought, and ideally affixes a "non breakable except by cutting" wristband to his person; only then can Larry retrieve his beers, one at a time, for his own personal consumption. If any are left over at the end of the party, his fraternity will secure them until the next day, when Larry can be reunited with his unconsumed beers, unless his frat decided to "eliminate" them overnight. Weaknesses in the system include the fact that all of these people coming between Larry and his beer—the sober monitors and ID checkers and militarized barkeeps—are Larry's fraternity brothers, who are among his closest buddies and who have pledged him lifelong fealty during candlelit ceremonies rife with Masonic mumbo jumbo and the fluttering language of 19th-century romantic friendship. Note also that these policies make it possible for fraternities to be the one industry in the country in which every aspect of serving alcohol can be monitored and managed by people who are legally too young to drink it.

Clearly, a great number of fraternity members will, at some point in their undergraduate career, violate their frat's alcohol policy regarding the six beers—and just as clearly, the great majority will never face any legal consequences for doing so. But when the inevitable catastrophes do happen, that policy can come to seem more like a cynical hoax than a real-world solution to a serious problem. When something terrible takes place—a young man plummets from a roof, a young woman is assaulted, a fraternity brother is subjected to the kind of sexual sadism that appears all too often in fraternity lawsuits—any small violation of policy can leave fraternity members twisting in the wind. Consider the following scenario: Larry makes a small, human-size mistake one night. Instead of waiting for the slow drip of six warm beers, he brings a bottle of Maker's Mark to the party, and—in the spirit of not being a weirdo or a dick—he shares it, at one point pouring a couple of ounces into the passing Solo cup of a kid who's running on empty and asks him for a shot. Larry never sees the kid again that night—not many people do; he ends up drinking himself to death in an upstairs bedroom. In the sad fullness of time, the night's horror is turned into a lawsuit, in which Larry becomes a named defendant. Thanks in part to the guest/witness list, Larry can be cut loose, both from the expensive insurance he was required to help pay for (by dint of his dues) as a precondition of membership, and from any legal defense paid for by the organization. What will happen to Larry now?

Gentle reader, if you happen to have a son currently in a college fraternity, I would ask that you take several carbon dioxide–rich deep breaths from a paper bag before reading the next paragraph. I'll assume you are sitting down. Ready?

"I've recovered millions and millions of dollars from homeowners' policies," a top fraternal plaintiff's attorney told me. For that is how many of the claims against boys who violate the strict policies are paid: from their parents' homeowners' insurance. As for the exorbitant cost of providing the young man with a legal defense for the civil case (in which, of course, there are no public defenders), that is money he and his parents are going to have to scramble to come up with, perhaps transforming the family home into an ATM to do it. The financial consequences of fraternity membership can be devastating, and they devolve not on the 18-year-old "man" but on his planning-for-retirement parents.

Like the six-beer policy, the Fraternal Information and Programming Group's chillingly comprehensive crisis-management plan was included in its manual for many years. But in 2013, the plan suddenly disappeared from its pages. When asked why this was so, Dave Westol, a longtime FIPG board member, said, "Member organizations prefer to establish their own procedures, and therefore the section has been eliminated." However, many fraternities continue to rely on the group's advice for in-house risk management, and it is well worth examining if you want to know what takes place in the hours following many fraternity disasters. As it is described in the two most recent editions that I was able to obtain (2003 and 2007), the plan serves a dual purpose, at once benevolent and mercenary. The benevolent part is accomplished by the clear directive that injured parties are to receive immediate medical attention, and that all fraternity brothers who come into contact with the relevant emergency workers are to be completely forthright about what has taken place. And the rest? The plans I obtained recommend six important steps:

1. In the midst of the horror, the chapter president takes immediate, commanding, and inspiring control of the situation: "In times of stress, leaders step forward."
2. A call is made to the fraternity's crisis hotline or the national headquarters, no matter the hour: "Someone will be available. They would much rather hear about a situation from you at 3:27 a.m. than receive an 8:01 a.m. telephone call from a reporter asking for a comment about 'The situation involving your chapter at _____.'"
3. The president closes the fraternity house to outsiders and summons all members back to the house: "Unorthodox situations call for unorthodox responses from leaders. Most situations occur at night. Therefore, be prepared to call a meeting of all members and all pledged members as soon as possible, even if that is at 3 a.m."
4. One member—who has already received extensive media training—is put in charge of all relations with the press, an entity fraternities view as biased and often unscrupulous. The appointed member should be prepared to present a concise, factual, and minimally alarming account of what took place. For example: "A new member was injured at a social event."
5. In the case of the death of a guest or a member, fraternity brothers do not attempt direct contact with the deceased's parents. This hideous task is to be left to the impersonal forces of the relevant professionals. (I know of one family who did not know their son was in any kind of trouble until—many hours after his death, and probably long after his fraternity brothers had initiated the crisis-management protocol—their home phone rang and the caller ID came up with the area code of their boy's college and a single word: coroner.) If the dead person was a fraternity member who lived in the house, his brothers should return any borrowed items to his room and temporarily relocate his roommate, if he had one. Members may offer to pack up his belongings, but "it is more likely the family will want to do this themselves." Several empty boxes might thoughtfully be left outside the room for this purpose.
6. Members sit tight until consultants from the national organization show up to take control of the situation and to walk them through the

next steps, which often include the completion of questionnaires explaining exactly what happened and one-on-one interviews with the fraternity representatives. The anxious brothers are reminded to be completely honest and forthcoming in these accounts, and to tell the folks from national absolutely everything they know so that the situation can be resolved in the best possible manner.

As you should by now be able to see very clearly, the interests of the national organization and the individual members cleave sharply as this crisis-management plan is followed. Those questionnaires and honest accounts—submitted gratefully to the grown-ups who have arrived, the brothers believe, to help them—may return to haunt many of the brothers, providing possible cause for separating them from the fraternity, dropping them from the fraternity's insurance, laying the blame on them as individuals and not on the fraternity as the sponsoring organization. Indeed, the young men who typically rush so gratefully into the open arms of the representatives from their beloved national—an outfit to which they have pledged eternal allegiance—would be far better served by not talking to them at all, by walking away from the chapter house as quickly as possible and calling a lawyer.

So here is the essential question: In the matter of these disasters, are fraternities acting in an ethical manner, requiring good behavior from their members and punishing them soundly for bad or even horrific decisions? Or are they keeping a cool distance from the mayhem, knowing full well that misbehavior occurs with regularity ("most events take place at night") and doing nothing about it until the inevitable tragedy occurs, at which point they cajole members into incriminating themselves via a crisis-management plan presented as being in their favor?

The opposing positions on this matter are held most forcefully and expressed most articulately by two men: Douglas Fierberg, the best plaintiff's attorney in the country when it comes to fraternity-related litigation, and Peter Smithhisler, the CEO of the North-American Interfraternity Conference, a trade organization representing 75 fraternities, among them all 32 members of the Fraternal Information and Programming Group. In a parallel universe, the two men would be not adversaries but powerful allies, for they have much in common: both are robust midwesterners in the flush of vital middle age and at the zenith of their professional powers; both possess more dark knowledge of college-student life and collegiate binge drinking than many, if not most, of the experts hired to study and quantify the phenomenon; both have built careers devoted to the lives and betterment of young people. But two roads diverged in the yellow wood, and here we are. One man is an avenger, a gun for hire, a person constitutionally ill-prepared to lose a fight; the other is a conciliator, a patient explainer, a man ever willing to lift the flap of his giant tent and welcome you inside. I have had long and wide-ranging conversations with both men, in which each put forth his perspective on the situation.

Fierberg is a man of obvious and deep intelligence, comfortable—in the way of alpha-male litigators—with sharply correcting a fuzzy thought; with using obscenities; with speaking derisively, even contemptuously, of opponents. He is also the man I would run to as though my hair were on fire if I ever found myself in a legal battle with a fraternity, and so should you. In a year of reporting this story, I have not spoken with anyone outside of the fraternity system who possesses a deeper understanding of its inner workings; its closely guarded procedures and money trails; and the legal theories it has developed over the past three decades to protect itself, often very successfully, from lawsuits. Fierberg speaks frequently and openly with the press, and because of this—and because of the reticence of senior members of the fraternity system to speak at length with meddlesome journalists—the media often reflect his attitude.

For all these reasons, Fierberg is generally loathed by people at the top of the fraternity world, who see him as a money-hungry lawyer who has chosen to chase their particular ambulance, and whose professed zeal for reforming the industry is a sham: what he wants is his share of huge damages, not systemic changes that would cut off the money flow. But in my experience of him, this is simply not the case. Sure, he has built a lucrative practice. But he is clearly passionate about his cause and the plight of the kids—some of them horribly injured, others dead—who comprise his caseload, along with their shattered parents.

"Until proven otherwise," Fierberg told me in April of fraternities, "they all are very risky organizations for young people to be involved in." He maintains that fraternities "are part of an industry that has tremendous risk and a tremendous history of rape, serious injury, and death, and the vast majority share common risk-management policies that are fundamentally flawed. Most of them are awash in alcohol. And most if not all of them are bereft of any meaningful adult supervision." As for the risk-management policies themselves: "They are primarily designed to take the nationals' fingerprints off the injury and deaths, and I don't believe that they offer any meaningful provisions." The fraternity system, he argues, is "the largest industry in this country directly involved in the provision of alcohol to underage people." The crisis-management plans reveal that in "the *foreseeable future*" there may be "the death or serious injury" of a healthy young person at a fraternity function.

And then there is Peter Smithhisler, who is the senior fraternity man *ne plus ultra*: unfailingly, sometimes elaborately courteous; careful in his choice of words; unflappable; and as unlikely to interrupt or drop the f-bomb on a respectful female journalist as he would be to join the Communist Party. He is the kind of man you would want on your side in a tough spot, the kind of man you would want mentoring your son through the challenging passage from late adolescence to young manhood. He believes that the fraternity experience at its best constitutes an appeal to a young man's better angels: through service, leadership training, and accountability for mistakes, a brother can learn the valuable lessons he will need to become "a better dad, a better teacher, a better engineer, a better pilot, a better 'insert career here.'" Spend some time talking with Pete Smithhisler, and you can go from refusing to allow your son to join a fraternity to demanding he do so. Indeed, the day after I talked with him, I happened to be at a social gathering where I met two women whose sons had just graduated from college. "The fraternity was what saved him," one mother said with great feeling. Her son had waited until sophomore year to rush, and freshman year he had been so lonely and unsure of himself that she had become deeply worried about him. But everything changed after he pledged. He had friends; he was happy. When he'd had to have some surgery while at school, his brothers had visited him almost around the clock, bringing him food, keeping up his spirits, checking in with his doctors and charming his nurses. "If only I could have gotten my son to join one," the other mom said, wistfully. "I kept trying, but he wouldn't do it." Why had she wished he'd pledged a fraternity? "He would have been so much more connected to the college," she said. "He would have had so many other opportunities."

Smithhisler was honest about the fact that he is at the helm of an outfit that supports organizations in which young people can come to terrible fates. "I wrestle with it," he said, with evident feeling. His belief is that what's tarnishing the reputation of the fraternities is the bad behavior of a very few members, who ignore all the risk-management training that is requisite for membership, who flout policies that could not be any more clear, and who are shocked when the response from the home office is not to help them cover their asses but to ensure that—perhaps for the first time in their lives—they are held 100 percent accountable for their actions. And neither the fraternities nor the insurance company are hiding their warnings that a member could lose his coverage if he does anything outside of the policy. It's front and center in any discussion of a frat's alcohol policies; if you don't follow the policy or if you do anything illegal, you could lose your insurance.

One way you become a man, Smithhisler suggests, is by taking responsibility for your own mistakes, no matter how small or how large they might be. If a young man wants to join a fraternity to gain extensive drinking experience, he's making a very bad choice. "A policy is a policy is a policy," he said of the six-beer rule: either follow it, get out of the fraternity, or prepare to face the consequences if you get caught. Unspoken but inherent in this larger philosophy is the idea that it is in a young man's nature to court danger and to behave in a foolhardy manner; the fraternity experience is intended to help tame the baser passions, to channel protean energies into productive endeavors such as service, sport, and career preparation.

In a sense, Fierberg, Smithhisler, and the powerful forces they each represent operate as a check and balance on the system. Personal-injury lawsuits bring the hated media attention and potential financial losses that motivate fraternities to improve. It would be a neat, almost a perfect, system, if the people wandering into it were not young, healthy college students with everything to lose.

If you want an object lesson in how all of this actually works—how fraternities exert their power over colleges, how college and university presidents can be reluctant to move unilaterally against dangerous fraternities, and how students can meet terrible fates as a result—there can be no better example than the $10 million Title IX lawsuit filed against Wesleyan University and the Beta Theta Pi fraternity. The plaintiff was a young woman who had been assaulted in the house, and who—in one of the bizarre twists so common to fraternity litigation—ended up being blamed by the university for her own assault.

Wesleyan University, in Middletown, Connecticut, is undergoing the kind of institutional transformation that our relentless fixation on *U.S. News & World Report* rankings has wrought for a number of colleges and universities in the past three decades. As great as its faculty may be—and it has included, over the years, some of the most renowned scholars in the world—it is the undergraduate population itself that constitutes its most impressive resource. Wesleyan is one of those places that has by now become so hard to get into that the mere fact of attendance is testament, in most cases, to a level of high-school preparation—combined with sheer academic ability—that exists among students at only a handful of top colleges in this country and that is almost without historical precedent. Wesleyan is a school with a large number of aspiring artists—many of whom took, and aced, AP Calculus as 11th-graders.

Still, what the university is perhaps most broadly famous for is its progressive politics, manifest in any number of actions, from the hiring of five Muslim chaplains in the years since 9/11; to the use of the gender-neutral pronouns *ze* and *hir* in the campus newspaper; to the creation of a Diversity Education Facilitation Program. *The Princeton Review*, among other publications, has named Wesleyan America's most politically active campus, an encomium that appears on the university's Web site.

Given these sensibilities, Wesleyan might not seem the type of institution likely to have a typical fraternity scene, but as we have observed, fraternities are older than political correctness. There are three all-male residential frats at Wesleyan, all founded in the 19th century and occupying a row of large houses on High Street; over the years, they have counted some of the university's most accomplished and loyal alumni among their members. If you raise the topic of fraternity alumni with a college president in a private moment, he or she will emit the weary sigh of the ancients. The group includes some of the most financially generous and institutionally helpful former students a school may have. But try to do some small thing to bring the contemporary fraternity scene in line with current campus priorities, and you will hear from them—loudly—before you even hit send on the e-mail.

By 2005, Wesleyan had taken such an action: it had pressured all three fraternities to offer residence, although not membership, to female students, if they wanted to be part of university-approved Program Housing. Wesleyan has a rare requirement. All undergraduates, barring those few who receive special allowances, must live either in dorms or in Program Housing. Integrating affinity group housing had lately been on the mind of the administration; recent lack of student interest in living in the Malcolm X House, for example, had ultimately led to that residence's becoming racially integrated, a charged and in many respects unpopular administration decision. But there was no shortage of fraternity brothers wishing to live in their houses—nor were the houses owned by the university or located on university property, as the Malcolm X House was. Predictably, and perhaps not irrationally, many in the Greek community viewed this new edict as antagonistic toward their way of life.

Two of the fraternities nonetheless agreed to the new directive, retaining access to the buffet of advantages offered to frats that maintain an official relationship with their host universities. Alone among the group, Beta Theta Pi hewed to the oldest of fraternity values: independence. It refused to admit women residents, and thus forfeited its official recognition by the university. Strangely, however, Beta was able to have its cake and eat it too: its members continued to live and party in the house much as they previously had, renting dorm rooms on campus but living at the fraternity, with the full knowledge of the university. This put Wesleyan in a difficult spot; the house remained a popular location for undergraduate revelry, yet the school's private security force, Public Safety (or PSafe), had lost its authority to monitor behavior there. Meanwhile, fraternity alumni registered their disapproval of the new housing policy in time-honored fashion: "I will reluctantly shift my Wesleyan contributions to the Beta house, to do my part to provide students with the opportunities I was afforded during my time at Wesleyan," wrote a Beta alum from the class of 1964 to the university's then-president, Douglas Bennet. (Due to the potential for the appearance of a conflict of interest, James Bennet, Douglas Bennet's son and the editor in chief of *The Atlantic*, was recused from involvement with this piece.)

What followed was a long, strained period in which Beta brothers— among them a large percentage of the school's lacrosse team—ran an increasingly wild house. In turn, the administration became increasingly concerned about what was happening there, and through back channels began pressuring the fraternity to rejoin Program Housing. But the brothers didn't budge, and reports of dangerous activity—including assaults, burglaries, extreme drinking, and at least two car accidents linked to the house—mounted. Wesleyan had a powerful weapon at its disposal: at any time, it could have ordered the brothers to live in the dorm rooms they had paid for, consistent with the university's housing policy. But for whatever reason, it was loath to do so.

Why wouldn't the university act unilaterally to solve this problem? The answer may involve the deep power that fraternities exert over their host universities and the complex mix of institutional priorities in which fraternities are important stakeholders. Chief among them, typically, is fundraising. Shortly after the university tightened the housing policy for its fraternities, a new president, Michael Roth, was inaugurated. He came to Wesleyan—his own alma mater, where he had served as the president of his fraternity, Alpha Delta Phi—with an audacious goal: doubling the university's endowment. A man of prodigious personal, intellectual, and administrative talents, with a powerful love of Wesleyan, he was uniquely suited to this grand vision. But no sooner had he taken office than the world economy crashed, dragging down the Wesleyan endowment with it. The endowment was slowly recouping its losses when the university's odd and secretive chief investment officer and vice president of investments was abruptly fired and then sued for allegedly profiting from his position—the kind of scandal that can make potential donors think twice before committing money to an institution. (He denied the charges; the case settled for an undisclosed amount in April 2012.) In this challenging fund-raising environment, taking decisive and punitive action against a fraternity would almost certainly come at a financial cost.

In February of 2010, the university tried a new tack: Wesleyan suddenly dropped the requirement for fraternities to house women. And yet still Beta refused to rejoin the fold and enter Program Housing. By March, the university at last took a decisive action. It sent a strongly worded e-mail to the entire Wesleyan community, including the parents of all undergraduates, warning students to stay away from the Beta house. The e-mail described "reports of illegal and unsafe behavior on the premises," although it specified only one such behavior, a relatively minor one: the overconsumption of alcohol, leading to hospital visits. This one example hardly matched the tone and language of the rest of the e-mail, which was alarming: "We advise all Wesleyan students to avoid the residence"; "our concern for the safety and well-being of Wesleyan students living at the residence or visiting the house has intensified"; "we remain deeply concerned about the safety of those students who choose to affiliate with the house or attend events there against our advice."

The university was entirely in the right to send this e-mail; it was an accurate report of a dangerous location. But many parents of Beta brothers were incensed—they felt that their sons had been unfairly maligned to a wide group of people by their own university. Thirty-seven Beta parents signed a letter of protest and sent it to Michael Roth. In it, the parents asked the university to "issue a clarification which retracts the unsupported statements." No such e-mail was sent—nor, in my view, should it have been. But that angry letter, sent by those outraged parents, was surely noted in the offices of the administration. The Beta brothers, meanwhile, had announced a plan to hire an off-duty Middletown cop to oversee their events, while continuing to deny PSafe access to their house. Roth was unsatisfied, saying, "The notion that Public Safety would have to get permission to enter a place where Wesleyan students, as Wesleyan students, are congregating is unacceptable."

The school year rolled on. Final exams came, and graduation, and then the students dispersed to their homes and internships and first jobs. Summer ripened into fall, and Wesleyan's newest students bid goodbye to their high-school selves, packed up their bags and crates, and—with excitement and anxiety—traveled to Middletown. Surely these youngest, least experienced, and most vulnerable of Wesleyan's students would be sent the important e-mail that the older ones and their parents had received about the dangerous and unaffiliated fraternity?

They were not. Yes, there undoubtedly would have been a cost to resending the e-mail: more angry Beta parents, fraternity discontent, pressure from Beta alumni and the national organization. But just as clearly, great good could have come from sending it; student safety was at risk. University trepidation and fraternity intransigence were about to produce a tort case. Its plaintiff: a young woman known to us as Jane Doe—18 years old, freshly arrived at Wesleyan from her home in Maryland, as eager as any other new student to experience the excitement of college life.

During Halloween weekend, Jane Doe got dressed up and went out with some of her friends to sample the student parties on and around campus. "I didn't have any alcohol to drink all night," she later told a police investigator in a sworn statement. "I usually don't drink, and I hang out with people who don't drink either." At the Beta house, she was "immediately spotted by this guy" who did not introduce himself but started dancing with her. "I was happy that someone was dancing with me," she told the policeman, "because I got all dressed up." The man she was dancing with would turn out not to be a Beta member or even a Wesleyan student at all. His name was John O'Neill, and he was the ne'er-do-well high-school-lacrosse teammate of one of the Beta brothers. O'Neill lived in his mother's basement and, according to a Yorktown, New York, police detective, had been arrested for selling pot out of an ice-cream truck earlier that year. That wild fraternity houses are often attractive party locations for unsavory characters is a grim reality. After O'Neill had danced with Jane Doe for about 30 minutes, half a dozen of his pals came over (dressed, as he was, in Halloween costumes consisting of old soccer uniforms) and asked him whether he wanted to smoke some pot upstairs. Jane agreed to go along, although she had no plans to smoke. The group arranged itself in a small bedroom, with Jane sitting next to O'Neill on a couch. He put his arm around her, which was fine with her, and she slipped off her shoes because her feet hurt.

The group then moved to a second room, where the men continued smoking. When the other men had finished smoking, they got up to leave, and Jane, too, stood up and began putting on her shoes, preparing to follow them out, but O'Neill closed the bedroom door and locked it. "What's up?" she asked. He began kissing her, which she at first submitted to, but then pulled away. "He probably thought that I wanted to hook up with him, but I didn't," she reported. She started for the door again, but he grabbed her by the shoulders and pushed her down onto the couch. "What are you doing?" she cried. "Stop it."

According to the victim's sworn statement, here's what happened next. O'Neill got on top of Jane, straddling her chest and shoulders so she couldn't move; pulled down his shorts; and shoved his penis into her mouth. She struggled, and bit his penis. He slapped her and called her a bitch. Then he pulled up her dress, yanked off her tights, and forced his penis into her vagina. "The more you try, the faster you are going to get out of here," he said, and covered her mouth with his hand so she couldn't scream for help. Some 10 minutes later, it was over. Jane pulled on her tights and ran downstairs and out of the fraternity house. On the street, hysterical, she ran into a male friend and asked him to walk her back to her dorm. Inside, she found a girlfriend who comforted her, staying nearby while she showered, giving her cookies, reading to her until she fell asleep. Following some spectacular bungling on Wesleyan's part (for instance, no one was at Health Services to help her, because it was a weekend), Jane went to the health center on Monday, then to two deans and eventually, after her parents and brother strongly encouraged her to do so, to the police. The criminal-justice system began its swift, efficient process, resulting in O'Neill's conviction. (He was initially charged with first-degree sexual assault and first-degree imprisonment, but eventually pleaded no contest to lesser charges of third-degree assault and first-degree imprisonment. He was sentenced to 15 months in prison.)

John O'Neill was not a member of Beta Theta Pi, but fraternities are no strangers to acts of violence committed in their houses by nonmembers. The fraternity followed the standard playbook, expressing sympathy for all victims of sexual assault and reasserting its zero-tolerance policy for such crimes. The brothers cooperated fully with the police and other authorities, which led to the capture of the criminal; and the actions of the individual assailant were forcefully asserted to have been in no way conducted under the auspices of the fraternity.

But back on campus, this level of coolheaded professionalism was nowhere to be seen. A second e-mail regarding Beta was sent out, this one attesting to *reports* (plural) of sexual assaults at the fraternity house "during recent parties"; noting that these reports "renewed our concern" expressed in the e-mail sent before Jane Doe's enrollment; and strongly encouraging students to stay away from the house. Next, Michael Roth issued an edict that he would come to regret: no Wesleyan student could so much as visit *any* private society lacking recognition by the university. His declaration was obviously intended to shut down Beta or bring it into the fold—but it did so in the same roundabout manner in which the university had been dealing with Beta all along. Its implications were unintentionally far-reaching, and Wesleyan students immediately protested it, holding "Free Beta" rallies; in one instance, a car full of young men shouted the slogan as Jane Doe walked miserably back to campus after visiting the police station. That student sympathies would array themselves so strongly on the side of a fraternity in whose chapter house a sexual assault had occurred, and so negligibly on the side of the young victim of that assault, was the kind of eccentric Wesleyan reaction that no one could have predicted.

Meanwhile, a nonprofit organization called FIRE, the Foundation for Individual Rights in Education, got involved, sending an open letter to President Roth informing him that his action posed a grave threat to Wesleyan students' right to the freedom of association, violated the university's own "Joint Statement on the Rights and Freedoms of Students," and might have consequences extending even to the local Elks Lodge and the Middletown Italian Society—hardly hives of Wesleyan undergraduate activity, but the organization had made its point.

The embattled president retrenched: he published a statement titled "Housing Policy and Threats to Student Freedom," in which he deemed his previous policy "just too broad," retracted most of it, and—in what has become a hallmark of his tenure—lavishly praised the student activism that it had engendered. "I want to thank the vocal Wesleyan undergraduates for reminding their president to be more careful in his use of language, and to be more attentive to student culture. Of course, I should have known this already, but hey, I try to keep learning."

Strictly speaking, the newest policy should not have ended the Free Beta protests, nor should it have assuaged activists' concern about threats to student freedom—because Roth also asserted in his statement that nothing had changed in regards to Beta: if the fraternity did not join Program Housing by the start of the next semester, the fraternity would be "off limits" to all students. Anyone who violated this rule would face "significant disciplinary action." It was high-handed treatment, it trampled on students' freedom of association, and it was entirely within Roth's rights. Wesleyan is a private university, and as such can establish requirements about students' private behavior essentially at the whim of the administration—the "Joint Statement on the Rights and Freedoms of Students" be damned. And it worked. The Free Beta protests ended, the fraternity agreed to rejoin Program Housing, student activism moved on to its next pressing target of opportunity, and the Beta brothers enjoyed a defrosting of their relationship with the university.

It turned out that in the heel of the hunt, with the situation at the Beta house becoming so out of control that the Middletown police department was aggressively investigating the alleged violent rape of a Wesleyan student, the university finally decided to act unilaterally against Beta, imposing a potentially unpopular decision that would surely go a long way toward improving student safety. Why hadn't it done so earlier? Why had it spent so many years in protracted, back-channel negotiations with the fraternity, in a pointless campaign to cajole it into voluntarily rejoining Program Housing, when it could have pulled the trigger on this effective solution at any time? And—most pressing of all—why had it taken the assault of a freshman to get the university to finally take decisive action?

All of these questions were perhaps most pressing to Jane Doe, who had not gone back home to Maryland to nurse her wounds in private. Justly outraged by what had happened to her, as well as by what she saw as her own university's complicity in it, she had joined forces with Douglas Fierberg, and together they built a case of formidable moral rightness.

Jane Doe filed a $10 million lawsuit in federal court against, in the main, Wesleyan and Beta Theta Pi, asserting that the events leading up to, including, and following Halloween weekend 2010 constituted a violation of the rights guaranteed her through Title IX legislation. It's hard to see how she wasn't right about this. She ended up withdrawing from a top university because that institution refused to take actions that could have prevented the assault, or, at the very least, to provide her with information she could have used to protect herself from it.

Wesleyan's affirmative defense—part of its answers to the lawsuit's complaint—was of a mien familiar to anyone with knowledge of how the civil litigation of rape cases unfolds. It was expedient, a shrewd legal strategy designed to protect the university from a guilty verdict and a huge settlement. It was also morally repugnant. Wesleyan's president has said the university is engaged in a "battle against sexual assault"; has averred—as recently as last April—that "survivors of assault must be supported in every way possible"; and has committed himself to ending the "epidemic" of sexual violence at Wesleyan. But here's how the university supported this particular survivor of sexual violence, who dared to stand up against the mighty force of Wesleyan with her claim of mistreatment: it blamed her for getting raped.

According to Wesleyan—courageous combatant in the "battle against sexual assault"—Jane Doe was responsible for her own rape because she was "not alert to situations that could be misinterpreted"; "did not remain in a public place [but rather went to a private room] with a person with whom she was unfamiliar"; "failed to make reasonable and proper use of her faculties and senses"; and failed "to exercise reasonable care for her own safety." I disagree. Jane Doe's sworn statement describes a series of sound actions taken toward the care of her own safety—including making the decision not to drink or use drugs, attempting to exit a room when she was about to be left alone in it with an unfamiliar man who had used drugs, and attempting to fight him off when he began attacking her. But she was physically restrained by a powerfully built man intent on assaulting her.

Surely there are many collegiate sexual encounters that fall into legally ambiguous territory; a number of Americans, among them reasonable people of good will, believe that "regretted sex" on the part of jilted coeds is as responsible for college "rape culture" as is male aggression. This is not one of those cases. This was a violent assault that occasioned a police investigation, an arrest, criminal charges, a conviction, and a jail sentence. To suggest—let alone to assert in federal court—that this event was the result of Jane Doe's negligence would be ugly if it were part of a rape case involving, say, the U.S. military. For it to be asserted on behalf of an American university against one of its own young students is even more astonishing. What it reveals is less Wesleyan's true attitude toward assault and its victims (surely there was distaste within the Wesleyan inner sanctum for the line of attack waged in the university's name against its former student) than the marshy ground of the progressive politics that underpins so much of the university's rhetoric. It's fine to announce a war against sexual violence—but, once the chips are down, it's quite another thing to write a $10 million check. Wesleyan's sexual-assault victims could be forgiven for assuming that, no matter what, their institution would never blame them for their attack. (Michael Roth and Wesleyan repeatedly declined to discuss the case, or anything related to this article, on the grounds that they did not want to comment on confidential matters pertaining to a lawsuit. Later, when *The Atlantic* sent President Roth an advance copy of the article a few days before publication, the university provided an official response. Douglas Fierberg, Jane Doe's attorney, also declined to talk about her case or anything relating to it, citing similar reasons.)

This January, after publishing a withering series of reports on fraternity malfeasance, the editors of Bloomberg.com published an editorial with a surprising headline: "Abolish Fraternities." It compared colleges and universities to companies, and fraternities to units that "don't fit into their business model, fail to yield an adequate return or cause reputational harm." The comparison was inexact, because colleges aren't businesses, and fraternities do not operate as divisions of a corporate structure helmed by institutions of higher learning. They are private societies, old and powerful, as deeply woven into the history of American higher education as nonreligious study. A college or university can choose, as Wesleyan did, to end its formal relationship with a troublesome fraternity, but—if that fiasco proves anything—keeping a fraternity at arm's length can be more devastating to a university and its students than keeping it in the fold.

Clearly, the contemporary fraternity world is beset by a series of deep problems, which its leadership is scrambling to address, often with mixed results. No sooner has a new "Men of Principle" or "True Gentlemen" campaign been rolled out—with attendant workshops, measurable goals, initiatives, and mission statements—than reports of a lurid disaster in some prominent or far-flung chapter undermine the whole thing. Clearly, too, there is a Grand Canyon–size chasm between the official risk-management policies of the fraternities and the way life is actually lived in countless dangerous chapters.

Articles like this one are a source of profound frustration to the fraternity industry, which believes itself deeply maligned by a malevolent press intent on describing the bad conduct of the few instead of the acceptable—sometimes exemplary—conduct of the many. But when healthy young college students are gravely injured or killed, it's newsworthy. When there is a common denominator among hundreds of such injuries and deaths, one that exists across all kinds of campuses, from private to public, prestigious to obscure, then it is more than newsworthy: it begins to approach a national scandal.

Universities often operate from a position of weakness when it comes to fraternities—for far too long, this is what happened with Wesleyan and Beta Theta Pi. The one force that may exert pressure on the fraternities to exact real change is the lawsuit. Plaintiffs have stories to tell that are so alarming, fraternities may, perhaps, be forced to do business differently because of them.

Perhaps.

Last spring, Wesleyan sent yet another e-mail about Beta Theta Pi to the student body. It reported that in the early-morning hours of April 7, a Wesleyan student contacted PSafe to report that she had been attacked at the Beta house. Interviewed by Wesleyan campus police, she reported that while she was at the house, an unknown male had knocked her to the floor, kicked and hit her, and then attempted to sexually assault her. During the assault, the suspect was distracted by a loud noise, and the young woman escaped. She was later treated at the Middletown hospital for several minor injuries.

In August, quietly and while students were away, Wesleyan and Beta Theta Pi settled with Jane Doe, who now attends college in another state.

Analyze

1. The college years are often considered a period of experimentation with alcohol and sexual experience, sometimes approaching aspects of hedonism. For previous generations, specifically those coming of age between 1900 and 1940, these same years have been years of

meaningful employment in which individuals begin families. What has changed in our culture so that these years are now considered the "party" years? Consider media influences, changing expectations for college, and levels of national wealth.

2. According to the article, one of the largest problems associated with fraternity life concerns drinking—such as over-drinking, binge drinking, and so forth. What are some practical ways that your university can reduce problems with alcohol both on and around campus?

3. The article asks the question "Who assumes the risks of college life?" In your opinion, how much responsibility should universities carry for drinking-related injuries and assaults that occur in university-affiliated fraternity and sorority houses, even if those houses are located off campus?

4. In your opinion, would universities provide a better experience to students with or without fraternities and sororities? How do fraternities and sororities contribute to (or detract from) the meaningful development of students between the ages of 18 and 23 years?

Explore

1. The article claims that "there is a common denominator among hundreds of such injuries and deaths, one that exists across all kinds of campuses, from private to public, prestigious to obscure," with that common denominator being fraternities. Do you agree that fraternity culture may lead to their parties being potentially more dangerous than other college-related events?

2. The article suggests that colleges may be unwilling to limit fraternity and sorority activities because Greek house members, after graduation, are often significant college supporters. What aspects of your college experience would—or would not—persuade you to financially support your alma mater after you graduate?

3. SHORT WRITING PROMPT: Propose ten improvements that would better tie fraternity and sorority life to the educational mission of your college.

4. FULL WRITING PROMPT: Agree or disagree—your college should remove fraternities and sororities from its official campus life. Consider the social, educational, intellectual, and financial implications of your position.

Editors of Bloomberg.com
Bloomberg: Ban Fraternities

During their periodic bouts of consultant-managed angst, U.S. companies are often encouraged to confront a single question: What business are we in? It's a process that might also benefit U.S. colleges and universities with fraternities.

Such self-examination can lead firms to scale back or abandon units that don't fit into their business model, fail to yield an adequate return or cause reputational harm. So: What is the business of an institution of higher learning? If your answer is to help young adults gain the knowledge and skills they need to prosper (or something close; this is a short essay question), then go to the head of the class.

The next question is: How do fraternities fit into that mission? As it turns out, the fraternities that dominate so much of collegiate social life are of dubious value.

University presidents and administrators don't even have to pay expensive consultants to reach this conclusion. They can just look at the data, both statistical and anecdotal: On balance, most campuses would be better off without fraternities.

Start with alcohol consumption. Although a majority of college students drink, abusive drinking is far more prevalent in fraternities. One study of 17,000 students at 140 four-year colleges found that almost 90 percent of fraternity house residents engage in binge drinking (five or more drinks at a time), compared with 45 percent for nonmembers. Binge drinking is associated with a host of ills, from neurological damage to assaults.

Alcohol abuse also plays a central role in one of the most corrosive aspects of fraternities: hazing of new members in initiation rituals that are often brutal and vile. Sadly, at least one student has died in hazing episodes in each of the past 43 years. Although it's unclear whether alcohol played a part in the death of a student at New York's Baruch College in November—the third hazing-related death last year—alcohol is often involved.

Hazing is illegal in 44 states, but the existing laws are largely ineffectual or treat hazing little more than jaywalking. A federal law that made serious hazing a felony offense might help deter this underreported scourge. It might also help college administrators overcome their reluctance to enforce bans on hazing for fear of offending alumni who threaten to withhold contributions. Unfortunately, fraternities have banded together to thwart the passage of national anti-hazing legislation in the past.

The anti-intellectualism that dominates so much of fraternity life—the frat-boy culture of spring-break lore and "Animal House"—also takes a toll on its members' academic performance. Even adjusting for differences in ability, age and other factors, fraternity members tend to have lower grades and underperform compared with their nonmember peers in tests of cognitive skills.

Fraternities also are at cross-purposes with the goal of promoting campus diversity. As a whole, they are more homogenous than the overall college student population.

University officials and fraternity alumni have long maintained that fraternities yield benefits, both for students and campus life, and that hazing is a rare and isolated event. The organizations, they say, help students adjust to life away from home, build camaraderie among members, and participate in volunteer and charitable work.

These benefits are undeniable, at least for some students some of the time. Two questions, however: Are students in fraternities more likely to get these benefits than those that aren't? And are there not other ways to encourage such behavior and fellowship?

At any rate, this much is clear: Too often, fraternities are at odds with the mission of a college or university. Focusing on that mission may be the best way for colleges and universities to see their way clear to the reform and, when necessary, abolition of campus fraternities.

Analyze

1. How do fraternities fit into a college's mission—assuming that its mission is to "help young adults gain the knowledge and skills they need to prosper?"

2. One study, cited by the article, found that "almost 90 percent of fraternity house residents engage in binge drinking," roughly double that of non-fraternity members. Explain this correlation: how, in your opinion, does living at a fraternity relate to substantially higher engagement with binge drinking?

3. The article claims that fraternities often inculcate a system of "anti-intellectualism" in its members that leads to "lower grades and [underperformance] compared with their nonmember peers in tests of cognitive skills." Do you agree with this claim?

Explore

1. Supporters of Greek life often claim that fraternity membership has social, civic, and charitable benefits. In your opinion, do these benefits adequately offset the potential dangers associated with fraternity life?

2. Greek letter houses have been enormously successful in creating a feeling of community for students living away from family. What other opportunities for a deep sense of community exist at your college?

3. SHORT WRITING PROMPT: The essay explores the importance of a college's mission statement in determining how it should conduct business. For a college, a mission statement defines the aims and values of the institution. In a writing assignment of no more than one page, create a "personal" mission statement for *your* college, defining those aspects central to its identity as an institution of higher learning as *you* understand them.

Peter Jacobs
I Still Think Joining a Fraternity Was One of the Best Decisions I've Ever Made

Peter Jacobs, a graduate of Cornell University, is currently a reporter at *Business Insider*, where he covers issues relating to education.

Disclosure: I was in a fraternity in college. **Further disclosure:** It was one of the best decisions I made in my four years on campus.

My second semester at Cornell University—where about a quarter of the campus is Greek—I joined my fraternity, Phi Kappa Tau, living in the house or off-campus with brothers during the next three years. The fraternity became a core part of my social life in college, and I'm still very close friends with many of my brothers.

The common reaction to my fraternity membership from people who weren't in a house is to dismiss Greek life as a childish indulgence or even destructive.

Anti-Greek sentiment has only increased in the wake of various fraternity controversies this academic year. Greek systems have been suspended for at least four schools—Clemson University, West Virginia University, University of Virginia, and San Diego State University—and Wesleyan University made the bold move to co-educate its campus fraternities.

There's no doubt that danger lurks in certain fraternities across the US.

At least one hazing death every year for the past 43 years is a very scary statistic, as is the often cited study from 2007 showing that fraternity members are three times more likely to commit rape than other college students. These trends need to be addressed.

However, Greek life also has some amazing benefits that go beyond just parties and easy access to booze. It is crucial to note, though, that this may not be the right social outlet for every student.

That said, here are some reasons why I'm still proud I joined a frat.

Fraternities Are Already Starting to Self-Regulate

Sigma Alpha Epsilon—branded in 2013 as America's deadliest fraternity—made headlines in March when the national organization announced it was abolishing pledging, and with it, hopefully, hazing.

Recently, fraternities at the University of Virginia worked with the school's administration to develop new protocols to increase safety at Greek events, including mandating sober brothers at frat parties and restricting the type of alcohol served.

Fraternities are also stepping up to fight other problems with frats, with eight national organizations banding together last year to announce a program designed to educate members about sexual assault, hazing, and binge drinking.

The program—called the Fraternal Health and Safety Initiative—uses proven prevention techniques, such as bystander intervention training.

Bystander intervention trains students to identify and intervene in potentially harmful situations. For example, bystander training teaches students to interject themselves if they see a clearly incapacitated friend being led off into a sexual situation they would likely have no control over.

In my chapter, we went through "Wingman 101," a university-sponsored training program designed to help male students learn to prevent sexual assault.

Many, if not all, of the fraternities on my campus went through this, learning techniques such as bystander intervention. While we may have heard some of the topics discussed before, I think the program was particularly effective because the conversations were led by other male students, rather than an administrator or authority figure.

These changes arguably make a frat house the safest place on campus to drink, especially compared with other student parties where alcohol and security are not as strictly regulated.

Greeks Have Higher GPAs at Many Schools and Are more Likely to Graduate

In a Bloomberg View editorial last year calling for banning fraternities, the authors wrote that frat brothers tend to have lower grades than their non-affiliated brothers. This isn't true at many schools, though.

As this helpful guide from Total Frat Move shows, frat boys actually have higher GPAs than non-affiliated students at a majority of schools across the country. According to the North American Interfraternity Conference, where TFM originally got its data, male Greek students overall have a higher GPA nationally than the entire male student population.

Greeks may have more of an incentive to keep their grades up.

Most schools have minimum GPA requirements for students to participate in rush and join a house, as well as minimum average GPA for the chapter overall. At the University of Georgia, for example, a fraternity needs to maintain a 2.90 average GPA to keep social privileges. Perhaps not coincidentally, UGA fraternities members have had a higher GPA than the campus' non-affiliated male students for the past 20 years.

Many fraternities—such as mine—also organize group study hours in the library and inform the brotherhood of interesting speakers on campus.

Another academic advantage for Greeks is a higher retention rate. A study from a group of Harvard University and Syracuse University professors found that joining a Greek organization "had a dramatically positive effect on persistence to graduation."

According to the study, 90% of fraternity and sorority members were still enrolled during their senior year, compared to only 70% of non-Greek students.

Additionally, Greek students have much higher graduation rates compared to their peers, according to USA Today. Greeks' graduation rates are 20% higher than non-Greek students.

A study released last year from professors at Middle Tennessee State University and Niagara University also affirmed that Greeks have a higher graduation rate than non-affiliated students. Not only are the numbers higher, according to the report, but Greeks are also more eager to complete their degrees.

"The increased likelihoods of graduating on time may stem from Greek members having an added incentive to stay enrolled and keep a minimum GPA, so that they can continue to belong to the organization," the study found, according to Pacific Standard magazine.

Greeks Are More Fulfilled in Their Professional Life

A study from Gallup last year found that fraternity and sorority members are significantly more engaged in their workplace and overall happier than students who were not part of a Greek organization.

According to Gallup Education Director Brandon H. Busteed, "the overall results suggest that the Greek experience could be beneficial for the vast majority of those involved in it."

The survey also found that fraternity and sorority members are more likely to be thriving in all of Gallup's five elements of well-being—purpose, social, financial, community, and physical.

On my fraternity listserv, it was not unusual to get emails sent out to the house from alumni whose companies had openings. It's a mutually beneficial relationship. The current student hears about a potential job opportunity and the older graduate can recommend someone they know.

Now an alumnus myself, I still get mass emails from my brothers informing us about jobs, or asking if anyone knows somebody at a company they're applying to.

Greek Life Is Becoming Much More Diverse

A common argument against Greek life—one that appeared in the Bloomberg editorial—is that fraternities and sororities are homogeneous, a claim that may have been true in the past but is actively changing now.

Probably the best example of this is the Greek community at the University of Alabama, whose racial segregation was uncovered by student newspaper the Crimson White last year. After a series of revealing reports from the paper and student protests, several black women were offered—and accepted—membership into previously all-white UA sororities.

This year, close to 200 minority women accepted bids at UA's historically white sororities, including each of the 21 black women who registered for rush.

For another perspective, check out this great guest post in BroBible ["Why I'm a Gay Bro, and Why You Should Be Friends with One"] from a self-styled "Gay Bro," who notes, "A lot has changed in the past 10 years."

While there are no firm statistics on the diversity of Greek houses nationally, it appears fraternities are starting to value having a group of brothers who don't all look the same.

Speaking from my own four years in a fraternity, the makeup of my house shifted during my tenure, with openly gay brothers in the house and seemingly increased racial diversity.

Joining a Greek Organization Can Help Fight Loneliness and Depression

For many students, the first year of college can be difficult because you're separated from your family and close friends for the first time. To combat this, experts suggest socializing to avoid depression.

Especially on a large college campus, where Greek life tends to be most popular, fraternities can offer a home away from home for students who might otherwise feel lost in the crowd.

College can be a tricky time for anyone, myself included, and a fraternity is often a built-in support system for students who are struggling. I know it made my college years a lot easier knowing there was a place on campus where I would always be welcome—and a group of guys who would always have my back.

Analyze

1. While agreeing that long-standing problems of drinking and aggression exist in fraternity systems overall, the author, Peter Jacobs, points to social and civic benefits enjoyed by fraternity brothers. He also points to recent social safeguards to prevent irresponsible drinking

and sexual assault. In your opinion, are these benefits and safeguards substantial enough to merit fraternities a continued presence at American universities?

2. The author's fraternity chapter required its members to take Wingman 101, "a university-sponsored training program designed to help male students learn to prevent sexual assault." Name three areas of concern that a course like Wingman 101 would need to cover to reduce instances of sexual assault and keep all students safe on your campus.

3. The article claims that Greek students are more likely to complete college due to the social cohesion provided by a fraternity or sorority compared with non-Greek members. In your opinion, why does membership in a sorority or fraternity relate so strongly to positive graduation rates?

Explore

1. The article points out that the social network of fraternities and sororities often extends beyond the college years. Why are fraternities and sororities so successful at moving college connections beyond college compared to other college organizations?

2. Do you believe that most college students are naturally drawn to a party atmosphere of experimentation and drinking—that is, is this a natural part of a young adult's experience? Or do you believe that students have absorbed this desire through movies, TV shows, music, and other media? Perhaps this blending of college and partying comes from some other source: consider that before 1950 very few American colleges struggled with problems related to excessive drinking and partying.

3. SHORT WRITING PROMPT: Interview a junior or senior who is actively involved in a Greek house to learn what, in that person's perspective, are the two best things about Greek membership and the two worst.

Risa C. Doherty
Greek Letters at a Price

Risa C. Doherty is a freelance journalist whose work appears in *The New York Times*, *Working Mother*, and *The Social Critic*.

Imagine finding a bill for $200 in your mailbox because your daughter was late to a couple of sorority events. Imagine, too, that those who snitched were her new best friends. This is one of the unwelcome surprises of sorority membership.

Depending on the generosity of the vice president of standards, a fine can be reversed with proof of a qualifying reason, such as a funeral, doctor's appointment or medical emergency, so long as a doctor's note is forthcoming. A paper due or a test the next day? No excuse. (Fraternities, by the way, rarely impose even nominal fines to enforce punctuality.)

Now imagine attending mandatory weekend retreats, throwing yourself into charitable work, making gifts for your sisters and, at tradition-thick schools like the University of Alabama and University of Missouri, investing 30 to 40 hours pomping—threading tissue paper through chicken wire to create elaborate homecoming decorations or parade floats that outdo rivals'.

During fall or winter rush, sororities court starry-eyed freshmen. They showcase their joyful conviviality with skits and serenades. They stress the benefits of joining, and brag about attracting the prettiest, smartest or most athletic. At many traditional sororities, however, not much energy is spent explaining what is expected, leaving many pledges unaware of the considerable time commitment and costs.

Do the math: Official charges include Panhellenic dues, chapter fees, administrative fees, nonresident house/parlor fees, a onetime pledging and initiation fee and contribution toward a house bond. Members must also buy a pin (consider the diamond-encrusted one) and a letter jersey. Without housing, basic costs for the first semester (the most expensive) average $1,570 at University of Georgia sororities, $1,130 at the University of Tennessee, Knoxville, and $1,580 at Syracuse University.

But such fees are only a portion of the real cost. Add in fines, philanthropy and the incidentals that are essential to participate in sorority life and the total spirals upward, especially when a closetful of designer party dresses is part of the mix.

"You think it is just a school club," said Jessica Rodgers, a Georgia State junior and Alpha Xi Delta pledge in 2012. "I wasn't expecting such a burden every month." The first year, she said, she paid about $1,100 in basic fees and $100 to $200 a month over that on sorority-related incidentals. "For someone who pays for all their own expenses, it's alarming," she said. "I was 17 and not thinking about billing and the huge time commitment of joining. It was like signing up for a loan—they said the debt could go to a collections agency if you failed to pay."

Georgia State, American University and Syracuse are among campuses that publish a range of fees covering all their chapters, but information on specific sororities can often be hard to come by before the midst of rush.

Syracuse's Alpha Phi chapter distributes a sheet with financials on the second day of recruitment and then promptly collects it, according to Cameron Boardman, Alpha Phi's 2014 president. She wishes she could email financial information earlier so students could "have an open and frank conversation with their parents about it," but she says she does not have approval from the campus Panhellenic Council to do so.

At the same time, she voices concern that members might be scared off by the cost (which she doesn't want made public) without understanding the benefits and realizing that other Syracuse sororities that seem cheaper impose hefty fines.

Expenses can mushroom with incidentals.

For example, sisters spend a significant amount of time and money on one another. It's a loving relationship, to be sure. Once Bigs choose one or more new members to mentor (Littles), they take them out regularly. They secretly decorate their Littles' rooms, and bake and craft gifts to shower on them. Essential tools are a glue gun and Puffy Paint to adorn anything imaginable—boxes for sorority pins, tumblers, door hangers, T-shirts— with the sorority's letters or mascot. Mod Podge mavens make decoupages with Lilly Pulitzer and Vera Bradley patterns, trimmed with official colors like straw, salmon pink, vieux green and Carolina blue.

With the pressure on, students troll Facebook and Pinterest for the hottest trends in sorority artwork.

Ms. Rodgers received a personalized picture frame, painted wooden Greek letters and a giant initial for her wall from her Big, who she estimates spent $200 to $300 on her. Her second year, the sorority standardized gifts to put an end to competitive spending.

Hannah Hembree, a recent University of Oklahoma graduate and an Alpha Chi Omega, says her spending exceeded $1,000 for gift baskets, coordinated pajamas and treating Littles to meals, movies, bowling, ice cream and coffee.

After a 2009 assessment at the College of William & Mary found that sisters were spending $500 per Little and deemed it excessive, the campus

Panhellenic Council capped such expenditures at $250, though it relinquished enforcement to the individual sororities.

Syracuse's Alpha Phi suggests a $100 cap on spending on Littles. "It is the culture of the school to really spoil them," Ms. Boardman said. "You can't stop girls who want to spend $500." Alpha Phi has two basket days, when Littles discover treats from secret Bigs, and a reveal day, when they find out the identity of their Big.

To help with all this crafting, a cottage industry has sprung up, offering a dizzying array of custom items. Designergreek.com sells canvas totes with appliquéd sorority letters for $23.95; Etsy.com showcases a bejeweled paddle for $65. Avoid trips to Michael's with Diygreek.com's "supply sacks" for $24.99 containing paint, glue, scrapbook paper, wire, charms, ribbons, ceramic beads and stencils with a sorority's symbols and colors.

Recruitment is particularly onerous. Some hopefuls attend an event a day during Rush Week or dedicate two full weekends to activities. Following rush, Gamma Phi Beta pledges must participate in an eight-week program with meetings at least three times a week, according to Krista Spanninger Davis, international president of the sorority, which has more than 130 chapters. Among the activities are lectures about sorority history and tradition. Yes, there's a test at the end (open book).

Nicole Davies, a former peer adviser at American University's career center who rushed Alpha Chi Omega, observes that many students' grades suffers as they pledge, with almost a full week of all-nighters. She had to work two jobs to pay her expenses—she had been "clueless" about the hundreds of dollars in extras—and found it too stressful. She dropped out of her sorority.

Ms. Rodgers, too, left hers. As she was struggling to get everything done on her overcommitted schedule, she would miss class or pull an all-nighter, and she started to resent being made to feel guilty when she would try to get out of an event. When she left she had to return all letter items, including shirts, bags and a $130 pin, without reimbursement.

For her 2004 exposé, "Pledged: The Secret Life of Sororities," Alexandra Robbins interviewed hundreds of sorority members. "It is a massive time commitment, but they also want the girls to pare down their non-Greek activities," she said recently. She estimates that the demands "take more time than an extra class."

Even though the word "optional" is attached to social mixers and dances, many sisters fear being treated with disapproval or left out of emerging social circles if they aren't present. Leah Jordan, a senior at Georgia State, says she does not know anyone at Alpha Omicron Pi, her former sorority, who skips those events. "That's why you join."

Ms. Jordan says she reached her breaking point at the beginning of sophomore year. She says it's not usual for people to drop out and she got some grief for leaving, but she had no choice. She had skipped classes and watched her grades slip while prepping for sorority events and attending meetings, socials and fund-raisers like "Strike Out Arthritis," at a bowling alley, for juvenile arthritis.

With an assist from mandatory weekly study hall, members must maintain a minimum grade-point average or are placed on academic probation by the chapter.

Laura Wright, an associate professor at Western Carolina University and a Chi Omega at Appalachian State, remembers once trying to hide at the back of a meeting to study and being called out for not behaving "in a sisterly way." She said: "I felt there was a strange line and I was not sure how to stay on the right side of it."

Miss enough of those weekly meetings or seminal events and risk not only possible fines but exclusion from formal, the semester highlight. Meetings, which run one to two hours, often take place on Sunday nights, leaving members scrambling right before assignments come due, especially if they follow an overnight weekend retreat.

What to do?

Sorority veterans recommend students do research before joining, to get different perspectives. Ms. Davis of Gamma Phi Beta encourages pledge candidates to visit sororities' social media pages and websites, and to ask the meatier questions. "You need to collect all the info you can to make the best decision that works for you," she says. She acknowledges, however, that freshmen clamoring for a bid can lack the confidence to ask about attendance policies and finances.

Gamma Phi Beta chapters are supposed to help with time management skills, she said. She proposes sorority members skip a required Sunday night chapter meeting if work necessitates and expresses the hope that members understand that "academic and family values should come first."

Sororities are governed according to their own guidelines, and colleges do not intervene to limit their demands on students. But Ms. Robbins believes it is the colleges' role to take action. She says they could do a much better job reporting what sorority life is like by requiring that each chapter supply recruits with a realistic list of time commitments and average yearly costs.

Universities are hesitant to crack down, Ms. Robbins suggests, because Greek alumni have strong bonds to the university and make sizable contributions.

Sororities can provide young women with a lively social life, engagement in community and the satisfaction of supporting worthy causes, but they're clearly not for everyone. "If you're going to join a sorority," Ms. Rodgers said, "you must dedicate your life to it."

Analyze

1. Much of the negative attention falling on the Greek system in recent years has been focused almost exclusively on fraternities. How is sorority culture different from that of fraternities?
2. Considering that most sororities and fraternities are connected to universities, what information should be presented to prospective pledges before they join a house? Consider money, social and civic obligations, and time commitments.
3. Why, in your opinion, are sororities so interested in "branding" their members with their Greek letters? Why is visual identification such a substantial part of sorority life?

Explore

1. Sororities tend to use the word "mixer" whereas fraternities tend to use the word "party." Both define "gatherings." How do the names define different social experiences?
2. Sororities and fraternities, along with some sports teams, are one of the few remaining areas of gender segregation at coed public universities. What are the pros and cons of a gender-segregated experience while in college? What can men best learn in a community of men? What can women best learn in an environment of women? Consider, briefly, that until the mid-1800s, most American colleges were single-sex institutions.
3. SHORT WRITING ASSIGNMENT: Sorority veterans, according to the article, recommend that students do research before joining a

house. Using informal interviews, the webpages of local sororities, and information from your college's Panhellenic association (or other student council group that regulates sorority life on your campus), estimate the total cost of joining a sorority for one year. Include various fees, the cost of social mixers, required (or suggested) attire, and other social expenditures (such as gifts, group activities, and meals out).

Forging Connections

1. Much of the public concern about the Greek system is focused on fraternities, with less emphasis on sororities. How does the culture of fraternities differ from that of sororities? Why has more public concern—and at times outrage—been focused on fraternities?

2. Risa C. Doherty in her article "Greek Letters at a Price" suggests that students should not be unknowingly burdened with expenses that don't directly relate to their academic program. Many students struggle to make ends meet, often working part-time jobs, to support themselves while studying for a degree. With this in mind, (a) what is a reasonable amount of money an average college student should spend each month on social activities? (b) how does the environment around a college often encourage students toward higher levels of spending? and (c) would the college experience be better for you if each student had an identical monthly allowance (such as $100) for social spending, with no possibility of receiving extra money from family members or a job?

Looking Further

1. In Caitlin Flanagan's article "The Dark Power of Fraternities," one central problem concerns party drinking off campus. To better manage this problem, some colleges have either moved Greek houses on campus, where they are managed by university professionals, or created drinking areas on campus (such as a pub) where students can party in a supervised environment. Do you believe that your campus would benefit from a system in which centers of drinking were moved from unsupervised off-campus locations to supervised on-campus

settings? In your opinion, what would be the pros and cons of this system?

2. In this book, many articles that examine the future of college fail to make a place for the Greek system. For example, in "The Future of College?" by Graeme Wood, the Minerva Project excludes the concept of a Greek system in favor of focusing on academics and international travel. Do you believe that the Greek system will have a robust life twenty years in the future? Or do you believe that colleges in the near future—and college students as well—will focus their attention more on education, training, and artistic exploration as opposed to organized social experiences?

6 College Sports

In September 2013, Johnny Manziel, the first freshman to win the Heisman Trophy, appeared on the cover of *Time Magazine*. Wearing cleats and cradling a football, he was dressed in the Texas A&M school colors, maroon and white. Aside from his youth and his surprising Heisman win, the cover of this weekly magazine might have passed through newsstands relatively unnoticed—except for its caption. In large white letters, the magazine announced: "It's Time to Pay College Athletes," rekindling a long-standing controversy about the role of athletes in college, particularly at powerhouse football and basketball schools: should they be classified as amateurs who play for the love of the sport or as employees who contribute to a multibillion-dollar industry and are therefore deserving of compensation, workplace insurance, and other rights usually afforded workers?

In this chapter, three authors examine the complex relationship between college and sports, especially stadium sports. Taylor Branch explores the history of college athletics and the rise of the NCAA (the National Collegiate Athletic Association), with an eye toward understanding how players have been excluded from the profits in college sports and have even been deprived of owning their own likeness. Ian Crouch investigates the distinctions between amateur and employee status as it relates to college sports. Lastly Dr. Alan Kadish argues that big-money sports not only spoil the academic atmosphere at some colleges but also diminish the moral environment that he believes should be part of the college experience.

In sum, these articles examine a concern relevant to many colleges: how should institutions of learning behave when they discover big money in athletics?

Taylor Branch
The Shame of College Sports

Taylor Branch is the recipient of a Pulitzer Prize for History and is best known for his three-volume series chronicling the civil rights movement and the life of Martin Luther King, Jr.

"I'm not hiding," Sonny Vaccaro told a closed hearing at the Willard Hotel in Washington, D.C., in 2001. "We want to put our materials on the bodies of your athletes, and the best way to do that is buy your school. Or buy your coach."

Vaccaro's audience, the members of the Knight Commission on Intercollegiate Athletics, bristled. These were eminent reformers—among them the president of the National Collegiate Athletic Association, two former heads of the U.S. Olympic Committee, and several university presidents and chancellors. The Knight Foundation, a nonprofit that takes an interest in college athletics as part of its concern with civic life, had tasked them with saving college sports from runaway commercialism as embodied by the likes of Vaccaro, who, since signing his pioneering shoe contract with Michael Jordan in 1984, had built sponsorship empires successively at Nike, Adidas, and Reebok. Not all the members could hide their scorn for the "sneaker pimp" of schoolyard hustle, who boasted of writing checks for millions to everybody in higher education.

"Why," asked Bryce Jordan, the president emeritus of Penn State, "should a university be an advertising medium for your industry?"

Vaccaro did not blink. "They shouldn't, sir," he replied. "You sold your souls, and you're going to continue selling them. You can be very moral and righteous in asking me that question, sir," Vaccaro added with irrepressible good cheer, "but there's not one of you in this room that's going to turn down any of our money. You're going to take it. I can only offer it."

William Friday, a former president of North Carolina's university system, still winces at the memory. "Boy, the silence that fell in that room," he recalled recently. "I never will forget it." Friday, who founded and co-chaired two of the three Knight Foundation sports initiatives over the past 20 years, called Vaccaro "the worst of all" the witnesses ever to come before the panel.

But what Vaccaro said in 2001 was true then, and it's true now: corporations offer money so they can profit from the glory of college athletes, and the universities grab it. In 2010, despite the faltering economy, a single college athletic league, the football-crazed Southeastern Conference (SEC), became the first to crack the billion-dollar barrier in athletic receipts. The Big Ten pursued closely at $905 million. That money comes from a combination of ticket sales, concession sales, merchandise, licensing fees, and other sources—but the great bulk of it comes from television contracts.

Educators are in thrall to their athletic departments because of these television riches and because they respect the political furies that can burst from a locker room. "There's fear," Friday told me when I visited him on the University of North Carolina campus in Chapel Hill last fall. As we spoke, two giant construction cranes towered nearby over the university's Kenan Stadium, working on the latest $77 million renovation. (The University of Michigan spent almost four times that much to expand its Big House.) Friday insisted that for the networks, paying huge sums to universities was a bargain.

"We do every little thing for them," he said. "We furnish the theater, the actors, the lights, the music, and the audience for a drama measured neatly in time slots. They bring the camera and turn it on." Friday, a weathered idealist at 91, laments the control universities have ceded in pursuit of this money. If television wants to broadcast football from here on a Thursday night, he said, "we shut down the university at 3 o'clock to accommodate the crowds." He longed for a campus identity more centered in an academic mission.

The United States is the only country in the world that hosts big-time sports at institutions of higher learning. This should not, in and of itself, be controversial. College athletics are rooted in the classical ideal of *Mens sana in corpore sano*—a sound mind in a sound body—and who would argue with that? College sports are deeply inscribed in the culture of our nation. Half a million young men and women play competitive intercollegiate sports each year. Millions of spectators flock into football stadiums each Saturday in the fall, and tens of millions more watch on television. The March Madness basketball tournament each spring has become a major national event, with upwards of 80 million watching it on television and talking about the games around the office water cooler. ESPN has spawned ESPNU, a channel dedicated to college sports, and Fox Sports and other cable outlets are developing channels exclusively to cover sports from specific regions or divisions.

With so many people paying for tickets and watching on television, college sports has become Very Big Business. According to various reports, the football teams at Texas, Florida, Georgia, Michigan, and Penn State— to name just a few big-revenue football schools—each earn between $40 million and $80 million in profits a year, even after paying coaches multimillion-dollar salaries. When you combine so much money with such high, almost tribal, stakes—football boosters are famously rabid in their zeal to have their alma mater win—corruption is likely to follow.

Scandal after scandal has rocked college sports. In 2010, the NCAA sanctioned the University of Southern California after determining that star running back Reggie Bush and his family had received "improper benefits" while he played for the Trojans. (Among other charges, Bush and members of his family were alleged to have received free airfare and limousine rides, a car, and a rent-free home in San Diego, from sports agents who wanted Bush as a client.) The Bowl Championship Series stripped USC of its 2004 national title, and Bush returned the Heisman Trophy he had won in 2005. Last fall, as Auburn University football stormed its way to an undefeated season and a national championship, the team's star quarterback,

Cam Newton, was dogged by allegations that his father had used a recruiter to solicit up to $180,000 from Mississippi State in exchange for his son's matriculation there after junior college in 2010. Jim Tressel, the highly successful head football coach of the Ohio State Buckeyes, resigned last spring after the NCAA alleged he had feigned ignorance of rules violations by players on his team. At least 28 players over the course of the previous nine seasons, according to *Sports Illustrated*, had traded autographs, jerseys, and other team memorabilia in exchange for tattoos or cash at a tattoo parlor in Columbus, in violation of NCAA rules. Late this summer, Yahoo Sports reported that the NCAA was investigating allegations that a University of Miami booster had given millions of dollars in illicit cash and services to more than 70 Hurricanes football players over eight years.

The list of scandals goes on. With each revelation, there is much wringing of hands. Critics scold schools for breaking faith with their educational mission, and for failing to enforce the sanctity of "amateurism." Sportswriters denounce the NCAA for both tyranny and impotence in its quest to "clean up" college sports. Observers on all sides express jumbled emotions about youth and innocence, venting against professional mores or greedy amateurs.

For all the outrage, the real scandal is not that students are getting illegally paid or recruited, it's that two of the noble principles on which the NCAA justifies its existence—"amateurism" and the "student-athlete"— are cynical hoaxes, legalistic confections propagated by the universities so they can exploit the skills and fame of young athletes. The tragedy at the heart of college sports is not that some college athletes are getting paid, but that more of them are not.

Don Curtis, a UNC trustee, told me that impoverished football players cannot afford movie tickets or bus fare home. Curtis is a rarity among those in higher education today, in that he dares to violate the signal taboo: "I think we should pay these guys something."

Fans and educators alike recoil from this proposal as though from original sin. Amateurism is the whole point, they say. Paid athletes would destroy the integrity and appeal of college sports. Many former college athletes object that money would have spoiled the sanctity of the bond they enjoyed with their teammates. I, too, once shuddered instinctively at the notion of paid college athletes.

But after an inquiry that took me into locker rooms and ivory towers across the country, I have come to believe that sentiment blinds us to what's before our eyes. Big-time college sports are fully commercialized. Billions of dollars flow through them each year. The NCAA makes money, and enables universities and corporations to make money, from the unpaid labor of young athletes.

Slavery analogies should be used carefully. College athletes are not slaves. Yet to survey the scene—corporations and universities enriching themselves on the backs of uncompensated young men, whose status as "student-athletes" deprives them of the right to due process guaranteed by the Constitution—is to catch an unmistakable whiff of the plantation. Perhaps a more apt metaphor is colonialism: college sports, as overseen by the NCAA, is a system imposed by well-meaning paternalists and rationalized with hoary sentiments about caring for the well-being of the colonized. But it is, nonetheless, unjust. The NCAA, in its zealous defense of bogus principles, sometimes destroys the dreams of innocent young athletes.

The NCAA today is in many ways a classic cartel. Efforts to reform it—most notably by the three Knight Commissions over the course of 20 years—have, while making changes around the edges, been largely fruitless. The time has come for a major overhaul. And whether the powers that be like it or not, big changes are coming. Threats loom on multiple fronts: in Congress, the courts, breakaway athletic conferences, student rebellion, and public disgust. Swaddled in gauzy clichés, the NCAA presides over a vast, teetering glory.

Founding Myths

From the start, amateurism in college sports has been honored more often in principle than in fact; the NCAA was built of a mixture of noble and venal impulses. In the late 19th century, intellectuals believed that the sporting arena simulated an impending age of Darwinian struggle. Because the United States did not hold a global empire like England's, leaders warned of national softness once railroads conquered the last continental frontier. As though heeding this warning, ingenious students turned variations on rugby into a toughening agent. Today a plaque in New Brunswick, New Jersey, commemorates the first college game, on November 6, 1869, when Rutgers beat Princeton 6–4.

Walter Camp graduated from Yale in 1880 so intoxicated by the sport that he devoted his life to it without pay, becoming "the father of American football." He persuaded other schools to reduce the chaos on the field by trimming each side from 15 players to 11, and it was his idea to paint measuring lines on the field. He conceived functional designations for players, coining terms such as quarterback. His game remained violent by design. Crawlers could push the ball forward beneath piles of flying elbows without pause until they cried "Down!" in submission.

In an 1892 game against its archrival, Yale, the Harvard football team was the first to deploy a "flying wedge," based on Napoleon's surprise concentrations of military force. In an editorial calling for the abolition of the play, *The New York Times* described it as "half a ton of bone and muscle coming into collision with a man weighing 160 or 170 pounds," noting that surgeons often had to be called onto the field. Three years later, the continuing mayhem prompted the Harvard faculty to take the first of two votes to abolish football. Charles Eliot, the university's president, brought up other concerns. "Deaths and injuries are not the strongest argument against football," declared Eliot. "That cheating and brutality are profitable is the main evil." Still, Harvard football persisted. In 1903, fervent alumni built Harvard Stadium with zero college funds. The team's first paid head coach, Bill Reid, started in 1905 at nearly twice the average salary for a full professor.

A newspaper story from that year, illustrated with the Grim Reaper laughing on a goalpost, counted 25 college players killed during football season. A fairy-tale version of the founding of the NCAA holds that President Theodore Roosevelt, upset by a photograph of a bloodied Swarthmore College player, vowed to civilize or destroy football. The real story is that Roosevelt maneuvered shrewdly to preserve the sport—and give a boost to his beloved Harvard. After *McClure's* magazine published a story on corrupt teams with phantom students, a muckraker exposed Walter Camp's $100,000 slush fund at Yale. In response to mounting outrage, Roosevelt summoned leaders from Harvard, Princeton, and Yale to the White House, where Camp parried mounting criticism and conceded nothing irresponsible in the college football rules he'd established. At Roosevelt's behest, the three schools issued a public statement that college sports must reform to survive, and representatives from 68 colleges founded a new organization that would soon be called the National Collegiate Athletic Association. A Haverford College official was confirmed as secretary but then promptly resigned in favor of Bill Reid, the new Harvard coach, who instituted new rules that benefited Harvard's playing style at the expense of Yale's. At a stroke, Roosevelt saved football and dethroned Yale.

For nearly 50 years, the NCAA, with no real authority and no staff to speak of, enshrined amateur ideals that it was helpless to enforce. (Not until 1939 did it gain the power even to mandate helmets.) In 1929, the Carnegie Foundation made headlines with a report, "American College Athletics," which concluded that the scramble for players had "reached the proportions of nationwide commerce." Of the 112 schools surveyed, 81 flouted NCAA recommendations with inducements to students ranging from open payrolls and disguised booster funds to no-show jobs at movie studios. Fans ignored the uproar, and two-thirds of the colleges mentioned told *The New York Times* that they planned no changes. In 1939, freshman players at the University of Pittsburgh went on strike because they were getting paid less than their upperclassman teammates.

Embarrassed, the NCAA in 1948 enacted a "Sanity Code," which was supposed to prohibit all concealed and indirect benefits for college athletes; any money for athletes was to be limited to transparent scholarships awarded solely on financial need. Schools that violated this code would be expelled from NCAA membership and thus exiled from competitive sports.

This bold effort flopped. Colleges balked at imposing such a drastic penalty on each other, and the Sanity Code was repealed within a few years. The University of Virginia went so far as to call a press conference to say that if its athletes were ever accused of being paid, they should be forgiven, because their studies at Thomas Jefferson's university were so rigorous.

The Big Bluff

In 1951, the NCAA seized upon a serendipitous set of events to gain control of intercollegiate sports. First, the organization hired a young college dropout named Walter Byers as executive director. A journalist who was not yet 30 years old, he was an appropriately inauspicious choice for the vaguely defined new post. He wore cowboy boots and a toupee. He shunned personal contact, obsessed over details, and proved himself a bureaucratic master of pervasive, anonymous intimidation. Although discharged from the Army during World War II for defective vision, Byers was able to see an opportunity in two contemporaneous scandals. In one, the tiny College of William and Mary, aspiring to challenge football powers Oklahoma and Ohio State, was found to be counterfeiting grades to keep conspicuously pampered players eligible. In the other, a basketball point-shaving conspiracy (in which gamblers paid players to perform poorly) had spread from five New York colleges to the University of Kentucky, the reigning national champion, generating tabloid "perp" photos of gangsters and handcuffed basketball players. The scandals posed a crisis of credibility for collegiate athletics, and nothing in the NCAA's feeble record would have led anyone to expect real reform.

But Byers managed to impanel a small infractions board to set penalties without waiting for a full convention of NCAA schools, which would have been inclined toward forgiveness. Then he lobbied a University of Kentucky dean—A. D. Kirwan, a former football coach and future university president—not to contest the NCAA's dubious legal position (the association had no actual authority to penalize the university), pleading that college sports must do something to restore public support. His gambit succeeded when Kirwan reluctantly accepted a landmark precedent: the Kentucky basketball team would be suspended for the entire 1952–53 season. Its legendary coach, Adolph Rupp, fumed for a year in limbo.

The Kentucky case created an aura of centralized command for an NCAA office that barely existed. At the same time, a colossal misperception gave Byers leverage to mine gold. Amazingly in retrospect, most colleges and marketing experts considered the advent of television a dire threat to sports. Studies found that broadcasts reduced live attendance, and therefore gate receipts, because some customers preferred to watch at home for free. Nobody could yet imagine the revenue bonanza that television represented. With clunky new TV sets proliferating, the 1951 NCAA convention voted 161–7 to outlaw televised games except for a specific few licensed by the NCAA staff.

All but two schools quickly complied. The University of Pennsylvania and Notre Dame protested the order to break contracts for home-game television broadcasts, claiming the right to make their own decisions. Byers objected that such exceptions would invite disaster. The conflict escalated. Byers brandished penalties for games televised without approval. Penn contemplated seeking antitrust protection through the courts. Byers issued a contamination notice, informing any opponent scheduled to play Penn that it would be punished for showing up to compete. In effect, Byers mobilized the college world to isolate the two holdouts in what one sportswriter later called "the Big Bluff."

Byers won. Penn folded in part because its president, the perennial White House contender Harold Stassen, wanted to mend relations with fellow schools in the emerging Ivy League, which would be formalized in 1954. When Notre Dame also surrendered, Byers conducted exclusive negotiations with the new television networks on behalf of every college team. Joe Rauh Jr., a prominent civil-rights attorney, helped him devise a rationing system to permit only 11 broadcasts a year—the fabled Game of the Week. Byers and Rauh selected a few teams for television exposure, excluding the rest. On June 6, 1952, NBC signed a one-year deal to pay the NCAA $1.14 million for a carefully restricted football package. Byers routed all contractual proceeds through his office. He floated the idea that, to fund an NCAA infrastructure, his organization should take a 60 percent cut; he accepted 12 percent that season. (For later contracts, as the size of television revenues grew exponentially, he backed down to 5 percent.) Proceeds from the first NBC contract were enough to rent an NCAA headquarters, in Kansas City.

Only one year into his job, Byers had secured enough power and money to regulate all of college sports. Over the next decade, the NCAA's power grew along with television revenues. Through the efforts of Byers's deputy and chief lobbyist, Chuck Neinas, the NCAA won an important concession in the Sports Broadcasting Act of 1961, in which Congress made its granting of a precious antitrust exemption to the National Football League contingent upon the blackout of professional football on Saturdays. Deftly, without even mentioning the NCAA, a rider on the bill carved each weekend into protected broadcast markets: Saturday for college, Sunday for the NFL. The NFL got its antitrust exemption. Byers, having negotiated the NCAA's television package up to $3.1 million per football season—which was higher than the NFL's figure in those early years—had made the NCAA into a spectacularly profitable cartel.

"We Eat What We Kill"

The NCAA's control of college sports still rested on a fragile base, however: the consent of the colleges and universities it governed. For a time, the vast sums of television money delivered to these institutions through Byers's deals made them willing to submit. But the big football powers grumbled about the portion of the television revenue diverted to nearly a thousand NCAA member schools that lacked major athletic programs. They chafed against cost-cutting measures—such as restrictions on team size—designed to help smaller schools. "I don't want Hofstra telling Texas how to play football," Darrell Royal, the Longhorns coach, griped. By the 1970s and '80s, as college football games delivered bonanza ratings—and advertising revenue—to the networks, some of the big football schools began to wonder: Why do we need to have our television coverage brokered through the NCAA? Couldn't we get a bigger cut of that TV money by dealing directly with the networks?

Byers faced a rude internal revolt. The NCAA's strongest legions, its big football schools, defected en masse. Calling the NCAA a price-fixing cartel that siphoned every television dollar through its coffers, in 1981 a rogue consortium of 61 major football schools threatened to sign an independent contract with NBC for $180 million over four years.

With a huge chunk of the NCAA's treasury walking out the door, Byers threatened sanctions, as he had against Penn and Notre Dame three decades earlier. But this time the universities of Georgia and Oklahoma responded with an antitrust suit. "It is virtually impossible to overstate the degree of our resentment . . . of the NCAA," said William Banowsky, the president of the University of Oklahoma. In the landmark 1984 *NCAA v. Board of Regents of the University of Oklahoma* decision, the U.S. Supreme Court struck down the NCAA's latest football contracts with television—and any future ones—as an illegal restraint of trade that harmed colleges and viewers. Overnight, the NCAA's control of the television market for football vanished. Upholding Banowsky's challenge to the NCAA's authority, the Regents decision freed the football schools to sell any and all games the markets would bear. Coaches and administrators no longer had to share the revenue generated by their athletes with smaller schools outside the football consortium. "We eat what we kill," one official at the University of Texas bragged.

A few years earlier, this blow might have financially crippled the NCAA—but a rising tide of money from basketball concealed the structural damage of the Regents decision. During the 1980s, income from the March Madness college basketball tournament, paid directly by the television networks to the NCAA, grew tenfold. The windfall covered—and then far exceeded—what the organization had lost from football.

Still, Byers never forgave his former deputy Chuck Neinas for leading the rebel consortium. He knew that Neinas had seen from the inside how tenuous the NCAA's control really was, and how diligently Byers had worked to prop up its Oz-like façade. During Byers's tenure, the rule book for Division I athletes grew to 427 pages of scholastic detail. His NCAA personnel manual banned conversations around water coolers, and coffee cups on desks, while specifying exactly when drapes must be drawn at the NCAA's 27,000-square-foot headquarters near Kansas City (built in 1973 from the proceeds of a 1 percent surtax on football contracts). It was as though, having lost control where it mattered, Byers pedantically exerted more control where it didn't.

After retiring in 1987, Byers let slip his suppressed fury that the ingrate football conferences, having robbed the NCAA of television revenue, still expected it to enforce amateurism rules and police every leak of funds to college players. A lethal greed was "gnawing at the innards of college athletics," he wrote in his memoir. When Byers renounced the NCAA's pretense of amateurism, his former colleagues would stare blankly, as though he had gone senile or, as he wrote, "desecrated my sacred vows." But Byers was better positioned than anyone else to argue that college football's claim to amateurism was unfounded. Years later, as we will see, lawyers would seize upon his words to do battle with the NCAA.

Meanwhile, reformers fretted that commercialism was hurting college sports, and that higher education's historical balance between academics and athletics had been distorted by all the money sloshing around. News stories revealed that schools went to extraordinary measures to keep academically incompetent athletes eligible for competition, and would vie for the most-sought-after high-school players by proffering under-the-table payments. In 1991, the first Knight Commission report, "Keeping Faith With the Student Athlete," was published; the commission's "bedrock conviction" was that university presidents must seize control of the NCAA from athletic directors in order to restore the preeminence of academic values over athletic or commercial ones. In response, college presidents did take over the NCAA's governance. But by 2001, when the second Knight Commission report ("A Call to Action: Reconnecting College Sports and Higher Education") was issued, a new generation of reformers was admitting that problems of corruption and commercialism had "grown rather than diminished" since the first report. Meanwhile the NCAA itself, revenues rising, had moved into a $50 million, 116,000-square-foot headquarters in Indianapolis. By 2010, as the size of NCAA headquarters increased yet again with a 130,000-square-foot expansion, a third Knight Commission was groping blindly for a hold on independent college-athletic conferences that were behaving more like sovereign pro leagues than confederations of universities. And still more money continued to flow into NCAA coffers. With the basketball tournament's 2011 television deal, annual March Madness broadcast revenues had skyrocketed 50-fold in less than 30 years.

The Myth of the "Student-Athlete"

Today, much of the NCAA's moral authority—indeed much of the justification for its existence—is vested in its claim to protect what it calls the "student-athlete." The term is meant to conjure the nobility of amateurism, and the precedence of scholarship over athletic endeavor. But the origins of the "student-athlete" lie not in a disinterested ideal but in a sophistic formulation designed, as the sports economist Andrew Zimbalist has written, to help the NCAA in its "fight against workmen's compensation insurance claims for injured football players."

"We crafted the term student-athlete," Walter Byers himself wrote, "and soon it was embedded in all NCAA rules and interpretations." The term came into play in the 1950s, when the widow of Ray Dennison, who had died from a head injury received while playing football in Colorado for the Fort Lewis A&M Aggies, filed for workmen's-compensation death benefits. Did his football scholarship make the fatal collision a "work-related" accident? Was he a school employee, like his peers who worked part-time as teaching assistants and bookstore cashiers? Or was he a fluke victim of extracurricular pursuits? Given the hundreds of incapacitating injuries to college athletes each year, the answers to these questions had enormous consequences. The Colorado Supreme Court ultimately agreed with the school's contention that he was not eligible for benefits, since the college was "not in the football business."

The term *student-athlete* was deliberately ambiguous. College players were not students at play (which might understate their athletic obligations), nor were they just athletes in college (which might imply they were professionals). That they were high-performance athletes meant they could be forgiven for not meeting the academic standards of their peers; that they were students meant they did not have to be compensated, ever, for anything more than the cost of their studies. *Student-athlete* became the NCAA's signature term, repeated constantly in and out of courtrooms.

Using the "student-athlete" defense, colleges have compiled a string of victories in liability cases. On the afternoon of October 26, 1974, the Texas

Christian University Horned Frogs were playing the Alabama Crimson Tide in Birmingham, Alabama. Kent Waldrep, a TCU running back, carried the ball on a "Red Right 28" sweep toward the Crimson Tide's sideline, where he was met by a swarm of tacklers. When Waldrep regained consciousness, Bear Bryant, the storied Crimson Tide coach, was standing over his hospital bed. "It was like talking to God, if you're a young football player," Waldrep recalled.

Waldrep was paralyzed: he had lost all movement and feeling below his neck. After nine months of paying his medical bills, Texas Christian refused to pay any more, so the Waldrep family coped for years on dwindling charity.

Through the 1990s, from his wheelchair, Waldrep pressed a lawsuit for workers' compensation. (He also, through heroic rehabilitation efforts, recovered feeling in his arms, and eventually learned to drive a specially rigged van. "I can brush my teeth," he told me last year, "but I still need help to bathe and dress.") His attorneys haggled with TCU and the state worker-compensation fund over what constituted employment. Clearly, TCU had provided football players with equipment for the job, as a typical employer would—but did the university pay wages, withhold income taxes on his financial aid, or control work conditions and performance? The appeals court finally rejected Waldrep's claim in June of 2000, ruling that he was not an employee because he had not paid taxes on financial aid that he could have kept even if he quit football. (Waldrep told me school officials "said they recruited me as a student, not an athlete," which he says was absurd.)

The long saga vindicated the power of the NCAA's "student-athlete" formulation as a shield, and the organization continues to invoke it as both a legalistic defense and a noble ideal. Indeed, such is the term's rhetorical power that it is increasingly used as a sort of reflexive mantra against charges of rabid hypocrisy.

Last Thanksgiving weekend, with both the FBI and the NCAA investigating whether Cam Newton had been lured onto his team with illegal payments, Newton's Auburn Tigers and the Alabama Crimson Tide came together for their annual game, known as the Iron Bowl, before 101,821 fans at Bryant-Denny Stadium. This game is always a highlight of the football season because of the historic rivalry between the two schools, and the 2010 edition had enormous significance, pitting the defending national champion Crimson Tide against the undefeated Tigers, who were aiming for their first championship since 1957. I expected excited fans; what I encountered was the throbbing heart of college sports. As I drove before daybreak toward the stadium, a sleepless caller babbled over WJOX, the local fan radio station, that he "couldn't stop thinking about the coin toss." In the parking lot, ticketless fans were puzzled that anyone need ask why they had tailgated for days just to watch their satellite-fed flat screens within earshot of the roar. All that morning, pilgrims packed the Bear Bryant museum, where displays elaborated the misery of Alabama's 4–24 run before the glorious Bryant era dawned in 1958.

Finally, as Auburn took the field for warm-ups, one of Alabama's public-address-system operators played "Take the Money and Run" (an act for which he would be fired). A sea of signs reading $CAM taunted Newton. The game, perhaps the most exciting of the season, was unbearably tense, with Auburn coming from way behind to win 28–27, all but assuring that it would go on to play for the national championship. Days later, Auburn suspended Newton after the NCAA found that a rules violation had occurred: his father was alleged to have marketed his son in a pay-for-play scheme; a day after that, the NCAA reinstated Newton's eligibility because investigators had not found evidence that Newton or Auburn officials had known of his father's actions. This left Newton conveniently eligible for the Southeastern Conference championship game and for the postseason BCS championship bowl. For the NCAA, prudence meant honoring public demand.

"Our championships," NCAA President Mark Emmert has declared, "are one of the primary tools we have to enhance the student-athlete experience."

"Whoremasters"

NCAA v. Regents left the NCAA devoid of television football revenue and almost wholly dependent on March Madness basketball. It is rich but insecure. Last year, CBS Sports and Turner Broadcasting paid $771 million to the NCAA for television rights to the 2011 men's basketball tournament alone. That's three-quarters of a billion dollars built on the backs of amateurs—on unpaid labor. The whole edifice depends on the players' willingness to perform what is effectively volunteer work. The athletes, and the league officials, are acutely aware of this extraordinary arrangement. William Friday, the former North Carolina president, recalls being yanked from one Knight Commission meeting and sworn to secrecy about what might happen if a certain team made the NCAA championship basketball game. "They were going to dress and go out on the floor," Friday told me, "but refuse to play," in a wildcat student strike. Skeptics doubted such a diabolical plot. These were college kids—unlikely to second-guess their coaches, let alone forfeit the dream of a championship. Still, it was unnerving to contemplate what hung on the consent of a few young volunteers: several hundred million dollars in television revenue, countless livelihoods, the NCAA budget, and subsidies for sports at more than 1,000 schools. Friday's informants exhaled when the suspect team lost before the finals.

Cognizant of its precarious financial base, the NCAA has in recent years begun to pursue new sources of revenue. Taking its cue from member schools such as Ohio State (which in 2009 bundled all its promotional rights—souvenirs, stadium ads, shoe deals—and outsourced them to the international sports marketer IMG College for a guaranteed $11 million a year), the NCAA began to exploit its vault of college sports on film. For $29.99 apiece, NCAA On Demand offers DVDs of more than 200 memorable contests in men's ice hockey alone. Video-game technology also allows nostalgic fans to relive and even participate in classic moments of NCAA Basketball. NCAA Football, licensed by the NCAA through IMG College to Electronic Arts, one of the world's largest video-game manufacturers, reportedly sold 2.5 million copies in 2008. Brit Kirwan, the chancellor of the Maryland university system and a former president at Ohio State, says there were "terrible fights" between the third Knight Commission and the NCAA over the ethics of generating this revenue.

All of this money ultimately derives from the college athletes whose likenesses are shown in the films or video games. But none of the profits go to them. Last year, Electronic Arts paid more than $35 million in royalties to the NFL players union for the underlying value of names and images in its pro football series—but neither the NCAA nor its affiliated companies paid former college players a nickel. Naturally, as they have become more of a profit center for the NCAA, some of the vaunted "student-athletes" have begun to clamor that they deserve a share of those profits. You "see everybody getting richer and richer," Desmond Howard, who won the 1991 Heisman Trophy while playing for the Michigan Wolverines, told USA Today recently. "And you walk around and you can't put gas in your car? You can't even fly home to see your parents?"

Some athletes have gone beyond talk. A series of lawsuits quietly making their way through the courts cast a harsh light on the absurdity of the system—and threaten to dislodge the foundations on which the NCAA rests. On July 21, 2009, lawyers for Ed O'Bannon filed a class-action anti-trust suit against the NCAA at the U.S. District Court in San Francisco. "Once you leave your university," says O'Bannon, who won the John Wooden Award for player of the year in 1995 on UCLA's national-championship basketball team, "one would think your likeness belongs to you." The NCAA and UCLA continue to collect money from the sales of videos of him playing. But by NCAA rules, O'Bannon, who today works at a Toyota dealership near Las Vegas, alleges he is still not allowed to share the revenue the NCAA generates from his own image as a college athlete. His suit quickly gathered co-plaintiffs from basketball and football, ex-players featured in NCAA videos and other products. "The NCAA does not license student-athlete likenesses," NCAA spokesperson Erik Chris-tianson told The New York Times in response to the suit, "or prevent former student-athletes from attempting to do so. Likewise, to claim the NCAA profits off student-athlete likenesses is also pure fiction."

The legal contention centers on Part IV of the NCAA's "Student-Athlete Statement" for Division I, which requires every athlete to authorize use of "your name or picture . . . to promote NCAA championships or other NCAA events, activities or programs." Does this clause mean that athletes clearly renounce personal interest forever? If so, does it actually undermine the NCAA by implicitly recognizing that athletes have a property right in their own performance? Jon King, a lawyer for the plaintiffs, expects the NCAA's core mission of amateurism to be its "last defense standing."

In theory, the NCAA's passion to protect the noble amateurism of col-lege athletes should prompt it to focus on head coaches in the high-revenue sports—basketball and football—since holding the top official account-able should most efficiently discourage corruption. The problem is that the coaches' growing power has rendered them, unlike their players, ever more immune to oversight. According to research by Charles Clotfelter, an econ-omist at Duke, the average compensation for head football coaches at public universities, now more than $2 million, has grown 750 percent (adjusted for inflation) since the Regents decision in 1984; that's more than 20 times the cumulative 32 percent raise for college professors. For top bas-ketball coaches, annual contracts now exceed $4 million, augmented by assorted bonuses, endorsements, country-club memberships, the occasional private plane, and in some cases a negotiated percentage of ticket receipts. (Oregon's ticket concessions netted former football coach Mike Bellotti an additional $631,000 in 2005.)

The NCAA rarely tangles with such people, who are apt to fight back and win. When Rick Neuheisel, the head football coach of the Washington Huskies, was punished for petty gambling (in a March Madness pool, as it happened), he sued the NCAA and the university for wrongful termination, collected $4.5 million, and later moved on to UCLA. When the NCAA tried to cap assistant coaches' entering salary at a mere $16,000, nearly 2,000 of them brought an antitrust suit, *Law v. NCAA*, and in 1999 settled for $54.5 million. Since then, salaries for assistant coaches have commonly exceeded $200,000, with the top assistants in the SEC averaging $700,000. In 2009, Monte Kiffin, then at the University of Tennessee, became the first assistant coach to reach $1 million, plus benefits.

The late Myles Brand, who led the NCAA from 2003 to 2009, defended the economics of college sports by claiming that they were simply the result of a smoothly functioning free market. He and his colleagues deflected criticism about the money saturating big-time college sports by focusing attention on scapegoats; in 2010, outrage targeted sports agents. Last year *Sports Illustrated* published "Confessions of an Agent," a firsthand account of dealing with high-strung future pros whom the agent and his peers courted with flattery, cash, and tawdry favors. Nick Saban, Alabama's head football coach, mobilized his peers to denounce agents as a public scourge. "I hate to say this," he said, "but how are they any better than a pimp? I have no respect for people who do that to young people. None."

Saban's raw condescension contrasts sharply with the lonely penitence from Dale Brown, the retired longtime basketball coach at LSU. "Look at the money we make off predominantly poor black kids," Brown once reflected. "We're the whoremasters."

"Picayune Rules"

NCAA officials have tried to assert their dominion—and distract attention from the larger issues—by chasing frantically after petty violations. Tom McMillen, a former member of the Knight Commission who was an All-American basketball player at the University of Maryland, likens these officials to traffic cops in a speed trap, who could flag down almost any passing motorist for prosecution in kangaroo court under a "maze of picayune rules." The publicized cases have become convoluted soap operas. At the start of the 2010 football season, A. J. Green, a wide receiver at Georgia, confessed that he'd sold his own jersey from the Independence Bowl the year before, to raise cash for a spring-break vacation. The NCAA sentenced Green to a four-game suspension for violating his amateur status with the illicit profit generated by selling the shirt off his own back. While he served the suspension, the Georgia Bulldogs store continued legally selling replicas of Green's No. 8 jersey for $39.95 and up.

A few months later, the NCAA investigated rumors that Ohio State football players had benefited from "hook-ups on tatts"—that is, that they'd gotten free or underpriced tattoos at an Ohio tattoo parlor in exchange for autographs and memorabilia—a violation of the NCAA's rule against discounts linked to athletic personae. The NCAA Committee on Infractions imposed five-game suspensions on Terrelle Pryor, Ohio State's tattooed quarterback, and four other players (some of whom had been found to have sold their Big Ten championship rings and other gear), but did permit them to finish the season and play in the Sugar Bowl. (This summer, in an attempt to satisfy NCAA investigators, Ohio State voluntarily vacated its football wins from last season, as well as its Sugar Bowl victory.) A different NCAA committee promulgated a rule banning symbols and messages in players' eyeblack—reportedly aimed at Pryor's controversial gesture of support for the pro quarterback Michael Vick, and at Bible verses inscribed in the eyeblack of the former Florida quarterback Tim Tebow.

The moral logic is hard to fathom: the NCAA bans personal messages on the bodies of the players, and penalizes players for trading their celebrity status for discounted tattoos—but it codifies precisely how and where commercial insignia from multinational corporations can be displayed on college players, for the financial benefit of the colleges. Last season, while the NCAA investigated him and his father for the recruiting fees they'd allegedly sought, Cam Newton compliantly wore at least 15 corporate logos—one on his jersey, four on his helmet visor, one on each wristband, one on his pants, six on his shoes, and one on the headband he wears under his helmet—as part of Auburn's $10.6 million deal with Under Armour.

"Restitution"

Obscure NCAA rules have bedeviled Scott Boras, the preeminent sports agent for Major League Baseball stars, in cases that may ultimately prove more threatening to the NCAA than Ed O'Bannon's antitrust suit. In 2008, Andrew Oliver, a sophomore pitcher for the Oklahoma State Cowboys, had been listed as the 12th-best professional prospect among sophomore players nationally. He decided to dismiss the two attorneys who had represented him out of high school, Robert and Tim Baratta, and retain Boras instead. Infuriated, the Barattas sent a spiteful letter to the NCAA. Oliver didn't learn about this until the night before he was scheduled to pitch in the regional final for a place in the College World Series, when an NCAA investigator showed up to question him in the presence of lawyers for Oklahoma State. The investigator also questioned his father, Dave, a truck driver.

Had Tim Baratta been present in their home when the Minnesota Twins offered $390,000 for Oliver to sign out of high school? A yes would mean trouble. While the NCAA did not forbid all professional advice—indeed, Baseball America used to publish the names of agents representing draft-likely underclassmen—NCAA Bylaw 12.3.2.1 prohibited actual negotiation with any professional team by an adviser, on pain of disqualification for the college athlete. The questioning lasted past midnight.

Just hours before the game was to start the next day, Oklahoma State officials summoned Oliver to tell him he would not be pitching. Only later did he learn that the university feared that by letting him play while the NCAA adjudicated his case, the university would open not only the baseball team but all other Oklahoma State teams to broad punishment under the NCAA's "restitution rule" (Bylaw 19.7), under which the NCAA threatens schools with sanctions if they obey any temporary court order benefiting a college athlete, should that order eventually be modified or removed. The baseball coach did not even let his ace tell his teammates the sad news in person. "He said, 'It's probably not a good idea for you to be at the game,'" Oliver recalls.

The Olivers went home to Ohio to find a lawyer. Rick Johnson, a solo practitioner specializing in legal ethics, was aghast that the Baratta brothers had turned in their own client to the NCAA, divulging attorney-client details likely to invite wrath upon Oliver. But for the next 15 months, Johnson directed his litigation against the two NCAA bylaws at issue. Judge Tygh M. Tone, of Erie County, came to share his outrage. On February 12, 2009, Tone struck down the ban on lawyers negotiating for student-athletes as a capricious, exploitative attempt by a private association to "dictate to an attorney where, what, how, or when he should represent his client," violating accepted legal practice in every state. He also struck down the NCAA's restitution rule as an intimidation that attempted to supersede the judicial system. Finally, Judge Tone ordered the NCAA to reinstate Oliver's eligibility at Oklahoma State for his junior season, which started several days later.

The NCAA sought to disqualify Oliver again, with several appellate motions to stay "an unprecedented Order purporting to void a fundamental Bylaw." Oliver did get to pitch that season, but he dropped into the second round of the June 2009 draft, signing for considerably less than if he'd been picked earlier. Now 23, Oliver says sadly that the whole experience "made me grow up a little quicker." His lawyer claimed victory. "Andy Oliver is the first college athlete ever to win against the NCAA in court," said Rick Johnson.

Yet the victory was only temporary. Wounded, the NCAA fought back with a vengeance. Its battery of lawyers prepared for a damages trial, ultimately overwhelming Oliver's side eight months later with an offer to resolve the dispute for $750,000. When Oliver and Johnson accepted, to extricate themselves ahead of burgeoning legal costs, Judge Tone was compelled to vacate his orders as part of the final settlement. This freed NCAA officials to reassert the two bylaws that Judge Tone had so forcefully overturned, and they moved swiftly to ramp up rather than curtail enforcement. First, the NCAA's Eligibility Center devised a survey for every drafted undergraduate athlete who sought to stay in college another year. The survey asked whether an agent had conducted negotiations. It also requested a signed release waiving privacy rights and authorizing professional teams to disclose details of any interaction to the NCAA Eligibility Center. Second, NCAA enforcement officials went after another Scott Boras client.

The Toronto Blue Jays had made the left-handed pitcher James Paxton, of the University of Kentucky, the 37th pick in the 2009 draft. Paxton decided to reject a reported $1 million offer and return to school for his senior year, pursuing a dream to pitch for his team in the College World Series. But then he ran into the new NCAA survey. Had Boras negotiated with the Blue Jays? Boras has denied that he did, but it would have made sense that he had—that was his job, to test the market for his client. But saying so would get Paxton banished under the same NCAA bylaw that had derailed Andrew Oliver's career. Since Paxton was planning to go back to school and not accept their draft offer, the Blue Jays no longer had any incentive to protect him—indeed, they had every incentive to turn him in. The Blue Jays' president, by telling reporters that Boras had negotiated on Paxton's behalf, demonstrated to future recruits and other teams that they could use the NCAA's rules to punish college players who wasted their draft picks by returning to college. The NCAA's enforcement staff raised the pressure by requesting to interview Paxton.

Though Paxton had no legal obligation to talk to an investigator, NCAA Bylaw 10.1(j) specified that anything short of complete cooperation could be interpreted as unethical conduct, affecting his amateur status. Under its restitution rule, the NCAA had leverage to compel the University of Kentucky to ensure obedience.

As the 2010 season approached, Gary Henderson, the Kentucky coach, sorely wanted Paxton, one of Baseball America's top-ranked players, to return. Rick Johnson, Andrew Oliver's lawyer, filed for a declaratory judgment on Paxton's behalf, arguing that the state constitution—plus the university's code of student conduct—barred arbitrary discipline at the request of a third party. Kentucky courts deferred to the university, however, and Paxton was suspended from the team. "Due to the possibility of future penalties, including forfeiture of games," the university stated, it "could not put the other 32 players of the team and the entire UK 22-sport intercollegiate athletics department at risk by having James compete." The NCAA appraised the result with satisfaction. "When negotiations occur on behalf of student-athletes," Erik Christianson, the NCAA spokesperson, told The New York Times in reference to the Oliver case, "those negotiations indicate that the student-athlete intends to become a professional athlete and no longer remain an amateur."

Paxton was stranded. Not only could he not play for Kentucky, but his draft rights with the Blue Jays had lapsed for the year, meaning he could not play for any minor-league affiliate of Major League Baseball. Boras wrangled a holdover job for him in Texas with the independent Grand Prairie AirHogs, pitching against the Pensacola Pelicans and Wichita Wingnuts. Once projected to be a first-round draft pick, Paxton saw his stock plummet into the fourth round. He remained unsigned until late in spring training, when he signed with the Seattle Mariners and reported to their minor-league camp in Peoria, Arizona.

"You Might As Well Shoot Them in the Head"

"When you dream about playing in college," Joseph Agnew told me not long ago, "you don't ever think about being in a lawsuit." Agnew, a student at Rice University in Houston, had been cut from the football team and had his scholarship revoked by Rice before his senior year, meaning that he faced at least $35,000 in tuition and other bills if he wanted to complete his degree in sociology. Bereft of his scholarship, he was flailing about for help when he discovered the National College Players Association, which claims 7,000 active members and seeks modest reforms such as safety guidelines and better death benefits for college athletes. Agnew was struck by the NCPA scholarship data on players from top Division I basketball teams, which showed that 22 percent were not renewed from 2008 to 2009—the same fate he had suffered.

In October 2010, Agnew filed a class-action antitrust suit over the cancellation of his scholarship and to remove the cap on the total number of scholarships that can be awarded by NCAA schools. In his suit, Agnew did not claim the right to free tuition. He merely asked the federal court to strike down an NCAA rule, dating to 1973, that prohibited colleges and universities from offering any athletic scholarship longer than a one-year commitment, to be renewed or not, unilaterally, by the school—which in practice means that coaches get to decide each year whose scholarships to renew or cancel. (After the coach who had recruited Agnew had moved on to Tulsa, the new Rice coach switched Agnew's scholarship to a recruit of his own.) Agnew argued that without the one-year rule, he would have been free to bargain with all eight colleges that had recruited him, and each college could have decided how long to guarantee his scholarship.

Agnew's suit rested on a claim of an NCAA antitrust violation combined with a laudable academic goal—making it possible for students to finish their educations. Around the same time, lawyers from President Obama's Justice Department initiated a series of meetings with NCAA officials and universities in which they asked what possible educational rationale there was for allowing the NCAA—an organization that did not itself pay for scholarships—to impose a blanket restriction on the length of scholarships offered by colleges. Tidbits leaked into the press. In response, the NCAA contended that an athletic scholarship was a "merit award" that should be reviewed annually, presumably because the degree of "merit" could change. Justice Department lawyers reportedly suggested that a free market in scholarships would expand learning opportunities in accord with the stated rationale for the NCAA's tax-exempt status—that it promotes education through athletics. The one-year rule effectively allows colleges to cut underperforming "student-athletes," just as pro sports teams cut their players. "Plenty of them don't stay in school," said one of Agnew's lawyers, Stuart Paynter. "They're just gone. You might as well shoot them in the head."

Agnew's lawsuit has made him a pariah to former friends in the athletic department at Rice, where everyone identified so thoroughly with the NCAA that they seemed to feel he was attacking them personally. But if the premise of Agnew's case is upheld by the courts, it will make a sham of the NCAA's claim that its highest priority is protecting education.

"They Want to Crush These Kids"

Academic performance has always been difficult for the NCAA to address. Any detailed regulation would intrude upon the free choice of widely varying schools, and any academic standard broad enough to fit both MIT and Ole Miss would have little force. From time to time, a scandal will expose extreme lapses. In 1989, Dexter Manley, by then the famous "Secretary of Defense" for the NFL's Washington Redskins, teared up before the U.S. Senate Subcommittee on Education, Arts, and Humanities, when admitting that he had been functionally illiterate in college.

Within big-time college athletic departments, the financial pressure to disregard obvious academic shortcomings and shortcuts is just too strong. In the 1980s, Jan Kemp, an English instructor at the University of Georgia, publicly alleged that university officials had demoted and then fired her because she refused to inflate grades in her remedial English courses. Documents showed that administrators replaced the grades she'd given athletes with higher ones, providing fake passing grades on one notable occasion to nine Bulldog football players who otherwise would have been ineligible to compete in the 1982 Sugar Bowl. (Georgia lost anyway, 24–20, to a University of Pittsburgh team led by the future Hall of Fame quarterback Dan Marino.) When Kemp filed a lawsuit against the university, she was publicly vilified as a troublemaker, but she persisted bravely in her testimony. Once, Kemp said, a supervisor demanding that she fix a grade had bellowed, "Who do you think is more important to this university, you or Dominique Wilkins?" (Wilkins was a star on the basketball team.) Traumatized, Kemp twice attempted suicide.

In trying to defend themselves, Georgia officials portrayed Kemp as naive about sports. "We have to compete on a level playing field," said Fred

Davison, the university president. During the Kemp civil trial, in 1986, Hale Almand, Georgia's defense lawyer, explained the university's patronizing aspirations for its typical less-than-scholarly athlete. "We may not make a university student out of him," Almand told the court, "but if we can teach him to read and write, maybe he can work at the post office rather than as a garbage man when he gets through with his athletic career." This argument backfired with the jurors: finding in favor of Kemp, they rejected her polite request for $100,000, and awarded her $2.6 million in damages instead. (This was later reduced to $1.08 million.) Jan Kemp embodied what is ostensibly the NCAA's reason for being—to enforce standards fairly and put studies above sports—but no one from the organization ever spoke up on her behalf.

The NCAA body charged with identifying violations of any of the Division I league rules, the Committee on Infractions, operates in the shadows. Josephine Potuto, a professor of law at the University of Nebraska and a longtime committee member who was then serving as its vice chair, told Congress in 2004 that one reason her group worked in secret was that it hoped to avoid a "media circus." The committee preferred to deliberate in private, she said, guiding member schools to punish themselves. "The enforcement process is cooperative, not adversarial," Potuto testified. The committee consisted of an elite coterie of judges, athletic directors, and authors of legal treatises. "The committee also is savvy about intercollegiate athletics," she added. "They cannot be conned."

In 2009, a series of unlikely circumstances peeled back the veil of secrecy to reveal NCAA procedures so contorted that even victims marveled at their comical wonder. The saga began in March of 2007, shortly after the Florida State Seminoles basketball team was knocked out of the NIT basketball tournament, which each spring invites the best teams not selected for the March Madness tournament. At an athletic-department study hall, Al Thornton, a star forward for the team, completed a sports-psychology quiz but then abandoned it without posting his written answers electronically by computer. Brenda Monk, an academic tutor for the Seminoles, says she noticed the error and asked a teammate to finish entering Thornton's answers onscreen and hit "submit," as required for credit. The teammate complied, steaming silently, and then complained at the athletic office about getting stuck with clean-up chores for the superstar Thornton (who was soon to be selected by the Los Angeles Clippers in the first round of the NBA draft). Monk promptly resigned when questioned by FSU officials, saying her fatigue at the time could not excuse her asking the teammate to submit the answers to another student's completed test.

Monk's act of guileless responsibility set off a chain reaction. First, FSU had to give the NCAA preliminary notice of a confessed academic fraud. Second, because this would be its seventh major infraction case since 1968, FSU mounted a vigorous self-investigation to demonstrate compliance with NCAA academic rules. Third, interviews with 129 Seminoles athletes unleashed a nightmare of matter-of-fact replies about absentee professors who allowed group consultations and unlimited retakes of open-computer assignments and tests. Fourth, FSU suspended 61 of its athletes in 10 sports. Fifth, the infractions committee applied the byzantine NCAA bylaws to FSU's violations. Sixth, one of the penalties announced in March of 2009 caused a howl of protest across the sports universe.

Twenty-seven news organizations filed a lawsuit in hopes of finding out how and why the NCAA proposed to invalidate 14 prior victories in FSU football. Such a penalty, if upheld, would doom coach Bobby Bowden's chance of overtaking Joe Paterno of Penn State for the most football wins in Division I history. This was sacrosanct territory. Sports reporters followed the litigation for six months, reporting that 25 of the 61 suspended FSU athletes were football players, some of whom were ruled ineligible retroactively from the time they had heard or yelled out answers to online test questions in, of all things, a music-appreciation course.

When reporters sought access to the transcript of the infractions committee's hearing in Indianapolis, NCAA lawyers said the 695-page document was private. (The NCAA claimed it was entitled to keep all such records secret because of a landmark Supreme Court ruling that it had won in 1988, in *NCAA v. Tarkanian*, which exempted the organization from any due-process obligations because it was not a government organization.) Media outlets pressed the judge to let Florida State share its own copy of the hearing transcript, whereupon NCAA lawyers objected that the school had never actually "possessed" the document; it had only seen the transcript via a defendant's guest access to the carefully restricted NCAA Web site. This claim, in turn, prompted intercession on the side of the media by Florida's attorney general, arguing that letting the NCAA use a technical loophole like this would undermine the state's sunshine law mandating open public records. After tumultuous appeals, the Florida courts agreed and ordered the NCAA transcript released in October of 2009.

News interest quickly evaporated when the sports media found nothing in the record about Coach Bowden or the canceled football victories. But the transcript revealed plenty about the NCAA. On page 37, T. K. Wetherell, the bewildered Florida State president, lamented that his university had hurt itself by cooperating with the investigation. "We self-reported this case," he said during the hearing, and he later complained that the most ingenuous athletes—those who asked "What's the big deal, this happens all the time?"—received the harshest suspensions, while those who clammed up on the advice of lawyers went free. The music-appreciation professor was apparently never questioned. Brenda Monk, the only instructor who consistently cooperated with the investigation, appeared voluntarily to explain her work with learning-disabled athletes, only to be grilled about her credentials by Potuto in a pettifogging inquisition of remarkable stamina.

In January of last year, the NCAA's Infractions Appeals Committee sustained all the sanctions imposed on FSU except the number of vacated football victories, which it dropped, ex cathedra, from 14 to 12. The final penalty locked Bobby Bowden's official win total on retirement at 377 instead of 389, behind Joe Paterno's 401 (and counting). This carried stinging symbolism for fans, without bringing down on the NCAA the harsh repercussions it would have risked if it had issued a television ban or substantial fine.

Cruelly, but typically, the NCAA concentrated public censure on powerless scapegoats. A dreaded "show cause" order rendered Brenda Monk, the tutor, effectively unhirable at any college in the United States. Cloaking an old-fashioned blackball in the stately language of law, the order gave notice that any school hiring Monk before a specified date in 2013 "shall, pursuant to the provisions of Bylaw 19.5.2.2(l), show cause why it should not be penalized if it does not restrict the former learning specialist [Monk] from having any contact with student-athletes." Today she works as an education supervisor at a prison in Florida.

The Florida State verdict hardly surprised Rick Johnson, the lawyer who had represented the college pitchers Andrew Oliver and James Paxton. "All the NCAA's enforcements are random and selective," he told me, calling the organization's appeals process a travesty. (Johnson says the NCAA has never admitted to having wrongly suspended an athlete.) Johnson's scalding experience prompted him to undertake a law-review article on the subject, which in turn sent him trawling through NCAA archives. From the summary tax forms required of nonprofits, he found out that the NCAA had spent nearly $1 million chartering private jets in 2006. "What kind of nonprofit organization leases private jets?," Johnson asks. It's hard to determine from tax returns what money goes where, but it looks as if the NCAA spent less than 1 percent of its budget on enforcement that year. Even after its plump cut for its own overhead, the NCAA dispersed huge sums to its 1,200 member schools, in the manner of a professional sports league. These annual payments are universal—every college gets something—but widely uneven. They keep the disparate shareholders (barely) united and speaking for all of college sports. The payments coerce unity within the structure of a private association that is unincorporated and unregulated, exercising amorphous powers not delegated by any government.

Searching through the archives, Johnson came across a 1973 memo from the NCAA general counsel recommending the adoption of a due-process procedure for athletes in disciplinary cases. Without it, warned the organization's lawyer, the association risked big liability claims for deprivation of rights. His proposal went nowhere. Instead, apparently to limit costs to the universities, Walter Byers had implemented the year-by-year scholarship rule that Joseph Agnew would challenge in court 37 years later. Moreover, the NCAA's 1975 convention adopted a second recommendation "to discourage legal actions against the NCAA," according to the minutes. The members voted to create Bylaw 19.7, Restitution, to intimidate college athletes in disputes with the NCAA. Johnson recognized this provision all too well, having won the temporary court judgment that the rule was illegal if not downright despotic. It made him nearly apoplectic to learn that the NCAA had deliberately drawn up the restitution rule as an obstacle to due process, contrary to the recommendation of its own lawyer. "They want to crush these kids," he says.

The NCAA, of course, has never expressed such a desire, and its public comments on due process tend to be anodyne. At a congressional hearing in 2004, the infractions-committee vice chair, Josephine Potuto, repeatedly argued that although the NCAA is "not bound by any judicial due process standards," its enforcement, infractions, and hearing procedures meet and "very likely exceed" those of other public institutions. Yet when pressed, Potuto declared that athletes would have no standing for due process even if the Supreme Court had not exempted the NCAA in the 1988 Tarkanian decision. "In order to reach due-process issues as a legal Constitutional principle, the individual challenging has to have a substantive property or liberty interest," she testified. "The opportunity to play intercollegiate athletics does not rise to that level."

To translate this from the legal jargon, Potuto used a circular argument to confine college athletes beneath any right to freedom or property in their own athletic effort. They have no stake to seek their rights, she claimed, because they have no rights at stake.

Potuto's assertion might be judged preposterous, an heir of the Dred Scott dictum that slaves possessed no rights a white person was bound to respect. But she was merely being honest, articulating assumptions almost everyone shares without question. Whether motivated by hostility for students (as critics like Johnson allege), or by noble and paternalistic tough love (as the NCAA professes), the denial of fundamental due process for college athletes has stood unchallenged in public discourse. Like other NCAA rules, it emanates naturally from the premise that college athletes own no interest in sports beyond exercise, character-building, and good fun. Who represents these young men and women? No one asks.

The debates and commissions about reforming college sports nibble around the edges—trying to reduce corruption, to prevent the "contamination" of athletes by lucre, and to maintain at least a pretense of concern for academic integrity. Everything stands on the implicit presumption that preserving amateurism is necessary for the well-being of college athletes. But while amateurism—and the free labor it provides—may be necessary to the preservation of the NCAA, and perhaps to the profit margins of various interested corporations and educational institutions, what if it doesn't benefit the athletes? What if it hurts them?

"The Plantation Mentality"

"Ninety percent of the NCAA revenue is produced by 1 percent of the athletes," Sonny Vaccaro says. "Go to the skill positions"—the stars. "Ninety percent African Americans." The NCAA made its money off those kids, and so did he. They were not all bad people, the NCAA officials, but they were blind, Vaccaro believes. "Their organization is a fraud."

Vaccaro retired from Reebok in 2007 to make a clean break for a crusade. "The kids and their parents gave me a good life," he says in his peppery staccato. "I want to give something back." Call it redemption, he told me. Call it education or a good cause. "Here's what I preach," said Vaccaro. "This goes beyond race, to human rights. The least educated are the most exploited. I'm probably closer to the kids than anyone else, and I'm 71 years old."

Vaccaro is officially an unpaid consultant to the plaintiffs in O'Bannon
v. NCAA. He connected Ed O'Bannon with the attorneys who now represent him, and he talked to some of the additional co-plaintiffs who have
joined the suit, among them Oscar Robertson, a basketball Hall of Famer
who was incensed that the NCAA was still selling his image on playing
cards 50 years after he left the University of Cincinnati.

Jon King, an antitrust lawyer at Hausfeld LLP in San Francisco, told me
that Vaccaro "opened our eyes to massive revenue streams hidden in college
sports." King and his colleagues have drawn on Vaccaro's vast knowledge of
athletic-department finances, which include off-budget accounts for shoe
contracts. Sonny Vaccaro and his wife, Pam, "had a mountain of documents," he said. The outcome of the 1984 Regents decision validated an
antitrust approach for O'Bannon, King argues, as well as for Joseph Agnew
in his continuing case against the one-year scholarship rule. Lawyers for
Sam Keller—a former quarterback for the University of Nebraska who is
featured in video games—are pursuing a parallel "right of publicity" track
based on the First Amendment. Still other lawyers could revive Rick
Johnson's case against NCAA bylaws on a larger scale, and King thinks
claims for the rights of college players may be viable also under laws
pertaining to contracts, employment, and civil rights.

Vaccaro had sought a law firm for O'Bannon with pockets deep enough
to withstand an expensive war of attrition, fearing that NCAA officials
would fight discovery to the end. So far, though, they have been forthcoming. "The numbers are off the wall," Vaccaro says. "The public will see for
the first time how all the money is distributed."

Vaccaro has been traveling the after-dinner circuit, proselytizing
against what he sees as the NCAA's exploitation of young athletes. Late in
2008, someone who heard his stump speech at Howard University mentioned it to Michael Hausfeld, a prominent antitrust and human-rights
lawyer, whose firm had won suits against Exxon for Native Alaskans and
against Union Bank of Switzerland for Holocaust victims' families. Someone tracked down Vaccaro on vacation in Athens, Greece, and he flew
back directly to meet Hausfeld. The shoe salesman and the white-shoe
lawyer made common cause.

Hausfeld LLP has offices in San Francisco, Philadelphia, and London.
Its headquarters are on K Street in Washington, D.C., about three blocks
from the White House. When I talked with Hausfeld there not long ago, he
sat in a cavernous conference room, tidy in pinstripes, hands folded on a

spotless table that reflected the skyline. He spoke softly, without pause, condensing the complex fugue of antitrust litigation into simple sentences. "Let's start with the basic question," he said, noting that the NCAA claims that student-athletes have no property rights in their own athletic accomplishments. Yet, in order to be eligible to play, college athletes have to waive their rights to proceeds from any sales based on their athletic performance.

"What right is it that they're waiving?," Hausfeld asked. "You can't waive something you don't have. So they had a right that they gave up in consideration to the principle of amateurism, if there be such." (At an April hearing in a U.S. District Court in California, Gregory Curtner, a representative for the NCAA, stunned O'Bannon's lawyers by saying: "There is no document, there is no substance, that the NCAA ever takes from the student-athletes their rights of publicity or their rights of likeness. They are at all times owned by the student-athlete." Jon King says this is "like telling someone they have the winning lottery ticket, but by the way, it can only be cashed in on Mars." The court denied for a second time an NCAA motion to dismiss the O'Bannon complaint.)

The waiver clause is nestled among the paragraphs of the "Student-Athlete Statement" that NCAA rules require be collected yearly from every college athlete. In signing the statement, the athletes attest that they have amateur status, that their stated SAT scores are valid, that they are willing to disclose any educational documents requested, and so forth. Already, Hausfeld said, the defendants in the Ed O'Bannon case have said in court filings that college athletes thereby transferred their promotional rights forever. He paused. "That's ludicrous," he said. "Nobody assigns rights like that. Nobody can assert rights like that." He said the pattern demonstrated clear abuse by the collective power of the schools and all their conferences under the NCAA umbrella—"a most effective cartel."

The faux ideal of amateurism is "the elephant in the room," Hausfeld said, sending for a book. "You can't get to the bottom of our case without exposing the hypocrisy of amateurism, and Walter Byers says it eloquently." An assistant brought in Byers's memoir. It looked garish on the shiny table because dozens of pink Post-its protruded from the text. Hausfeld read to me from page 390:

> The college player cannot sell his own feet (the coach does that) nor can he sell his own name (the college will do that). This is the plantation mentality resurrected and blessed by today's campus executives.

He looked up. "That wasn't me," he said. "That was the NCAA's architect." He found a key recommendation on page 388:

> Prosecutors and the courts, with the support of the public, should use antitrust laws to break up the collegiate cartel—not just in athletics but possibly in other aspects of collegiate life as well.

Could the book become evidence? Might the aged Byers testify? (He is now 89.) Was that part of the plaintiffs' strategy for the O'Bannon trial? Hausfeld smiled faintly. "I'd rather the NCAA lawyers not fully understand the strategy," he said.

He put the spiny book away and previewed what lies ahead. The court soon would qualify his clients as a class. Then the Sherman Antitrust Act would provide for thorough discovery to break down exactly what the NCAA receives on everything from video clips to jerseys, contract by contract. "And we want to know what they're carrying on their books as the value of their archival footage," he concluded. "They say it's a lot of money. We agree. How much?"

The work will be hard, but Hausfeld said he will win in the courts, unless the NCAA folds first. "Why?" Hausfeld asked rhetorically. "We know our clients are foreclosed: neither the NCAA nor its members will permit them to participate in any of that licensing revenue. Under the law, it's up to them [the defendants] to give a pro-competitive justification. They can't. End of story."

In 2010 the third Knight Commission, complementing a previous commission's recommendation for published reports on academic progress, called for the finances of college sports to be made transparent and public—television contracts, conference budgets, shoe deals, coaches' salaries, stadium bonds, everything. The recommendation was based on the worthy truism that sunlight is a proven disinfectant. But in practice, it has not been applied at all. Conferences, coaches, and other stakeholders resisted disclosure; college players still have no way of determining their value to the university.

"Money surrounds college sports," says Domonique Foxworth, who is a cornerback for the NFL's Baltimore Ravens and an executive-committee member for the NFL Players Association, and played for the University of Maryland. "And every player knows those millions are floating around only because of the 18-to-22-year-olds." Yes, he told me, even the second-string punter believes a miracle might lift him into the NFL, and why not? In all the many pages of the three voluminous Knight Commission reports, there is but one paragraph that addresses the real-life choices for college athletes. "Approximately 1 percent of NCAA men's basketball players and 2 percent of NCAA football players are drafted by NBA or NFL teams," stated the 2001 report, basing its figures on a review of the previous 10 years, "and just being drafted is no assurance of a successful professional career." Warning that the odds against professional athletic success are "astronomically high," the Knight Commission counsels college athletes to avoid a "rude surprise" and to stick to regular studies. This is sound advice as far as it goes, but it's a bromide that pinches off discussion. Nothing in the typical college curriculum teaches a sweat-stained guard at Clemson or Purdue what his monetary value to the university is. Nothing prods students to think independently about amateurism—because the universities themselves have too much invested in its preservation. Stifling thought, the universities, in league with the NCAA, have failed their own primary mission by providing an empty, cynical education on college sports.

The most basic reform would treat the students as what they are—adults, with rights and reason of their own—and grant them a meaningful voice in NCAA deliberations. A restoration of full citizenship to "student-athletes" would facilitate open governance, making it possible to enforce pledges of transparency in both academic standards and athletic finances. Without that, the NCAA has no effective checks and balances, no way for the students to provide informed consent regarding the way they are governed. A thousand questions lie willfully silenced because the NCAA is naturally afraid of giving "student-athletes" a true voice. Would college players be content with the augmented scholarship or allowance now requested by the National College Players Association? If a player's worth to the university is greater than the value of his scholarship (as it clearly is in some cases), should he be paid a salary? If so, would teammates in revenue sports want to be paid equally, or in salaries stratified according to talent or value on the field? What would the athletes want in Division III, where athletic budgets keep rising without scholarships or substantial sports revenue? Would athletes seek more or less variance in admissions standards? Should non-athletes also have a voice, especially where involuntary student fees support more and more of college sports? Might some schools choose to specialize, paying players only in elite leagues for football, or lacrosse? In athletic councils, how much would high-revenue athletes value a simple thank you from the tennis or field-hockey players for the newly specified subsidies to their facilities?

University administrators, already besieged from all sides, do not want to even think about such questions. Most cringe at the thought of bargaining with athletes as a general manager does in professional sports, with untold effects on the budgets for coaches and every other sports item. "I would not want to be part of it," North Carolina Athletic Director Dick Baddour told me flatly. After 44 years at UNC, he could scarcely contemplate a world without amateur rules. "We would have to think long and hard," Baddour added gravely, "about whether this university would continue those sports at all."

I, too, once reflexively recoiled at the idea of paying college athletes and treating them like employees or professionals. It feels abhorrent—but for reasons having to do more with sentiment than with practicality or law. Not just fans and university presidents but judges have often found cursory, non-statutory excuses to leave amateur traditions intact. "Even in the increasingly commercial modern world," said a federal-court judge in *Gaines v. NCAA* in 1990, "this Court believes there is still validity to the Athenian concept of a complete education derived from fostering the full growth of both mind and body." The fact that "the NCAA has not distilled amateurism to its purest form," said the Fifth Circuit Court of Appeals in 1988, "does not mean its attempts to maintain a mixture containing some amateur elements are unreasonable."

But one way or another, the smokescreen of amateurism may soon be swept away. For one thing, a victory by the plaintiffs in O'Bannon's case would radically transform college sports. Colleges would likely have to either stop profiting from students or start paying them. The NCAA could also be forced to pay tens, if not hundreds, of millions of dollars in damages. If O'Bannon and Vaccaro and company win, "it will turn college sports on its ear," said Richard Lapchick, the president of the National Consortium for Academics and Sports, in a recent interview with *The New York Times*.

Though the O'Bannon case may take several years yet to reach resolution, developments on other fronts are chipping away at amateurism, and at the NCAA. This past summer, *Sports Illustrated* editorialized in favor of allowing college athletes to be paid by non-university sources without jeopardizing their eligibility. At a press conference last June, Steve Spurrier, the coach of the South Carolina Gamecocks football team (and the winner of the 1966 Heisman Trophy as a Florida Gator), proposed that coaches start paying players $300 a game out of their own pockets. The coaches at six other SEC schools (Alabama, Florida, Ole Miss, Mississippi State, LSU, and Tennessee) all endorsed Spurrier's proposal. And Mark Emmert, the NCAA president, recently conceded that big changes must come. "The integrity of collegiate athletics is seriously challenged today by rapidly growing pressures coming from many directions," Emmert said in July. "We have reached a point where incremental change is not sufficient to meet these challenges. I want us to act more aggressively and in a more comprehensive way than we have in the past. A few new tweaks of the rules won't get the job done."

Threats to NCAA dominion also percolate in Congress. Aggrieved legislators have sponsored numerous bills. Senator Orrin Hatch, citing mistreatment of his Utah Utes, has called witnesses to discuss possible antitrust remedies for the Bowl Championship Series. Congressional committees have already held hearings critical of the NCAA's refusal to follow due process in disciplinary matters; other committees have explored a rise in football concussions. Last January, calls went up to investigate "informal" football workouts at the University of Iowa just after the season-ending bowl games—workouts so grueling that 41 of the 56 amateur student-athletes collapsed, and 13 were hospitalized with rhabdomyolysis, a life-threatening kidney condition often caused by excessive exercise.

The greatest threat to the viability of the NCAA may come from its member universities. Many experts believe that the churning instability within college football will drive the next major change. President Obama himself has endorsed the drumbeat cry for a national playoff in college football. This past spring, the Justice Department questioned the BCS about its adherence to antitrust standards. Jim Delany, the commissioner of the Big Ten, has estimated that a national playoff system could produce three or four times as much money as the existing bowl system does. If a significant band of football schools were to demonstrate that they could orchestrate a true national playoff, without the NCAA's assistance, the association would be terrified—and with good reason. Because if the big sports colleges don't need the NCAA to administer a national playoff in football, then they don't need it to do so in basketball. In which case, they could cut out the middleman in March Madness and run the tournament themselves. Which would deprive the NCAA of close to $1 billion a year, more than 95 percent of its revenue. The organization would be reduced to a rule book without money—an organization aspiring to enforce its rules but without the financial authority to enforce anything.

Thus the playoff dreamed of and hankered for by millions of football fans haunts the NCAA. "There will be some kind of playoff in college football, and it will not be run by the NCAA," says Todd Turner, a former athletic director in four conferences (Big East, ACC, SEC, and Pac-10). "If I'm at the NCAA, I have to worry that the playoff group can get basketball to break away, too."

This danger helps explain why the NCAA steps gingerly in enforcements against powerful colleges. To alienate member colleges would be to jeopardize its own existence. Long gone are television bans and the "death penalty" sentences (commanding season-long shutdowns of offending teams) once meted out to Kentucky (1952), Southwestern Louisiana (1973), and Southern Methodist University (1987). Institutions receive mostly symbolic slaps nowadays. Real punishments fall heavily on players and on scapegoats like literacy tutors.

A deeper reason explains why, in its predicament, the NCAA has no recourse to any principle or law that can justify amateurism. There is no such thing. Scholars and sportswriters yearn for grand juries to ferret out every forbidden bauble that reaches a college athlete, but the NCAA's ersatz courts can only masquerade as public authority. How could any statute impose amateur status on college athletes, or on anyone else? No legal definition of amateur exists, and any attempt to create one in enforceable law would expose its repulsive and unconstitutional nature—a bill of attainder, stripping from college athletes the rights of American citizenship.

For all our queasiness about what would happen if some athletes were to get paid, there is a successful precedent for the professionalization of an amateur sports system: the Olympics. For years, Walter Byers waged war with the NCAA's older and more powerful nemesis, the Amateur Athletic Union, which since 1894 had overseen U.S. Olympic athletes. Run in high-handed fashion, the AAU had infamously banned Jesse Owens for life in 1936—weeks after his four heroic gold medals punctured the Nazi claim of Aryan supremacy—because instead of using his sudden fame to tour and make money for the AAU at track meets across Europe, he came home early. In the early 1960s, the fights between the NCAA and the AAU over who should manage Olympic athletes become so bitter that President Kennedy called in General Douglas MacArthur to try to mediate a truce before the Tokyo Olympic Games.

Ultimately, Byers prevailed and effectively neutered the AAU. In November 1978, President Jimmy Carter signed the bipartisan Amateur Sports Act. Amateurism in the Olympics soon dissolved—and the world did not end. Athletes, granted a 20 percent voting stake on every Olympic sport's governing body, tipped balances in the United States and then inexorably around the world. First in marathon races, then in tennis tournaments, players soon were allowed to accept prize money and keep their Olympic eligibility. Athletes profited from sponsorships and endorsements. The International Olympic Committee expunged the word *amateur* from its charter in 1986. Olympic officials, who had once disdained the NCAA for offering scholarships in exchange for athletic performance, came to welcome millionaire athletes from every quarter, while the NCAA still refused to let the pro Olympian Michael Phelps swim for his college team at Michigan.

This sweeping shift left the Olympic reputation intact, and perhaps improved. Only hardened romantics mourned the amateur code. "Hey, come on," said Anne Audain, a track-and-field star who once held the world record for the 5,000 meters. "It's like losing your virginity. You're a little misty for a while, but then you realize, Wow, there's a whole new world out there!"

Without logic or practicality or fairness to support amateurism, the NCAA's final retreat is to sentiment. The Knight Commission endorsed its heartfelt cry that to pay college athletes would be "an unacceptable surrender to despair." Many of the people I spoke with while reporting this article felt the same way. "I don't want to pay college players," said Wade Smith, a tough criminal lawyer and former star running back at North Carolina. "I just don't want to do it. We'd lose something precious."

"Scholarship athletes are already paid," declared the Knight Commission members, "in the most meaningful way possible: with a free education." This evasion by prominent educators severed my last reluctant, emotional tie with imposed amateurism. I found it worse than self-serving. It echoes masters who once claimed that heavenly salvation would outweigh earthly injustice to slaves. In the era when our college sports first arose, colonial powers were turning the whole world upside down to define their own interests as all-inclusive and benevolent. Just so, the NCAA calls it heinous exploitation to pay college athletes a fair portion of what they earn.

Analyze

1. What are the pros and cons of corporations sponsoring college athletics—a situation in which colleges become an "advertising medium" for brands and apparel?
2. What legal obligation should universities have to "student-athletes" who are injured while playing a school sport?
3. In your opinion, does the NCAA do more to help students (such as by creating exposure for student-athletes) or more to harm students?
4. Overall, do you believe that universities would be better institutions with or without the type of competitive, corporate-sponsored sports that are played in large stadiums and broadcast on TV?

Explore

1. Many colleges construct a college image around their sports identity or sports mascot. Without sports or a sports mascot, how might your college develop a new public identity?
2. In your opinion, why are supporters of some large universities—such as Florida State University and the University of Oklahoma—more likely to focus their attention on a school's football or basketball team than they are on the same school's theatrical or film productions, cancer research program, or engineering achievements?
3. SHORT WRITING PROMPT: Create your own working definition of "amateurism" as it should be applied to student-athletes at your college. Consider the number of hours per week required by a sport, the level of compensation (financial aid), ownership of one's image, emphasis on winning, commercialism as expressed through corporate sponsorships, and levels of sports profit enjoyed by an institution.
4. FULL WRITING PROMPT: Agree or disagree: your college would be a better institution without corporate-sponsored, spectator-focused athletics.

Ian Crouch
Are College Athletes Employees?

Ian Crouch writes for NewYorker.com, where he covers sports, culture, and books. He lives in Boston.

March Madness resumes on Thursday, and you'll be hearing the announcers celebrate the talent and dedication of the so-called amateur student athletes on the court. That phrase used to be considered an honorific, but in recent years—owing to stagnant graduation rates, high-profile academic scandals, and the ever-increasing revenues that sports such as men's basketball and football bring to their schools—it has been more like a feeble euphemism. It reflects an outmoded myth about amateurism that leaves players unpaid, unable to advocate for their health and safety, and without even the normal freedoms that other college students have.

We need a more accurate vocabulary to talk about these players. A decision this week by the Chicago district office of the National Labor Relations Board offers one plain, useful term: employees. In a ruling issued on Wednesday, the N.L.R.B. regional director Peter Sung Ohr found that scholarship players on the Northwestern University football team are employees of the school, and therefore have the right to form a union. That finding, which Northwestern opposes and says it will appeal, applies only to private schools. (Students at public universities are subject to state labor laws.) Although the decision specifically concerns the Northwestern football program, its description of the life of college athletes calls the N.C.A.A.'s entire amateur model into question.

In January, Kain Colter, who had just finished a season as Northwestern's quarterback, filed a petition on behalf of his teammates to form a union. The players were backed by a new organization called the College Athletes Players Association, and received financial support from the United Steelworkers. In testimony before the board in February, Colter said plainly that playing football had been a job.

Ohr, in his spirited and at times feisty decision, agreed: "Under the common law definition, an employee is a person who performs services for another under a contract of hire, subject to the other's control or right of control, and in return for payment." In the case of Northwestern's scholarship players, the contract is the scholarship agreement that they sign with the university; the control is the pervasive and constant oversight by coaches; and the payment is the dollar value of the scholarship itself, which amounts to sixty-one thousand dollars per year for most players and seventy-six thousand dollars for those who also enroll in summer classes. Northwestern had argued that, rather than a payment, a scholarship should be considered a grant. Ohr, however, wrote that "the scholarship is clearly tied to the player's performance of athletic services as evidenced by the fact that scholarships can be immediately canceled if the player voluntarily withdraws from the team or abuses team rules."

The number here is the revenue that Northwestern's players generated for the school—two hundred and thirty-five million dollars between 2003 and 2012—and the comparative unfairness of a capped scholarship system that makes no distinction among players' abilities or contributions to the team. Scholarships fail to cover all the expenses that players incur during their years in college. And yet the N.C.A.A. forbids these players from entering into their own endorsement deals or otherwise profiting from their temporary status as local football heroes. It punishes them when they do.

On Wednesday, the N.C.A.A. was quick to emphasize the financial implications of the decision: "We frequently hear from student-athletes, across all sports, that they participate to enhance their overall college experience and for the love of their sport, not to be paid." This statement is almost obscene in its feigned naïveté, as if major college sports were still just some intramural frolic on the green after dinner. Tell that to the gamblers in Las Vegas—and to the coaches, athletic directors, administrators, and business interests that profit from these games played by supposedly grateful amateurs. The N.C.A.A. has a ten-billion-dollar television contract for the men's basketball tournament. At Northwestern, players sign away rights to their image to the school and to the Big Ten conference.

The statement also misrepresents the demands of the players in this case. Colter and his former Northwestern teammates weren't asking for more compensation. Instead, they sought the right to bargain collectively with the school over the conditions of their services as players. Ohr goes into great detail about the ways in which the lives of football players are different from those of other students at Northwestern. It is a striking portrait of a paternalistic and isolating experience. They must comply with the team's regulations regarding the use of social media, and aren't allowed to give interviews that aren't scheduled by the athletic department. Upperclassmen living off campus must get their leases approved by the coach. Players need to obtain approval from the athletic department before getting an off-campus job. They have to tell their coaches about the cars that they drive.

These are examples of the kind of control that employers exert over employees, Ohr argues, and those subject to such control should have the right to bargain.

The College Athletes Players Association, which is hoping to represent Northwestern's players, has said that it is also interested in "guaranteeing coverage of sports-related medical expenses for current and former players, ensuring better procedures to reduce head injuries and potentially letting players pursue commercial sponsorships," according to the Associated Press. These measured demands only serve to make the opposition from the N.C.A.A. and its member schools look more retrograde and extreme. There isn't even a guarantee that Northwestern's players would choose to unionize; they simply want the chance to vote.

In a way, Northwestern football is an odd test case. The program's graduation rate (above ninety-seven per cent) is the best in the country. Yet, based on the testimony of players, Ohr figured that students devoted between forty and fifty hours a week to football, and just twenty to school. And, he writes:

> The fact that the players undoubtedly learn great life lessons from participating on the football team and take with them important values such as character, dedication, perseverance, and team work, is insufficient to show that their relationship with the Employer is primarily an academic one.

Ivan Maisel, of ESPN, raises a smart series of concerns. There is, for example, a potential problem of scope. Ohr's decision covers only scholarship players on the football team. What about athletes who play other sports? "The workload of the college athletes in non-revenue sports is also extreme," he writes. "They also sign that contract to perform services. They are subject to the control of the coaches, and in return for payment. By these criteria, they deserve to join the union, too." And the decision covers only men. Women's sports often lose money. Does that mean that the female athletes in these sports are students, rather than employees, and thus undeserving of union protection?

But that's no argument in favor of maintaining a vastly flawed and unfair status quo. This week's decision joins a legal conversation that includes several other cases—including an antitrust suit originally filed by the former U.C.L.A. basketball player Ed O'Bannon over the rights of players to be paid for the use of their likeness, and, more recently, a case filed by the labor lawyer Jeffrey Kessler which argues that scholarships unfairly suppress player compensation.

Ohr's decision may get overturned by the full board, in Washington, on appeal; it may be fought in the courts. But, at the very least, it has added a cogent voice to the debate over the role of sports in American higher learning (and vice versa). College players may not be "student athletes," but they are something more remarkable: students *and* athletes, who have managed to go to college while working rigorous, full-time jobs.

Analyze

1. In your opinion, should some college athletes be classified as employees of the university? Employee here is defined as "a person who performs services for another under a contract of hire, subject to the other's control or right of control, and in return for payment."

2. What makes a college athlete an employee more than an enthusiastic amateur? Must the sport in question be a revenue sport—that is, one that produces a profit?

3. If college athletes are employees, to what, then, are they entitled: a salary, participation in any profits, workers' compensation for sports injuries, general health insurance, employer contributions to a retirement account, the right to collectively bargain for better work conditions?

Explore

1. What "great life lessons" might students learn through athletics that they might not learn elsewhere in college?

2. The article focuses on the amateur status of college athletes. Are there other "amateurs" who provide services for your college that should be considered employees? Consider actors in school productions, student senators, lab assistants, musicians, journalists for the student paper, website developers, and so forth. If your college offered protections of formal employment to its athletes, what other students might be

protected by that designation? And would a campus filled with student-employees likely improve or damage the academic environment at your college?

3. SHORT WRITING PROMPT: By interviewing students at your university (or in your class), write a short essay that explains how the life of a college athlete is different from that of most other students.

Dr. Alan Kadish
Colleges Prepare Athletes for Bad Behavior in the NFL

Dr. Alan Kadish, a professor of cardiology, is currently the president of the Touro College System in New York.

Pro football star Ray Rice is caught on tape punching his then-fiancée and casually dragging her unconscious body out of an elevator. Another one of the National Football League's biggest stars is indicted for beating his four-year-old son with a tree branch. Just days later, another player is arrested on domestic violence charges for assaulting his wife.

There are many troubling questions about each of these events: Did the National Football League try to cover up the Ray Rice incident? Are star athletes given special treatment when accused of a crime? Does the punishment always fit the crime?

The most recent—and the one that got most of the headlines—was the spectacle of Heisman Trophy–winning Florida State quarterback Jameis Winston, who has a history of bad behavior, jumping onto a table on campus and yelling obscene lyrics that were derogatory to women.

The school's original response to Winston's latest offense was to suspend him for the first half of Florida State's game against Clemson last Saturday night. School officials changed the punishment to a full game under pressure, but either way the punishment was absurd. Someone with Jameis Winston's history of transgressions should not have been suspended for half of a football game; he should have been suspended for half the season.

To me, as a college administrator, the underlying problem is that many big-sport schools fail to educate student-athletes on proper behavior, which leads to delinquency in the pros.

The NFL may be the subject of most of the upsetting headlines, but look closely and you'll see that their understudies in college don't shine in comparison. Winston was just the latest in a string of college football players to act inappropriately.

College athletics is a big business that in some schools outstrips academic achievements. At the very least, colleges that sponsor major athletic programs should ensure that they also educate student-athletes. Education also is about learning proper behavior and in these cases—and many others like them over the years—colleges are simply not doing enough.

We need to change the culture, best described by former Tampa Bay Buccaneers cornerback Troy Vincent, who told ESPN two years ago: "By the time the player is drafted, there's a pretty good chance he's thoroughly spoiled and surrounded by enablers."

So how do we accomplish this? Some suggestions:

- Colleges should adopt a zero-tolerance policy for inappropriate behavior, be it a violation of school rules, poor academic standing, offensive or derogatory remarks, misdemeanors or criminality. We need to send the message early on that such actions are will not be tolerated.
- We must apply discipline equally to everyone, from the star quarterback to a third-string lineman. This sense of entitlement evident in so many top players has to stop.
- Schools should implement mandatory counseling throughout the year to help athletes deal with the pressures of being in the public eye, give them an outlet to voice their frustrations and, hopefully, correct bad behavior before it manifests into something far worse.

Finally, punishments must fit the offense and take into account a player's past problems. For some that may mean a one-game suspension; for others it may mean getting kicked off the team.

Colleges have the responsibility of educating all of our students, whether they're star athletes or not. For athletics to be an appropriate part of a college's mission, it must also serve as a didactic tool. We need to start teaching the right lessons or our students will become adults who spend more time in courtrooms than on the field or at work.

Analyze

1. Do certain college sports (such as football and boxing) that glamorize violence contribute to a culture of violence on college campuses?

2. Some college sports (such as football and basketball) bring celebrity status to student-athletes. Describe both the benefits of and problems with this system.

3. The author believes that college sports must provide "a didactic tool." By this, he likely means that colleges must demonstrate the consequences of destructive or illegal activity foremost with student-athletes as they are often the most visible students at a university. Do you agree?

Explore

1. In the essay, Dr. Alan Kadish suggests that colleges have a civic responsibility to educate students in ethical conduct—or what the author calls "proper behavior." Most college students are legally adults and therefore outside traditional systems of civic paternalism. What role should a college play in the moral and civic education of its students, particularly when these lessons relate to activities that occur off school property?

2. The United States is the only country where college sports rise to the level of national entertainment. In your opinion, how do American values or customs allow for a blending of education, entertainment, and even spectacle when in other countries education is protected from these concerns?

3. FULL WRITING PROMPT: Dr. Kadish believes that, in addition to academic disciplines, colleges have a civic responsibility to offer students a moral education and instruction on "proper behavior" to ensure that their graduates become upstanding citizens. Do you agree? Or should college instruction be limited to academic topics?

Forging Connections

1. In 2014 the National Labor Relations Board ruled that football players at Northwestern University were "employees," not amateur athletes, and therefore had the right to unionize and collectively bargain for better working conditions. Using the Internet, read five news articles related to this ruling. How do you think the players' right to

organize will change the environment of college sports? (Note: As discussion of college athletes' legal standing as either amateurs or employees will continue after this book is published, feel free to refer to more recent rulings or relevant court cases to explore the changing status of the college athlete.)

2. Much of the discussion in these articles concerns men's sports, which are traditionally more lucrative than those of women. Assuming a university's athletic department produces a profit and that profit benefits athletes, discuss ways that women athletes and women's sports programs can benefit. Also discuss if financial support should be limited to athletes—or should it extend to other members of the larger sports experience, such as cheerleaders, the marching band, the mascot, and so forth?

Looking Further

1. Much of the debate about amateurism in college sports is related to colleges presenting themselves as nonprofit institutions. In other words, most colleges claim to be interested in benefiting the public through education rather than in producing a profit. Yet with stadium sports, many colleges act like for-profit companies, paying coaches six- or even seven-figure salaries and managing branded sports-centered enterprises. The conflict is obvious. Do you believe that colleges, over the next ten years, will evolve more into for-profit institutions or better entrench themselves into their traditional nonprofit identities?

2. Much of the debate also assumes that college sports will continue in their role as feeder programs that produce talent for professional football, basketball, and baseball teams. Do you think that colleges would be better served if stadium sports were removed from the university entirely—replaced with privately owned, minor-league teams where young players, both students and non-students alike, could train toward possible careers on a pro team?

7 Campus Life

The core college experience for most students is the opportunity to educate themselves. They sign up for courses in computer science, biology, algebra, engineering, and British literature. But the college experience, as touched on in previous chapters, is not solely a collection of academic classes. The college experience is a social one, an experience in which many students transition from childhood to their roles as adults, an experience in which they investigate possible careers, an experience in which they explore new social options. The college experience is a defining set of years that, for many individuals, shapes them for later life.

In this chapter, we gather together areas of campus life not yet examined in this book. Scott Carlson discusses how colleges attract students with luxury facilities, such as an ultramodern gym or spacious dorms that resemble urban condos. Abigail Sullivan Moore and Julie Turkewitz investigate how the legalization of marijuana is changing college life for students in Colorado. Phyllis Korkki considers the relationship between internships and coursework in finding employment after graduation. Jonathan Lash proposes that academic coursework by itself is not enough to prepare students for success: they will need a wide range of skills, including activism and artistry, to thrive in a rapidly changing world. Carla Rivera asks how the admission of transgender students will change the landscape at women's colleges, colleges that traditionally have found unity and identity through sisterhood. And Nathan Deuel eulogizes single-gender education as his alma mater transitions from a men's college to a coed campus.

Collectively these authors explore layers of the collegiate experience, aspects of which will forever stay with students as they move away from home and fall into facets of campus life.

Scott Carlson
Spending Shifts as Colleges Compete on Students' Comfort

Scott Carlson is a senior writer for *The Chronicle of Higher Education*, where he writes on college management, the cost of higher education, and sustainability.

When someone stops by Bethany College, claiming that they're just passing through, Scott D. Miller knows they're lying. This West Virginia college, where he has been president since 2007, is only 39 miles from Pittsburgh, but it's a long 39 miles, down one of three winding country roads. (There was a fourth road some years ago, but when a bridge on that route washed out in a rainstorm, state officials didn't bother replacing it.)

In this town of about 1,000 people, a visitor finds two businesses aside from the college: a general store, which sells everything from air filters to filet mignon, and a college watering hole that seems to sell beer and not much else. Even more than 170 years after the college's founding, the remote mountainside is just the sort of place that the clergyman Alexander Campbell had in mind when he created Bethany.

"There's this quote that Campbell had in the 1830s, before he founded the college," Mr. Miller says, "where he talked about wanting a location that was secluded, free from distraction."

These days Bethany is trying to drum up a little distraction, to bring students in and keep them around: In the past several years, the college has revived an equestrian program, expanded its athletics programs (adding sports like lacrosse and field hockey), started a marching band, offered a broader range of campus jobs for students, and added various student activities. For those who get a little too distracted, Bethany also put a significant sum into a new academic-counseling center.

The programs come out of a bucket of money known as "student services," a category that can include athletics, student organizations, admissions, financial-aid administration, and various kinds of counseling. On a ledger of expenditures, the new emphasis is plain to see: In 2007, Bethany was spending about $3,800 per full-time-equivalent student on such services; in 2008, after Mr. Miller arrived, it was spending $5,800 per student.

Mr. Miller, taking over after years of financial instability at the college, decided that giving students more amenities and activities was a way to help stabilize enrollment. A student's 168-hour week, he notes, consists of 18 hours in the classroom and 50 spent sleeping. "For the extra 100 hours a week, it's up to us to provide an educational experience."

Other colleges might not be as remote as Bethany, but they are trying the same things, as indicated by a new report from the American Institutes for Research. The report, covering college spending from 2001 to 2011, shows that increases in student services outpaced those in other categories at most types of colleges—a trend that has held for years in studies conducted by the institutes' Delta Cost Project, which looks at college finances. Although student-services spending can be modest compared with other categories, it has grown 20 to 30 percent at many colleges, outpacing any other category.

What's driving growth in that area? Many speculate that it's a facet of the amenities race—comforts and resources that go along with swanky dorms, cornucopian dining halls, and the infamous climbing walls (spending on which falls under a different category). Some say it represents colleges' commitment to a new population of students who need more help getting through college—first-generation students, or those with learning disabilities, depression, or anxiety. Some financial experts look at data from recent years and conclude that colleges are spending more on enrollment resources.

It's surely some combination of all of those priorities. But in the end, the growth in student services is certainly a sign of an intensifying competition among colleges. And even if the amenities, activities, and support cost many thousands of dollars per student, especially at elite institutions, they represent a college cost that students and their parents have asked for—either explicitly or through their decisions in enrollment.

Colleges are, more than ever, measuring their offerings and services against what peer institutions might provide, Mr. Miller says. The race is hardest on rural, less-selective colleges, he argues, which have to provide more support and more amenities to differentiate themselves.

"Competition is more intense now than I have seen in my 23 years as a college president," he says. "Colleges have to be more student-centered."

If that's true, surely most colleges are feeling the heat. The American Institutes for Research report shows that only public baccalaureate colleges and community colleges did not increase their spending on student services over the 10-year period. For the rest—public research and master's colleges, and all private institutions—the spending went up considerably.

For example, at private baccalaureate colleges, average spending on student services increased more than 21 percent per full-time-equivalent student, while spending on instruction went up only 5.5 percent, and on operations and maintenance by 9 percent. Spending on research, public service, and institutional support declined. At public master's institutions, student-services spending increased 15 percent, while that on instruction went up 6 percent, and in most other categories went down. Public research institutions spent 16 percent more on student services. At private master's institutions the increase was 24 percent, and at private research universities nearly 30 percent.

Spending on student services also grew faster at nearly all institutions compared with instruction and "overhead" expenses like academic support and maintenance.

Donna Desrochers, an author of the report and a researcher at the institutes, points out that the data lines up with a report by the group on administrator hiring, released in February. It said that new administrator hires—particularly in student services—were what drove a 28 percent expansion of the higher-education workforce from 2000 to 2012. Student-services positions also commanded the expansion of wages and salaries, as pay in other areas was either flat or declining.

Analyses of the increases should come with a caveat: Around 2006, a number of colleges began reporting athletics expenditures under student services for the first time—they had previously reported that spending under another category. Many institutions where spending on student services spiked explained to *The Chronicle* that they had previously categorized athletics under instruction, in most cases because coaches also taught classes.

However, says Ms. Desrochers, even if you examine subsequent expenditures, increases in student-services spending are still higher than in other areas. What she doesn't know is where, exactly, the money is going. Her data, from the Integrated Postsecondary Education Data System, or Ipeds, don't provide figures at that granular a level.

"If colleges are making investments in services that help students learn and graduate, that is a good investment," she says. (She is less positive about spending in athletics, because she doesn't believe it helps retention.) "The difficult part is that it is a broad category, and it's hard to determine what the money is being spent on."

For the details, one has to go to people who handle college finances or work in student services—and even there, the answers might come in broad brushstrokes. Patricia A. Whitely, vice president for student affairs at the University of Miami and chair of the board of National Association of Student Personnel Administrators, can point to a handful of areas where Miami's student services have expanded, and she hears the same from peers across the country. Start with mental-health counseling: Use of those services goes up 3 to 4 percent per year, and Miami has hired not only counselors but also social workers. Students show up at college with depression, hyperactivity disorders, Asperger's syndrome, or a history of therapy that goes back years—without the sense of shame that may have accompanied those conditions in the past.

"It's not a big deal to seek counseling," Ms. Whitely says. "It's all good news. But we have had to ramp up our support so they can persist, retain, and graduate."

The growing numbers of first-generation students present their own challenges, and many colleges are putting more effort into programming for them. Compliance with regulations is another factor—Miami has added two staff members in the past three years to help deal with Title IX regulations, not to mention staff added to deal with Title IV, the Clery Act, and other laws.

The university has also added activities of various kinds. "In 1995 we had 18 sports clubs at Miami. We have 48 now. Think about that," Ms. Whitely says. In the mid-1990s, the university had about 190 student organizations; it has 274 now. Forty are devoted to community service, she says, because today's college students "have been doing that since they were in fifth grade."

Her office handles educational programs in substance abuse and sexual assault. The university has added other programming to help build a sense of community on the campus and to keep students out of trouble in the city—late-night dining on the campus, till 2 a.m., is one such option, she notes. "Students are coming to us and saying, 'We want this.'"

At any institution, spending levels and priorities depend on a college's choice and scale of services. Empire State College, a branch of the State University of New York for adult and online learning, went from spending $306 per full-time-equivalent student in 2001 to $1,004 in 2011, adjusted for inflation, according to the American Institutes for Research. In recent years, the college has established an office to handle disability, wellness, and other student-services issues; a call center for student queries; a health-services fee; and a major expansion of tutoring services.

Private colleges—particularly elite ones—spend much more per student. Colgate University's spending on student services went from $3,200 per student in 2001 to $8,000 in 2011. Colgate is one of the institutions that transferred athletics spending from instruction to student services, which explains some of the jump. But Suzy M. Nelson, dean of the college, who supervises student affairs, ticks off some of the same cost drivers that Ms. Whitely does: expanded efforts in student life, career counseling, and regulation compliance. Colgate spent $24.8 million on student services in 2013. A little more than half of that went to sports programs, and $3.4 million to admissions. Of the remaining $8.7 million, 12 percent went to career planning, a portion that has grown slightly over time. The biggest growth has been in the 27 percent chunk that includes various deans' offices, seminars, drug and alcohol committees, a multicultural-affairs office, volunteer programs, and fall orientation.

Wellness is a big focus at a college that attracts high-achieving students—Colgate sees about 20 percent of its students in the counseling center, and health and counseling absorb 23 percent of the budget.

"Since 1988, the likelihood of college students' suffering depression has doubled, suicidal ideation has tripled, and sexual assault has quadrupled," Ms. Nelson says. "I can add to that alcohol abuse, sleep deprivation, anxiety disorders—any number of things that we may not have seen 10 to 20 years ago, at least in quantity."

She is clear that student services involves more than mitigating problems or checking off boxes on federal forms. The operation is a vital partner in creating the college experience. Ms. Nelson cites research by Richard J. Light, a Harvard University education professor, who asked people to recall a defining experience in college. The vast majority of them pointed to something outside of the classroom.

"If we cut out all of that stuff, it wouldn't be as expensive, but what I am suggesting is that this actually is the educational experience—in class and out of class," she says. "It's less learning from an expert and more about what you integrate and synthesize yourself. That is the goal."

The increasing emphasis on services and amenities began in the mid-1980s, says John Thelin, a historian of higher education at the University of Kentucky. Colleges had just come through an enrollment slump starting in the late 1970s, during which even careful observers of the industry predicted that many institutions would close. As a result, they started going after more middle-class and upper-middle-class kids, "from families where they just presume that you have certain amenities," Mr. Thelin says. Admissions offices, which had been passive in the 1950s and 60s, started staffing up and sending emissaries to high schools near and far.

Some believe that professors once helped provide academic counseling and extracurricular activities that were eventually professionalized under student-services administrations, but Mr. Thelin says that's a nostalgic view. Regardless, he has begun to notice that his former graduate students who went into student services have given their work more of a professional veneer.

"They started describing student services not as extracurricular but co-curricular," he says. "I think the idea was to legitimize and ensure the survival of some of the things they were offering."

Compare campus life today with the "spartan experience" it was in the 1950s, Mr. Thelin says. Colleges did not have elaborate counseling programs to help students get through—in fact, professors promoted a sink-or-swim environment, and attrition rates were high, even at selective colleges.

Go back even further, and the whole notion of a ready-made college experience for incoming students would have been totally foreign. College
administrations coordinated academic instruction, and that was about it.

"If you go back to the 1890s and early 1900s, it was widely agreed that the
interesting part of the college experience was the student clubs—athletics,
society, and debating clubs—and a lot of that stuff was done by students
and for students, and it was done outside of official institutional budgets,"
Mr. Thelin says. Students had to figure out where to live and eat on their
own. "That's how eating co-ops were started at Princeton. They originally
were very pragmatic arrangements—rent a place to eat, hire a cook, throw
in your share. It was an innovative and resilient student culture."

For Bethany, enriching the campus experience was a matter of survival.
When Mr. Miller was hired, seven years ago, he asked a consulting group of
former college presidents to visit and provide guidance on what the college
needed to survive. A main recommendation focused on giving students
more support and amenities.

"The small town and the rural location is one of the major contributors
on the attrition side," says Mr. Miller. "So it's up to us to be more responsive
to our consumers and our marketplace, to provide greater activities outside
of the classroom."

On a tour of the campus, Mr. Miller points out new hangouts for students, the equestrian fields, and new sports facilities, where some of the
college's annual $5 million in student-services money might be spent.

The most expensive additions to Bethany's programming are not necessarily fun stuff. The college now devotes $400,000 a year to jobs for stu-
dents who don't qualify for Federal Work-Study. It puts $326,000 per year
into an academic-counseling program for both mainstream students and
those with learning disabilities. And, with $155,000 a year, it has beefed up
a center for enrollment management, admissions, and financial aid.

When seen on a tour, the results of those expenditures don't seem particularly opulent, especially by the standards of what one finds at elite universities these days. (A new workout room for students, for example,
consists of a collection of equipment arranged in a low-ceilinged room of an
underutilized building.)

What the college gets for the investment is unclear. Officials point to
data showing that Bethany has some of the best graduation rates among its
34 peers in the Appalachian College Association. But according to Ipeds data,

its graduation rates have been falling, from a six-year-graduation rate of 70 percent in 2006, to 68 percent in 2009, to 48 percent in 2012. Mr. Miller says the decline is mostly due to a stagnant economy and students who are stretched financially.

While Mr. Miller is certain that Bethany needed the student-services investments to remain competitive, he seems ambivalent about the competition with other colleges. The Internet, he says, has changed the game during his career—students check out what each of their potential choices has to offer, and colleges look at what the institution across town is advertising.

In building and adding programs to remain attractive, "some schools will see the bubble burst and not be able to keep pace," Mr. Miller says. Bethany got a windfall a few years ago, when it leased out a natural-gas well on a patch of the college's 1,300 acres, ensuring a steady flow of money for the next 30 to 40 years. Still, Mr. Miller says, the college depends on enrollment, and it has to be responsive. "Students walk and talk with their checkbooks."

Perhaps students are both more demanding and more fragile today. Perhaps colleges are more committed to their students. Perhaps it's part of a trend that has turned college into a luxury-resort experience, a consumer-oriented product. Maybe it's a complicated mixture of all of those motivations.

Part of it is on the colleges, says Steve Schneider, a counselor at Sheboygan South High School, in Wisconsin, who was a finalist for a national school-counselor-of-the-year award in 2014.

The college search starts with the student focusing on what he or she wants to do and which college has the right academic program. Then the college brochures start showing up, describing the amenities and services each place provides. "It isn't until students start to enter into that portion of this process when they begin to realize, 'Hang on a second, maybe there is a school that can provide something that is more cool, or something I don't know I need until I know they have it,'" Mr. Schneider says.

Colleges position themselves to offer a unique angle, and since math, history, literature, and science are not typically unique, it's the extracurricular experience that has to be. First-generation students are particularly susceptible, he says, because their parents can't guide them regarding which amenities and support services are vital and which are just frills.

Many colleges, the counselor says, are fishing for students who might need a little more time before they are ready for the college experience. Statistics on graduation rates attest to that.

Colleges attracting those students "ignore the reality that a lot of kids are uncomfortable with college because they probably shouldn't be going," Mr. Schneider says. The amenities and services are, in that case, just a salve: "If we know you're not going to be comfortable educationally, because that's going to be a real struggle for you, we are going to make sure that you are comfortable in other ways."

But students and their parents are clearly a factor as well. This is the era of the "super kid," says Ms. Nelson, from Colgate. "Every kid is going to take ballet lessons and do three sports and be in the play—all of these things that were not typical of years ago. That drives the expectations of the students who come here and the expectations of the parents who send their kids here."

And parents are very involved in their kids' lives. "Some would argue that students are becoming less and less resilient because of the way that they are parented and because their childhood is extended into late adolescence," Ms. Nelson says. Maybe college-bound kids in the good old days were more self-reliant, but they were also predominantly male and predominantly elite. The landscape has changed, and colleges have had to change with it. "Students are able to perform really well," she says, "when they know that they are adequately supported personally and professionally."

Analyze

1. Student services add substantial charges to the overall cost of college. In the example of Bethany College, the cost of student services comes to nearly $6,000 per year per student. Student services (also called student affairs and student support) is an umbrella department that usually covers many non-academic areas of the student experience, including the health center, student gym, recreation areas, on-campus dining, counseling services, student clubs and organizations, new student orientation, escort vans, Greek affairs, student union activities, veterans' programs, career development, wellness education, disability support services, multicultural services, faith-based services, substance abuse services, intermural sports, and often athletics. Keeping in mind that these programs add to the cost of college for all students, are there any programs that you would add to student services at your school?

Are there any "optional" areas—such as "swanky gyms," Greek life, intermural sports, or the "cornucopian dining halls"—that you might remove to lower the cost of college?

2. Do you believe that competition in "student services" is a positive or negative force in terms of creating a quality experience for most college students? Does it improve the value of college—or just increase the cost?

3. Are prospective students more likely to select a college with reasonably good academic programs but excellent student services (luxury dorms, wide range of dining options, modern gym, etc.) or are they more likely to attend a college with reasonably good student services (average dorms, modest dining programs, small or perhaps no gym) but excellent academic programs?

4. Should some student services be "unbundled"? That is, for nonessential services, should students pay only for those they use (e.g., intermural sports, the gym, Greek life, late-night dining, recreational programs, student clubs)?

Explore

1. In your opinion, why are students accustomed to more services on campus today than they were thirty years ago?

2. As a prospective student exploring college options, how important were student services to you—particularly the "cool factor" of the dorms, gym, and so forth—in selecting a college?

3. SHORT WRITING PROMPT: Propose one new student service for your college. Explain the benefit to students. Estimate the overall cost and then (dividing the overall cost by the total number of students at your college) the cost per student.

4. FULL WRITING PROMPT: Suzy B. Nelson, a dean at Colgate University, explains that students today need more services because "their childhood is extended into late adolescence." Do you agree that students today have a longer period of childhood and adolescence? What services are essential for college students today? What services at your college are unessential or luxury items? To balance costs, student desires, and marketability, what student services should your college offer, considering that the needs of students today may differ from the needs of past generations? What services, if any, should be removed?

Abigail Sullivan Moore and Julie Turkewitz
Legally High at a Colorado Campus

Abigail Sullivan Moore is the co-author of *The iConnected Parent: Staying Close to Your Kids in College (and Beyond) While Letting Them Grow Up*. As a journalist, she is a regular contributor to *The New York Times*'s coverage on educational life. **Julie Turkewitz** is a staff reporter for *The New York Times* who lives in Denver.

In an apartment complex just outside the western edge of the University of Colorado's flagship campus, a 22-year-old psychology major named Zach has just leaned over an expensive oil rig—a twisting glass tube that he will use to smoke shatter, a hash oil concentrate. Once he lights up, his high will be rapid and intense.

Zach spends hundreds of dollars on smoking devices. But he has a side income. This evening's session was preceded by visits to three medical marijuana dispensaries, where, using his state-issued card, he bought pot products to sell to friends at a markup. "Runners"—campus argot, as in running around buying for others—are an open secret on campus.

Zach takes a seat on his overstuffed sectional and tells how it happened: His first day living on campus, a sophomore had taken him to a dispensary for a pizza with marijuana baked in. He asked how he could get his own card, and friends coached him on telling a doctor about anxiety, nausea or back pain. "I just said I had a bike accident when I was younger, and that caused lower back pain, which caused nausea and that caused anxiety," he recalls. "I was afraid it wouldn't happen, so I just got all three knocked out." He presented a bill mailed to his dorm as proof he was a state resident, which he wasn't, and received a card allowing him to access medical marijuana immediately, two ounces at a time.

Some of Zach's clients are under 21 and cannot buy recreational cannabis legally. But others are older students who simply don't want to pay the hefty tax—three times that levied on medical marijuana. So despite the abundance of recreational cannabis products since the first retail shops opened in January, there is still a vibrant black market for medical marijuana, which has been legal in Colorado since 2001 with a doctor's recommendation.

"There's definitely still the demand," says Zach, who is on track to graduate in December. He makes anywhere from a few dollars to a thousand a month, depending on how much he hustles, but he says that overall sales have declined a bit, what with retail shops, student growers and all the medical cards.

It's difficult to say if students are smoking more. There is no long-term data by age, but statewide about 16,000 18- to 24-year-olds are on the medical marijuana registry. That's 14 percent of all cardholders. City of Boulder tax revenue for medical marijuana for the first six months of 2014 was up 30 percent, at $500,000—about equal to revenue on recreational marijuana.

Nationally, marijuana use among young adults has clearly been trending upward. The percentage of college students who reported smoking within the previous year plummeted from a high of 51 percent in 1981 to a low of 26.5 percent in 1991, and has been zigzagging back up, to some 36 percent in 2013, according to the Monitoring the Future Study at the University of Michigan. Data released in September show that one of 20 college students (one of 11 men) gets high daily or near daily, the highest rate since 1981. To put that in perspective, from 1990 to 1994, fewer than one in 50 students used pot that frequently.

Experts say that the increase is surely a reflection of relaxed laws governing marijuana in some states, a movement gaining momentum. Floridians will face a ballot initiative on Tuesday on whether to legalize medical marijuana, which is allowed in almost half the states. Alaska, Oregon and District of Columbia voters will decide whether to follow Colorado and Washington State, where recreational marijuana has been legal since 2012.

The amendments ban smoking in public—on streets and in parks, shops and restaurants. The same holds for campuses, including university housing.

Dr. Donald A. Misch, associate vice chancellor for health and wellness at the University of Colorado, says that his main concern about the way legalization will affect students is that the industry—and associated advertising and commercialization—promotes the notion that cannabis is harmless. Monitoring the Future asks high school seniors if they see "great harm" in smoking regularly: 60 percent do not. In 2005, 42 percent did not.

Dr. Misch is working with other campus officials to increase awareness about the effects of the substance, including its impact on learning. "It is not going to turn you into an ax murderer," he says, "but what I tell people is: 'The good news is that marijuana is in many ways better than alcohol. The bad news is it's not as benign as many people want you to believe.' "

Tucked away in a windowless basement room in the university's Wardenburg Health Center, three clean-cut undergraduates are examining how marijuana is affecting them. "Breathe," a sign suggests in the softly lit room. Backpacks slung to the floor, the students form a restless crescent—pencils tapping, legs jiggling—around a new-age rug of concentric circles.

"Did anybody get in more trouble over the weekend?" asks Stephen Bentley, a substance abuse counselor. They hadn't. The session, designed to help them see the discrepancy between getting high and reaching their goals, is one of three they have been mandated to attend. All are under 21 and were caught smoking.

Marijuana citations by the campus police are, in fact, down—154 as of Oct. 3, compared with almost 256 in the same period last year. Christina Gonzales, dean of students, says the university is moving from a punitive stance to a more educational approach, easing up on enforcement. But last year, 718 students who had been sent to the health center by the courts or university after a substance-related offense (mostly alcohol) were found to be engaged in pot use that put them at risk.

Michael, a sophomore from Colorado, was caught over the summer in a Boulder park for possession. "A bike cop came up and saw me exhale." He paid fines and fees of about $150, performed 24 hours of community service and had to complete Mr. Bentley's three-part class. If he stays out of trouble for several months, the court will wipe his record clean. During the summer, he was smoking about five times a week but has slowed down with the start of classes.

Mr. Bentley asks the group about problems with memory, which seems to resonate with Michael. "If I get high a number of times per week," he says, "I notice that my memory slumps a little."

Mr. Bentley empathizes. "You can't remember your car keys, phone?"

"No, it's not like that. If a friend tells me an answer to a problem when I'm working on homework and I'm not quite there yet, I can't remember it."

"So, you can't hold it in your mind," Mr. Bentley affirms. No judgment, no confrontation, no labels. This is the mantra.

Mr. Bentley and counselors at other universities say they are seeing a small but growing number of students who have been smoking since age 14 and are serious users. He mentions dabs, an exponentially powerful form of marijuana. Last year, he got an email from a member of the housing staff.

Students were wielding a butane torch in the dorm. "The kids were saying, 'We're making crème brûlée on the hot plate.'"

Not exactly. The torches heat a nail. A dab of pot concentrate is placed on the head. Vapors are inhaled.

"That's the way things work in this culture," says Mr. Bentley, who has more than 20 years in the addiction field, 10 at Boulder. "People on the front lines are playing catch-up a lot of times." Word spread quickly through the staff of the potential fire hazard.

Universities are searching for ways to respond to marijuana, the most abused substance on campuses after alcohol. But interventions are often adaptations of programs for heavy drinkers that don't capture the marijuana experience, says Jason R. Kilmer, an assistant professor of psychiatry at the University of Washington. In a typical program for experienced smokers, students answer questions adapted from a widely used index of alcohol-related problems: Has the student ever passed out after using? Got into a fight? But they aren't asked about eating too much, coughing and problems with sleep, motivation, memory and attention—top unwanted effects of marijuana named in a recent survey of students by Dr. Kilmer and colleagues. Helping students recognize problems can prompt them to reduce consumption.

Some colleges, including the University of North Carolina at Wilmington, Boston College and the University of Southern Indiana, have been adding programs tailored to marijuana users. C.U.-Boulder offers a tier of psycho-educational options—two levels of individual sessions for mild and more serious users, and a group program for moderate and heavier users. For students unable to curb their use, a more extensive program is being planned to help them add structure to their lives and find relaxation alternatives—yoga, maybe.

"It's a retention strategy as well," Mr. Bentley says. Users, even infrequent, are more likely to drop out, according to a 2013 report from the University of Maryland.

Alan J. Budney, a researcher and professor at the Geisel School of Medicine at Dartmouth, ticks off academic fallout: "Not getting to class, changing majors, the B average becomes a C average—they are small things that aren't disastrous but they can change the course of where you are heading."

Research on universities' efforts is scant. Several studies have shown encouraging, if short-term results. Three months after a brief intervention, students from two campuses in the Northwest reported smoking less and experiencing fewer pot-related consequences; ditto for Wilmington students one month after their program.

At the heart of the sessions is motivational interviewing, which gets students to voice their own ambivalence about their use and eventually consider changing it.

Students first discuss what's good about getting high, how it lubricates social interactions and dissipates boredom and stress. Michael, a driven computer engineering major, tells Mr. Bentley's group that pot helps him feel his emotions. "Marijuana changed my point of view on life, not to take things so hard and go easier on myself." And, of course, there are the perception-altering qualities. Ben, a junior, smiles and says: "When you're high, watching a movie or going to a concert is freaking awesome."

They also discuss what's "not so good" (words like "bad" are taboo). Spending too much: "I don't want to even think about that," says Kevin, the third member of the group, who smoked multiple times a day as a freshman but has cut back to three or four times a week. Lack of motivation scores, too. And anxiety. "If you have anxiety in your life regularly, it amplifies it," Ben offers.

As students reveal their dislikes, counselors listen intently for signs of self-medication for anxiety, depression, attention deficit hyperactivity disorder or post-traumatic stress disorder. But mostly, they listen for any hook that might motivate a student to cut back.

Relationship troubles caused by a partner's disapproval of their marijuana use is a "biggie," says Rebecca Caldwell, director of the substance abuse program in Wilmington. So are slipping grades, a factor motivating the three in Mr. Bentley's session. For an athlete, it might be diminished lung capacity.

Because marijuana's effects are subtle, some students don't connect the dots with, say, feeling tired after a night's sleep. Some don't want to see the connection. Pot becomes part of who they are. Oregon State University shut down its group program two years ago and now offers only individual sessions because participants were enabling one another, says Robert C. Reff, director of the substance abuse program.

"I ask: 'Who are your friends? How many smoke marijuana?' And they say, 'All of them.'"

Ask students what has changed at the University of Colorado since legalization and most will say: not much.

Boulder has a long history with cannabis. Hippies flocked to this oasis of independent thought, drawn by a bustling music scene and student protests. As the city morphed into a counterculture outpost and activist hotbed—passing strict environmental laws, relaxing drug enforcement and opening one of the state's first abortion clinics—getting high was not just a way to tune out but also a political statement.

"The only rules here are no rules," Rob Pudim, a resident, told a Newsweek reporter in a 1980 piece entitled "Where the Hip Meet to Trip." "The only people in town who aren't comfortable," he said, "are straight people who need boundaries."

The campus still draws from afar. Nearly 40 percent of its 26,000 undergraduates are from out of state—a high percentage for a public university. They are attracted by mountain adventure and a stunning setting. The Flatirons, the steep slabs of rock that dominate the landscape, feel close enough to touch. Many students are here because of the robust science programs; C.U. is a member of the Association of American Universities, an exclusive group of research institutions. And because of its party-school reputation.

On a recent Friday, a clutch of students and friends gather around a table garnished for an evening of casual indulgence: beers, playing cards, tubes of medical marijuana and a bong. All are 21, or almost there, and from other states.

Several voice sentiments that are shared in other corners of campus. They didn't come here simply because it's located in a permissive pot town, but cannabis culture certainly played a role. "I could have went to a bunch of sweet public schools," says Erik Mingo, "and I chose this one because I knew it was pretty accepted here. I knew people had an open mind."

Mr. Mingo dropped out after the spring semester to work at a start-up. He has largely quit smoking, and isn't indulging on this night. "I just didn't really need it anymore," he explains. "It helped me relax and think about myself and the world, and I just wasn't getting the same return." His priority now is excelling at a demanding job, he says. "I was moving on just naturally in my life."

The campus is not under a cannabis cloud. Sometimes one sees a lit joint in the open or a "vape" pen in class, drawing ire from professors. But students and others talk about a shift in how they view cannabis consumption. Once an act of rebellion, it no longer seems to hold symbolic power. "Now it's just part of everyday life," says Joseph Kaley, 27, who graduated in 2009 and manages a Mexican restaurant on the Hill, an off-campus gathering spot. Mr. Kaley attended three of the campus's famous April 20 smoke-outs, lighting up each time to protest marijuana's criminal status at the time.

In 2012, the university successfully shut down "4/20," saying it had grown so large it was disrupting academic life. Many were angered, particularly by the methods used to ward smokers away: Workers spread smelly fish fertilizer on the quad and anyone without a student identification card was turned away.

New students, when asked, see the smoke-out as a piece of quirky campus history. "It's just kind of fading from people's memories," says Wyatt Ryder, 20, the chief of staff of the student government, which last April held a symposium offering "an all-inclusive inside dive into the realm of cannabis culture."

"The goal was to have a very nuanced discussion about marijuana," said Caitlin Pratt, 23, Mr. Ryder's colleague in student government. Panelists discussed making money in the industry, the effects of cannabis on the mind and efforts to legalize the substance in other states. One of the most popular panels was led by Nolan Kane, a C.U. professor attempting to map the cannabis genome to better understand marijuana's medical, fuel and biotechnology potential.

A few months later, Mr. Ryder attended a national conference for student government representatives. He was accosted with questions—and jokes—about pot culture at his university. Mr. Ryder, who doesn't even smoke, was shocked to be appointed the conference's unofficial marijuana expert.

"I just think it's fascinating," he said, "because to us in Colorado, it's not such a big deal. But to other people, it's a major issue."

Analyze

1. In your opinion, will the legalization of marijuana lower graduation rates of students? Will it lower their overall GPA?
2. The article suggests that there are significant lifestyle differences between heavy drinkers and marijuana users. In a college environment, what are the primary lifestyle or usage differences between the two groups?
3. How is drug and alcohol use different at college than it was at your high school?

Explore

1. Universities see themselves mostly as an environment where students explore educational interests and learn skills that will benefit them for the rest of their lives; however, popular films—such as *Animal House*—sometimes present college as an environment primarily focused on social experiences. In your opinion, what percentage of your freshman class *primarily* came to college to explore educational interests and what percentage *primarily* came for the social experience?

2. Some colleges designate campus as an alcohol-free, drug-free environment, even in areas where marijuana is legal. What would be the pros and cons of designating your campus, including dorms and other residential areas, as both an alcohol- and drug-free environment?

3. SHORT WRITING PROMPT: Using your college's webpage as a starting point, create a list of non-academic services your college offers students. Services may include various substance abuse groups (such as Alcoholics Anonymous and Marijuana Anonymous), money management programs, health services (often including flu shots and wellness classes), nutrition counseling, family and relationship counseling, and safe sex education. List the services and their location.

Phyllis Korkki
The Internship as Inside Track

Phyllis Korkki in an assignment editor for *The New York Times*, where she writes on employment-related issues.

Want to land a full-time job after college? Get an internship or two, or even four or more.

Internships have long been a part of the collegiate learning experience, but have never been more closely tied to permanent hiring than they are today, said Trudy Steinfeld, executive director of career development at New York University.

Of course, internships aren't the only route to employment. But companies increasingly view them as a recruiting tool because they are a way to test-drive potential employees, she said. Conversely, interns can test-drive the company to see if it's a good fit, professionally and culturally.

Not only do college interns garner more job offers than applicants without that experience, but jobs that grow out of internships tend to command higher starting salaries, said Edwin W. Koc, research director at the National Association of Colleges and Employers.

But while more companies are offering internships, the competition has become more intense. And more high school students, too, are seeking them, adding to the competitive pressure, said Lauren Berger, chief executive of Internqueen.com, an online internship listing site. Ms. Berger herself had 15 internships while attending the University of Central Florida, mostly in public relations, entertainment and communications, she said.

So what is the best way to find an internship? It sounds so basic, but many students don't take the logical first step—visiting career services centers at their colleges, Ms. Berger said. Career centers in each major, and for the college as a whole, can offer leads, and free services like mock interviews and help with résumés.

Beyond checking with your college, use Web sites, social media and networking. Another option is to call a company that interests you and ask whether it needs an intern. "If the employer tells you they've never had an intern before," Ms. Berger said, "ask them if you can be the first."

She recommends making a list of 10 companies where you could see yourself working, then finding their Web sites and the contact information for their internship coordinators. Then note the materials needed to apply, as well as any deadlines.

Treat each application individually, she said. "I always recommend a cover letter even if the employer doesn't require one." she said. If you don't hear back from the company in two weeks, she advised, send a follow-up e-mail.

On Internships.com, which posts openings, just 34 percent of the internships listed by employers are paid positions, said Robin Richards, chief executive of the company. But that varies widely by industry. Glamorous jobs like those in fashion and entertainment tend not to pay, whereas fields like engineering, technology and finance are more likely to offer money.

Students need to view unpaid internships as an investment in the future, by perhaps working 15 or 20 hours a week at them and taking a part-time job to support themselves, Ms. Berger said.

Check whether your school can help with financial aid. New York University is among the institutions that award stipends to students with unpaid internships.

The stereotype is that the intern makes the coffee and the copies—and that can still be true in some cases. But Ms. Steinfeld said that now more than ever she sees interns perform professionally meaningful tasks like managing projects and making presentations. That is partly because many of today's employees have growing workloads and are happy to delegate assignments, she said.

An internship should always have a learning component, Ms. Steinfeld said, and most companies are good about providing it. But to avoid an unfulfilling experience, ask questions during your interview and when you get the offer. Find out what tasks you will perform, what past interns have accomplished, which decision makers you will work with, whether you'll have a mentor or another advocate, and how the internship might fit in with your long-term career goals, Ms. Steinfeld said.

At the same time, realize that some of your tasks will be mundane, and make sure to do them well and without complaint, said Ms. Berger, who once caused a coffee machine to explode during an internship. "Students need to absorb everything they can," she said, "from the small tasks to the big ones."

At times, you may have nothing to do—one of the top complaints that Ms. Berger hears from interns. If that happens, knock on doors and ask people if they need help, she said, or see if you can sit in on meetings. Don't surf the Web, check Facebook or text your friends, she said—that shows you're not taking the internship seriously.

When the internship is over, there is still work to do. Ms. Berger, 26, has a decidedly old-fashioned suggestion: send a handwritten thank you note to the internship coordinator. Then send e-mail updates throughout the year to the people you've worked for, so that you'll be in their minds when a job becomes available.

Analyze

1. The article suggests that there should be a strong connection between a college education and pre-career training. In your opinion, what role does pre-career training play in a well-rounded college experience?
2. The article explains that "internships aren't the only route to employment." What are other paths that lead college students to a job?

3. What valuable skills can be acquired through an internship? How are these different from skills developed in a classroom environment?

Explore

1. In your opinion, which is more important for students: college experiences such as internships and technical training that lead directly into a specified career or college experiences that develop robust though non-career-specific skills (such as critical thinking, verbal and presentation skills, and the ability to approach problems creatively)?
2. In your opinion, should colleges offer course credit for internships, even though the type of "learning" that happens in an internship is often different than the type of learning associated with college classes and even though a college has very little oversight about the level of learning that may (or may not) occur in an internship?
3. SHORT WRITING PROMPT: After visiting career services at your college, develop a list of five to seven internships that might interest you later in your academic career. You might also check with academic departments that interest you. At some colleges, individual departments (e.g., Business, Engineering, English) keep a separate list of internships better directed for students in their major.

Jonathan Lash
Educating for Change

Jonathan Lash, who holds an AB from Harvard College and graduate degrees from the Catholic University of America, is the president of Hampshire College.

Here we are, midway into the second decade of the 21st century and growing ever closer, by connection if not through understanding. Money, goods, ideas and images flow freely across borders, creating both acquaintance and conflict.

The pace of change is accelerating. By one estimate, the amount of new technical information doubles every two years, and 70 percent of today's students will end up in jobs that have not yet been invented. They will collaborate with people on multiple continents through institutions not yet created, struggling to solve problems we do not yet recognize. The skills needed for our rapidly changing world will not be learned through the old models.

Preparation to succeed and contribute in this fast paced, often confusing global environment requires education that provides more than narrow job training and efficient information transfer. Such rapid change requires intelligence that is creative, adaptive, and thrives on challenge. More than ever before, students will need to know how to think, evaluate, and explore, even as what they think about may change and expand. They will need the creativity and the courage to challenge traditional ways of doing and working, and forge new paths and solutions.

The boundaries of traditional academic disciplines no longer map onto the radically interdisciplinary topography of today's pressing problems and concerns. Climate change, the nature of consciousness, income inequality, the challenge of providing more and healthier food to a growing global population, the discovery of new planets: All of these issues demand collaborative, cross-disciplinary responses.

Every responsible and informed citizen will need to be able to understand and assess the scientific findings that inform every facet of our lives, from global politics, public policy and medicine, to what we eat, what we throw away, and how we get to work.

Historical, cultural, and geopolitical frameworks are profoundly important to the 21st-century citizen navigating changing landscapes locally and globally. Culture shapes reality. Literature and the arts enable us to understand and address the complexity, contradictions, and challenges of our world. Information is changing—more, faster, unfiltered, leaving the individual to sort through and make sense of it all.

Emphasizing direct pre-professional training at the undergraduate level is the worst possible idea for today's 18-year-old, placing short-term employability above long-term outcomes for both the individual and society. Stressing marketability over creativity runs contrary to the demands of tomorrow's economy. One recent survey of global business leaders ranked creativity as the most important factor for future success, and high tech companies increasingly search for graduates with broad backgrounds and creative skills, rather than narrow technical training.

In a global marketplace of ideas students will need to take up different perspectives and forge an ethical stance that is sensitive to cultural difference while guided by principles of fairness, justice, and welfare.

What educational approach will work for this world?

- One in which students are actively involved in their education. Knowledge is not something to be passively received and codified; it is to be sought out, questioned, created, and investigated. Students need to be engaged in the processes of asking, acquiring, analyzing, and adding to knowledge. What one needs to know is subject to a rapidly changing world, but the "how" and the "why"—the core skills needed to acquire, evaluate, and add to knowledge—once instilled become the basis for creative engagement with the world. Don't just sit there: Ask, question, explore, rethink, argue—learn the process of learning!

- One in which students build on their curiosity, transcend disciplinary boundaries, follow ideas where they lead, and join a community of co-discoverers. Students need to negotiate their own educational paths with their teachers, working together to forge an educational plan that is rigorous, coherent, and interesting. Learning in this way is reciprocal and hands-on. Collaboration and dialogue mark the learning environment. The imperative to work with and persuade mentors makes students entrepreneurial, self-reliant, and adaptive. They will be comfortable finding new approaches and inventing new careers.

- One that is not merely interdisciplinary, but also intellectually and artistically agile. The question or problem, not the structure of an academic field, drives the student's inquiry. They are encouraged to see how artistic endeavors are enriched and informed by ideas in mathematics and the sciences, or how scientific findings might be contextualized and made more complex by the humanities and social sciences. The hallmark is: inquiry and discovery without boundaries.

- One that creates lifelong learners who have internalized their motivations and goals. Education for the whole person creates informed citizens who act to create positive change in the world, whether through political activism, scientific discovery, artistic creation, or sustainable entrepreneurship—people with a moral compass and a passionate belief in their capacity to make a difference.

Graduates who are trained to address tough situations with ingenuity, entrepreneurship, and a capacity for mobilizing collaborative thinking and cooperative action are the most valuable contribution any school can make to society. Such students live with a fierce sense of the obligation of justice.

Analyze

1. The essay claims that the "skills needed for our rapidly changing world" will not be provided by "narrow job training" in college. What skills, specifically, should students acquire in college to become life-long learners and active members of society and to prepare for future employment opportunities? What classes best prepare students for these new roles?

2. In Jonathan Lash's view of the near future, "every responsible and informed citizen will need to be able to understand and assess the scientific findings that inform every facet of our lives." Based on this statement—and other opinions in his article—what role do you believe that general education courses play in preparing students for Lash's vision of the future?

3. Why does Jonathan Lash believe that problems in the near future cannot be adequately addressed within traditional academic programs but "demand collaborative, cross-disciplinary responses"? Have the world's problems changed? Are companies demanding that workers have wider-ranging academic experience before employment? Is the focus of business moving in new directions?

Explore

1. The author believes that new jobs will rise out of "interdisciplinary topography of today's pressing problems and concerns"—that is, out of the space between established programs, such as the space between engineering and the liberal arts or the space between architecture and biology. How can students prepare themselves to engage these cross-disciplinary or interdisciplinary opportunities with programs at your college?

2. The author suggests that change in the twenty-first century will be so dramatic that colleges should reconsider their approach to education.

Consider this: at the start of the twentieth century most people used horses for transportation and pencils to solve simple math problems, but by the end of the century, mankind had conquered the moon, invented passenger jets, and developed computers small enough to fit in a backpack. Do you agree with the author that change in the future will outstrip anything we experienced in the past? And if so, how can we best prepare for it?

3. SHORT WRITING PROMPT: Traditionally, many students widen their academic experience through a well-selected minor. After discussing your options with an academic adviser on campus, write a short essay on how a minor can expand your "core skills" and better prepare you for the civic, cultural, and employment opportunities of the future.

Carla Rivera
Women's Colleges Lead Push to Redefine Gender Rules

Carla Rivera, a member of the staff that received a Pulitzer Prize for their work on the 1992 Los Angeles riots, is a reporter covering higher education for *The Los Angeles Times*.

At a women's college, gender should be the easiest qualification for entry.

That's no longer the case. Women's colleges across the country are reconsidering their admission policies to adapt to a changing world in which gender norms are being challenged and more transgender students are seeking to enroll. It's a complicated calculus for many colleges, prompting concerns that these new considerations could affect the nature of single-gender schools.

Pressured by proactive student groups, some of the nation's 40-plus women's colleges are debating enrollment changes but also how to accommodate students who identify as men, such linguistics questions as the use of feminine pronouns, and whether school mission statements should be rewritten.

Mills College in Oakland last summer became the first in the nation to adopt a written policy on admitting transgender students, setting off a wave of self-examinations at many colleges. The latest to deal with the issue was Scripps College in Claremont.

Trustees there approved a new policy this month to admit applicants identified as female on their birth certificates. The school also will admit those who self-identify as women, which could include those born male who identify as female. The policy is effective for students applying for fall 2016.

College officials said the changes mostly reflect current practice and that the campus has graduated transgender students in the past, including some who transitioned while in school. Scripps, they insist, still will be a women's college.

"College and universities have always led the way in policy discussions about social justice and expanding access," said Scripps President Lori Bettison-Varga. "It's not a surprise that students who we charge with thinking critically about institutions in general would be having these conversations at women's colleges right now. We're laying the foundation for a broader discussion about what it means to be a women's college in the 21st century."

Many alumnae agree but are troubled by the implications.

In a letter to the trustees, more than 100 alumnae raised several concerns, chiefly that these changes are part of a "systematic erasure of the female identity from women's colleges."

"Trans students argue that gender neutral language should be used to encompass their presence," the letter said. "But are we not, by erasing feminized language from our documents and rhetoric, erasing the female identities from a women's college? What could be more ironic?"

Scripps was founded in 1926 as part of the Claremont Colleges, a closely clustered consortium of five private liberal arts undergraduate campuses and two graduate campuses noted for academic excellence. Scripps alumnae include former Arizona legislator Gabrielle Giffords; the first female chief justice of the United States District Court for the Southern District of California, Judith N. Keep; and human rights attorney Karen I. Tse.

Many current students sought a stronger policy. A petition presented to the board in October and signed by more than half of the 1,000 students urged trustees to include applicants who don't identify as either male or female, regardless of the gender they were assigned at birth.

Still, "as a first step it's really exciting," said student government President Alex Frumkin, 21, a senior majoring in environment, economics and politics.

Frumkin acknowledged the disconnect for many as to how a women's college can remain true to its mission while admitting students who identify as men. Is it still a sisterhood if brothers are included?

But the evolution has already been underway, she said. The student association changed its bylaws four years ago to adopt language that's gender inclusive—referring, for example, to Scripps "students" rather than Scripps "women." Most bathrooms are gender neutral, and male students from other Claremont campuses have long been a presence in Scripps classrooms.

At other prominent women's colleges such as Smith and Wellesley, both in Massachusetts, the application and supporting materials, including transcripts and letters of recommendation, must identify the applicant as a woman. Both colleges recently announced the formation of advisory groups to study evolving gender issues and make recommendations to trustees.

Mount Holyoke, in South Hadley, Mass., the first of the Seven Sisters women's colleges, in September adopted a formal policy to welcome transgender students, including those whose gender identity is not clear.

Mount Holyoke President Lynn Pasquerella upheld the position as a human rights issue. Transgender students and women share a history of being marginalized based on their sex, Pasquerella said, and many transgender students suffer verbal and physical harassment at coed campuses.

Her campus, she said, is sensitive to those with philosophical or religious differences. She pointed to a case of a Muslim whose request to change dorms was accommodated after her roommate transitioned to a man.

"We want to make clear that if people feel uncomfortable, there are ways to address these issues," Pasquerella said.

Women's colleges began as a counter to a patriarchal social structure that excluded women from higher education. In the 1960s, these campuses became symbols of women's empowerment, graduating future judges, senators, business tycoons and astronauts.

The threat, argue some critics, is that the presence of trans men—and their potential to adopt the trappings of male privilege—may once again relegate the voices of women to the back of the classroom. Trans men have taken leadership roles at women's colleges, including the current student body president at Mills.

The alumnae coalition at Scripps unsuccessfully asked trustees to allow more time for those opposed to make their case. The group had advocated a more restrictive policy to admit only students who identify as female at the time of application.

"For many alumnae, the approval of the new admissions policy at Scripps is not just disappointing. It is heartbreaking," said Kelsey Phipps, a Washington, D.C. attorney and advocate in the LGBTQ community who graduated from Scripps in 2001. "With its decision to admit male-identified students, many alumnae who believe deeply in women's education feel abandoned by the college. . . . In the end, no argument, logic or passion could derail that hurtling train. We were steamrolled."

Some transgender students, meanwhile, say that adopting a more inclusive policy won't necessarily change attitudes. Eli Erlick is a trans woman enrolled at Pitzer College but attends most of her classes at Scripps because of her major in feminist, gender and sexuality studies. Attitudes toward transgender students at the women's campus are not always welcoming, said Erlick, a national transgender advocate.

"I'm very leery that a policy change is being used as a representation of actual change," Erlick, 19, said. "The atmosphere on campus is still very focused on gendered people, on women assigned female at birth. Change is still going to require a lot of education."

Adriana di Bartolo, director of the Queer Resource Center of the Claremont Colleges, said a big part of education is demystifying the language around gender identity and understanding that transgender students have a variety of experiences, and even appearances. The center provided training for Scripps trustees and faculty.

"What is amazing about the students at Scripps is that they're ready for this change, ready to have a more inclusive policy and to welcome new folks on campus," Di Bartolo said. "People are afraid of a tidal wave of trans students going to Scripps, and that's just not going to happen. But women's colleges are absolutely leading the way."

Analyze

1. Discuss some advantages women students may find on a campus with an exclusively female population. How might a single-gender education experience differ from a blended-gender experience?

2. The article explores the ways the admission of transgender students—trans men in particular—might change the atmosphere of women's

colleges. In your opinion, what would be the largest cultural and environmental change in admitting transgender students to an all-women's college?

3. How can your college better accommodate and welcome students who identify as transgender?

Explore

1. Colleges have traditionally divided students into two gender groups—male and female, a system that excluded many transgender students. In your opinion, as society moves toward greater inclusiveness, how should colleges understand gender in terms of admission, dorm assignments, eligibility for sports teams, locker accommodations, and other considerations?

2. A mid-twentieth-century cultural definition of gender divided all people into two sharply defined categories, male and female. In your opinion, how will our cultural definition of gender likely change in the twenty-first century?

3. SHORT WRITING PROMPT: Examine your college's webpage for prospective students. Do you find it gender-inclusive and welcoming for all students? If not, how would you improve it?

Nathan Deuel
On Maleness and Deep Springs College

Nathan Deuel has written for *Harper's*, *GQ*, *The Paris Review*, and *The New York Times Magazine*. He is the author of *Friday Was the Bomb* and teaches in the MFA program at Mount Saint Mary's University.

Deep Springs College has been around for almost a hundred years. In 1917, a crew of about a dozen students, mostly ruddy young things from back east, were brought to a remote desert basin halfway between

Yosemite and Death Valley by an entrepreneur and educator named L. L. Nunn. His idea was to form "whole men"—and only men, it being Nunn's contention that a single-sex institution was the ideal way to achieve his goals—who would be as comfortable at a desk as in the field. He offered the boys two free years of education in exchange for a pledge to devote their lives to serving humanity. The first group built the dormitory by hand.

I'm pretty sure kids built the concrete building where I lived on campus last year, too—a place so cold in the winter that I dragged an oil-filled heater around my apartment like it was an IV pole. Nowadays, though, architects usually draw up the school's building plans, and professional crews handle the construction. This is but one of the changes to the place over the years. Soon enough will come the biggest one yet: pending a final ruling by the Superior Court of California on a challenge to a decision made by trustees in 2011, Deep Springs College will soon begin admitting women.

There are now seven hundred living alumni of the school, among them aspiring New York congressman and Facebook husband Sean Eldridge, as well as authors William T. Vollmann, Benjamin Kunkel, and, well, me. Last September, I was hired on to teach a semester of creative writing, to live once again in a community of fifty people in a valley the size of Manhattan, at 5,000 feet above sea level. All of the college's housing is clustered around a main circle, surrounded by mountains that extend another 2,000 feet up. The nearest town lies over a difficult mountain pass. Whether you like the college or not—and I've loved it most of my adult life, first as a fresh-faced student from Miami in 1997, less so a few summers ago when I learned the college would go co-ed, and then as much as ever when I returned as a thirty-four-year-old professor—being at Deep Springs has always meant facing a certain level of rugged discomfort. Which: fun, romantic. Which in winter: very cold.

When I'd driven into the valley in the summer, a farm team of half a dozen students was out irrigating some of the college's 150 acres of alfalfa, which they would then process into large bales for sale. In addition to their studies, pupils here work at least twenty hours a week in the Labor program, which stands with Academics and Self-Governance as the college's so-called three pillars.

First thing, I sought out Adam, one of my old classmates and the school's current farm manager. When we were students together, we called him Cyborg. He could do fifty pull-ups with weights strapped to his chest. Now he's a father, as I am. We took his girls to the swimming hole where he and

I had graduated fifteen years earlier, in a small ceremony for which members of a younger class burned an item from each of us on a raft—things that marked who we'd been when we arrived and that we would no longer need. For me, it was the boots I'd worn when I was dairy boy; for a friend, a copy of St. Augustine's *Confessions*; for another, a well-worn early music CD.

Adam and I swam alongside his girls, the older one cutting through the water like a peach-colored dolphin. Then we walked back to the boarding house just ahead of the dinner bell. I learned that one of my writing students was the school's butcher. Another was cooking most of the food. We sat down to a meal of pork chops, salad, and applesauce, with milk from the college's cows. As a student, dairy was my favorite job—I came to love the intimacy of laying my head each morning against a giant mammal's heaving warmth, and it didn't hurt that milking made my forearms hard as steel.

Surrounded by young man-boys with ripped T-shirts, dirty hair, and sunburns, I thought about the fact that as students we'd shower together unselfconsciously, that there was a lot of hugging, and that we all achieved a kind of closeness and tenderness that, at the time, felt like a direct and special byproduct of the college being single-sex. Once, we held a wrestling competition in a makeshift ring lit up by the headlights of three pickups. Something like twenty Deep Springers came to my wedding, and I consider at least ten my best friends. I'm protective of what I think I gained. But sitting there at dinner, a father of a daughter, I began to understand the questions—about inequality, purpose, privilege—that came with attending an institution this exclusive and inessential and fragile and ridiculous.

For nearly 100 years, the Deep Springs formula has been simple: students stayed for two years, three at most, and during that time they hired and fired faculty, and constituted a majority of the admissions committee. Faculty typically stayed for a semester or a year, and the cap was seven. A few of the nonacademic staff—there's typically a ranch manager, a farm manager, a cook, and a mechanic—have lasted a couple of decades, but life here is isolated and repetitive, and the charms of a student-run school wear thin, so most staff log a couple of years and move on. For everything wonderful about Deep Springs, it's not always easy to live in a place that's trying to be paradise.

As a student I both dreaded and loved the idea of going into the real world. During a trip to Harvard and other East Coast schools—we needed to transfer to a four-year university in order to complete our bachelor's degrees—we'd hand-roll cigarettes, strike matches on belt buckles, and ash in our hats, feeling dazzling even as alfalfa fell from our pockets. Now I'd been out for a long time. I'd earned my degree, married, thrived in and then abandoned various jobs in New York. I'd lived in half a dozen cities, including Beirut, Istanbul, and Riyadh. I was a dad.

When the semester got underway, I settled into a routine, drinking coffee at night until I couldn't see straight, printing out and marking up endless copies of a book manuscript. My wife began a new job in Los Angeles; our daughter started preschool. It pained me that they couldn't be with me, but they were starting normal lives that didn't involve social utopias in the middle of the desert. Within weeks, I was going through long stretches of not shaving or changing my clothes. Being alone was wonderful and awful. It afforded me tremendous amounts of time to work. But soon I forgot why and for whom I was working. One night, I spilled beer all over my manuscript. I began to think more and more about isolation, and how males act in the absence of females.

In class, everyone got sick. A tall, reedy guy from Michigan—one of my best students—handed a coughing classmate a lozenge. The cougher, who wore a denim jacket and a natural snarl, ignored the lozenge. His essay that week was called "In Defense of Shitholes." During the response period, a student from Mali, a former special-forces paratrooper, asked, "What is 'real America'?" We struggled to explain what a shithole was. Later, the butcher told us how, just before class, they'd gone to drop off the guts of a freshly slaughtered cow at the Dead Animal Dump, and the truck nearly fell in. The dump lies in the desert just beyond campus, and at night, coyotes circle the place, howling. When I was a student, I carried a gun and went to class with blood on my hands, too.

What it might mean to become a man at Deep Springs turned into a rather more urgent matter one night, when one of my other students decided to eat a spider. It was a Tuesday night, when the entire community traditionally gathers to hear students give talks, and he walked up to the podium with a hot plate, a cup of oil, and a jar containing a live black widow. When the oil was hot enough, he tipped the jar. There was a sizzle, and then he plucked out the cooked spider. I held my breath, hoping it was dead. Then he ate it (and survived). It was hard to imagine this happening at any other college.

Not long after I'd graduated, a student one year below me died in a tractor accident in the hills above the college. As a result, Deep Springs developed new regulations, covering who could use a power tool, how much instruction was required before a student could drive the backhoe, and the number of students required before a college vehicle could be used for an official trip. The black-widow incident was a rare show of risk. By contrast, in my first few weeks as a student, I was handed a chainsaw and pointed toward a pile of boards. When I hit a nail, the saw kicked back and nearly tore me in half. Whatever we built back then, it was ours. But at least some of what we built could have been better.

On Thanksgiving, I brought out my family for the first time. The meal was astonishing—delicate baked goods, mounds of steaming meat, deep bowls of fresh ice cream. My daughter found a deer's tooth lying on my porch. She was both terrified and thrilled. "Daddy, is that a dead tooth from a dead animal? And when am I going to die? Daddy?? Tell me!!!" She fell in love with three different students and was overcome with a joy I hadn't previously seen.

I realized, holding her hand, walking around a campus I'd known and idealized and wanted to protect my entire adult life, that maybe the most basic purpose of Deep Springs was to teach us to welcome challenge, and to do so with grace. Because of how much I'd loved the place, my line had always been this: I don't want it to change. Deep Springs had been very good to me. I'd learned how to be at home in the field and at a desk. Now, as the father of a little girl, I was ready to see what else it could do.

Analyze

1. The previous article, "Women's Colleges Lead Push to Redefine Gender Rules," and its discussion questions explored the benefits of same-gender education for women. What are the benefits of same-gender education for men, as described in this article, "On Maleness and Deep Springs College?" In what ways might they be similar to same-gender education for women? In what ways might they be different?

2. What valuable experience might students have at Deep Springs that they could not have at a traditional college?

3. In the article "Women's Colleges Lead Push to Redefine Gender Rules," female alumnae of a women's college fear that new admission criteria might create a "systematic erasure of the female identity from women's colleges." In this article, the author, an alumnus of Deep Springs, claims that he loved the college "less so a few summers ago when I learned the

college would go co-ed." What do these alumni value in single-gender education? What is lost when the option for single-gender college experience is diminished?

Explore

1. The Deep Springs experience is isolated, with students removed from many urban comforts. Students run the dairy, plow the fields, and work as butchers, preparing food for the entire college. Students enjoy long hours of solitude, without TV and other common distractions. Why does the author describe this isolated experience as a type of utopia and feel that the modern comforts of Los Angeles somehow offer a less meaningful experience?

2. The author describes Deep Springs as a school with minimal reliance on technology, including the Internet. Do you think you would have a better educational experience with less technology, including the Internet? In what ways would this change your learning experience? Consider ways that you read, ways that you multitask on a computer, the level of helpfulness or distraction provided by the Internet, and the type of learning required in a technology-limited environment versus the type of learning pursued on a technology-rich campus?

3. SHORT WRITING PROMPT: The article describes a ceremony in which students release possessions once essential to their identity (a book, a CD, a favorite item of clothing) that they've now outgrown. In a short essay, describe a possession that was central to your identity the summer before you attended college but no longer figures in to your personality. Why does this item no longer represent part of your character? How have you changed since arriving at college?

Forging Connections

1. In this section are two essays that explore the benefits and limitations of single-gender education ("Women's Colleges Lead Push to Redefine gender Roles" and "On Maleness and Deep Springs College"). Assuming you currently attend a coed college, write an essay in which you explore ways that your educational experience would be different if you attended a single-gender college (either a women's college or a men's college). What benefits might you find in that environment? What

limitations? How would it change your relationship to the process of learning? Would you be more assertive in a single-gender classroom? Do you believe it would improve or diminish your social experience on campus? Would you be more or less concerned with your appearance in a single-gender environment?

2. In the essay "Spending Shifts as Colleges Compete on Students' Comfort," the author documents a system in which administrators vie for prospective students by offering luxury amenities, such as an ultramodern gym, a climbing wall, resort-style pools, and organic dining options. Conversely, in "Educating for Change," the author argues that students should engage in "political activism, scientific discovery, artistic creation, or sustainable entrepreneurship" as well as classes in which they explore pure interests, divorced from any consideration of marketable skills. Which collegiate vision do you believe would be more compelling for prospective students shopping for a college?

Looking Further

1. The campus experience is forever changing. Students today are surrounded by conveniences and modern technology, similar to young professionals in an urban setting. Based on your own ideas about how culture will change in the future, how will the college experience be different ten years from now? Explore two ideas and discuss how these changes will benefit or damage campus life as you know it.

2. After both the Great Depression (1929–39) and the Great Recession (2007–09), college students showed a heightened interest in business internships and technical skills that would immediately translate into sustainable employment. Do you think that students in the next ten years will be as interested in business internships and technical skills—as opposed to majoring in the humanities and arts—as they are at present?

Researching and Writing About College

Todd James Pierce with Barbara Rockenbach
and Aaron Ritzenberg[1]

Research-based writing lies at the heart of the mission of higher education: to discover, transform, and share ideas. As a college student, it is through writing and research that you will become an active participant in an intellectual community. Doing research in college involves not only searching for information but also digesting, analyzing, and synthesizing what you find in order to create new knowledge. Your most successful efforts as a college writer will report on the latest and most important ideas in a field as well as make new arguments and offer fresh insights.

It may seem daunting to be asked to contribute new ideas to a field in which you are a novice. After all, creating new knowledge seems to be the realm of experts. In this guide, we offer strategies that demystify the research and writing process, breaking down some of the fundamental steps that scholars take when they do research and make arguments. You'll see that contributing to scholarship involves strategies that can be learned and practiced.

Throughout this guide we imagine doing research and writing as engaging in a scholarly conversation. When you read academic writing, you'll see

---

[1]Barbara Rockenbach, Director of Humanities & History Libraries, Columbia University. Aaron Ritzenberg, Associate Director of First-Year Writing, Columbia University.

that scholars reference the studies that came before them and allude to the studies that will grow out of their research. When you think of research as engaging in a conversation, you quickly realize that scholarship always has a social aspect. Even if you like to find books in the darkest corners of the library, even if you like to draft your essays in deep solitude, you will always be awake to the voices that helped you form your ideas and to the audience who will receive your ideas. As if in a conversation at a party, scholars mingle: they listen to others and share their most recent ideas, learning and teaching at the same time. Strong scholars, like good conversationalists, will listen and speak with an open mind, letting their own thoughts evolve as they encounter new ideas.

You may be wondering, "what does it mean to have an open mind when I'm doing research? After all, aren't I supposed to find evidence that supports my thesis?" We'll be returning to this question soon, but the quick answer is: To have an open mind when you're doing research means that you'll be involved in the research process well before you have a thesis. We realize this may be a big change from the way you think about research. The fact is, though, that scholars do research well before they know any of the arguments they'll be making in their papers. Indeed, scholars do research even before they know what specific topic they'll be addressing and what questions they'll be asking.

When scholars do research they may not know exactly what they are hunting for, but they have techniques that help them define projects, identify strong interlocutors, and ask important questions. This guide will help you move through the various kinds of research that you'll need at the different stages of your project. If writing a paper involves orchestrating a conversation within a scholarly community, there are a number of important questions you'll need to answer: How do I choose what to write about? How do I find a scholarly community? How do I orchestrate a conversation that involves this community? Whose voices should be most prominent? How do I enter the conversation? How do I use evidence to make a persuasive claim? How do I make sure that my claim is not just interesting but important?

GETTING STARTED

You have been asked to write a research paper. This may be your first research paper at the college level. Where do you start? The important thing when embarking on any kind of writing project that involves research is to find something that you are interested in learning more about. Writing and research is easier if you care about your topic. Your instructor may have given you a topic, but you can make that topic your own by finding something that appeals to you within the scope of the assignment.

Academic writing begins from a place of deep inquiry. When you are sincerely interested in a problem, researching can be a pleasure, since it will satisfy your own intellectual curiosity. More important, the intellectual problems that seem most difficult—the questions that appear to resist obvious answers—are the very problems that will often yield the most surprising and most rewarding results.

Presearching to Generate Ideas

When faced with a research project, your first instinct might be to go to Google or Wikipedia, or even to a social media site. This is not a bad instinct. In fact, Google, Wikipedia, and social media can be great places to start. Using Google, Wikipedia, and social media to help you discover a topic is what we call "presearch"—it is what you do to warm up before the more rigorous work of academic research. Academic research and writing will require you to go beyond these sites to find resources that will make the work of researching and writing both easier and more appropriate to an academic context.

Google   Let's start with Google (Figure A.1). You use Google because you know that you are going to find a simple search interface and that your search will produce many results. These results may not be completely relevant to your topic, but Google helps in the discovery phase of your work. For instance, you are asked to write about the possible role of a new alcohol education class at your college.

This Google search for "college and alcohol education" will produce articles from many diverse sources, magazines, government sites, and corporate reports among them. It's not a bad start. Use these results to begin to hone in on a topic you are interested in pursuing. A quick look through these results may yield a more focused topic: alcohol education and Greek-letter houses. A particular source mentions the relationship between college alcohol use and driving. while others examine how a required class in alcohol use changes drinking patterns among students.

Wikipedia   A Wikipedia search on "alcohol education and college" will lead you to several articles that address many issues within the topic

Figure A.1   Results of a Google search for "alcohol use and college."

(Figure A.2). The great thing about Wikipedia is that it is an easy way to gain access to a wealth of information about thousands of topics. However, it is crucial to realize that Wikipedia itself is not an authoritative source in a scholarly context. Even though you may see Wikipedia cited in mainstream newspapers and popular magazines, academic researchers do not consider Wikipedia a reliable source and do not consult or cite it in their own research. Wikipedia itself says that "Wikipedia is not considered a credible source . . . This is especially true considering that anyone can edit the information given at any time." For research papers in college, you should use Wikipedia only to find basic information about your topic and to point you toward scholarly sources. Wikipedia may be a great starting point for presearch, but it is not an adequate ending point for research. Use the References section at the bottom of the Wikipedia article to find other, more substantive and authoritative resources about your topic.

Using Social Media   Social media such as Facebook and Twitter can be useful in the presearch phase of your project, but you must start thinking about these tools in new ways. You may have a Facebook or Twitter account

References [edit]

- Pedersen, Eric; LaBrie, Josephy; Kilmer, Jason (June 2009). "Before You Slip in to the Night, You'll Want Something to Drink: Exploring the Reasons for Prepartying Behavior Among College Student Drinkers" 🔗. *Issues in Mental Health Nursing* **30** (6): 354–363. doi:10.1080/01612840802422623 🔗. PMID 19499435 🔗. Retrieved 20 October 2011.

- "School Rankings- Party Schools" 🔗. The Princeton Review. Retrieved 20 October 2011.

- Spoth, Richard; Greenberg, Mark; Turrisi, Robert (2009). "Overview of Preventive Interventions Addressing Underage Drinking" 🔗. *Alcohol Research & Health* **32** (1): 53–66. Retrieved 20 October 2011.

- Brazy, David (29 September 2010). "Wisconsin Drinking Culture Across UW System" 🔗. *The Badger Herald*. Retrieved 20 October 2011.

- Windle, Michael; Zucker (2010). "Robert" 🔗. *Alcohol Research & Health* **33** (1/2): 29–44. Retrieved 20 October 2011.

Figure A.2 List of references from a Wikipedia search on alcohol use among college students. Use these links to further your research.

and use it to keep in touch with friends, family, and colleagues. These social networks are valuable, and you may already use them to gather information to help you make decisions in your personal life and your workplace. Although social media is not generally useful to your academic research, both Facebook and Twitter have powerful search functions that can lead you to resources and help you refine your ideas.

After you log in to Facebook, use the "Search for people, places, and things" bar at the top of the page to begin. When you type search terms into this bar, Facebook will first search your own social network. To extend beyond your own network, try adding the word "research" after your search terms to find articles and posts that relate to this topic. This is not necessarily the scholarly conversation we referred to at the start of this guide, but it is a social conversation that can still be useful in helping you determine what you want to focus on in the research process.

Twitter is an information network where users can post short messages (or "tweets"). While many people use Twitter simply to update their friends ("I'm going to the mall" or "Can't believe it's snowing!"), more and more individuals and organizations use Twitter to comment on noteworthy events or link to interesting articles. You can use Twitter as a presearch tool because it aggregates links to sites, people in a field of research, and noteworthy sources. Communities, sometimes even scholarly communities, form around topics on Twitter. Users group posts together by using hashtags—words or phrases that follow the # sign. Users can respond to other users by using the @ sign followed by a user's twitter name. When searching for specific individuals or organizations on Twitter, you search using their handle (such as @barackobama or @whitehouse). You will re-trieve tweets that were created either by the person or organization, or tweets that mention the person or organization. When searching for a topic to find discussions, you search using the hashtag symbol, #. For in-stance, a search on #alcoholeducation will take you to tweets and threaded discussions on the topic of alcohol education.

There are two ways to search Twitter. You can use the search book in the upper right-hand corner and enter either a @ or # search as described above. Once you retrieve results, you can search again by clicking on any of the words that are hyperlinked within your results, such as #college or #collegealcoholuse.

If you consider a hashtag (the # sign) as an entry point into a commu-nity, you will begin to discover a conversation around topics. For instance, a search on Twitter for #alcoholeducation leads you to Alcohol Education Trust (@talkalcohol), a community that facilitates discussions on alcohol. News agencies such as Reuters are also active in Twitter, so an article from a Reuters publication will be retrieved in a search. Evaluating information and sources found in social media is similar to how you evaluate any infor-mation you encounter during the research process. And, as with Wikipedia and Google searches, this is just a starting point to help you get a sense of the spectrum of topics. This is no substitute for using library resources. Do not cite Facebook, Twitter, or Wikipedia in a research paper; use them to find more credible, authoritative sources. We'll talk about evaluating sources in the sections that follow.

Create a Concept Map

Once you have settled on a topic that you find exciting and interesting, the next step is to generate search terms, or keywords, for effective searching. Keywords are the crucial terms or phrases that signal the content of any given source. Keywords are the building blocks of your search for information. We have already seen a few basic keywords such as "alcohol" and "alcohol education." One way to generate keywords is to tell a friend or classmate what you are interested in. What words are you using to describe your research project? You may not have a fully formed idea or claim, but you have a vague sense of your interest. A concept map exercise can help you generate more keywords and, in many cases, narrow your topic to make it more manageable.

A concept map is a way to visualize the relationship between concepts or ideas. You can create a concept map on paper, or there are many free programs online that can help you do this (see, for instance, http://vue .tufts.edu/, http://www.wisemapping.com, or http://www.freeplane.org). There are many concept mapping applications available for mobile devices.

Here is how you use a concept map. First, begin with a term or phrase like "college alcohol education." Put that term in the first box. Then think of synonyms, related words or ideas to describe alcohol education and its effects such as "binge drinking," "student services," "paternalism," "behavior management," "substance abuse," "drinking prevention," "MADD," "SADD," "underage drinking," "college legal responsibility and drinking," "college attrition and alcohol," "alcohol effect on community," "alcohol and grades," and "student counseling." This brainstorming process will help you develop keywords for searching. Notice that keywords can also be short phrases.

After some practice, you'll discover that some phrases make for excellent keywords and others make for less effective search tools. The best keywords are precise enough to narrow your topic so that all of your results are relevant, but are not so specific that you might miss helpful results. Concept maps created using apps such as SimpleMind allow you to use templates, embed hyperlinks, and attach notes, among other useful functions.

Keyword Search

One of the hardest parts of writing is coming up with something to write about. Too often, we make the mistake of waiting until we have a fully formed idea before we start writing. The process of writing can actually help you discover what your idea is, and most important, what is interesting about your idea.

Keyword searches are most effective at the beginning stages of your research. They generally produce the most number of results and can help you determine how much has been written on your topic. You want to use keyword searches to help you achieve a manageable number of results. What is manageable? This is a key question when beginning research. Our keyword search in Google on "college alcohol education" produced over 13 million results. The same search in JSTOR.org produces over 41,000 results. These are not manageable result sets. Let's see how we can narrow our search.

Keyword searches, in library resources or on Google, are most effective if you employ a few search strategies that will focus your results.

First, use AND when you are combining multiple keywords. We have used this search construction previously:

alcohol AND freshmen

The AND ensures that all your results will contain both "alcohol" and "freshmen." Many search engines and databases will assume an AND search, meaning if you type

alcohol freshmen

the search will automatically look for both terms. However, in some cases the AND will not be assumed and "alcohol freshmen" will be treated as a phrase. This means that "alcohol" will have to be next to the word "freshmen" to return results. Worse yet, sometimes the search automatically assumes an OR. That would mean that all your results would come back with either "alcohol" or "freshmen." This will produce a large and mostly irrelevant set of results. Therefore, use AND whenever you want two or more words to appear in a result.

Second, using OR can be very effective when you want to use several terms to describe a concept, such as:

freshmen OR first-year

A search on "alcohol" and "freshmen" assumes that all colleges refer to incoming students as "freshmen," but administrators often refer to incoming students as "first-year students." The following search casts a broader net because results will come back with "alcohol" and either "freshmen" or "first-year":

alcohol AND (freshmen OR first-year)

Not all of these words will appear in each record. Note also that the parentheses set off the OR search, indicating that "alcohol" must appear in each record and then either "freshmen" or "first-year" needs to appear along with "alcohol."

Third, use quotation marks when looking for a phrase. For instance, if you are looking for information on alcohol and freshmen in a California state university, you can ensure that the search results will include all of these concepts and increase the relevance by using the following search construction:

alcohol AND freshmen AND "California state university"

This phrasing will return results that contain both the words "alcohol" and "freshmen" and the exact phrase "California state university."

Finally, use NOT to exclude terms that will make your search less relevant. You may find that a term or a phrase keeps appearing in your search that is not useful. Try this:

"alcohol education" NOT "high school"

This will return results that contain the phrase "alcohol education" while excluding results that include the phrase "high school." By excluding the keyword phrase "high school," you will retrieve far fewer sources, and, we hope, more relevant results.

Researchable Question

In a college research paper, it is often important that you make an argument, not just offer a report. In high school you may have found some success by merely listing or cataloging the data and information you found; you might have offered a series of findings to show your teacher that you investigated your topic. In college, however, your readers will not be interested in data or information merely for its own sake; they will want to know what you make of this data and why they should care.

To satisfy the requirements of a college paper, you'll need to distinguish between a topic and a research question. You will likely begin with a topic, but it is only when you move from a topic to a question that your research will begin to feel motivated and purposeful. A topic refers only to the general subject area that you'll be investigating. A researchable question, on the other hand, points toward a specific problem in the subject area that you'll be attempting to answer by making a claim about the evidence you examine.

"Alcohol education and college" is a topic but not a researchable question. It is important that you ask yourself, "What aspect of the topic is most interesting to me?" It is even more important that you ask, "What aspect of the topic is it most important that I illuminate for my audience?"

A strong researchable question will not lead to an easy answer, but rather will lead you into a scholarly conversation in which there are many competing claims. For instance, the question, "is alcohol education valuable on a college campus?" is not a strong research question because it is too general. What type of alcohol education program? What campus? What is meant by "valuable"?

When you are interested in developing a college-level argument, try to use concrete language and specific ideas. Preresearch will likely have revealed that there are many types of alcohol education courses designed for college: online courses, a one-time lecture, an educational unit delivered through a college skills course, a required course for fraternity and sorority members, and so forth. Each of these options will provide different levels of exposure to the potential dangers of alcohol use during college. Each will also have its own cost.

Likewise, the term "college campus" is too broad. A private liberal arts campus in Vermont is nothing like a state university campus in California.

Lastly, the term "valuable" is imprecise. What is "valuable" in terms of this argument?

A more specific question may be: "Will a required two-hour online alcohol education course reduce drinking for students at a California state university campus in San Diego?"

This is a much better question. It gives the argument shape and direction. But even this question is, in ways, limiting. It seeks a simple "yes" or "no" answer. An open-ended question may be a better place to begin an inquiry into the subject.

Try using the words "why" and "how" rather than "will." Instead of leading to a definitive answer, the words "why" and "how" will often lead to complex, nuanced answers for which you'll need to marshal evidence in order to be convincing. "How will a required two-hour online alcohol education program affect binge drinking at a California state university campus in San Diego? " is a question that has a number of complex and competing answers that might draw from a number of different disciplines (sociology, economics, education, and psychology, among others).

Once you have come up with an interesting researchable question, your first task as a researcher is to figure out how scholars are discussing your question. Many novice writers think that the first thing they should do when beginning a research project is to articulate an argument, then find sources that confirm their argument. This is not how experienced scholars work. Instead, strong writers know that they cannot possibly come up with a strong central argument until they have done sufficient research. So, instead of looking for sources that confirm a preliminary claim you might want to make, look for the scholarly conversation.

Looking at the scholarly conversation is a strong way to figure out if you've found a research question that is suitable in scope for the kind of paper you're writing. Put another way, reading the scholarly conversation can tell you if your research question is too broad or too narrow. Most novice writers begin with research questions that are overly broad. If your question is so broad that there are thousands of books and articles participating in the scholarly conversation, it's a good idea for you to focus your question so that you are asking something more specific. If, on the other hand, you are asking a research question that is so obscure that you cannot find a corresponding scholarly conversation, you will want to broaden the scope of your project by asking a slightly less specific question.

Keep in mind the metaphor of a conversation. If you walk into a room and people are talking about alcohol education and college, it would be out of place for you to begin immediately by making a huge, vague claim, like, "online seminars can change the way students act." It would be equally out of place for you to begin immediately by making an overly specific or personal claim, like, "you can understand all our campus problems by simply standing outside Fraternity Row on any Saturday night." Rather, you would gauge the scope of the conversation and figure out what seems like a reasonable contribution.

Your contribution to the conversation, at this point, will likely be a focused research question. This is the question you take with you to the library. In the next section, we'll discuss how best to make use of the library. Later, we'll explore how to turn your research question into an argument for your essay.

Your Campus Library

You have probably used libraries all your life, checking out books from your local public library and studying in your high school library. The difference between your previous library experiences and your college library experience is one of scale. Your college library has more stuff. It may be real stuff like books, journals, and videos, or it may be virtual stuff, like online articles, ebooks, and streaming video. Your library pays a lot of money every year to buy or license content for you to use for your research. By extension, your tuition dollars are buying a lot of really good research material. Resorting to Google and Wikipedia means you are not getting all you can out of your college experience.

Not only will your college library have a much larger collection, it will have a more up-to-date and relevant collection than your high school or community public library. Academic librarians spend considerable time acquiring research materials based on classes being taught at your institution. You may not know it, but librarians carefully monitor what courses are being taught each year and are constantly trying to find research materials appropriate to those courses and your professor's research interests. In many cases, you will find that the librarians will know about your assignment and will already have ideas about the types of sources that will make you most successful.

Get To Know Your Librarians!   The most important thing to know during the research process is that there are people to help you. While you may not yet be in the habit of going to the library, there are still many ways in which librarians and library staff can be helpful. Most libraries now have an email or chat service set up so you can ask questions without even setting foot in a library. No question is too basic or too specific. It's a librarian's job to help you find answers, and all questions are welcome. The librarian can even help you discover the right question to ask given the task you are trying to complete.

Help can also come in the form of consultations. Librarians will often make appointments to meet one on one to offer in-depth help on a research paper or project. Chances are you will find a link on your library website for scheduling a consultation.

Among the many questions fielded by reference librarians, three stand out as the most often asked. Because librarians hear these questions with such regularity, we suggest that students ask these questions when they begin their research. You can go to the library and ask these questions in person, or you can ask vie email or online chat.

The first question is, **How do I find a book relevant to my topic?** The answer to this question will vary from place to place, but the thing to remember is that finding a book can be either a physical process or a virtual process. Your library will have books on shelves somewhere, and the complexity of how those shelves are organized and accessed depends on factors of size, number of libraries, and the system of organization your library uses. You will find books by using your library's online catalog and carefully noting the call number and location of a book.

Your library is also increasingly likely to offer electronic books (ebooks). You can discover these books in your library's online catalog as well. When looking at the location of a book you will frequently see a link for ebook versions. You will not find an ebook in every search, but when you do the advantage is that ebook content is searchable, making your job of finding relevant material in the book easier.

If you find one book on your topic, use it as a jumping-off point for finding more books or articles on that topic. Most books will have bibliographies either at the end of each chapter or the end of the book in which the author has compiled all the sources he or she used. Consult these bibliographies to find other materials on your topic that will help support your claim.

Another efficient way to find more sources once you've identified a particularly authoritative and credible book is to go back to the book's listing in your library's online catalog. Once you find the book, look carefully at the record for links to subjects. By clicking on a subject link you are finding other items in your library on the same subject. For instance, a search on

"alcohol education" and college

will lead you to items with subjects such as

alcohol abuse

binge drinking

student behaviors

social drinking

The second important question is, **What sources can I use as evidence in my paper?** There are many types of resources out there to use as you orchestrate a scholarly conversation and support your paper's argument. Books, which we discussed earlier, are great sources if you can find them on your topic, but often your research question will be something that is either too new or too specific for a book to cover. Books are very good for historical questions and overviews of large topics. For current topics, you will want to explore articles from magazines, journals, and newspapers.

Magazines or periodicals (you will hear these terms interchangeably) are published on a weekly or monthly schedule and contain articles of popular interest. These sources can cover broad topics, like the news in magazines such as *Newsweek, Time,* and *U.S. News and World Report*. They can also be more focused for particular groups, like farmers (*Dairy Farmer*) or photographers (*Creative Photography*). Articles in magazines or periodicals are by professional writers who may or may not be experts. Magazines typically are not considered scholarly and generally do not contain articles with bibliographies, endnotes, or footnotes. This does not mean they are not good sources for your research. In fact, there may be very good reasons to use a magazine article to help support your argument. Magazines capture the point of view of a particular group on a subject, like how members of MADD want colleges to provide more education concerning alcohol use. This point of view may offer support for your claim or an opposing viewpoint to counter. Magazines can also highlight aspects of a topic at a particular point in time. Comparing a *Newsweek* article from 1986 on drinking patterns on college campuses to an article on the same topic in 2016 allows you to draw conclusions about how alcohol use has changed over time.

Journals are intended for a scholarly audience of researchers, specialists, or students of a particular field. Journals such as *American Educational Research Journal* and *The Journal of College and Character* are examples of scholarly journals focused on a particular field or research topic. You may hear the term "peer-reviewed" or "refereed" in reference to scholarly journals. This means that the articles contained in a journal have been reviewed by a group of scholars in the same field before the article is published in the journal. This ensures that the research has been vetted by a group of peers before it is published. Articles from scholarly journals can help provide some authority to your argument. By citing experts in a field you are bolstering your argument and entering into the scholarly conversation we talked about at the beginning of this guide.

Newspaper articles are found in newspapers that are generally published daily. There is a broad range of content in newspapers, ranging from articles written by staff reporters, to editorials written by scholars, experts, and general readers, to reviews and commentary written by experts. Newspapers are published more frequently and locally than magazines or journals, making them excellent sources for very recent topics and events as well as those with regional significance. Newspaper articles can provide you with a point of view from a particular part of the country or world (how do Texans feel about underage drinking vs. New Yorkers?) or a strong opinion on a topic from an expert (an economist writing an editorial on the effects of alcohol use and the community around UC Berkeley).

A good argument uses evidence from a variety of sources. Do not assume you have done a good job if your paper only cites newspaper articles. You need a broad range of sources to fill out your argument. Your instructor will provide you with guidelines about the number of sources you need, but it will be up to you to find a variety of sources. Finding two or three sources in each of the categories above will help you begin to build a strong argument.

The final important question is, **Where should I look for articles on my topic?** The best way to locate journal, magazine, or newspaper articles is to use a database. A database is an online resource that organizes research material of a particular type or content area. For example, *PsycINFO* is a psychology database where you would look for journal articles (as well as other kinds of sources) in the discipline of psychology. Your library licenses or subscribes to databases on your behalf. Finding the right database for your topic will depend upon what is available at your college or university because every institution has a different set of resources. Many libraries will provide subject or research guides that can help you determine what database would be best for your topic. Look for these guides on your library website. Your library's website will have a way to search databases. Look for a section of the library website on databases, and look for a search box in that section. For instance, if you type "language" in a database search box, you may find that your library licenses a database called *MLA International Bibliography* (Modern Language Association). A search for "history" in the database search box may yield *American History and Life* or *Historical Abstracts*. In most instances, your best bet is to ask a librarian which database or databases are most relevant to your research.

When using these databases that your library provides for you, you will know that you are starting to sufficiently narrow or broaden your topic when you begin to retrieve thirty to fifty sources during a search. This kind of narrow result field will rarely occur in Google, which is one of the reasons why using library databases is preferable to Google when doing academic research. Databases will help you determine when you have begun to ask a manageable question.

When you have gotten down to thirty to fifty sources in your result list, begin to look through those results to see what aspects of your topic are being written about. Are there lots of articles on online education and alcohol and college? If so, that might be a topic worth investigating since there is a lot of information for you to read. This is where you begin to discover where your voice might add to the ongoing conversation on the topic.

Using Evidence

The quality of evidence and how you deploy the evidence is ultimately what will make your claims persuasive. You may think of evidence as that which will help prove your claim. But if you look at any scholarly book or article you'll see that evidence can be used in a number of different ways. Evidence can be used to provide readers with crucial background information. It can be used to tell readers what scholars have commonly thought about a topic (but which you may disagree with). It can offer a theory that you use as a lens. It can offer a methodology or an approach that you would like to use. And finally, evidence can be used to back up the claim that you'll be making in your paper.

Novice researchers begin with a thesis and try to find all the evidence that will prove that their claim is valid or true. What if you come across evidence that doesn't help with the validity of your claim? A novice researcher might decide not to take this complicating evidence into account. Indeed, when you come across complicating evidence, you might be tempted to pretend you never saw it! But rather than sweeping imperfect evidence under the rug, you should figure out how to use this evidence to complicate your own ideas.

The best scholarly conversations take into account a wide array of evidence, carefully considering all sides of a topic. As you probably know, often the most fruitful and productive conversations occur not just when you are talking to people who already agree with you, but when you are fully engaging with the people who might disagree with you.

Coming across unexpected, surprising, and contradictory evidence, then, is a good thing! It will force you to make a complex, nuanced argument and will ultimately allow you to write a more persuasive paper.

Other Forms of Evidence

We've talked about finding evidence in books, magazines, journals, and newspapers. Here are a few other kinds of evidence you may want to use.

Interviews can be a powerful form of evidence, especially if the person you are interviewing is an expert in the field that you're investigating. Interviewing can be intimidating, but it might help to know that many people (even experts!) will feel flattered when you ask them for an interview. Most scholars are deeply interested in spreading knowledge, so you should feel comfortable asking a scholar for his or her ideas. Even if the scholar doesn't know the specific answer to your question, he or she may be able to point you in the right direction.

Remember, of course, to be as courteous as possible when you are planning to interview someone. This means sending a polite email that fully introduces yourself and your project before you begin asking questions. Email interviews may be convenient, but an in-person interview is best, since this allows for you and the interviewee to engage in a conversation that may take surprising and helpful turns.

It's a good idea to write down a number of questions before the interview. Make sure not just to get facts (which you can likely get somewhere else). Ask the interviewee to speculate about your topic. Remember that "why" and "how" questions often yield more interesting answers than "what" questions.

If you do conduct an in-person interview, act professionally. Be on time, dress respectfully, and show sincere interest and gratitude. Bring something to record the interview. Many reporters still use pens and a pad, since these feel unobtrusive and are very portable.

Write down the interviewee's name, the date, and the location of the interview, and have your list of questions ready. Don't be afraid, of course, to veer from your questions. The best questions might be the follow-up questions that couldn't have occurred to you before the conversation began. You're likely to get the interviewee to talk freely and openly if you show real intellectual curiosity. If you're not a fast writer, it's certainly OK to ask the interviewee to pause for a moment while you take notes. Some people like to record their interviews. Just make sure that you ask permission if you choose to do this. It's always nice to send a brief thank-you note or email after the interview. This would be a good time to ask any brief follow-up questions.

Because we live in a visual age, we tend to take **images** for granted. We see them in magazines, on TV, and on the Internet. We don't often think about them as critically as we think about words on a page. Yet, a critical look at an image can uncover helpful evidence for a claim. Use Google Image search or flickr.com to find images using the same keywords you used to find books and articles. Ask your instructor for guidance on how to properly cite and acknowledge the source of any images you wish to use. If you want to present your research outside of a classroom project (for example, publish it on a blog or share it at a community event), ask a research librarian for guidance on avoiding any potential copyright violations.

Like images, **multimedia** such as video, audio, and animations are increasingly easy to find on the Internet and can strengthen your claim. There are several audio and video search engines available such as Vimeo (vimeo. com) or Blinkx (blinkx.com), a search engine featuring audio and video from the BBC, Reuters, and the Associated Press among others. As with images, ask your instructor for guidance on how to properly cite and acknowledge the source of any multimedia you wish to use. If you want to present your research outside of a classroom project (for example, publish it on a blog or share it at a community event), ask a research librarian for guidance on avoiding any potential copyright violations.

Evaluating Sources

A common problem in research isn't a lack of sources, but an overload of information. Information is more accessible than ever. How many times have you done an online search and asked yourself the question: "How do I know what is good information?" Librarians can help. Evaluating online sources is more challenging than traditional sources because it is harder to make distinctions between good and bad online information than with print sources. It is easy to tell that *Newsweek* magazine is not as scholarly as an academic journal, but online everything may look the same. There are markers of credibility and authoritativeness when it comes to online information, and you can start to recognize them. We'll provide a few tips here, but be sure to ask a librarian or your professor for more guidance whenever you're uncertain about the reliability of a source.

1. **Domain**: The "domain" of a site is the last part of its URL. The domain indicates the type of website. Noting the web address can tell you a lot. A .edu site indicates that an educational organization created that content. This is no guarantee that the information is accurate, but it does suggest less bias than a .com site, which will be commercial in nature. with a motive to sell you something, including ideas.

2. **Date**: Most websites include a date somewhere on the page. This date may indicate a copyright date, the date something was posted, or the date the site was last updated. These dates tell you when the content on the site was last changed or reviewed. Older sites might be outdated or contain information that is no longer relevant.

3. **Author or editor**: Does the online content indicate an author or editor? Like print materials, authority comes from the creator of the content. It is now easier than ever to investigate an author's credentials. A general Google search may lead you to a Wikipedia entry on the author, a LinkedIn page, or even an online résumé. If an author is affiliated with an educational institution, try visiting the institution's website for more information.

Managing Sources

Now that you've found sources, you need to think about how you are going to keep track of the sources and prepare the bibliography that will accompany your paper. Managing your sources is called "bibliographic citation management," and you will sometimes see references to bibliographic citation management on your library's website. Don't let this complicated phrase deter you; managing your citations from the start of your research will make your life much easier during the research process and especially the night before your paper is due when you are compiling your bibliography.

Chances are your college library provides software, such as *EndNote* or *RefWorks*, to help you manage citations. These are two commercially available citation management software packages that are not freely available to you unless your library has paid for a license. *EndNote* and *RefWorks* enable you to organize your sources in personal libraries. These libraries help you manage your sources and create bibliographies. Both *EndNote* and *RefWorks* also enable you to insert endnotes and footnotes directly into a Microsoft Word document.

If your library does not provide *EndNote* or *RefWorks*, a freely available software called *Zotero* (Zotero.org) will help you manage your sources. *Zotero* helps you collect, organize, cite, and share your sources, and it lives right in your web browser where you do your research. As you are searching *Google*, your library catalog, or library database, *Zotero* enables you to add a book, article, or website to a personal library with one click. As you add items to your library, *Zotero* collects both the information you need for your bibliography and any full-text content. This mean that the content of journal articles and ebooks will be available to you right from your *Zotero* library.

To create a bibliography, simply select the items from your *Zotero* library you want to include, right-click and select "Create Bibliography from Selected Items . . .," and choose the citation style your instructor asked you to use for the paper. To get started, go to *Zotero.org* and download *Zotero* for the browser of your choice.

Taking Notes

It is crucial that you take good, careful notes while you are doing your research. Not only is careful note taking necessary to avoid plagiarism, but it can also help you think through your project while you are doing research.

While many researchers used to take notes on index cards, most people now use computers. If you're using your computer, open a new document for each source that you're considering using. The first step in taking notes is to make sure that you gather all the information you might need in your bibliography or works cited. If you're taking notes from a book, for instance, you'll need the author, the title, the place of publication, the press, and the year. Be sure to check the style guide assigned by your instructor to make sure you're gathering all the necessary information.

After you've recorded the bibliographic information, add one or two keywords that can help you sort this source. Next, write a one- or two-sentence summary of the source. Finally, have a section on your document that is reserved for specific places in the text that you might want to work with. When you write down a quote, remember to be extra careful that you are capturing the quote exactly as it is written, and that you enclose the quote in quotation marks. Do not use abbreviations or change the punctuation. Remember, too, to write down the exact page numbers from the source you are quoting. Being careful with small details at the beginning of your project can save you a lot of time in the long run.

WRITING ABOUT COLLEGE

In your writing, as in your conversations, you should always be thinking about your audience. While your most obvious audience is the instructor, most college instructors will want you to write a paper that will be interesting and illuminating for other members of the college community. For example, if you are exploring ways that an online alcohol education program will change attitudes about drinking at your college, you will find many realistic audience groups around you, such as students at your college, the administration and other key decision makers, and professionals who study systems of higher education. Each of these groups will have its own interests and concerns about a proposed alcohol education program. You should, therefore, carefully consider how to employ voice and examples to best engage the members of your specific audience. For example, an intimate conversational voice may be an effective way to engage but not the most effective strategy to capture the interest of scholars.

College Newspaper as Audience

In terms of a public audience outside of a class, some instructors and students may find it useful to submit finished papers to a college newspaper or news website, especially when class projects speak directly to concerns on campus. Many of the prompts in the Analyze, Explore, Forging Connections, and Looking Further sections are a good starting point for interesting campus-wide conversations—conversations that might include a campus newspaper or news website as a place to showcase excellent work completed in class.

From Research Question to Thesis Statement

Many students like to begin the writing process by writing an introduction. Novice writers often use an early draft of their introduction to guide the shape of their paper. Experienced scholars, however, continually return to their introduction, reshaping it and revising it as their thoughts evolve. After all, since writing is thinking, it is impossible to anticipate the full thoughts of your paper before you have written it. Many writers, in fact, only realize the actual argument they are making after they have written a draft or two of the paper. Make sure not to let your introduction trap your thinking. Think of your introduction as a guide that will help your readers down the path of discovery—a path you can only fully know after you have written your paper.

A strong introduction will welcome readers to the scholarly conversation. You'll introduce your central interlocutors and pose the question or problem that all of you are interested in resolving. Most introductions contain a thesis statement, which is a sentence or two that clearly states the main argument. Some introductions, you'll notice, do not contain the argument, but merely contain the promise of a resolution to the intellectual problem.

Is Your Thesis an Argument?

So far, we've discussed a number of steps for you to take when you begin to write a research paper. We started by strategizing about ways to use presearch to find a topic and ask a researchable question, and then we looked at ways to find a scholarly conversation by using your library's resources. Now we'll discuss a crucial step in the writing process: coming up with a thesis.

Your thesis is the central claim of your paper—the main point that you'd like to argue. You may make a number of claims throughout the paper; when you make a claim, you are offering a small argument, usually about a piece of evidence that you've found. Your thesis is your governing claim, the central argument of the whole paper. Sometimes it is difficult to know if you have written a proper thesis. Ask yourself, "Can a reasonable person disagree with my thesis statement?" If the answer is no, then likely you have written an observation rather than an argument. For instance, the statement, "There are six official languages of the UN" is not a thesis, since this is a fact. A reasonable person cannot disagree with this fact, so it is not an argument. The statement, "Arabic became an official language of the UN for economic reasons" is a thesis, since it is a debatable point. A reasonable person might disagree (by arguing, for instance, that "Arabic became an official language of the UN for political reasons"). Remember to keep returning to your thesis statement while you are writing. Not only will you be thus able to make sure that your writing remains on a clear path, but you'll also be able to keep refining your thesis so that it becomes clearer and more precise.

Make sure, too, that your thesis is a point of persuasion rather than one of belief or taste.

"Chinese food tastes delicious" is certainly an argument you could make to your friend, but it is not an adequate thesis for an academic paper, because there is no evidence that you could provide that might persuade a reader who doesn't already agree with you.

Organization

In order for your paper to feel organized, readers should know where they are headed and have a reasonable idea of how they are going to get there. An introduction will offer a strong sense of organization if it:

- introduces your central intellectual problem and explains why it is important
- suggests who will be involved in the scholarly conversation
- indicates what kind of evidence you'll be investigating
- offers a precise central argument.

Some readers describe well-organized papers as having a sense of flow. When readers praise a sense of flow, they mean that the argument moves easily from one sentence to the next and from one paragraph to the next. This allows your reader to follow your thoughts easily. When you begin writing a sentence, try using an idea, keyword, or phrase from the end of the previous sentence. The next sentence, then, will appear to have emerged smoothly from the previous sentence. This tip is especially important when you move between paragraphs. The beginning of a paragraph should feel like it has a clear relationship to the end of the previous paragraph.

Keep in mind, too, a sense of wholeness. A strong paragraph has a sense of flow and a sense of wholeness: not only will you allow your reader to trace your thoughts smoothly, but you will ensure that your reader understands how all your thoughts are connected to a large, central idea. Ask yourself, as you write a paragraph, what the paragraph has to do with the central intellectual problem that you are investigating. If the relationship isn't clear to you, then your readers will likely be confused.

Novice writers often use the form of a five-paragraph essay. In this form, each paragraph offers an example that proves the validity of the central claim. The five-paragraph essay may have worked in high school, since it meets the minimum requirement for making an argument with evidence. You'll quickly notice, though, that experienced writers do not use the five-paragraph essay. Indeed, your college instructors will expect you to move beyond the five-paragraph essay. This is because a five-paragraph essay relies on static examples rather than fully engaging new evidence. A strong essay will grow in complexity and nuance as the writer brings in new evidence. Rather than thinking of an essay as something that offers many examples to back up the same static idea, think of an essay as the evolution of an idea that grows ever more complex and rich as the writer engages with scholars who view the idea from various angles.

Integrating Your Research

As we have seen, doing research involves finding an intellectual community by looking for scholars who are thinking through similar problems and may be in conversation with one another. When you write your paper, you will not merely be reporting what you found; you will be orchestrating the conversation that your research has uncovered. To orchestrate a conversation involves asking a few key questions: Whose voices should be most prominent? What is the relationship between one scholar's ideas and another scholar's ideas? How do these ideas contribute to the argument that your own paper is making? Is it important that your readers hear the exact words of the conversation, or can you give them the main ideas and important points of the conversation in your own words? Your answers to these questions will determine how you go about integrating your research into your paper.

Using evidence is a way of gaining authority. Even though you may not have known much about your topic before you started researching, the way you use evidence in your paper will allow you to establish a voice that is authoritative and trustworthy. You have three basic choices to decide how best you'd like to present the information from a source: summarize, paraphrase, or quote. Let's discuss each one briefly.

You should **summarize** a source when the source provides helpful background information for your research. Summaries do not make strong evidence, but they can be helpful if you need to chart the intellectual terrain of your project. Summaries can be an efficient way of capturing the main ideas of a source. Remember, when you are summarizing, to be fully sympathetic to the writer's point of view. Put yourself in the scholar's shoes. If you later disagree with the scholar's methods or conclusions, your disagreement will be convincing because your reader will know that you have given the scholar a fair hearing. A summary that is clearly biased is not only inaccurate and ethically suspect, it will make your writing less convincing because readers will be suspicious of your rigor.

Let's say you come across the following quote that you'd like to summarize. Here's an excerpt from *The Language Wars: A History of Proper English*, by Henry Hitchings:

> No language has spread as widely as English, and it continues to
> spread. Internationally the desire to learn it is insatiable. In the

twenty-first century the world is becoming more urban and more middle class, and the adoption of English is a symptom of this, for increasingly English serves as the lingua franca of business and popular culture. It is dominant or at least very prominent in other areas such as shipping, diplomacy, computing, medicine and education. (300)

Consider this summary:

In *The Language Wars*, Hitchings says that everyone wants to learn English because it is the best language in the world (300). I agree that English is the best.

If you compare this summary to what Hitchings actually said, you will see that this summary is a biased, distorted version of the actual quote. Hitchings did not make a universal claim about whether English is better or worse than other languages. Rather, he made a claim about why English is becoming so widespread in an increasingly connected world.

Now let's look at another summary:

According to Hitchings, English has become the go-to choice for global communications and has spread quickly as the language of commerce and ideas. (300)

This is a much stronger summary than the previous example. The writer shortens Hitchings's original language but is fair to his original meaning and intent.

Paraphrasing involves putting a source's ideas into your own words. It's a good idea to paraphrase if you think you can state the idea more clearly or more directly than the original source does. Remember that if you paraphrase you need to put the entire idea into your own words. It is not enough for you to change one or two words. Indeed, if you only change a few words, you may put yourself at risk of plagiarizing.

Let's look at how we might paraphrase the Hitchings quote that we've been discussing. Consider this paraphrase:

Internationally the desire to learn English is insatiable. In today's society, the world is becoming wealthier and more urban, and the use of English is a symptom of this. (Hitchings 300)

You will notice that the writer simply replaced some of Hitchings's original language with synonyms. Even with the parenthetical citation, this is unacceptable paraphrasing. Indeed, this is a form of plagiarism, because the writer suggests that the language is his or her own, when it is in fact an only slightly modified version of Hitchings's own phrasing.

Let's see how we might paraphrase Hitchings in an academically honest way:

> Because English is used so frequently in global communications, many people around the world want to learn English as they become members of the middle class. (Hitchings 300)

Here the writer has taken Hitchings's message but has used his or her own language to describe what Hitchings originally wrote. The writer offers Hitchings's ideas with fresh syntax and new vocabulary, and the writer is sure to give Hitchings credit for the idea in a parenthetical citation.

The best way to show that you are in conversation with scholars is to quote them. **Quoting** involves capturing the exact wording and punctuation of a passage. Quotations make for powerful evidence, especially in humanities papers. If you come across evidence that you think will be helpful in your project, you should quote it. You may be tempted to quote only those passages that seem to agree with the claim that you are working with. But remember to write down the quotes of scholars who may not seem to agree with you. These are precisely the thoughts that will help you build a powerful scholarly conversation. Working with fresh ideas that you may not agree with can help you revise your claim to make it even more persuasive, since it will force you to take into account potential counterarguments. When your readers see that you are grappling with an intellectual problem from all sides and that you are giving all interlocutors a fair voice, they are more likely to be persuaded by your argument.

To make sure that you are properly integrating your sources into your paper, remember the acronym ICE: Introduce, Cite, and Explain. Let's imagine that you've found an idea that you'd like to incorporate into your paper. We'll use a quote from David Harvey's *A Brief History of Neoliberalism* as an example. On page 7, you find the following quote that you'd like to use: "The assumption that individual freedoms are guaranteed by freedom of the market and of trade is a cardinal feature of neoliberal thinking, and it has long dominated the US stance towards the rest of the world."

The first thing you need to do is **introduce** the quote ("introduce" gives us the "I" in ICE). To introduce a quote, you must provide context so that your readers know where it is coming from, and you must integrate the quote into your own sentence. Here are some examples of how you might do this:

In his book *A Brief History of Neoliberalism*, David Harvey writes . . .

One expert on the relationship between economics and politics claims . . .

Professor of Anthropology David Harvey explains that . . .

In a recent book by Harvey, he contends . . .

Notice that each of these introduces the quote in such a way that readers are likely to recognize it as an authoritative source.

The next step is to **cite** the quote (the "C" in ICE). Here is where you indicate the origin of the quotation so that your readers can easily look up the original source. Citing is a two-step process that varies slightly depending on the citation style that you're using. We'll offer an example using MLA style. The first step involves indicating the author and page number in the body of your essay. Here is an example of a parenthetical citation that gives the author and page number after the quote and before the period that ends the sentence:

> One expert on the relationship between economics and politics claims that neoliberal thinking has "long dominated the US stance towards the rest of the world." (Harvey 7)

If it is already clear to readers which author you're quoting, you need only to give the page number:

> In *A Brief History of Neoliberalism*, David Harvey contends that neoliberal thinking has "long dominated the US stance towards the rest of the world." (7)

The second step of citing the quote is providing proper information in the works cited or bibliography of your paper. This list should include the complete bibliographical information of all the sources you have cited. An essay that includes the quote by David Harvey should also include the following entry in the Works Cited:

Harvey, David. *A Brief History of Neoliberalism.* New York: Oxford UP, 2005. Print.

Finally, the most important part of integrating a quote is **explaining** it. The "E" in ICE is often overlooked, but a strong explanation is the most important step to involve yourself in the scholarly conversation. Here is where you will explain how you interpret the source you are citing, what aspect of the quote is most important for your readers to understand, and how the source pertains to your own project. For example:

> David Harvey writes, "The assumption that individual freedoms are guaranteed by freedom of the market and of trade is a cardinal feature of neoliberal thinking, and it has long dominated the US stance towards the rest of the world" (7). As Harvey explains, neoliberalism suggests that free markets do not limit personal freedom but actually lead to free individuals.

Or:

> David Harvey writes, "The assumption that individual freedoms are guaranteed by freedom of the market and of trade is a cardinal feature of neoliberal thinking, and it has long dominated the US stance towards the rest of the world" (7). For Harvey, before we understand the role of the United States in global politics, we must first understand the philosophy that binds personal freedom with market freedom.

Novice writers are sometimes tempted to end a paragraph with a quote that they feel is especially compelling or clear. But remember that you should never leave a quote to speak for itself (even if you love it!). After all, as the orchestrator of this scholarly conversation, you need to make sure that readers are receiving exactly what you'd like them to receive from each quote. Notice, in the above examples, that the first explanation suggests that the writer quoting Harvey is centrally concerned with neoliberal philosophy, while the second explanation suggests that the writer is centrally concerned with U.S. politics. The explanation, in other words, is the crucial link between your source and the main idea of your paper.

Avoiding Plagiarism

Scholarly conversations are what drive knowledge in the world. Scholars using each other's ideas in open, honest ways form the bedrock of our intellectual communities and ensure that our contributions to the world of thought are important. It is crucial, then, that all writers do their part in maintaining the integrity and trustworthiness of scholarly conversations. It is crucial that you never claim someone else's ideas as your own, and that you always are extra careful to give the proper credit to someone else's thoughts. This is what we call responsible scholarship.

The best way to avoid plagiarism is to plan ahead and keep careful notes as you read your sources. Remember the advice above on *Zotero* and taking notes: find the way that works best for you to keep track of what ideas are your own and what ideas come directly from the sources you are reading. Most acts of plagiarism are accidental. It is easy when you are drafting a paper to lose track of where a quote or idea came from; plan ahead and this won't happen. Here are a few tips for making sure that confusion doesn't happen to you.

1. Know what needs to be cited. You do not need to cite what is considered common knowledge such as facts (the day Lincoln was born), concepts (the earth orbits the sun), or events (the day Martin Luther King was shot). You do need to cite the ideas and words of others from the sources you are using in your paper.
2. Be conservative. If you are not sure if you should cite something, either ask your instructor or a librarian, or cite it. It is better to cite something you don't have to than not cite something you should.
3. Direct quotations from your sources need to be cited as well as anytime you paraphrase the ideas or words from your sources.
4. Finally, extensive citation not only helps you avoid plagiarism, but it also boosts your credibility and enables your reader to trace your scholarship.

Citation Styles

It is crucial that you adhere to the standards of a single citation style when you write your paper. The most common styles are MLA (Modern

Language Association, generally used in the humanities), APA (American Psychological Association, generally used in the social sciences), and Chicago (*Chicago Manual of Style*). If you're not sure which style you should use, ask your instructor. Each style has its own guidelines regarding the format of the paper. While proper formatting within a given style may seem arbitrary, there are important reasons behind the guidelines of each style. For instance, while MLA citations tend to emphasize authors' names, APA citations tend to emphasize the date of publications. This distinction make sense, especially given that MLA standards are usually followed by departments in the humanities and APA standards are usually followed by departments in the social sciences. While papers in the humanities value original thinking about arguments and texts that are canonical and often old, papers in the social sciences tend to value arguments that take into account the most current thought and the latest research.

There are a number of helpful guidebooks that will tell you all the rules you need to know in order to follow the standards for various citation styles. If your instructor hasn't pointed you to a specific guidebook, try the following online resources:

Purdue Online Writing Lab: owl.english.purdue.edu/
Internet Public Library: www.ipl.org/div/farq/netciteFARQ.html/
Modern Language Association (for MLA style): www.mla.org/style/

American Psychological Association (for APA style): www.apastyle.org/

The Chicago Manual of Style Online: www.chicagomanualofstyle.org/ tools_citationguide.html

credits

Chapter 1

"Getting in College" by Malcolm Gladwell, *The New Yorker*, November 10, 2005. Copyright © 2005 by Malcolm Gladwell. Reprinted by permission of Malcolm Gladwell/Pushkin Enterprises, Inc.

"Application Inflation: When Is Enough Enough?" by Eric Hoover, *The New York Times*, November 7, 2010. Copyright © 2010 by The New York Times. All rights reserved. Used by permission and protected by the Copyright Laws of the United States. The printing, copying, redistribution, or retransmission of this Content without express permission is prohibited.

"College Admissions, Beyond the No. 2 Pencil (How Admissions Really Works)" by Robert J. Sternberg, *The Washington Post*, November 21, 2010. Copyright © 2010 by Robert J. Sternberg. Reprinted by permission of the author.

"When Roommates Were Random" by Dalton Conley, *The New York Times*, August 29, 2011. Copyright © 2011 by The New York Times. All rights reserved. Used by permission and protected by the Copyright Laws of the United States. The printing, copying, redistribution, or retransmission of this Content without express permission is prohibited.

Chapter 2

"The Future of College?" by Graeme Wood, *The Atlantic Magazine*, September 8, 2014. Copyright © 2014 by The Atlantic Media Co., as first published in The Atlantic Magazine. All rights reserved. Distributed by Tribune Content Agency, LLC.

"The Day the Purpose of College Changed" by Dan Berrett, *The Chronicle of Higher Education*, January 26, 2015. Copyright © 2015 by The Chronicle of Higher Education. Reprinted by permission of The YGS Group for the publisher.

"The Disadvantages of an Elite Education" by William Deresiewicz, *The American Scholar*, June 1, 2008. Copyright © 2008 by William Deresiewicz. Reprinted by permission of the author.

"Is College the New High School?" by Vauhini Vara, *The New Yorker*, January 13, 2015. Copyright © 2015 by Conde Nast. Reprinted by permission of Conde Nast.

Chapter 3

Chapter 4

of Rajat Bhageria, the author of "What High School Didn't Teach Me." http://
www.huffingtonpost.com/rajat-bhageria/computer-science-class_b_6395870.
html.Read his blog at RajatBhageria.com.

"Why College Freshman Need to Take Emotions 101" by Diana Divecha and Robin
Stern, *The Washington Post*, November 21, 2010. Copyright © 2010 by Diana
Divecha and Robin Stern. Reprinted by permission of the authors.

"BU Mandates Online Alcohol Course for First Year Students" by Rich Barlow, *BU
Today*, June 13, 2013. Copyright © 2013 by Boston University. Reprinted by permission of BU Today.

"When Colleges Abandon Phys Ed, What Else Is Lost?" by Scott Carlson, *The Chronicle of Higher Education*, January 16, 2015. Copyright © 2015 by The Chronicle of
Higher Education. Reprinted by permission of The YGS Group for the publisher.

Chapter 5

"The Dark Power of Fraternities" by Caitlin Flanagan, *The Atlantic Magazine*, March 2,
2014. Copyright © 2014 by The Atlantic Media Co., as first published in The
Atlantic Magazine. All rights reserved. Distributed by Tribune Content Agency,
LLC.

"Bloomberg: Ban Fraternities" by The Editors, *Bloomberg News,* January 7, 2014.
Copyright © 2014 by Bloomberg Content. Reprinted by permission of the
publisher. <http://www.bloombergview.com/articles/2014-01-07/dean-wormer-
s-favorite-editorial>.

"I Still Think Joining a Fraternity Was One of the Best Decisions I've Ever Made" by
Peter Jacobs, *Business Insider*, January 8, 2014. Copyright © 2014 by Wright's
Media. Reprinted by permission of the publisher. http://www.businessinsider.
com/don't-ban-fraternities-2014-1.

"Greek Letters at a Price" by Risa C. Doherty, *The New York Times*, November 2,
2014. Copyright © 2014 by The New York Times. All rights reserved. Used by
permission and protected by the Copyright Laws of the United States. The printing, copying, redistribution, or retransmission of this Content without express
permission is prohibited.

Chapter 6

"The Shame of College Sports" by Taylor Branch, *The Atlantic Magazine*, September 10,
2011. Copyright © 2011 by The Atlantic Media Co., as first published in The
Atlantic Magazine. All rights reserved. Distributed by Tribune Content Agency,
LLC.

"Are College Athletes Employees?" by Ian Crouch, *The New Yorker*, March 27, 2014.
Copyright © 2014 by Conde Nast. Reprinted by permission of Conde Nast.

"Colleges Prepare Athletes for Bad Behavior in the NFL" by Dr. Alan Kadish,
Huffington Post, September 22, 2014. Copyright © 2014 by Huffington Post.
Reprinted by permission of Dr. Alan Kadish, Touro College.

Chapter 7

"Spending Shifts as Colleges Compete on Students' Comfort" by Scott Carlson, *The
Chronicle of Higher Education*, June 28, 2014. Copyright © 2014 by The Chronicle
of Higher Education. Reprinted by permission of The YGS Group for the
publisher.

index